THE RATIONALE DIVINORUM OFFICIORUM

THE RATIONALE DIVINORUM OFFICIORUM

The Foundational Symbolism of the Early Church, its Structure, Decoration, Sacraments and Vestments

Books I, III, and IV

BY GUILIELMUS DURANDUS
(1230-1296CE)

including

selections from

THE MYSTICAL MIRROR OF THE CHURCH

BY HUGO DE SANCTO VICTORE
(1096-1141CE)

FONS VITAE

First published in 2007 by
Fons Vitae
49 Mockingbird Valley Drive
Louisville, KY 40207
http://www.fonsvitae.com

Library of Congress Control Number: 2007937223

ISBN 1-887752-92-7

This book was typeset by Neville Blakemore, Jr.

Owned by the Habsburgs. The codex was originally written for Duke Albrecht III (1365-1395), it remained the property of the Habsburgs, was kept in the library at Ambras castle (Innsbruck) and handed over to the Imperial Library, Vienna in 1665. It is a major key work in the history of Viennese book art. The decoration of this monumental manuscript was interrupted several times and must have taken about twenty years to complete- thus, it documents notable changes in Viennese book art at the turn of the 14th - 15th centuries. It shows the decorative concept of the illumination with historiated initials and borders. The contents of this folio also document the possible occasion that inspired the creation of the codex: namely, the papal concession for the study of theology at Vienna University applied for by Duke Albrecht III.

TABLE OF CONTENTS

TABLE OF CONTENTS, continued

TABLE OF CONTENTS, continued

(Germany, 1070, Treasury of St. Liudger, Essen-Werden, Germany)

"The 'Chief corner-stone is Christ.' Upon this, not besides this, is the 'foundation of the apostles and Prophets.'"

– Hugo de Sancto Victore (1096-1141)

DEDICATION

Dedicated to Archbishop Thomas C. Kelly, O.P. who has served his community for over a quarter of a century with a breadth of Spirit and Learning that continues the great tradition of his predecessor, William Durandus. We honor his restoration of the historic Cathedral of the Assumption as part of his ministry to the parish and the diocese and we celebrate his vision in creating an international model for interfaith work by committing the Cathedral to the work of the Cathedral Heritage Foundation/Center for Interfaith Relations.

> "Notice must be taken of how a great many different practices are utilized in celebrating divine worship; almost every Church has its own observances which are appropriate and full of meaning. These should never be rejected as reprehensible or absurd, for God and the saints can be venerated by innumerable harmonies and modulations, by different observances, for the Church Triumphant is, as the prophet says, "ornamented with vestments of diverse colors," and even when it comes to the administration of the Sacraments, the Church allows for a variety of ceremonies established by the law of custom."

From the Proeme
of The Rationale Divinorum Officiorum
William Durandus, Bishop of Mende

A WORD FROM THE PUBLISHER

This volume contains translations from three of the eight books of *The Rationale Divinorum Officiorum* by Guilielmus Durandus (1230-1296CE). These were translated from the Latin through the effort of different scholars, each of whose style, punctuation, spelling, and systems of capitalization, differed from one another. Out of respect for the integrity of each contributor and the literary conventions of his time, we have chosen to admit these inconsistencies and to leave the texts unaltered.

We are indebted to the Reverends John M. Neale, B.A., and Benjamin Webb, B.A., of Trinity College Cambridge, for their translation in 1842 of Book I, *The Symbolism of Churches and Church Ornaments*, to the Reverend T.H. Passmore, M.A., 1899, for Book III, *The Sacred Vestments* , and to the Reverend Father Rama Coomaraswamy for his translation of eight chapters from Book IV, *The Mass*, on which he was working at the time of his death in 2005, making use of the 1854 French translation. We are grateful to these four scholars for making this rare and inspiring treasure available. We hope that the experience of those seeking to deepen their own spiritual lives and awareness, and those who attend church services will be greatly enriched. May it also be that those of other faith traditions will enjoy a more profound understanding of the Christian faith, while students of the history of art and architecture will appreciate and benefit from this unique opening into the medieval mind and the Christian Middle Ages at which time the symbolism of the sacred structures and rites were being consolidated and were still understood.

Fons Vitae wishes to thank Father Chrysogonus Waddell, a hermit monk and organist at the monastery of Our Lady of Gethsemani in Kentucky, where Thomas Merton lived, for his generous contribution of time and his thoughtful and important suggestions, he being a recognized medievalist.

We also gratefully acknowledge Robert Carter, a Swedish physicist who spent years laboriously typing out this material, Anne Ogden for her editing, Carlyn Nugent for preparing the text, Reverend Karen Francis for proofreading, Nasra Hasan for helping to obtain the magnificent cover illustration from the National Library of Vienna where one of the finest early copies of the Durandus manuscript is kept, G. John Champoux, editor of the forthcoming *The Way to Our Heavenly Father, A Contemplative Telling of the Lord's Prayer*, for his guidance, and Lord George, Earl of St. Andrews for his encouragement of this effort, begun twenty years ago at the Cambridge Univeristy Library.

For the illustrations and photography Fons Vitae would like to thank the accomplished photographer Brother Paul Quenon, a monk at the Gethsemani Monastery, as well as the Abbey for use of its archives; William Dallas Jones, a student at Lewis & Clark College, for climbing the tower of Notre Dame in Paris to photograph ancient bells; from Saudi Arabia, Princess Reem Faisal and Tereen Ali Reza, a recent graduate from Brown University, for her important contribution of simply marvelous photos taken at Notre Dame and the Cluny Museum in Paris; as well as Christopher Wheatly, Pamela Swisher, and Steven Stivers for the preparation of the photographic material from the Fons Vitae archives. For help with some of the illustrations of the sacred vestments, we are grateful to the Holy Rood Guild and Paul Negri of Dover Publications. Though not for the lack of trying, the illustrations could not all depict medieval architecture, ornaments, liturgical vessels, and the like; therefore, some photographs are of objects sustaining and continuing that earlier tradition.

Appreciation is extended to Mary and Bob Griffith as well as my family for their patience while endless photographs were taken and excursions made to museums, libraries, and sacred sites throughout Europe and Great Britain. For any low quality pictures and mistaken identifications I ask for your forbearance.

Lastly, it is interesting to note that we are dealing with scholarship which stretched over a period of one thousand years. The different world views of these writers, all men steeped in their own time and traditions as we are in ours, are reflected in the particular conventions and attitudes of the time in which they lived. While the role and place of women or the regard for other faith traditions, for example, may have changed, this work continues to be remarkable for its comprehensiveness, historical significance, and value as regards the spiritual life and world of Christianity.

MEMOIR OF DURANDUS

This piece, authored by Reverend T. H. Passmore, M.A., was included in the 1899 translation and publication of *The Sacred Vestments, An English Rendering of the Third Book of the 'Rationale Divinorum Officiorum' of Durandus, Bishop of Mende*, pages xix–xxii.

William Durandus was born at Puy-moisson, in the diocese of Béziers, in Languedoc. There is some uncertainty as to the date of his birth; it was about the year 1230. Having studied canon law at the university of Bologna, he obtained his doctor's degree, and afterwards taught both at Bologna and Modena. By the year 1265 the fame of his skill and learning had reached the ear of Pope Clement IV, who appointed him Auditor of the Sacred Palace, Subdeacon, and Chaplain to the Pope, and Canon of Beauvais and Narbonne. He rendered good service to Pope Gregory X, as his secretary, at the Council of Lyons in 1274. In 1277 he was made spiritual and temporal legate of the patrimony of S. Peter; and in 1281 he became Vicar Spiritual, and in 1283 governor of the temporalities of the rebellious province of Romagna, taking the lead of the war against the rebels, and exerting himself to the utmost, as Captain of the Papal forces, to secure the Pope's authority. In pacifying this province Durandus gave proof of great military and administrative powers. In 1286 Pope Honorius IV made him Bishop of Mende, in Languedoc; but he took possession of the see by proxy, and so remained in Italy until 1291. During this time he wrote much, and (it is thought) completed the *Rationale*. In 1295 Pope Boniface VIII offered him the Bishopric of Ravenna, which he refused. About this time his strength began to fail, and compelled him to resign office. He retired to Rome, and closed a brilliant career by death on All Saints' Day, 1296. His monument is still to be seen in the Church of Santa Maria sopra Minerva, with a lengthy inscription enumerating his writings and good deeds. He was the survivor of sixteen Popes, and the favourite of many.

Some of the most famous works of Durandus are the following:

•*Speculum Judiciale* or *Juris*, first published at Rome in folio, 1474; a practical treatise on civil and canon law, which earned for its young author, at 34 years of age, the names *Father of Practice*, and *Speculator*. This work passed through thirty-eight editions between the years 1474 and 1678.

•*Repertorium Aureum* or *Breviarium*, dedicated to Cardinal Matthaeus.

•De Modo Concilii in Generalis habendi.

•Commentarius in Concilium Lugdunense.

The *Rationale Divinorum Officiorum*, of whose Third Book a translation is now presented to the reader, is an exhaustive treatise covering the whole range of Christian worship. It is divided into eight Books, to which the theme is apportioned as follows:

The First Book treats of the Church and its parts.
The Second, of Church Ministers and Orders.
The Third, of the Vestments of Bishops, Priests, and Deacons.
The Fourth, of the Holy Mass and its parts.
The Fifth, of the Divine Offices of the Day and Night.
The Sixth, of the Sundays and Festivals of the year.
The Seventh, of Saints' Days.
The Eighth, of the Calendar.

It may be of interest to mention that the *Rationale* was the first book, from the pen of an uninspired writer, ever printed. The *editio princeps*, a magnificently beautiful book, and perhaps as rare as a book can be, was printed by Fust in 1459; being preceded only by the Psalters of 1457 and 1459. Besides this, Chalmers mentions thirteen editions in the fifteenth, and thirteen in the sixteenth century, all of which are very rare.

The chief writers on Sacred Vestments with whose works Durandus gives evidence of familiarity, are as follows: Josephus, Philo, S. Jerome (Letter to Fabiola, A.D. 396), Pope Celestine (A.D. 423-432), S. Isidore of Pelusium (*c.* A.D. 412), S. Gregory the Great (A.D. 590-604), S. Isidore of Seville (*c.* A.D. 560-636), Venerable Bede (*c.* A.D. 673-735), S. Germanus of Constantinople (*c.* A.D. 715), Rabanus Maurus (*c.* A.D. 822), Amalarius of Metz (*c.* A.D. 824), Walafrid Strabo (A.D. 842), Alcuin (*c.* A.D. 800), S. Ivo Carnotensis (*c.* A.D. 1100), Ps.-Hugh of S. Victor (A.D. 1096-1140), Honorius of Autun (*c.* A.D. 1120), Pope Innocent III. (*c.* A.D. 1200).

***

Other authors known by Durand could be mentioned: Bruno of Segni (c. 1040–1123); John Beleth (d. 1182); Sicard of Cremona (c. 1150–1215); William of Auxerre (c. 1150–1231); the anonymous author of the 11th century *Liber Quare*: Praepositinus of Cremona (c. 1150–1210); Hugh of St. Cher (c. 1195–1263); Gilbert of Tournai (d. 1284).

Father Chrysogonus Waddell
Abbey of Our Lady of Gethsemani
Trappist, Kentucky

AN HISTORICAL NOTICE ON THE LIFE OF WILLIAM DURAND

By Charles Barthélemy for the 1854 French edition of the *Rationale*

William Durand,* the celebrated author of *The Mirror of the Law* (*Speculum Judiciale*), which led to his being called the "Speculator," and of the *Manual of Divine Worship*, or "Rationale", was born at Puymission (Puimoisson) in the diocese of Béziers, France, probably around 1230. He received an excellent education from his family, which was of distinguished ancestry. Interested especially in the study of canon and civil law, the popularity of which had been spreading rapidly for a century in Italy and southern France, he went to hear the best teachers, perhaps at Montpellier† above all, where the chairs of jurisprudence were already famous. In 1251 he became a canon regular of the cathedral of Maguellone which was then still a town, an episcopal town located some nine or ten miles from his native land and where he pursued his early studies: then, around 1254, he became a cleric in the church at Narbonne.

At twenty-five, he came to the University of Paris to attend lessons for some time, as he himself informs us.‡ And it was in the schools of this city that he became acquainted with Giacomo Savelli, who was subsequently elevated to the Chair of Peter under the name of Honorius IV, and who approved Durand's election to the bishopric of Mende.§

His desire to round out his knowledge of both canon and civil law led him, in 1255, to leave for Italy where Stephen of Tournai, Alexander of Saint-Gilles, and Bernard Dorna had previously gone to study law; where similar motives would soon draw James of Révigny, John of Moissac, and

---

*One can read about this illustrious individual in the fine work that Victor Le Clerc has devoted to him in volume twenty of the *Histoire Littéraire de France* (1842, pp. 411–497), a series started by the Benedictines and continued by the members of the Institut (Académie Royale des Inscriptions et Belles-Lettres). It is from this work that we have taken the significant details of his life. The biography provided by Le Clerc is the one and only work in our literary history devoted to this individual who is one of the great encyclopedists of the middle ages, and we should be grateful to this scholar for knowing how to lay the foundations for his work and, lastly, sort out the true from the false in such numerous and sometimes contradictory documents. Out of this he has shaped a perfect whole that is both learned and engaging.

†Subsequent research finds his presence at Montpellier pure conjecture. –ED.

‡*Rationale*, Bk. VI, chap. 77, num. 17.

§Du Boulay, *Hist. Univ.*, Paris, Bk. III, p. 473, 532.

William of Mandagot, and where the two illustrious professors of the University of Bologna, Bernard of Parma and Henry of Suze, afterwards Cardinal of Ostia, counted him among their disciples. He attained, after the highest examinations—among them a private examination still in vogue at this school—the degree of Doctor of Canon Law, and gained such a reputation for his knowledge and ability that he was appointed to teach law at Bologna and then later at Modena. It was during his public professorship in this last city that he edited his commentaries on the Decretals of Gratian.

In 1265, at the age of thirty-four, increasingly esteemed for his many gifts and engaged from that moment on in editing his *Mirror of the Law* (*Speculum Judiciale*), he was called by Pope Clement IV, his compatriot and protector, to be apostolic chaplain and general auditor of the sacred palace. At the same time he was appointed to two honorary positions as canon of the cathedrals of Beauvais and Narbonne.

Upon the death of Clement IV on November 29th, 1268, Durand was at Viterbo. After an interregnum of three years the cardinals elected a new pope, Gregory X. Durand, as a member of the pontifical court, assisted in 1274 at the Council of Lyons (the fourteenth General Council), where he functioned as an advisor on how to secure the Holy Land and end the Greek Schism. Already well known for his works on the law, the canon from Beauvais and Narbonne merited the confidence of those directing the Council. We know this because he has told us several times that he was among those prelates responsible for editing the acts of this Council. It was during the pontificate of Gregory X that he published his *Speculum Judiciale* which he dedicated to the Genoese Ottobuono de' Fieschi, who died in 1276 after reigning as pope for a brief period under the name of Adrian V. Adrian V had intended to raise him to the cardinalate.

Durand was appointed dean of Chartres in 1279. While there he was sent (in 1280) to various princes, nobles, and cities of Italy, by the cardinals reunited in conclave after the death of Nicholas III, in order to invite them to receive with appropriate dignity the daughter of the emperor Rudolph, Clementia, engaged to the eldest son of Charles, prince of Salerno.

Durand, until this time known and honored as a prelate and a specialist in the law, was from the second year of the reign of Nicholas III (1278) placed in charge as the spiritual and temporal administrator of the patrimony of Saint Peter with the title of legate. He continued to demonstrate his abilities in this difficult ministry throughout the reigns of Martin IV (1281), Honorius IV (1285), Nicholas IV (1288), and under Boniface VIII, elected Pope ten years later. William Durand, esteemed and respected by this long line of popes, showed himself the most energetic and skillful among the leaders of the French party who supported this series of successors to the Chair of Peter in their efforts to establish their authority over Romagna and on the March of Ancona.

We will not follow Durand of Mende through his political and diplomatic career. Le Clerc, always relying on definitive documentation, has most strikingly related this finest and most brilliant part of his life. We will simply direct our readers to his excellent work.

The functions with which the Holy See entrusted Durand were not limited to the spiritual realm. At times they involved military duties. The future author of the "Rationale" tells us the nature of his duties as governor of Romagna, over which he became Count in 1284 after the death of Jean d'Épe. "Durand's very words," says Le Clerc, "are much too important not to be quoted directly: 'A cleric can be appointed to conduct a just war—not to directly lead men of blood, but to be responsible for soldiers, to furnish them with money, to make treaties, to render sentences, and to dispose of all matters, as we have ourselves done in the war which the Church of Rome has sustained in Romagna against the cities in revolt.'"

It was during this period, in 1284, that the author of the *Speculum* "who possessed," as Cimarelli says,* "a wealthy monastery in the Apennines," constructed a castle at his own expense. Built on the plain and on the site of the *delle Ripe* fortress, which had been destroyed by the people of Urbino, who were inveterate Ghibellines, this castle bore his name, the Castel Durante, until 1635. At that time Pope Urban VIII created the episcopal town of Urbania, established on the Metro (the earlier name for the Metauro) about three leagues from Urbino.

In 1285 Durand was importuned, by the wish of the chapter of Mende, to govern this Church.† "His maturity in years combined with the gravity of his bearing and his knowledge of letters," says the Bull of Honorius IV, rendered him worthy of being chosen. As he was absent from France at the time, his consecration was postponed until the 16th of May at which time he received unction with the Holy Oils in the cathedral church of Clermont. Three years previously (1284) he had published his *Rationale of the Divine Offices* and the *Directory of Canon Law* (*Repertorium juris canonici*) as well as a completely re-edited version of his *Speculum*.

In this new charge Durand was the ever-zealous defender of the spiritual and temporal interests of Rome, the Rome that he had served and defended

---

**Istoria dello stato d'Urbino*, p. 141.

†Only in 1291, however, did he take possession of his see. –ED.

with his pen and arm for more than thirty years. He died in the capital of the Catholic world, where he had been called in the interests of the Church, on November 1, 1296 at the age of sixty-six.

He was buried in the Dominican Church of Our Lady *sopra la Minerva* in Rome. His epitaph, engraved on a marble tablet at the base of the tomb of this great bishop, is so valuable in providing historic and literary details on William Durand that we shall give the complete translation according to the reading of Echard and Sarti, which is more correct than other ones.

"Here lies an excellent doctor, the bishop of Mende, William Duranti,* the measure of morality. Sparkling virtue and all the guilelessness of pure love were joined in him with depth of counsel, outward beauty and serenity of soul. Calm amidst the storms of the world, pious, serious of speech, modest in his demeanor, he fought, like a dread lion, the enemies of the faith. He conquered unconquerable people, repelled the rebellious with a rod of iron and constrained the vanquished to obey the Church. Romagna during the reign of Martin IV bears witness to this; submitting itself to the scepter of this prelate who became a warlike count. This is he who is the author of the *Directory of the Law,* the *Mirror of the Law*, the *Episcopal Pontifical* and the *Rationale of the Divine Offices*. Through his writings, he has instructed the clergy, directed them by means of his statutcs; cnlightened the faithful by a continuous commentary on the constitutions of Gregory X and Nicholas, and illuminated his students by his teaching, inspiring them with the most profound thoughts. This worthy and glorious man was born in Puymission, in the diocese of Béziers. The court of a most illustrious pope called him while he rested from his labors in his bishopric of Mende; Boniface VIII wished to elevate him to a higher state, but the bishop refused to be archbishop of Ravenna. Ever invincible, he was a count, and lastly a marquis. Returning to Rome in the 1296th year of the Lord, he died and was buried in this tomb at the church of Minerva on the first day of November [All Saints Day]. This is why this prelate enjoys now here the heavenly life with all the saints and why a perpetual sacrifice is celebrated for him in this chapel."

---

*In Latin Durand is named: Guillelmus Durandus, Durandi, Durantes, Durantis or Duranti. We add below the Latin text of the epitaph preserved for us by Le Clerc:

Hic jacet egregius doctor, presul Mimatensis,
Nomini Duranti Guilielmus, regula morum,
Splendor honestatis, et casti candor amoris,
Altum consiliis, speciosum, mente serenum,
Hunc insignibant, Immotus turbine mundi,
Mente pius, sermone gravis, gestuque modestus,

Extitit infestus super hostes more elonis.
Indomitos domuit populos, ferroque rebelles
Impulit, Ecclesiae victos servire coegit.
Comprobat officiis, paruit Romaniasceptro
Belligeri comitis, Martini tempore quarti.
Ediidit in jure librum, quo jus reperitur.
Et Speculum juris, patrum quoque Pontificale,
Et Rationale Divinorum patefecit.
Instruxit clerum scriptis, monuitque statutis.
Gregorii deni, Nicolai scita perenni
Glossa diffudit populis, sensusque profundos
Scire dedit mentes corusca luce studentum.
Quem memori laudi genuit Provincia dignum,
Et dedit a Podio Missone dioecesis ilum
Inde Biterrensis. Praesignis curia papae,
Dum foret ecclesiae Mimatensis sede quietus,
Hunc vocat: octavus Bonifacius altius illum
Promovet; hic renuit Ravennae praesul haberi.
Fit comes invictus simul hinc, et marchio tandem.
Et Roman rediit Domini sub mille trecentis
Quatuor amotis annis, tumulante Minerva.
Subripit hunc festiva dies et prima novembris.
Gaudia cum Sanctis tenet omnibus inde sacerdos,
Pro quo perpetuo datur hac celebrare capella.

Baptismal font (1226 C.E., Germany)

THE PROEME FROM THE RATIONALE DIVINORUM OFFICIORUM WILLIAM DURAND, BISHOP OF MENDE

1. Everything that pertains to divine worship, the practices and vestments used by the Church are full of divine meanings and mysteries. Each and every one of them, when examined with care and love by an individual who knows how to draw honey from stones and oil from the hardest of rocks, pours forth a celestial fragrance. Who however can know the mandates of heaven, and who can apply to them the laws of this world? Clearly, anyone who wishes to investigate these divine realms would be overwhelmed by their glory; for it is a deep well and I do not have the means necessary to draw—unless He who gives most generously, and without reproach, provides me with the necessary container so that I might imbibe with a plenitude of joy from the fountains of the Savior which pour forth from the midst of the mountains.* However, it is impossible to give the explanation for everything which has been transmitted to us by our ancestors, and sometimes it is even necessary to pass over that which cannot be explained. This is why I, William Durand, elected bishop of the holy Church of Mende by the sole grace of God, knock and continuously knock at the door. Perhaps at some point the key of David will deign to open this door to me in order that the King might introduce me into the cellar where He guards His wine, and where the divine model, such as was shown to Moses on the mountain, is revealed to me so that I might be able to explain in precise and clear terms that which is hidden in all the things related to divine worship, and in the practices and vestments of the Church, and to determine the rules governing them. I pray that these things be revealed to me by our Lord, Who rendered the language of children eloquent and Whose Spirit blows where it will, giving to each person whatsoever He wills for the praise and the glory of the Holy Trinity.

2. We will consider the sacraments as signs or figures: these figures are not what gives the sacraments their power, but rather signs of their efficacious power; they are like the written word used to instruct. Among these signs some are natural, others are practical; a matter about which more will be

---

*It is only in the later editions of Durand's work that the Scriptural sources of his phrases are established—and this in a most tentative manner. We will follow the practice of Durand and give none: In this way we remain faithful to our principle of providing an exact translation. Moreover, indicating the Scriptural sources of his phrases for ecclesiastics and those likely to read his works seems rather futile. [Note by the editors of the 1854 French translation – ED].

said in the fourth part of this work, in the seventh section on the Canon when discussing the phrase *mysterium fidei* (mystery of the faith).

3. Now the priests and prelates of the Church, to whom it is given to know the mysteries, as can be read in Chapter 8 of Saint Luke, and who are the distributors and dispensers of the sacraments, should shine forth with the powers that they represent in order that others, reflecting their insights, might also be enlightened. If such is not the case then it is a matter of the blind leading the blind, or as the words of the prophet put it: "their eyes are darkened and they cannot see where they are going." But (and how sad) in these days many seem to have hardly any understanding of the things they engage in daily pertaining to the practices of the Church, or her divine worship. Nor do they know what they signify or why they were instituted. So much is this the case that the words of this prophet seem to be fulfilled to the letter: "The priest will be like the common people," for they bear the showbreads and mysteries to the Lord's altar without any understanding or respect, such that, beyond any doubt, they will be considered, by the just judgement of God, as beasts of burden who carry the food which provides for the sustenance of others. They will have to render an account of this ignorance on the day of judgment and then, while the very cedars of paradise tremble, what will happen to these reeds in the desert? For it is said of such by the Prophet: "They have not known my ways, and I will judge them in my anger, and they will not enter into my repose."

4. Professors of the liberal arts, regardless of their specialty, exert every effort to explain the causes and reasons for the things contained in these arts, be they ever so dry and colorless, and seek to both color and embellish them. The same is true of painters and every type of artisan and worker—each in their own area of expertise—who try to provide their profession or their art with true explanations, and have these readily available. Even according to the laws of the world, it is shameful for an official or a lawyer to be ignorant of the law with which he should be very familiar since he has chosen to make it a means of livelihood throughout his life.

5. Even though knowledge is most necessary to priests insofar as they are meant to teach others, one should not hold ignorant priests in any lower estimation than those knowing experts in the schools. According to the words of Exodus, "do not hold the judges of the law in contempt." This is why, as St. Augustine said, one should not deride, even by accident, bishops or ministers of the Church who invoke God in barbarous or degrading terms, even if it is clear that they do not understand the words which they

pronounce or only mumble them in a confused manner. Nor should those who are aware of these defects reprimand such individuals, but on the contrary, they should support them with charity and good will. We shall consider what is necessary for a priest to know in the second part of this book entitled "Treatise on the Priesthood."

6. It is possible that people do not understand just what occurs in the practices and divine worship of the Church because it is obscured by the use of symbols. This may be because the signs belong to a previous era, or because we now live in the times of truth and wish not to judaize. However, even if the symbols in which the truth is revealed are today passé, there are still many others that we do not see because they are hidden in obscurity, and it is for this reason that the Church returns yet again to symbols. Thus, for example, the white vestments to some degree lead us to understand the beauty of our souls, which is to say the glory of our immortality which is not openly manifest to us. And again, in the Mass, before the *Preface*, we have the preliminaries of the Passion of Christ in order that these episodes may be impressed more firmly and definitively on our memories.

7. It is important to note that some of those things which are contained in the ancient law are moral, while others are mystical. Things moral form customs and should therefore be comprised of the very words which give expression to them as for example, "You should love your God, honor your father and not kill" *etc.* Things mystical are allegorical and signify something other than the letter of the word: "Among those which are mystical, some are sacramentals and others ceremonial." The sacramentals are those for which one can give the reasons. This is why they must be followed to the letter as is the case with circumcision, the observance of the Sabbath and other things of that order. One cannot however explain the ceremonials, for they fall under the category of precepts such as, "you should not yoke the cow with the ass; you should not wear clothes of linen and wool; you should not sow your field with different seeds," *etc., etc.*

8. In moral matters, the law cannot be changed. But with regard to sacramentals and ceremonial matters, these have only been changed superficially: their mystical sense has not changed. This is why one does not say that the law has been changed, even though it has been transformed among us by the priesthood.

9. One must be aware of the fact that in the Holy Scriptures there exists an historical, an allegorical, a tropologic and an anagogic sense. This is why, according to Boethius, the fullness of divine authority is to be found either in the historical sense, or in the allegorical sense, or in one of the other

senses, and according to St. Jerome, we should examine divine Scripture in three ways: firstly, according the literal sense, secondly according to the allegorical meaning, which is to say, in the spiritual sense, and thirdly according to future blessedness. The historical sense is the meaning of the words attached to events, as for example, when a fact of any kind is reported as an event that has transpired according to the letter. For example, how the Israelites were saved from Egypt and built a temple to the Lord. The word history comes from the Greek *istorein*, which means to express a thing by actions, which is why historians are called "gesticulators," or actors.*

10. Allegory exists when a word conveys any sense to the mind that differs from its sound, or a fact which conveys a different meaning to the intelligence. If the object designated is visible, it is a simple allegory; if it is invisible and heavenly, then it is called an anagoge. It is also an allegory when a strange phrase gives expression to a strange state, as for example when the presence of Christ or the sacraments of the Church are designated by words or by mystical things, as for example, in the *Introit* when it says, "a branch grew of the root of Jesse," this means: "the Virgin Mary was born of the race of David" who was the son of Jesse. And again with regard to mystical things, when the Jews were delivered from Egyptian slavery by the blood of the Lamb, this signifies that the Church was snatched from the claws of the Devil by the Passion of Christ. The word allegory is derived from the Greek *goron* meaning "foreign" and *allo* meaning "sense"—in other words, a foreign sense.

11. Tropology turns discourse into morality. It is a way of speaking about morality so as to either form or correct behavior. One can do this in two ways, either mystically or openly. With regard to the mystical manner consider the following: "At all times your clothes should be as white as snow, and do not forget to anoint your head with oil," which means: "all your works should be pure, and charity should never be lacking in your soul." And again, "It is necessary that David should kill Goliath in us," which means: "our humility should kill our pride." Or in a clear manner: "bring and break your bread with those that are hungry"; or again, "do not love fine speeches and words, but rather works in truth." The word tropology comes from the Greek *tropos* signifying "change" and *logos* meaning "word", as if to say, a changed word.

12. Anagogic comes from the Greek *ano* meaning "on high" and *ago*, meaning "I lead", thus indicating that which leads on high. And so the

*An etymology, current in the West since Isidore of Seville (seventh century), mistakenly deriving a Greek word from the unrelated Latin *histrio* or "actor" –ED.

term anagogic pertains to that which achieves this, for it brings us from visible things to those that are invisible. For example the light which was created on the first day signifies something invisible, which is to say, angelic nature created from the beginning. An expression which leads us to higher things in the Church is anagogic, as for example the Trinity or the orders of the angels. It expresses itself by either clear or by mystical statements, with regard to the rewards of the future life in Heaven. An example of a clear statement is the following: "Happy are those whose hearts are pure because they will see God." As a mystical one, "Happy are those whose robes are washed in the blood of the Lamb for they shall gather the fruit of the tree of life, and they shall enter the city by means of the gate," which is to say more clearly: "Happy are those who purify their thoughts because they will have the ability to see God who is the life, the truth, and the way, and by doctrine, which is to say, the teaching of the Fathers, they will enter into the Heavenly kingdom." Similarly, Jerusalem signifies the historical and earthly city which carries this name and where pilgrims visit. Allegorically it refers to the Church Militant; and tropologically it refers to each faithful soul. In a similar manner one can find other examples in the lessons read on Holy Saturday as will be explained in the sixth part. Most of the time in this treatise the various senses are used and one passes from one to another in such a manner as to make it easy for the reader to follow.

13. Just as in law anyone can submit different exceptions or defenses, so also no one is forbidden to explain, in praise of God, the ceremonies of the Church in different ways, providing of course that the faith is not impugned and remains intact.

14. Notice must be taken of how a great many different practices are utilized in celebrating divine worship; almost every Church has its own observances which are appropriate and full of meaning. These should never be rejected as reprehensible or absurd, for God and the saints can be venerated by innumerable harmonies and modulations, by different observances, for the Church Triumphant is, as the prophet says, "ornamented with vestments of diverse colors," and even when it comes to the administration of the Sacraments, the Church allows for a variety of ceremonies established by the law of custom.

15. As St. Augustine has pointed out, we have received some of the teachings of the Church with regard to the Divine Office from the Holy Scriptures, others from apostolic tradition not found in Scripture, and which have been confirmed by their successors. Still others are fortified by cus-

tomary usage, even though their origin is unsure, and these should be observed, followed and respected.

16. The reader should not be surprised to come across, in this work, unfamiliar practices never observed in his own church. It is not our intention to treat of practices limited to any particular place, but rather to deal with those rites that are common and most often used, for it is our aim to provide an explanation of common rather than particular teachings. In any event, it would be impossible for us to consider each and every practice to be found in all the countries of the world. This is why we have decided, for the sake of our soul and for the benefit of the reader, to explain as clearly as possible, the mysteries hidden in the Divine Offices, and further, to provide clerics what seems essential for them to understand in the rites they utilize on a daily basis; to explain these intimately and profoundly, penetrating as it were to the kernal of the matter, just as I have previously composed the *Speculum Judiciale* [*Mirror of the Law*] to be used by those responsible for judging the affairs of these times, men placed in a state having nothing to do with the Church.

17. However, one should be aware that there are many ceremonies observed in the Divine Offices, the origin of which is unknown, and the moral and mystical sense of which is unclear. Some have come into use because of necessity, others for reasons of convenience, and still others in order to manifest the difference between the old and the new law. Still others because they are commodious or give the service greater dignity and reverence, and these have with time become customary. And thus it is that, as St. Augustine says, the ceremonies used in different lands are infinitely variable, as indeed are the customs in these lands. It would be impossible to determine the reasons why many of these were originally established.

18. Now this work is entitled the *Rationale*, for just as with the Rational [Breastplate] of Judgment that the High Priest of the Law bore upon his breast there was written "manifestation and truth", so in this work the reasons for the different ceremonies in the Divine Offices and their variations are clearly described and revealed, and so also the prelates and priests of the Churches should faithfully preserve them in the jewel-case of their hearts. Even more, just as there was a stone upon this Rational by whose sparkling the children of Israel knew when God would favor them, so the devout reader, by the splendors of this reading, having been instructed in the mysteries of the Divine Offices, will understand that God will favor us, providing of course we do not incur His indignation by the unforseen injury of sin. This Rational, or Breastplate, was also woven of four colors

with golden threads, while in this book (as mentioned above), the reasons for the variations in Church practices and offices are decorated as if with different colors, with the four senses to be found there, namely the historic, allegorical, tropologic and anagogic, and finally by the faith which is the groundwork in the midst of these four kinds of colors.

19. Finally, this work is divided into eight distinct parts which will be followed in sequence with the help of Our Lord. The first part treats of the Church and the principles on which it is founded, of its ornaments, its consecration, and its sacraments. The second will discuss the ministers of the Church and their offices; the third, priestly and other vestments; the fourth, the Mass and all the ceremonies that surround this rite; the fifth, the other Divine Offices. The sixth will give special consideration to the Sundays, ferias and feast days consecrated to our Savior. The seventh will treat of the festivals of the saints, and the feast and offices devoted to the dedication of a Church and to the dead. And lastly, the eighth will show how the calendar is computed.

Translated in 2005 by
the Reverend Father Rama Coomaraswamy,
from a volume of *Rationale ou Manuel des Divins Offices* 1854 (see p.177), originally kept in the monastery library of St. Benoît-sur-Loire, France.

(Notre Dame, Paris)

"The door is Christ; whence the Lord saith in the Evangel. 'I am the Door.' The pillars be doctors; who hold up spiritually the temple of God by their doctrine, as do the evangelists also the throne..." – HUGO DE SANCTO VICTORE (1096-1141)

THE MYSTICAL MIRROR OF THE CHURCH, MADE BY MASTER HUGH OF S. VICTOR (1096–1141)

The 1893 publication of *The Symbolism of Churches and Church Ornaments* included two chapters from the Mystical Mirror adding this explanation:

> [For the avoiding continual reference, for the extreme beauty of the treatise itself, for its value as an older document than the 'Rationale', and for the advantage of comparison with the latter in subject, sentiment, style, and often language, the Editors have subjoined a translation of the first and second chapters of the 'Mystical Mirror of the Church' of Hugo de Sancto Victore.]
>
> (*Folio Edition*, 237 E)

A PROLOGUE TO THE MYSTICAL MIRROR OF THE CHURCH,

Your love hath asked of me to treat of the sacraments of the Church, and to set forth unto you their mystical sweetness. But since with the more willingness, because with the more ease and boldness I do evolve (after my custom) points of logic rather than of theology; I began to doubt whether to withstand your admonition or the rather to write. But when I presently remembered how that every good thing when shared with others becometh more bright and beautiful when it is shared, I incontinently betook myself to my pen, having invoked the aid of 'Him Who openeth and no man shutteth, and shutteth and no man openeth.'[1] Wherefore I have put into the lips of your understanding the tractate which you did desire, flowing within with nectar like the honeycomb: and the same, because therein ye may see as in a mirror what every thing in the church doth mystically denote, I have called 'The Mystical Mirror of a Church.'

CHAPTER I: OF A CHURCH

The material church in which the people cometh together to praise God, signifieth the Holy Catholic Church, which is builded in the heavens of living stones. This is the Lord's house which is firmly builded. The 'chief corner-stone is Christ.' *Upon* this, not *besides* this, is the 'foundation of the apostles and Prophets'; as it is written, 'Her foundations are upon the holy hills.'[2] The walls builded thereon, be the Jews and Gentiles coming from the four quarters of the world unto Christ. All the stones be polished and squared; that is, all the saints be pure and firm: the which also be placed so as to last for ever by the hands of the Chief Workman. Of these some be borne and do not bear, as the more simple folk in the Church; some be borne and do also bear, as the middling sort; others do only bear, and be not borne, save by Christ alone, Who is the single Corner-stone. And in this house by how much anyone doth differ from and excel others, by so much being the more humble doth he hold up more of the building. One charity doth join all together after the fashion of cement: and the living stones be bound together by the bond of peace. The towers be the preachers and the prelates of the Church: who are her wards and defence. Whence saith the bridegroom unto his spouse in the *Song of Songs*: 'Thy neck is like the tower of David builded for an armoury.'[3] The cock which is placed thereon representeth preacher. For the cock in the deep watches of the night divideth the hours thereof with his song: he arouseth the sleepers; he foretelleth the approach of day; but first he stirreth up himself to crow by the striking of his wings. Behold ye these things mystically: for not one is there without meaning. The sleepers be the children of this world, lying in sins. The cock is the company of preachers, which do preach sharply, do stir up the sleepers to cast away the works of darkness, crying, 'Woe to the sleepers: awake thou that sleepest'; which also do foretell the coming of the light, when they preach of the day of judgment and future glory. But wisely before they preach unto others do they rouse themselves by virtues from the sleep of sin, and do chasten their bodies. Whence saith the Apostle, 'I keep under my body and bring it into subjection.'[4] The same also do turn themselves to meet the wind when they bravely do contend against and resist the rebellious by admonition and argument, lest they should seem to flee when the wolf cometh. The iron rod upon which the cock sitteth, showeth the straightforward speech of the preacher; that he doth not speak from the spirit of man, but according to the scriptures of God: as it is said, 'If any man speak, let him speak as the oracles of God.'[5] In that this rod is placed above the cross, it is shown that the words of Scripture be consummated and confirmed by the cross: whence our Lord said in His Passion, 'It is finished.'[6] And His title was indelibly written over Him. The ball (*tholus*) upon which the cross is placed doth signify perfection by its roundness: since the Catholic faith is to be preached and held perfectly and inviolably: 'Which faith, except a man do keep whole and undefiled, without doubt he shall perish everlastingly.' Or else the ball doth signify the world redeemed by the price of the Cross: on which account the cross is placed over it. The cock being set over the cross signifieth that the preacher ought to make sure this point, that Christ redeemed the world by His Cross. The pinnacle and turret show the mind or life of a prelate who tendeth unto things above. The bells, by the voice of which the people are called together unto the church, typify also preachers: the which being necessary for many uses are called by many names. The clapper, which causeth the sound from the two sides of the bell, is the tongue of the preacher which causeth both Testaments to resound. The wooden frame, whence the bell hangeth, signifieth the Cross; the cramps, charity; by which charity the preacher, being fast bound to the Cross, boasteth, saying, 'God forbid that I should glory save in the Cross of our Lord Jesus Christ.'[7] The rope is the life and humility of the preacher. Whence the Apostle saith, 'He condescendeth towards others. Whether we exalt ourselves it is for God; whether we abase ourselves it is for you.'[8] The rings on the rope are perseverance and the crown of reward. The glazed windows of the church be the Holy Scriptures, which do ward off the wind and the rain, that is, do repel all hurtful things; and when they do transmit the brightness of the True Sun by day into the church, they do give light to them that be therein. These be wider within than without, because the sense mystical is more ample and more pre-eminent than the sense literal. These be frequented of preachers, 'who do fly as a cloud and as the doves to the windows.'[9] Also by the windows the five senses of the body be signified: which ought to be narrow without, lest they should take in vanities, but should be wide within to receive spiritual good. The door is Christ: whence the Lord saith in the Evangele, 'I am the Door.'[10] The pillars be doctors; who do hold up spiritually the temple of God by their doctrine, as do the evangelists also the throne of God. These, for the harmony of divine eloquence, be called silver columns: according to that of the Song of Songs, 'He made the pillars thereof of silver.'[11] The stalls do denote the contemplative: in whom God doth rest without offence. These, for that they do contemplate the highest divinity and glory of the eternal life, be compared unto gold: whence in the aforesaid Song of Songs it is said, 'He made a golden bed.'[12] The beams be such as spiritually sustain the Church: the ceilings such as adorn it and strengthen it; of the which (because they be not corrupted by vices) the bride glorieth in the same Canticles, saying, 'The beams of our house are cedar and our rafters of fir.'[13] For God hath built His Church of living stones and imperishable wood: according to that, 'Solomon made himself a litter of the wood of Lebanon;'[14] that is Christ of His saints made white by chastity. The chancel, when lower than the body of the church, showeth mystically how great humility ought to be in the clergy: according to the saying, 'The greater thou art the more humble thyself.'[15] The altar signifieth Christ, without Whom no acceptable gift is offered unto the Father. Whence the Church uttereth her prayers unto the Father *through* Christ. The vestments with which the altar is adorned be the saints of whom the prophet speaketh unto God, saying, 'Thou shalt surely clothe Thee with them all as with an ornament.'[16] The steps by which we ascend unto the altar do spiritually denote the apostles and martyrs of Christ who have shed their blood for the love of Him. The bride in the Canticles saith, 'The ascent unto it is purple, the midst thereof being paved with love.'[17] Furthermore, the fifteen virtues be expressed by the fifteen steps with which they went up unto the temple of Solomon: and the same be shown by the prophet in the fifteen continuous Psalms, which the righteous man hath disposed as steps or degrees in his heart.[18] This is the ladder which Jacob saw, the top of which touched the heavens. The lights of the church be they by whose doctrine the Church shineth as the sun and the moon; unto whom it is said by our Lord's voice,[19] 'Ye are the light of the world.' They be also the examples of good works: whence He saith in His admonitions, 'Let your light so shine before men.'[20] In that the church is adorned joyfully within but not without, it is shown morally that its 'Glory is all from within.'[21] For although it be contemptible externally, yet doth it shine within in the soul, which is the abode of God: whence the Church saith, 'I am black but comely.'[22] And again, 'Yea, I have a goodly heritage.'[23] Which the Prophet considering, saith, 'Lord I have loved the habitation of Thy house: and the place where Thine honour dwelleth,'[24] which place also Faith, Hope, and Charity do spiritually adorn. The cross of triumph is placed in the middle of the church, because the Church loveth her Redeemer in the middle of her heart, and 'the midst thereof is paved with love for the daughters of Jerusalem.'[25] The which as a sign of victory, let all who see say one and all, 'Hail, salvation of the whole world: hail, life-giving Tree!' Wherefore, lest we should ever forget the love of God for us, 'Who gave His only-begotten Son' to redeem us His servants, the Church armeth herself in her bosom and forehead with this sign, signifying that the mystery of the cross must always be believed by us in our heart, and confessed openly with our mouth. The figure of which went before her in Egypt. But when we cross ourselves from the forehead downwards, and then from the left to the right, we do set forth this mystery, that God 'bowed the heavens and came down,' to teach us to prefer things eternal unto things temporal. But by this sign the army of the devil is overthrown; the Church triumpheth, 'terrible as an army with banners.'[26] 'How dreadful is this place: this is none other but the house of God.'[27] And the hymn saith, 'The banners of the King come forth: the Cross unfolds its mystery.'[28] Round this do the heavenly legions rally. Of this it is written, 'I saw the holy city, New Jerusalem, coming down from God out of heaven.'[29]

For the Church is militant here; in her home she doth reign: a part is in pilgrimage, a part in glory. That which is in pilgrimage coming up from her exile through the desert, doth sigh for her home, from the 'waters of Babylon for the heavenly Jerusalem;' while the other part, continually seeing peace, doth hold perpetual festival. Thus the heavenly city of Jerusalem is called the 'vision of peace.'[30] How glorious is her kingdom, 'glorious things are spoken of thee, thou city of God.'[31] Her guardians be the citizens of heaven, the legions of angels with the glorious company of the apostles, the Prophets, and the patriarchs, the armies of martyrs robed in purple, the flowers of virgins, the verdant choir of confessors, compassed about with the universal assembly of all the saints, chaste and glorified! And this wondrous court of heaven is yet more wondrously adorned by that one incomparable jewel, the Virgin Mother, 'whose like there ne'er hath been, whose like there ne'er shall be.' But how great is the admiration of all in beholding the King Himself, and how harmonious be the songs in praise of Him; this is known to those alone, who have deserved to stand amongst the happy throng, and to behold the mystery of the Trinity and the glory of Christ: Who is encircled by the angelic choirs; upon Whom the angels desire continually to gaze. To behold this the Immortal King face to face, the Church below is preparing herself: and while she keepeth here her feasts of time, she is remembering the festivals of her home and of eternity; in which the bridegroom is hymned by angelical instruments. And all the saints continually celebrating the day of great festivity 'which the Lord hath made,' cease not in their nuptial songs to laud the eternal bridegroom, the beautiful in form above the sons of men; Him who hath chosen the Church for Himself of His free mercy. Of whom, as He had seen her from eternity, He saith, 'I will get Me to the mountain of myrrh, and to the hill of frankincense and will speak unto my spouse.'[32] For whom 'He came forth as a bridegroom out of His chamber, and rejoiced as a giant to run his course';[33] when He went forth from His Father, and returned unto His Father—went forth indeed even unto Hades, returned unto the Throne of God—to make all His elect, from the beginning even unto the end of the world, one kindgom in the vision of the Supreme Trinity: in which is glorified 'one God world without end.'

(Notre Dame, Paris)

"The cross of triumph is placed in the middle of the church, because the Church loveth her Redeemer in the middle of her heart, and 'the midst thereof is paved with love for the daughters of Jerusalem."

(Berlin, Germany, 15th C.E.)

The Holy Trinity on the Thone

"...and to behold the mystery of the Trinity and the glory of Christ: Who is encircled by the angelic choirs; upon whom the angels desire continually to gaze. To behold this Immortal King face to face, the Church below is preparing herself; and while she keepeth her feasts of time, she is remembering the festivals..."

(Dresden, Germany)

(Dresden, Germany)

(Victoria and Albert Museum, London, England)

"This wondrous court of heaven is yet more wonderfully adorned by one incomparable jewel, the Virgin Mother..."

(Bohemia, 1260 C.E.)

(Minden Altar Piece, Berlin, Germany)

CHAPTER II: OF THE DEDICATION OF A CHURCH

With what carefulness and love Christ doth adorn the bride for Himself and prepare her for her heavenly dedication, is in part signified by the consecration of the material church. The bishop compasseth the church to be dedicated three times, sprinkling it with holy water, the clergy and people following him.

239 A. In the meanwhile without and within there be burning twelve lamps. So often as he cometh to the door (which for a mystical reason is shut), the bishop smiteth the lintel with his pastoral staff, saying 'Lift up your heads, O ye gates, and be ye lift up, ye everlasting doors, and the King of Glory shall come in.'[34] The deacon answereth, 'Who is the King of Glory?' To whom the bishop, 'The Lord of Hosts: He is the King of Glory.' At the third time, the door being thrown open, he entereth with the clergy and people, saying, 'Peace be to this house.' Then he performeth the other ceremonies which pertain to dedication. But whatever things be here done visibly, the same doth God work by His invisible power in the soul, which is the true Temple of God: wherein Faith layeth the foundation, Hope raiseth the buildings, and Charity finisheth it. Also the Church Catholic herself, being made one out of many stones, is the temple of God; because many temples make one temple, of which there is one Lord and one Faith. Wherefore the house must be dedicated; the soul sanctified. Water is penitence: salt, wisdom; the threefold aspersion, the threefold immersion in baptism; the twelve lights, the twelve apostles, preaching the mystery of the Cross; the bishop, Christ; his staff, Christ's power; the three strokes on the door, Christ's dominion over all things in heaven, earth, and hell: 'that all the threefold frame of things may bow the knee to Him, their Lord.' Again, the question of the deacon within is the ignorance of the people; the opening of the door, the ejection of sin. The bishop entering, prayeth for peace on the house, and Christ entering the world maketh peace between God and men. Then prostrate he prayeth unto the Lord for its sanctification: and so Christ, humbled in His Passion, prayed for His disciples and them that should believe, saying, 'Father, sanctify them in Thy truth.'[35] Arising he does not give the salutation but only prayeth: because they who be not yet sanctified must not be blessed but only prayed for. The writing of the alphabet upon the pavement is the simple teaching of faith in the heart of man. The line drawn from the left corner of the east unto the right corner of the west, and the other line from the right of the east unto the left of the west, do express the Cross, and also the gathering

in of both peoples: according as Jacob blessed the children of Joseph with his hands crossed.[36] For although Christ passing from the east did leave the Jews, because they would not believe, on His left hand, and did come unto the Gentiles; to whom, though they had been in the west, He granteth to be on the right hand: yet will he again, passing from the Gentiles who be placed in the right of the east, visit the Jews in the left hand corner: who, it is evident, be worse than He first found the Gentiles. The staff with which the alphabet is described typifieth the ministry of teachers, by which the conversion of the Gentiles is effected and that of Jews perfected. In that afterwards the bishop standing before the altar saith, 'O God, make speed to save us'; he doth signify those who having received the faith are preparing themselves to fight. And because they be still in conflict, and as it were amongst sighs, the Alleluia is not yet added. After this the water is blessed with salt and ashes; wine mixed with water being also added. The water is the people; the salt, doctrine; the ashes, the remembrance of the Passion of Christ. The wine mixed with water is Christ, God and Man; the wine His Godhead, the water His Manhood. Thus the people is sanctified by the doctrines of faith and remembrance of the Passion, being united with its Head both God and Man. Whence the altar and the church be sprinkled within; to show that within, as without, the spiritual Church must be sanctified. The aspersory, made of hyssop, denoteth humility; with which grace the Catholic Church being sprinkled is purified. The bishop compasseth the church in lustration and as if bestowing his care upon all. In the meanwhile is chanted the Psalm, 'Let God arise and his enemies be scattered,' with its proper response and antiphon, which is followed by another, 'Whoso dwelleth under the defence of the most high.' Then the bishop chanteth, 'My House shall be called an House of Prayer,' and also, 'I will tell out thy name among my brethren.' And because no work can prosper without God, he prayeth in conclusion that they may be heard who shall enter therein to pray for blessings. After this he approacheth unto the altar, saying, 'I will go up unto the altar of the Lord,' with the whole Psalm: and what remains of the water he poureth away at the base of the altar, committing unto God that which surpasseth human abilities in so great a sacrament. After this the altar is wiped with a linen cloth. The altar is Christ, the cloth is his flesh, brought by the beating of His Passion unto the whiteness and glory of immortality. Next the bishop offereth upon the altar frankincense, which is burnt in the shape of a cross in the middle thereof; and at its four corners he maketh crosses with sanctified oil. Then upon each of the four walls of the church there be made three crosses with the same oil: and the consecration being thus finished, the altar is covered with a white veil. Incense, prayers, and oil do denote the grace of the Holy Ghost, Whose fulness—'like the precious ointment upon the head that ran down unto the beard: even unto Aaron's beard,'[37]—came down upon the apostles and their disciples: who preached the mystery of the Cross through the four quarters of the world, the Lord working with them. The white covering doth typify the joy of immortality: concerning which the Son exulteth, saying unto the Father, 'Thou hast put off my sackcloth, and girded me with gladness.'[38]

"The ball (tholus) upon which the cross is placed doth signify perfection by its roundness . . . or else the ball doth signify the world redeemed by the price of the Cross; on which account the cross is placed over it."

– Hugo de Sancto Victore (1096-1141)

(Vezelay, France, 12th Century)

The mystic mill, Vezelay: the Apostle Paul turns the mill, 'urging us onward from the material to the immaterial', converting the words of the prophets into the message of the New Testament. (E. Panofsky, Abbot Suger, pp. 74 - 75)

THE SYMBOLISM OF CHURCHES AND CHURCH ORNAMENTS

A TRANSLATION OF THE FIRST BOOK OF THE

RATIONALE DIVINORUM OFFICIORUM

WRITTEN BY

WILLIAM DURANDUS
SOMETIME BISHOP OF MENDE

WITH AN INTRODUCTORY ESSAY AND NOTES

BY

THE REV. JOHN MASON NEALE, B.A.

AND

THE REV. BENJAMIN WEBB, B.A.

OF TRINITY COLLEGE, CAMBRIDGE

1893

(The Gothic Cathedral of Chartes. 1194 - 1260)

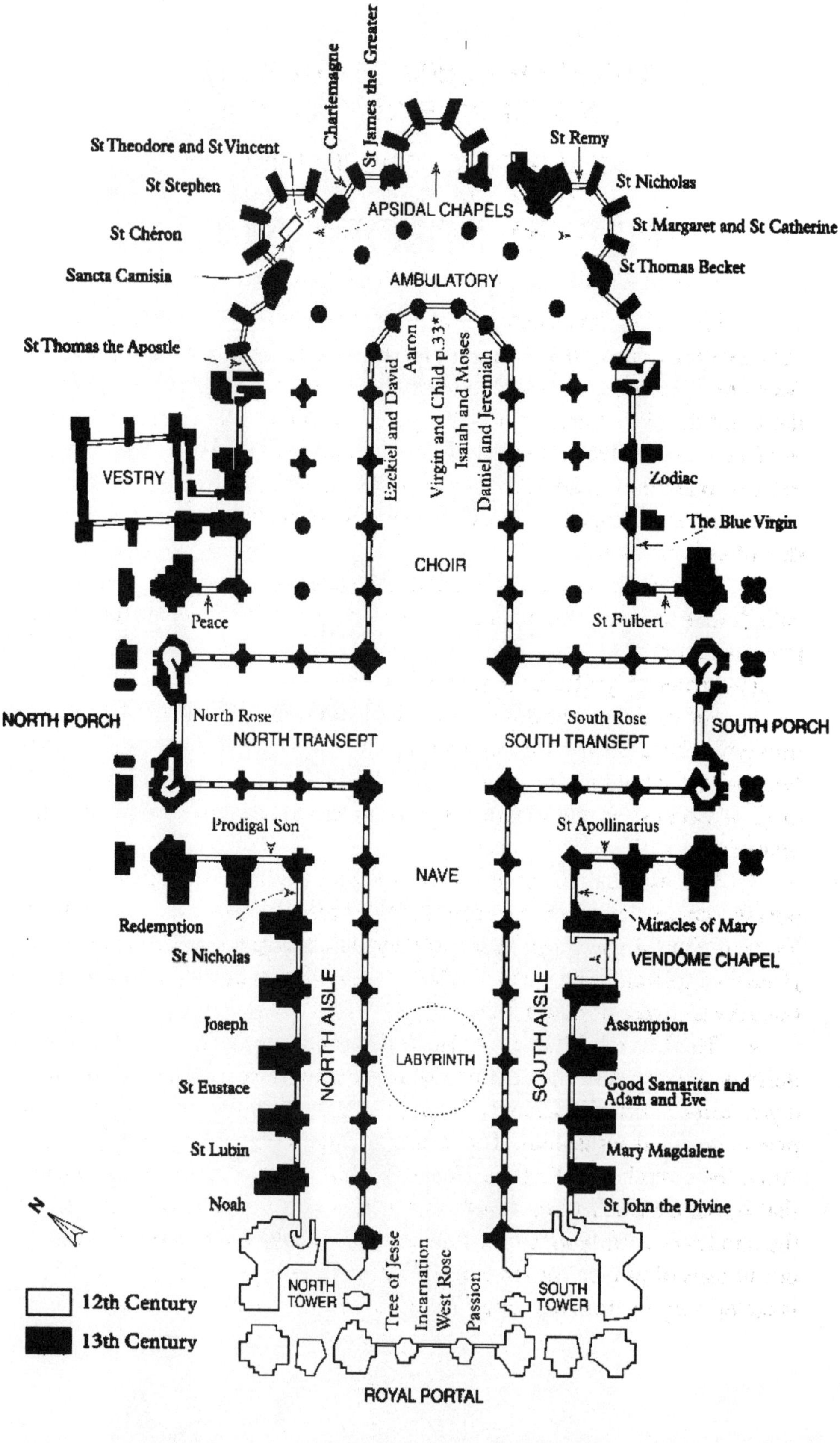

THE SYMBOLISM OF CHURCHES AND CHURCH ORNAMENTS

HERE BEGINNETH THE FIRST BOOK OF GULIELMUS DURANDUS, HIS RATIONALE OF THE DIVINE OFFICES.

CHAPTER I: OF A CHURCH AND ITS PARTS

1. First of all, let us consider a church[1] and its parts. The word church hath two meanings: the one, a material building, wherein the divine offices are celebrated: the other, a spiritual fabric, which is the collection of the faithful. The Church, *that* is the people forming it, is assembled by its ministers, and collected together into one place by 'Him who maketh men to be of one mind in an house'[2] For as the material church is constructed from the joining together of various stones, so is the spiritual Church by that of various men.

2. The Greek *ecclesia* is in Latin translated by *convocatio,* because it calleth men to itself: the which title doth better befit the spiritual than the material church.

The material typifieth the spiritual Church: as shall be explained when we treat of its consecration.[3] Again, the Church is called Catholic, that is universal, because it hath been set up in, or spread over, all the world, because the whole multitude of the faithful ought to be in one congregation, or because in the Church is laid up the doctrine necessary for the instruction of all.

3. It is also called in Greek *synagoga*, in Latin *congregatio*, which was the name chosen by the Jews for their place of worship: for to them the term synagogue more appropriately belongeth, though it be also applied to a church. But the Apostles never call a church by this title, perhaps for the sake of distinction.

4. The Church Militant is also called *Sion*: because, amidst its wanderings, it expecteth the promise of a heavenly rest: for Sion signifieth *expectation*. But the Church Triumphant, our future home, the land of peace, is called Jerusalem: for Jerusalem signifieth *the vision of peace*.[4] Also, the church is called the *House of God*: also, sometimes, κυριακή, that is, the *Lord's House*. At others *basilica* (in Latin, a royal palace), for the abodes of earthly kings are thus termed: and how much more fittingly our houses of prayer, the dwelling-places of the King of Kings! Again, it is called *temple*, from *tectum amplum*, where sacrifices are offered to God:

and sometimes the tabernacle of God, because this present life is a journey, and a progress to a lasting country: and a tabernacle is an hostelrie:[5] as will be explained when we speak of the dedication[6] of the church. And why it is called the *Ark of the Testimony*, we shall say in the ensuing chapter, under the title Altars. Sometimes it is called *Martyrium*, when raised in honour of any martyr; sometimes *capella*[7] (chapel), (see under the head Priest in the second part); sometimes *cœnobium*, at others *sacrificium;* sometimes *sacellum*; sometimes *the house of prayer*: sometimes *monastery*: sometimes *oratory*. Generally, any place set apart for prayers is called an oratory. Again, the church is called the *Body of* Christ: sometimes a *virgin*, as the Apostle saith, 'that I may present you as a chaste virgin to Christ'[8]: sometimes a *bride*, because Christ hath betrothed her to Himself, as saith the Gospel: 'he that hath the bride is the bridegroom'[9]: sometimes a *mother*, for daily in baptism she beareth sons to God: sometimes a *daughter*, according to that saying of the Prophet, 'Instead of thy fathers thou shalt have children'[10]: sometimes a *widow*, because 'she sitteth solitary through her afflictions, and, like Rachel, will not be comforted.' Sometimes she is set forth under the emblem of an *harlot*, because she is called out of many nations, and because she closeth not her bosom against any that return to her. Sometimes she is called a city, because of the communion of her holy citizens, being defended by the munitions of the Scriptures, whereby heretics are kept off: having stones and beams of divers kinds, because the merits of the saints are of divers kinds also, as shall be said below. Whatever the Jewish Church received by the law, that doth the Christian Church receive, and with large increase by grace, from Christ whose bride she is. The setting up of an oratory, or church, is not new. For the Lord commanded Moses in Mount Sinai, that he should make a tabernacle of curiously wrought materials. This was divided by a veil into two parts: the outer, called the holy place, where the people attended the sacrifices: the inner, the holy of the holies, where the priests and Levites ministered before the Lord (see the Preface to the Fourth Book and also Appendix A).

5. This tabernacle having decayed through age, the Lord commanded that a temple should be built, which Solomon accomplished with wonderful skill: this also had two parts, like the tabernacle. From both of these, namely, from the tabernacle and the temple, doth our material church take its form. In its outer portion, the laity offer their prayers, and hear the Word. In the sanctuary, the clergy pray, preach, offer praises and prayers.

6. The tabernacle, built as it was amidst the journeyings of the Israelites, is sometimes taken as a type of the world which 'passeth away, and

The Tabernacle

(from the Hortus Deliciarum, 1167- 85 C.E.)

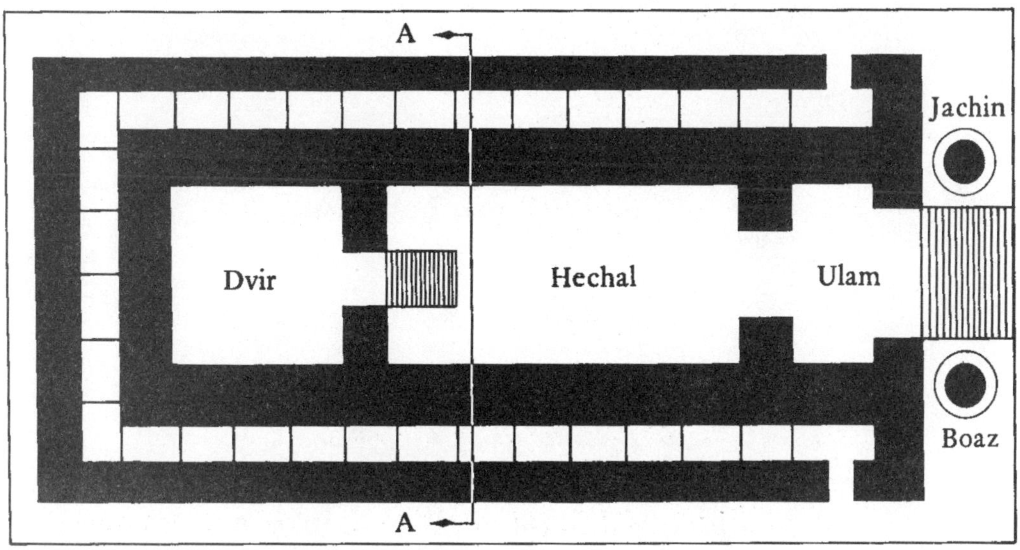

"The outer part of the tabernacle, where the people sacrificed, is the active life, wherein men give themselves up to the love of their neighbour: the interior, wherein the Levites ministered, is the contemplative life, where a band of religious men devote themselves to the love and contemplation of God. The tabernacle gave place to the temple..."

"The Lord commanded that a temple should be built, which Solomon accomplished with wonderful skill: this also has two parts, like the tabernacle. From both of these, namely, the tabernacle and the temple, doth our material church take its form. In its outer portion, the laity offer their prayers, and hear the Word. In the sanctuary, the clergy pray, preach, offer praises and prayers."

(A reconstruction of the Temple of Solomon based on the description of the Old Testament and archaeological evidence)

lust thereof.'[11] Whence it was formed with curtains of four colours, as the world is composed of four elements. 'God,' said the Prophet, 'is in His tabernacle':[12] God is in this world, as in a temple dyed scarlet by the blood of Christ. The tabernacle is, however, more especially symbolical of the Church Militant, which hath 'here no continuing city, but seeketh one to come.'[13] Therefore is it called a tabernacle, for tabernacles or tents belong to soldiers: and this saying, God is in his tabernacle, meaneth, God is among the faithful collected together in His name. The outer part of the tabernacle, where the people sacrificed, is the active life, wherein men give themselves up to the love of their neighbour: the interior, wherein the Levites ministered, is the contemplative life, where a band of religious men devote themselves to the love and contemplation of God. The tabernacle gave place to the temple: because after the warfare cometh the triumph.

7. Now a church is to be built on this fashion: The foundation being prepared, according to that saying, 'It fell not, for it was founded upon rock,'[14] the bishop or a priest[15] as the bishop's deputy, must sprinkle it with holy water, to banish the foul forms of evil spirits, and lay the first stone, whereon a cross must be engraved.[16]

8. The foundation must be so contrived, as that the head of the church may point due east (see Appendix B); that is, to that point of the heavens, wherein the sun ariseth at the equinoxes; to signify, that the Church Militant must[17] behave herself with moderation, both in prosperity and adversity: and not towards that point where the sun ariseth at the solstices, which is the practice of some. But if the walls of Jerusalem, 'which is built as a city that is at unity with itself,'[18] were, by the Prophet's command, raised by the Jews, with how much greater zeal should we raise the walls of our churches! For the material church, wherein the people assemble to set forth God's holy praise, symboliseth that Holy Church which is built in heaven of living stones.

9. This is that House of the Lord, built with all strength, 'upon the foundations of the apostles and Prophets, Jesus Christ Himself being the chief cornerstone.[19] Her[20] foundations are in the holy mountains.' The walls built upon these are the Jews and Gentiles; who come from the four parts of the world unto Christ, and who have believed, believe, or shall believe on Him.

The faithful predestined to eternal life, are the stones in the structure of this wall which shall continually be built up unto the world's end. And one stone is added to another, when masters in the Church teach and confirm and strengthen those who are put under them: and whosoever in Holy

Church undertaketh painful labours from brotherly love, he as it were beareth up the weight of stones which have been placed above him. Those stones which are of larger size, and polished, or squared, and placed on the outside and at the angles of the building, are men of holier life than others, who by their merits and prayers retain weaker brethren in Holy Church.

10. The cement, without which there can be no stability of the walls, is made of lime, sand, and water. The lime is fervent charity, which joineth to itself the sand, that is, undertakings for thc temporal welfare of our brethren: because true charity taketh care of the widow and the aged, and the infant, and the infirm: and they who have it study to work with their hands, that they may possess wherewith to benefit them. Now the lime and the sand are bound together in the wall by an admixture of water. But water is an emblem of the Spirit. And as without cement the stones cannot cohere, so neither can men be built up in the heavenly Jerusalem without charity, which the Holy Ghost worketh in them. All the stones are polished and squared—that is, holy and pure, and are built by the hands of the Great Workman into an abiding place in the Church: whereof some are borne, and bear nothing, as the weaker members: some are both borne and bear, as those of moderate strength: and some bear, and are borne of none save Christ, the cornerstone, as they that are perfect. All are bound together by one spirit of charity, as though fastened with cement; and those living stones are knit together in the bond of peace. Christ was our wall in His conversation: and our outer wall in His Passion.

11. When the Jews were rebuilding the walls of Jerusalem, their enemies strove hard to let the works: so that 'they built with one hand, and held their weapons of war in the other.' And round us too do enemies gather, while we are building the walls of our Church: our own sins , or ungodly men, willing to hinder our success. Whence, while we build our walls, that is, while we add virtue to virtue, we must fight with the enemy, and grasp our weapons firmly: we must 'take the helmet of salvation, the shield of faith, the breastplate of righteousness: and for our sword the word of God,'[21] that we may defend ourselves against them: and God's priest shall be unto us in Christ's stead, to teach us by his lessons, and defend us by his prayers.

12. Furthermore, of what the tabernacle was made the Lord hath told us, saying unto Moses, 'Take the first fruits,'—that is, the most precious gifts—'of the children of Israel: but from him alone who willingly offereth gold, and silver, and brass, and precious stones, and purple and linen twice dyed'; namely cloth of the colours of blue, purple, and scarlet: and of biss, which is a kind of Egyptian linen white and soft: 'and goat's hair, and

(Saint Vitus' Cathedral, Prague, 10th Century onwards)

"The arrangement of a material church resembleth that of a human heart: the chancel, or place where the altar is, representeth the head…The sacrifice of the altar denoteth the vows of the heart."

(Victoria and Albert Museum, London, England)

"Medieval sarcophagus with apse-shaped extension for head."

"Concerning this house saith the Lord, 'We will come unto him, and make our abode with him. But some chur are built in the shape of a cross, to signify that we are crucified to the world..."

(Notre Dame, Paris, France)

Altar and Throne

Rose Window (Cathedral Saint Vitus, Prague, 10th Century onwards)

Nave (Cathedral Saint Vitus, Prague, 10th Century onwards)

Example of Pier

rams' skins dyed red,' which we call Parthian, because the Parthians first dyed them thus, 'and purple skins and shittim wood' (shittim is the name of a mountain, and also of a tree: its leaves are like the white thorn, and to be injured neither by fire nor by decay): 'and oil for the lights, frankincense, and ointment of a sweet savour, onyx stones, and sard-onyxes, and jewels: and let them make Me a house, that I may dwell in the midst of them: and that they may not weary themselves in returning to this mountain.'[22]

14. The arrangement of a material church resembleth that of a human body: the chancel, or place where the altar is, representeth the head: the transepts, the hands and arms, and the remainder—towards the west—the rest of the body. The sacrifice of the altar denoteth the vows of the heart. Furthermore, according to Richard de Sancto Victore, the arrangement of a church typifieth the three states in a church: of virgins, of the continent, of the married. The sanctuary[23] is smaller than the chancel, and this than the nave: because the virgins are fewer in number[24] than the continent, and these than the married. And the sanctuary is more holy than the chancel: and the chancel than the nave: because the order of virgins is more worthy than that of the continent, and the continent more worthy than the married.

15. Furthermore, the church consisteth of four walls, that is, is built on the doctrine of the Four Evangelists; and hath length, breadth, and height: the height representeth courage, the length fortitude, which patiently endureth till it attaineth its heavenly home; the breadth is charity, which, with long suffering, loveth its friends in God, and its foes for God; and again, its height is the hope of future retribution, which despiseth prosperity and adversity, hoping 'to see the goodness of the Lord in the land of the living.'[25]

16. Again, in the temple of God, the foundation is faith, which is conversant with unseen things: the roof, charity, 'which covereth a multitude of sins.'[26] The door, obedience, of which the Lord saith, 'If thou wilt enter into life, keep the commandments.'[27] The pavement, humility, of which the psalmist saith, 'My soul cleaveth to the pavement.'[28]

17. The four side-walls, the four cardinal virtues, justice, fortitude, temperance, prudence. Hence the Apocalypse saith, 'The city lieth foursquare.'[29] The windows are hospitality with cheerfulness, and tenderness with charity. Concerning this house saith the Lord, 'We will come unto him, and make our abode with him.'[30] But some churches are built in the shape of a cross, to signify, that we are crucified to the world, and should tread in the steps of the Crucified, according to that saying, 'If any man come after Me, let him deny himself and take up his cross, and follow

Me.'[31] Some are also built in the form of a circle:[32] to signify that the Church hath been extended throughout the circle of the world, as saith the Psalmist: 'And their words unto the end of the world.'[33] Or because from the circle of this world, we reach forth to that crown of eternity which shall encircle our brows.

18. The choir is so called from the harmony of the clergy in their chanting, or from the multitude collected at the divine offices. The word *chorus* is derived from *chorea*, or from *corona*. For in early times they stood like a crown round the altar, and thus sung the Psalms in one body: but Flavianus and Theodorus taught the antiphonal method of chanting, having received it from S. Ignatius, who himself learned it by inspiration. The two choirs then typify the angels, and the spirits of just men, while they cheerfully and mutually excite each other in this holy exercise. Others derive *chorus* from *concord*, which consisteth of charity; because he who hath not charity, cannot sing with the spirit. But what this choir signifieth, and why the greatest in it sit last, shall be explained in the fourth book.[34] And observe, that when one sings, it is called in Greek a *monody*, in Latin *tycinium*. When two sing, it is called *bicinium*; when many, a *chorus*.

19. The exedra is an apis, separated a little from a temple or palace; so called because it projecteth a little from the wall (in Greek ἐξέδρα), and signifieth the lay portion of the faithful joined to Christ and the Church. The crypts, or subterranean caves, which we find in some churches, are hermits who are devoted to a solitary life.

20. The open court signifieth Christ, by Whom an entrance is administered into the heavenly Jerusalem: this is also called porch, from *porta*, a gate, or because it is *aperta*, open.

21. The towers are the preachers and prelates of the Church, which are her bulwark and defence. Whence the bridegroom in the Canticles saith to the bride, 'Thy neck is like the tower of David builded for an armoury.'[35] The pinnacles of the towers signify the life or the mind of a prelate which aspireth heavenwards.

22. The cock at the summit of the church is a type of preacher. For the cock, ever watchful even in the depth of night, giveth notice how the hours pass, wakeneth the sleepers, predicteth the approach of day, but first exciteth himself to crow by striking his sides with his wings. There is a mystery conveyed in each of these particulars. The night is this world: the sleepers are the children of this world who are asleep in their sins. The cock is the preacher, who preacheth boldly, and exciteth the sleepers to cast away the works of darkness, exclaiming, 'Woe to them that sleep! Awake thou that sleepest!'[36] And these foretell the approach of day when they speak of the

(Oxford, England)

"The cock at the summit of the church is a type of preacher. For the cock, ever watchful even in the depth of night, giveth notice how the hours pass..." "The night is this world: the sleepers are the children of this world who are asleep in their sins. The cock is the preacher, who preacheth boldly, and exciteth the sleepers to cast away the works of darkness, exclaiming, 'Woe to them that sleep! Awake thou that sleepest!'"

(Notre Dame, Paris

"By these windows the senses of the body are signified: which ought to be shut to the vanities of this world, and open to r
with all freedom, spiritual gifts."

(Notre Dame, Paris, France)

(Notre Dame, Paris, France)

(Church of St. Bartholomew, Bohemia, 1365)

glass windows in a church are Holy Scriptures, which expel the wind and the rain, that is, all things hurtful, but trans-
he light of the true Sun, that is, God, into the hearts of the faithful."

Day of Judgment, and the glory that shall be revealed: and like prudent messengers, before they teach others, arouse themselves from the sleep of sin by mortifying their bodies. Whence the Apostle, 'I keep under my body.'[37] And as the weathercock faceth the wind, they turn themselves boldly to meet the rebellious by threats and arguments: lest they should be guilty, 'when the wolf cometh, of leaving the sheep and fleeing.'[38] The iron rod, whereon the cock sitteth, representeth the discourse of the preacher, that he speaketh not of man but of God: according to that saying, 'If any man speak, let him speak as the oracles of God.'[39] But in that the iron rod is placed above the cross, on the summit of the church, it signifieth that Holy Scripture is now consummated and confirmed. Whence saith our Lord in His Passion, 'It is finished': and that title is written indelibly over Him.

23. The cone, that is the summit of the church, of great height, and of round shape, signifieth how perfectly and inviolably the Catholic faith must be held: which faith except a man do keep whole and undefiled, without doubt he shall perish everlastingly.

24. The glass windows in a church are Holy Scriptures, which expel the wind and the rain, that is all things hurtful, but transmit the light of the true Sun, that is, God, into the hearts of the faithful. These are wider[40] within than without, because the mystical sense is the more ample, and precedeth the literal meaning. Also, by the windows the senses of the body are signified: which ought to be shut to the vanities of this world, and open to receive with all freedom spiritual gifts.

25. By the lattice work[41] of the windows, we understand the Prophets or other obscure teachers of the Church Militant: in which windows there are often two shafts, signifying the two precepts of charity, or because the apostles were sent out to preach two and two.

26. The door of the church is Christ: according to that saying in the Gospel, 'I am the Door.'[42] The apostles are also called doors.

27. The piers of the church are bishops and doctors: who specially sustain the Church of God by their doctrine. These, from the majesty and clearness of their divine message, are called silver, according to that in the Song of Songs, 'He made me silver columns.'[43] Whence also Moses at the entering in of the tabernacle, placed five columns, and four before the oracle, that is, the holy of the holies. Although the piers are more in number than seven, yet they are called seven, according to that saying, 'Wisdom hath builded her house, she hath hewn out her seven pillars':[44] because bishops ought to be filled with the sevenfold influences of the Holy Ghost:[45] and SS. James and John, as the Apostle testifieth, 'seemed to be

pillars.'[46] The bases of the columns are the apostolic bishops,[47] who support the frame of the whole church. The capitals of the piers are the opinions of the bishops and doctors. For as the members are directed and moved by the head, so are our words and works governed by their mind. The ornaments of the capitals are the words of Sacred Scripture, to the meditation and observance of which we are bound.

28. The pavement of the church is the foundation of our faith. But in the spiritual Church, the pavement is the poor of Christ: the poor in spirit, who humble themselves in all things: wherefore on account of their humility they are likened to the pavement. Again, the pavement, which is trodden under foot, representeth the multitude, by whose labours the Church is sustained.

29. The beams[48] which join together the church are the princes of this world or the preachers who defend the unity of the Church, the one by deed, the other by argument.

30. The stalls in the church signify the contemplative, in whom God dwelleth without hindrance, who, from their high dignity and the glory of eternal life, are compared to gold. Whence He saith in the Canticles, 'He made a golden seat.'[49]

31. The beams in the church are preachers, who spiritually sustain it. The vaulting also, or ceiling representeth preachers, who adorn and strengthen it, concerning whom, seeing that they are not corruptible through vice, the bridegroom glorieth in the same Canticles, saying 'the beams of our house are cedar, and its ceiling, fir.' For God hath built His Church of living stones, and imperishable wood, according to that saying, 'Solomon made himself a litter of cedar wood;'[50] that is, Christ, of His saints who wear the white robe of chastity. The chancel, that is, the head of the church, being lower[51] than its body, signifieth how great humility there should be in the clergy, or in prelates, according to that saying, 'And the more thou art exalted, humble thyself in all things.' The rail, by which the altar[52] is divided from the choir, teacheth the separation of things celestial from things terrestrial.

32. The seats in the choir admonish us that the body must sometimes be refreshed: because that which hath not altarnate rest wanteth durability.

33. The pulpit in the church is the life of the perfect: and is so called from being public, or placed in a public place. For we read, 'Solomon made a brazen scaffold, and set it in the midst of the temple, and stood upon it, and stretching forth his hands spake to the people of God.' Esdras also made a wooden scaffold for speaking: in which when he stood, he was higher than the rest of the people.[53]

34. The analogium (rood-loft) is so called because in it the Word of God is read and delivered. Which also is called ambo, from *ambire*,[54] to surround, because it surroundeth him that entereth in.

35. The horologium, by means of which the hours are read, teacheth diligence that should be in priests to observe at the proper times the canonical hours: as he saith, "Seven times a day do I praise thee.'[55]

36. The tiles[56] of the roof which keep off the rain are the soldiers, who preserve the Church from paynim, and from enemies.

37. The circular staircases, which are imitated from Solomon's temple, are passages which wind among the walls, and point out the hidden knowledge which they only have who ascend to celestial things. Concerning the steps, by which ascent is made to the altar, hereafter.

38. The sacristy, or place where the holy vessels are deposited, or where the priest putteth on his robes, is the womb of the Blessed Mary, where Christ put on his robes of humanity. The priest, having robed himself, cometh forth into the public view, because Christ, having come from the womb of the Virgin, proceeded forth into the world.

The bishop's throne in the church is higher than the rest.

39. Near to the altar, which signifieth Christ, is placed the piscina, or lavacrum, that is, the pity of Christ, in which the priest washeth his hands, thereby denoting that by baptism and penitence we are purged from the filth of sin: which is drawn from the Old Testament. For he saith in Exodus, 'And Moses made a laver of brass, with his basin, in the which Aaron the priest and his sons should wash, before they went up to the altar, that they might offer an offering.[57]

40. The lamp in the church is Christ: as He saith, 'I am the light of the world'[58]; and again, 'That was the true light.'[59] Or the light in a church may denote the apostles and other doctors, by whose doctrine the Church is enlightened, as the sun and moon: concerning whom saith the Lord, 'Ye are the light of the world':[60] that is, an example of good works. Wherefore He saith to them in His admonitions, 'Let your light shine before men.'[61] But the Church is enlightened by the precepts of the Lord; wherefore it saith in the before-quoted place, 'Speak unto the sons of Aaron that they offer oil-olive most pure, that the lamp may burn continually in the tabernacle of the testimony.'[62] Moses made also seven lights, which are the seven gifts of the Holy Ghost: for they in the darkness of this world shine forth with brightness: and they rest in candlesticks, because in Christ rested 'the spirit of wisdom and knowledge, the spirit of counsel and might, the spirit of learning and piety, the spirit of the fear of the Lord, by which He

preached wisdom to the captives.'[63] The number of lights showeth the number of graces in the faithful.

41. In many places a triumphal cross is placed in the midst of the church; to teach us, that from the midst of our hearts we must love the Redeemer: who, after Solomon's pattern, 'paved the midst of his litter (*ferculum*) with love for the daughters of Jerusalem:'[64] and that all, seeing the sign of victory, might exclaim, Hail, thou Salvation of the whole world, Tree of our Redemption, and that should never forget the love of God, who, to redeem His servants, gave His only son, that we might imitate Him crucified. But the cross is exalted on high, to signify the victory of Christ. Why a church is ornamented within and not without, shall be said hereafter.

42. The cloisters, as Richard, Bishop of Cremona, testifieth, had their rise either in the watchings of the Levites around the tabernacle, or from the chambers of the priests, or from the porch of Solomon's temple. 'For the Lord commanded Moses, that he should not number the Levites with the rest of the children of Israel; but should set them over the tabernacle of the testimony to carry it and to keep it.'[65] On account of which divine commandment, while the Holy Mysteries are in celebration, the clergy should in the church stand apart from the laity. Whence the Council of Mayence ordained that the part which is separated with rails from the altar should be appropriated altogether to the priests choral. Furthermore, as the church signifieth the Church Triumphant, so the cloister signifieth the celestial Paradise, where there will be one and the same heart in fulfilling the commands of God and loving Him: where all things will be possessed in common, because that of which one hath less, he will rejoice to see more abounding in another, for 'God shall be all in all.'[66] Therefore the regular clergy who live in the cloisters, and are of one mind, rising to the service of God and leaving worldly things, lead their lives in common. The various offices in the cloister signify the different mansions, and the difference of rewards in the Kingdom: for 'In My Father's House are many mansions,'[67] saith our Lord. But in a moral sense the cloister is the contemplative state, into which the soul betaking itself, is separated from the crowd of carnal thoughts, and meditateth on celestial things only. In this cloister there are four sides: denoting, namely, contempt of self, contempt of the world, love of God, love of our neighbor. Each side hath his own row of columns. Contempt of self hath humiliation of soul, mortification of the flesh, humility of speech, and the like. The base of all the columns is patience.

43. In this cloister the diversity of office-chambers is the diversity of virtues. The chapter-house is the secret of the heart: concerning this,

(Notre Dame, Paris)

"In many places a triumphal cross is placed in the midst of the church; to teach us, that from the midst of our hearts we must love the Redeemer."

(Maximus' Throne: Ravenna, Italy)

"The Episcopal throne, which according to injunctions of Saint Peter has been of old consecrated in each city, the piety of our forefathers dedicated, not in memory of confessors, but to the honour of apostles and martyrs, and especially the Blesed Virgin Mary."

(Episcopal Throne: at S. Sabrina's Rome)

(Medieval Throne: France)

Sample of a Rood Screen (1620 C.E.)

Choir Stall (Switzerland, 17th Century)

Chancel Screen (11-12th C.E. Berlin)

Cloister (12th Century, Bologna. Italy)

"The cloister is the contemplative state, into which the soul betaking itself, is separated from the crowd of carnal thoughts, and meditateth on celestial things only."

however, we shall speak differently hereafter. The refectory is the love of holy meditation. The cellar, Holy Scripture. The dormitory, a clean conscience. The oratory, a spotless life. The garden of trees and herbs, the collection of virtues. The well, the dew of God's heavenly gifts; which in this world mitigateth our thirst, and hereafter will quench it.

44. The Episcopal throne, which according to the injunctions of Saint Peter has been of old consecrated in each city (as shall be said below), the piety of our forefathers dedicated, not in memory of confessors, but to the honour of apostles and martyrs, and especially of the Blessed Virgin Mary.

45. But we therefore go to church, that we may there ask for the pardon of our sins, and assist in the divine praises: as shall be said in the proeme of the fifth book, and that there we may hear God's proceedings[68] with the good and the ill, and learn and receive the knowledge of God, and that we may there feed on the Lord's body.

46. In church, men and women sit apart: which, according to Bede, we have received from the custom of the ancients: and thence it was that Joseph and Mary lost the Child Jesus; since the one who did not behold Him in his own company, thought Him to be with the other... But the men remain on the southern, the women on the northern side:[69] to signify that the saints who be most advanced in holiness should stand against the greater temptations of this world: and they who be less advanced, against the less; or that the bolder and the stronger sex should take their place in the position fittest for action: because the Apostle saith, 'God is faithful, Who will not suffer you to be tempted above that ye are able.'[70] To this also pertaineth the vision of S. John, who 'beheld a mighty angel placing his right foot in the sea.'[71] For the stronger members are opposed to the greater dangers. But, according to others, the men are to be in the fore part [*i.e.* eastward], the women behind: because 'the husband is the head of the wife,'[72] and therefore should go before her.

47. A woman must cover her head in the church, because she is not the image of God, and because by woman sin began. And therefore in the church, out of respect for the priest, who is the vicar of Christ, in his presence, as before a judge, she hath her head covered, and not at liberty: and on account of the same reverence she hath not the power of speaking in the church before him. Of old time, men and women wearing long hair stood in church with uncovered heads glorifying in their locks: which was a disgrace unto them.

48. But what should be our conversation in church the Apostle teacheth, saying, 'Speaking to yourselves in psalms and hymns and spiritual songs.'[73] Whence we must, when we be there, abstain from superfluous words: ac-

cording to that saying of S. Chrysostome, When thou goest into a king's palace, set in order thy conversation and thy habit. For the angels of the Lord are there: and the House of God is full of incorporeal virtues.[74] And the Lord saith to Moses, and so doth the angel to Joshua, 'Put off thy shoes from off thy feet: for the place where thou standest is holy ground.'[75]

49. In the last place, a consecrated church defendeth murderers who take sanctuary in it from losing life or limb, provided that they have not offended in it, or against it. Whence it is written that 'Joab fled to the tabernacle, and laid hold on the horns of the altar.'[76] The same privilege is possessed also by an unconsecrated church, if the divine offices be therein celebrated.

50. But the body of Christ received by such persons, doth not defend them nor those who fly to it: partly because the privilege is granted to a church as a church: and therefore not to be misbestowed on other things: partly because that food is the support of the soul, and not of the body: whence it freeth the soul and not the body.

51. Churches are moved from one place to another on three accounts. First, on account of the necessity arising from persecutors: secondly, on account of the difficulty of access or habitation, such as the unwholesomeness of air: thirdly, when they are oppressed with the society of evil men: and then with the consent of the Pope or the bishop. Wherefore he that entereth into a church fortifieth himself with the sign of the cross, shall be said in the proeme of the fifth book.[77]

(Vienna Codex, 1007 C.E.)

(Byzantine Ivory)

"According to that saying of S. Chrysostome, When thou goest into a king's palace, set in order thy conversation and thy habit. For the angels of the Lord are there: and the House of God is full of incorporeal virtues."

CHAPTER II: OF THE ALTAR

1. The altar hath a place in the church on three accounts, as shall be said in speaking of its dedication. We are to know that Noe[1] first, then Isaac[2] and Abraham[3] and Jacob made, as we read altars: which is only to be understood as stones set upright, on which they offered and slew the victims and burnt them with fire laid beneath them. Also Moses made an altar[4] of shittim wood: and the same was made as an altar of incense, and covered with pure gold: as we read in the xxvth chapter of Exodus, where also the form of the altar is described. From these of the ancient fathers, the altars of the moderns have their origin, being erected with four horns at the corners. Of which some are of one stone, and some are put together of many.

2. And sometimes the words altare and ara are used in the same sense. Yet is there a difference. For *altare*, derived *alta res*, or *alta ara*, is that on which the priests burnt incense. But *ara*, which is derived from *area*, or from *ardeo*, is that on which sacrifices were burnt.[5]

3. And note, that many kinds of altars are found in Scripture: as a higher, a lower, an inner, an outer; of which each hath both a plain and a symbolical signification. The higher altar is God the Trinity: of which it is written, 'Thou shalt not go up by steps to my altar.'[6] And it also signifieth the Church Triumphant: of which it is said, 'Then shall they offer bullocks upon mine altar.'[7] But the lower altar is the Church Militant, of which it is said, 'If thou wilt make an altar of stone, thou shalt not make it of hewn stone.'[8] Also it is the table of the temple. Of which he saith, 'Appoint a solemn day for your assembly even unto the horns of the altar.'[9] And in the Third of Kings, it is said that Solomon made a golden altar.[10] But the interior altar is a clean heart, as shall be said below. It is also a type of faith in the incarnation, of which in Exodus, 'An altar of earth ye shall make Me.'[11] And an interior altar is the altar of the cross. This is the altar on which they offered the evening sacrifice. Whence in the Canon of the Mass it is said, *Jube hoc in sublime Altare Tuum perferri.*[12] Moreover the external altar representeth the sacraments of the Church: of which it is said, 'Even thine altars, O Lord of hosts, my King, and my God.'[13] Again, the altar is our mortification in our heart, in which carnal motions are consumed by the fervour of the Holy Spirit.

4. Secondly, it also signifieth the Spiritual Church: and its four horns teach how she hath been extended into the four quarters of the world. Thirdly, it signifieth Christ, without whom no gift is offered acceptable to

the Father. Whence also the Church addresseth her prayers to the Father through Christ alone. Fourthly, it signifieth the body of Christ, as shall be explained in the fifth book. Fifthly, it signifieth the table at which Christ did feast with His disciples.

5. It is written in Exodus, that in the Ark of the Testament or of the Testimony the witness was laid up:[14] that is, the tables on which the law was written: and it is said that the *Testimony* was there laid up, because it was a bearing witness that the law imprinted on our hearts by nature God had reimprinted by writing. Also, there was laid up the golden pot full of manna, for a testimony that He had given the children of Israel bread from heaven. And the rod of Aaron, for a testimony that all power is from God. And the second tables of the law, in testimony of the covenant in which they had said, 'All that the Lord hath spoken we will do.'[15] And on these accounts it is called the Ark of the Testimony or Testament; and also the tabernacle of the testimony thence deriveth its title. But over the ark was made a mercy seat: of which we shall speak in the proeme of the fourth book. In imitation whereof some churches have over the altar an ark or tabernacle, in which the body of the Lord and relics are preserved. The Lord also commanded that a candlestick should be made of beaten pure gold. It is written in the third book of Kings, that in the Ark of the Covenant was nothing else than the two tables of stone which Moses put therein in Horeb: when the Lord made a covenant with the children of Israel in the day that they came out of the land of Egypt.

6. And note that in the time of S. Silvester, Pope,[16] Constantine the Emperor built the Lateran church, in which he placed the Ark of the Testament, which the Emperor Titus had brought from Jerusalem, and the golden candlestick with his seven branches. In which ark are these things: the rings and the staves of gold: the tables of the testimony: the rod of Aaron: manna: barley loaves: the golden pot: the seamless garment: the reed: a garment of S. John Baptist, and the scissors with which the hair of S. John the Evangelist was shorn.

7. Man, if he hath an altar, a table, a candlestick, and an ark, he is the temple of God. He must have an altar, whereon rightly to offer and rightly to distribute. The altar is our heart, on which we ought to offer. Whence the Lord commandeth in Exodus: 'Thou shalt offer burnt offerings on mine altar.'[17] Since from the heart words, set on fire of charity, ought to proceed. *Holocaust* is derived from *holos, whole*, and *cauma, a burning*: therein signifying a thing wholly burnt. On this altar we must rightly offer, and we must rightly divide. We offer rightly when we bring any good thought to perfection. But we do not rightly divide if we do it not dis-

(Palestine, Megiddo, Iron Age, 10th Century B.C.E.)

The Horned Altar

(Beersheba Horned Altar)

The Ark (Antwerp Bible, 1526 C.E.)

"From these of the ancient fathers, the altars of the moderns have their origin, being erected with four horns at the corners. Of which some are of one stone, and some are put together of many."

"Man, if he hath an altar, a table, a candlestick, and an ark, he is the temple of God. He must have an altar, whereon rightly to offer and rightly to distribute. The altar is the heart, on which we ought to offer. Whence the Lord commandeth in Exodus: 'Thou shalt offer burnt offerings on mine altar.' Since from the heart, words, set on fire of charity, ought to proceed."

(Beersheba Horned Altar)

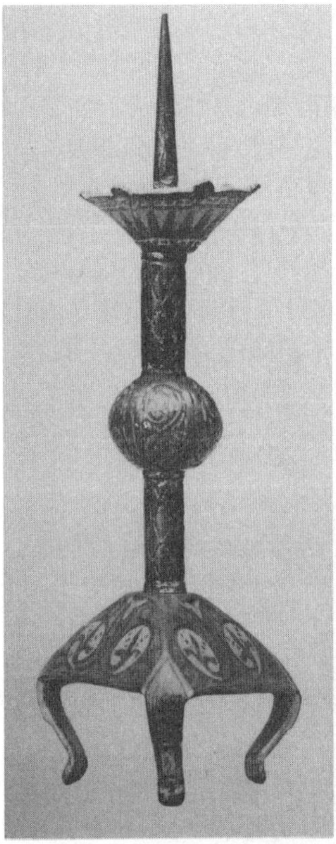

(Limoges, France, 13th Century)

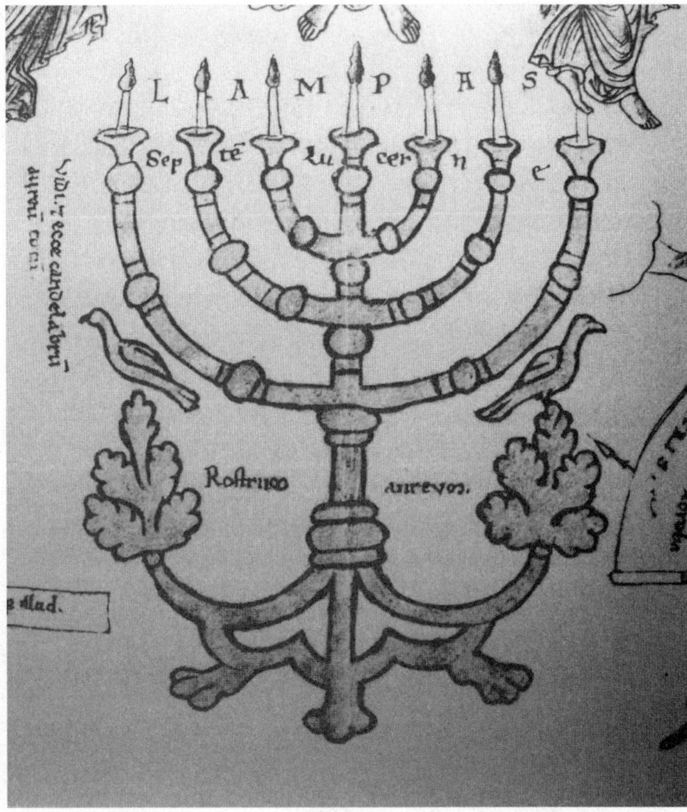

(from Hortus Deliciarum, 12th century)

"Moses made seven lights, which are the seven gifts of the of the Holy Ghost: for they in the darkness of this world shine forth with brightness: and they rest in candlesticks..."

(Essen Cathedral, 1000 C.E.)

creetly. For a man often thinketh to do good, and doeth ill: and sometimes with one hand he doeth good and with the other ill; and thus himself buildeth, and himself knocketh down. But we then rightly divide when the good which we do we attribute, not to ourselves, but to God alone.

8. It behoveth also man to have a table, whence he may take the bread of the Word of God. By the table we understand Holy Scripture, concerning which the Psalm, 'Thou preparest a table before me in the presence of mine enemies.'[18] That is, Thou hast given me Scripture against the temptations of the devil. This table then we must have, that is, must lay up in our minds, that thence we may take the Word of God. Of the deficiency of this bread saith Jeremiah: 'The little ones sought bread, and there was none to break it unto them.'[19] It behoveth man likewise to have a candlestick, that he may shine with good works.

9. A candlestick that giveth light without is a good work, which by its good example inflameth others. Of which it is said, 'No man lighteth a candle and putteth it under a bushel, but in a candlestick.'[20] This candle, according to the Word of the Lord, is a good intention: of which He saith Himself: 'Thine eye is a light.'[21] But the eye is the intention. Therefore we ought not to put the candle under a bushel, but in a candlestick. Because, if we have a good intention, we ought not to hide it: but to manifest our good deeds to others, for a light and an example.

10. Man must also have an ark. Now *arca* is derived from *arcendo*: discipline, therefore, and regular life may be called the ark; by which crimes are driven away (*arcentur*) from us. Now in the ark were the rod, the tables, and the manna: because in regular life there must be the rod of correction, that the flesh may be chastised; and the table of love, that God may be loved. For in the tables of the law were written the commands which pertain to the love of God. Therein must also be the manna of divine sweetness: that we may 'taste and see how gracious the Lord is: for it is good to have to do with Him.'[22] According to that proverb of the prudent woman, 'She tasted and saw that it was good.'[23] Therefore, that we may be the temple of God, let us have in ourselves an altar of oblation, lest we appear empty in His presence, according to that saying, 'Thou shalt not appear empty before the presence of thy God':[24] let us have a table for reflection lest we faint, through hunger, in the way: as saith the Evangelist, 'If I send them away empty, they will faint in the way,'[25] a candlestick by good works that we be not idle, as he saith in Ecclesiasticus, 'Idleness hath taught much mischief,'[26] let us have an ark, that we be not as sons of Belial, that is, undisciplined, and without the yoke: for discipline is necessary, as the Psalmist teacheth, saying, 'Be instructed, lest He be angry.'[27]

Concerning which, and other ornaments, we shall speak in the following chapter.

11. He buildeth this altar who adorneth his heart with true humility and other virtues. Whence Gregory: He who gathereth together virtues without humility, is as he who scattereth dust to the wind. For by the altar he understandeth our heart, as it shall be said when we treat of the dedication of the altar: it is in the middle of the body, as the altar is in the middle of the church.[28]

12. Concerning which altar the Lord commandeth in Leviticus: 'The fire shall always be burning upon Mine altar.'[29] The fire is charity. The altar is a clean heart. The fire shall always burn on the altar, because charity should always burn in our hearts. Whence Solomon in the Canticles: 'Many waters cannot extinguish charity,'[30] for that which ever burneth cannot be extinguished. Do thou, therefore, as the prophet commandeth, keep holy day and solemn assembly, even to the horns of the altar: because the rest of thy thoughts will keep holy day. Concerning this the Apostle showeth 'unto us a more excellent way.'[31] He calleth charity a more excellent way, because she is above all virtues: and whoever possesseth her possesseth all virtucs. This is the short word that the Lord speaketh over the earth: which is so short that it only saith, 'Have charity, and do whatsoever thou wilt. For from these two commandments hang all the law and the Prophets.'[32]

13. Or by the altar we understand the soul of everyman, which is by the Lord built up of various living stones, which are various and different virtues.

14. Furthermore, the white cloths wherewith the altar is covered signify the flesh of the Saviour, that is, His humanity: because it was made white with many toils, as also the flesh of Christ born of earth, that is, of Mary, which attained through many tribulations to the glory of the Resurrection, and the purity and joy of immortality. [Concerning which the Son exulteth, saying to the Father, 'Thou hast girded me with gladness, and exalted Me on every side.'[33] When, therefore, the altar is covered, it signifieth the joining of the soul to an immortal and incorruptible body.[34]] Again, the altar is covered with white and clean cloths, because the pure heart is adorned with good works. Whence the Apocalypse: 'And put on white garments, that the shame of thy nakedness does not appear.'[35] And Solomon: 'Let thy garments be always white,'[36] that is, let thy works be clean. [But it little profiteth him that approacheth to the altar to have high dignity, and a life sunk low in sins. Whence Benedict: It is a monstrous thing, exalted faith, and abandoned life. The highest step and the lowest

(Notre Dame, Paris, France)

"A candlestick that giveth light without is a good work, which by its good example inflameth others."

state, is mighty authority joined with instability of soul.[37] The silken coverings placed over the altar are the ornaments of divers virtues wherewith the soul is adorned. The hanging wherewith the altar is beautified setteth forth the saints, as below shall be said. [The beginning and the end of the Mass take place at the right side of the altar: the middle portion at the left: as shall be said when we treat of the changes of the priest. The ancients made their altars concave; as it is written in Ezekiel, that in the altar of God was a trench. And this, according to Gregory, lest the wind should scatter the sacrifices laid upon it. Also he saith in Ezekiel that the inner part of the altar was bent downwards in all its circumference.[38]

15. But the steps to the altar [spiritually set forth the apostles and martyrs of Christ, who for His love poured out their blood. The bride in the Canticles of Love calleth it a purple ascent. Also, the fifteen virtues are set forth by them: which were also typified by the fifteen steps by which they went up to the temple of Solomon:[39]] and by the prophet in fifteen Psalms of degrees, therein setting forth that he is blest who maketh ascents in his heart. This was the ladder that Jacob beheld: 'And his top reached to the heavens.' By these steps the ascent of virtues is sufficiently made manifest, by which we go up to the altar, that is, to Christ: according to that saying of the Psalmist, 'They go from virtue to virtue.'[40] And Job, 'I will seek him through all my steps.' Yet it is said in Exodus, 'Neither shalt thou go up by steps to my altar, that thy nakedness be not discovered thereon.'[41] For perhaps the ancients did not as yet use trousers. In the Council of Toledo, it is decreed that the priest, who for the sake of grief at the misfortune of another, strippeth the altar or any image of its garments, [or girdeth himself with a mourning vest, or with thorns,[42]] or extinguisheth the lights of the church, shall be disposed. But if his church be undeservedly spoiled, he is allowed to do this for grief: or, according to some, he may make bare the altars as a sign of grief. Which is, however, reprobated by the Council of Lyons. Lastly, altars which have been built at the instigation of dreams, or the empty revelations of men, are altogether reprobated.

(Jacob's Blessing: French Medieval Enamel)

"But we worship not images, nor account them to be gods, nor put any hope of salvation in them: for that were idolatry. Yet we adore them for the memory and remembrance of things long agone."

CHAPTER III: OF PICTURES, AND IMAGES, AND CURTAINS, AND THE ORNAMENTS OF CHURCHES

1. Pictures and ornaments in churches are the lessons and the Scriptures of the laity. Whence Gregory: It is one thing to adore a picture, and another by means of a picture historically to learn what should be adored. For what writing supplieth to him which can read, that doth a picture supply to him which is unlearned, and can only look. Because they are uninstructed thus see what they ought to follow: and *things* are read, though letters be unknown. True is it that the Chaldeans, which worship fire, compel others to do the same, and burn other idols. But Paynim adore images, as icons, and idols; which Saracens do not, who neither will possess nor look on images, grounding themselves on that saying, 'Thou shalt not make to thyself any graven image, nor the likeness of anything that is in heaven above, nor in the earth beneath, nor in the waters under the earth'[1] and on other the like authorities: these they follow incontinently, casting the same in our teeth. But we worship not images, nor account them to be gods, nor put any hope of salvation in them: for that were idolatry. Yet we adore them for the memory and remembrance of things done long agone.[2] Whence the verse,[3]

What time thou passest by the rood, bow humbly evermore;
Yet not the rood, but Him which there was crucified, adore.

And again:[4]

That thing, which hath his being given, 'tis fond for God to own:
A form material, carved out by cunning hands in stone.

And again:[5]

The form is neither God nor man, which here thou dost behold:
He very God and Man, of whom thou by that form art told.

2. The Greeks, moreover, employ painted representations, painting, it is said, only from the navel upwards, that all occasion of vain thoughts may be removed. But they make no carved image, as it is written, 'Thou shalt not make a graven image.'[6] And again: 'Thou shalt not make an idol, nor a graven image.'[7] And again, 'Lest ye be deceived, and make a graven image.'[8] And again: 'Ye shall not make unto you gods of silver:[9] neither shall ye make with Me gods of gold.' So also the Prophet, 'Their idols are silver and gold, the work of man's hand. They that make them are like unto them: and so are all they put their trust in them.'[10] And again: 'Con-

St. Peter and St. James (1270 C.E., Pisa, Italy)

(1135-1140 C.E., Church of S.Veno,Verona, Italy)

"Of pictures and images, some are in front of the church, as the ox and the cow, others within, as images, statues, and various kinds of painting and sculpture: and these be represented either in garments, or on walls, or in stained glass.

Doubting Thomas (Santo Domingo of Silos, 12th Century, Spain)

The Deposition (Santo Domingo of Silos, 12th Century, Spain)

St. Paul (from Augustinian Priory, 1160 C.E., Ivy Church, Wiltshire, England

Apostles (1240 C.E. from St. Agnes Convent, Prague)

Gloria Porch (from St. James in Compestela, Spain)

St. Phillip, St. Jude, and St. Bartholomew (1150 C.E., Catalan, Spain)

Romanesque Apse (12th Century, Spain)

founded be all they that worship graven images: and that put their glory in their idols.'[11]

3. Also, Moses saith to the children of Israel, 'Lest perchance thou shouldest be deceived, and shouldest worship that which the Lord thy God hath created.'[12] Hence also was it that Hezekiah King of Judah brake in pieces the brazen serpent which Moses set up: because the people, contrary to the precepts of the law, burnt incense to it.

4. From these forementioned and other authorities, the excessive use of images is forbidden. The Apostle saith also to the Corinthians, 'We know that an idol is nothing in the world: and there is no god but One.'[13] For they who are simple and infirm may easily by an excessive and indiscreet use of images, be perverted to idolatry. Whence he saith in Wisdom, 'There shall be no respect of the idols of the nations, which have made the creatures of God hateful, and temptations for the souls of men, and snares for the feet of the unwise.'[14] [15] But blame there is none in a moderate use of pictures, to teach how ill is to be avoided, and good followed. Whence saith the Lord to Ezekiel, 'Go in, and behold the abominations which these men do. And he went in, and saw the likeness of reptiles and beasts, and the abominations, and all the idols of the house of Israel portrayed on the wall.'[16] Whence saith Pope Gregory in his Pastorale: When the forms of external objects are drawn into the heart, they are as it were painted there, because the thoughts of them are their images. Again, He saith to the same Ezekiel, 'Take a tile, and lay it before thee, and describe in it the city of Jerusalem.'[17] But that which is said above, that pictures are the letters of the laity explaineth that saying in the Gospel, 'He saith, They have Moses and the Prophets: let them hear them.'[18] Of this, more hereafter. The Agathensian[19] Council forbids pictures in churches: and also that that which is worshipped and adored and worshipped should be painted on the walls. But Gregory saith, that pictures are not to be put away because they are not to be worshipped: for paintings appear to move the mind more than descriptions; for deeds are placed before the eyes in paintings, and so appear to be actually carrying on. But in description, the deed is done as it were by hearsay: which affecteth the mind less when recalled to memory. Hence, also, is it that in churches we pay less reverence to books than to images and pictures.

5. Of pictures and images some are above the church, as the cock and the eagle: somewhat without the church, namely, in the air in front of the church, as the ox and the cow: others within, as images, and statues, and various kinds of painting and sculpture: and these be represented either in garments, or on walls, or in stained glass. Concerning some of which we

have spoken in treating of the church: and how they are taken from the tabernacle of Moses and the temple of Solomon. For Moses made carved work, and Solomon made carved work, and pictures, and adorned the walls with paintings and frescoes.

6. The image of the Saviour is more commonly represented in churches three ways: as sitting on[20] His throne, or on His cross, or lying on the bosom of His Mother. And because John Baptist pointed to Him, saying, 'Behold the Lamb of God,'[21] therefore some represented Christ under the form of a lamb. But because the light passeth away, and because Christ is very man, therefore, saith Adrian, Pope, He must be represented in the form of a man. A holy lamb must not be depicted on the cross, as a principal object: but there is no let when Christ hath been represented as a man, to paint a lamb in a lower or less prominent part of the picture: since He is the true Lamb which 'taketh away the sins of the world.' In these and divers other manners is the image of the Saviour painted, on account of diversity of significations.

7. Represented in the cradle, the artist commemorateth His nativity: on the bosom of His Mother, His childhood: the painting or carving His cross signifieth His Passion (and sometimes the sun and moon are represented on the cross itself, as suffering an eclipse): when depicted on a flight of steps, His ascension is signified: when on a state or lofty throne, we be taught His present power: as if He said, 'All things are given to Me in Heaven and in earth:'[22] according to that saying, 'I saw the Lord sitting upon His throne:'[23] that is, reigning over the angels: as the text, 'Which sitteth upon the cherubim.'[24] Sometimes He is represented as He was seen of Moses and Aaron, Nadab and Abihu, on the mountain: when 'under His feet was as it were a paved work of sapphire stones, and as the body of heaven in His clearness:'[25] and as 'they shall see,' as saith S. Luke, 'the Son of Man coming in the clouds with power and great glory.[26] Wherefore sometimes He is represented surrounded by the seven angels that serve Him, and stand by His throne, each being portrayed with six wings, according to the vision of Isaiah, 'And by it stood the seraphim: each one had six wings: with twain he covered his feet, and with twain he did fly.'[27]

8. The angels are also represented as in the flower of youthful age: for they never grow old.[28] Sometimes S. Michael is represented trampling the dragon, according to that of John, 'There was war in heaven: Michael fought with the dragon.' Which was to represent the dissensions of the angels: the confirmation of them that were good, and the ruin of them that were bad: or the persecution of the faithful in the Church Militant. Sometimes the twenty-four elders are painted around the Saviour, according to

Christ Enthroned (Cathedral Porch of St. James, Compestela, Spain)

John the Baptist (Berlin, Germany)

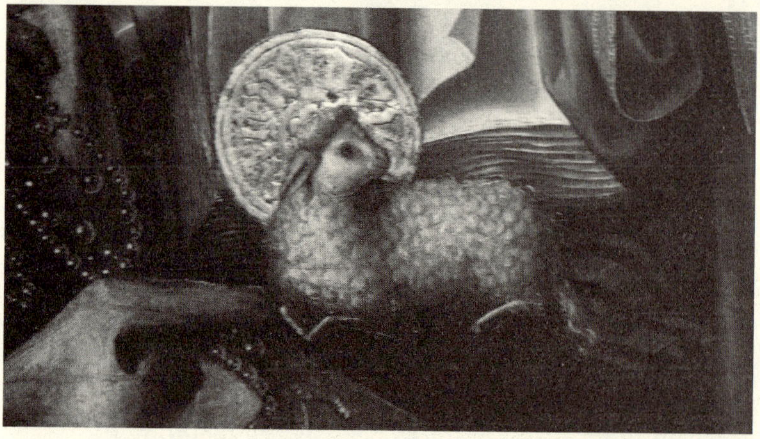

"The image of the Saviour is more commonly represented in churches three ways: as sitting on His throne, or on His cross, or lying on the bosom of his Mother."

"And because John Baptist pointed to Him, saying, 'Behold the Lamb of God,' therefore some represented Christ as of a lamb."

"Represented in the cradle, the artist commemoreth His nativity..."

The Nativity (from the Hortus Deliciarum, 1167-1175 C.E.)

(England, 11th Century)

(Germany, 12th Century)

"Wherefore sometimes He is represented surrounded by the seven angels that serve Him, and stand by His throne, each being portrayed with six wings, according to the vision of Isaiah, 'And by it stood the seraphim: each one had six wings...'"

(Italy)

"The painting or carving of His cross signifieth His Passion (and sometimes the sun and moon are represented on the cross itself, as suffering an eclipse."

Early Christian depiction of St. Michael (Berlin, Germany)

(Victoria and Albert Museum, London, England)

"Sometimes S. Michael is represented trampling the dragon, according to that of John, 'There was war in heaven: Michael fought with the dragon.'"

Ezekiel

The Cherub as Tetramorph (from the Hortus Deliciarum, 12th Century)

"Sometimes also representation is made of the four living creatures spoken of in the visions of Ezekiel...the face of a man, and the face of a lion on the right- the face of an ox on the left, and the face of an eagle above the four. These be the Four Evangelists."

the vision of the said John, with 'white garments, and they have on their heads crowns of gold.'[29] By which are signified the doctors of the Old and the New Testament; which are twelve, on account of faith in the Holy Trinity preached through the *four* quarters of the world: or twenty-four, on account of good works, and the keeping of the gospels.[30] If the seven lamps be added, the gifts of the Holy Spirit are represented: if the sea of glass, baptism.[31]

9. Sometimes also representation is made of the four living creatures spoken of in the visions of Ezekiel and the aforesaid John: the face of a man, and the face of a lion on the right,—the face of an ox on the left and the face of an eagle above the four. These be the Four Evangelists. Whence they be painted with books by their feet, because by their words and writings they have instructed the minds of the faithful, and accomplished their own works. Matthew hath the figure of a man, Mark of a lion. These be painted on the right hand: because the nativity and the resurrection of Christ were the general joy of all: whence in the Psalms: 'And gladness at the morning.'[32] But Luke is the ox: because he beginneth from Zachary the priest, and treateth more specially of the Passion and Sacrifice of Christ: now the ox is an animal fitted for sacrifice. He is also compared to the ox, because of the two horns,—as containing the two testaments; and the four hoofs, as having the sentences of the four Evangelists.[33] By this also Christ is figured, who was the sacrifice for us: and therefore the ox is painted on the left side, because the death of Christ was the trouble of the apostles. Concerning this, and how blessed Mark[34] is depicted, in the seventh part. But John hath the figure of the eagle: because, soaring to the utmost height, he saith, 'In the beginning was the word.'[35] This also representeth Christ, 'Whose youth is renewed like the eagle's':[36] because, rising from the dead, He ascendeth into heaven. Here, however, it is not portrayed as by the side, but as above, since it denoteth the ascension, and the word pronounced of God. But how, since each of the living creatures hath four faces and four wings, they can be depicted, shall be said hereafter.[37]

10. Sometimes there are painted around, or rather beneath, the Apostles; who were His witnesses by deed and word to the ends of the earth: and they are portrayed with long hair, as Nazarenes, that is, holy persons. For the law of the Nazarenes was this: from the time of their separation from the ordinary life of man, no razor passed upon their heads. They are also sometimes painted under the form of twelve sheep: because they were slain like sheep for the Lord's sake: and sometimes the twelve tribes of Israel are so represented. When, however, more or less sheep than twelve are painted, then another thing is signified, according to that saying of

Matthew, 'When the Son of Man shall come in His glory—then shall He sit on the throne of His glory: and before Him shall be gathered all nations, and He shall separate them one from the other, as a shepherd divideth the sheep from the goats.'[38] How the Apostles Bartholomew and Andrew are to be painted, shall be said hereafter.[39]

11. And note that the patriarchs and Prophets are painted with wheels in their hands. Some of the apostles with books and some with wheels: namely, because before the advent of Christ the faith was set forth under figures, and many things were not yet made clear; to represent this, the patriarchs and Prophets are painted with wheels, to signify that imperfect knowledge. But because the apostles were perfectly taught of Christ, therefore the books, which are the emblems of this perfect knowledge, are open. But because some of them reduced their knowledge in writing, to the instruction of others, therefore fittingly they are represented with books in their hands like doctors. So Paul, and the Evangelists, Peter, James, and Jude. But others, who wrote nothing which has lasted, or been received into the canon by the Church, are not portrayed with books but with wheels, as a type of their preaching. Whence the Apostle to the Ephesians, 'And he gave some apostles, and some Prophets, and some evangelists, and some pastors and teachers for the work of the ministry.'[40]

12. But the Divine Majesty is also portrayed with a closed book in hands: 'which no man was found worthy to open but the Lion of the tribe of Juda.'[41] And sometimes with an open book: that in it every one may read that 'He is the Light of the world':[42] 'and the Way, the Truth, and the Life':[43] and the Book of Life [is also portrayed]. But why Paul is represented at the right, and Peter at the left of the Saviour, we shall show hereafter.

13. John Baptist is painted as a hermit.

14. Martyrs with the instruments of their torture: as S. Laurence with the gridiron: S. Stephen with stones: and sometimes with palms, which signify victory, according to that saying, 'The righteous shall flourish like a palm-tree:[44] as a palm-tree[45] flourishes, so his memory is preserved. Hence is it that palmers, they who come from Jerusalem, bear palms in their hands in token that they have been the soldiers of the King Who was gloriously received in the earthly Jerusalem with palms: and Who afterwards, having in the same city subdued the devil in battle, entered the palace of heaven in triumph with His angels, where the just shall flourish like a palm-tree, and shall shine like stars.

15. Confessors are painted with their insignia, as bishops with their mitres, abbots with their hoods: and some with lilies,[46] which denote chas-

The Four Evangelists (Lower Rhine, Medieval)

St. Luke, represented by the ox (Chapel of Holy Cross, Prague, 1369)

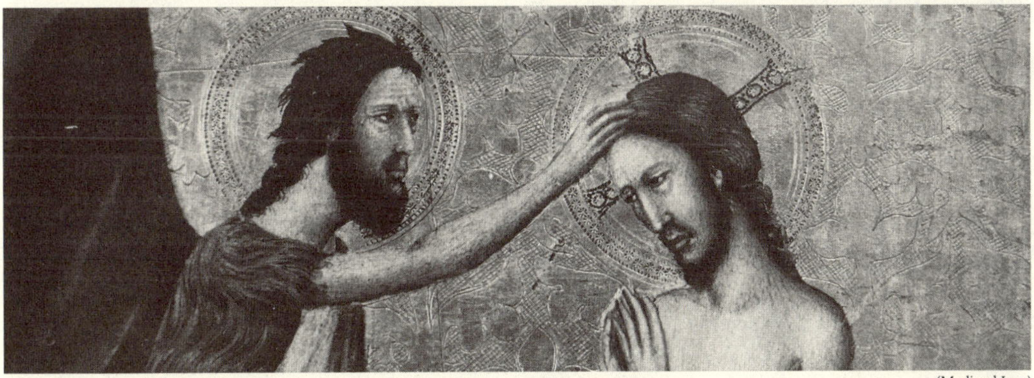

"John is painted as a hermit." (Medieval Icon)

(Convent of St. Agnes, Prague)

"The patriarchs and Prophets are painted with wheels in their hands."

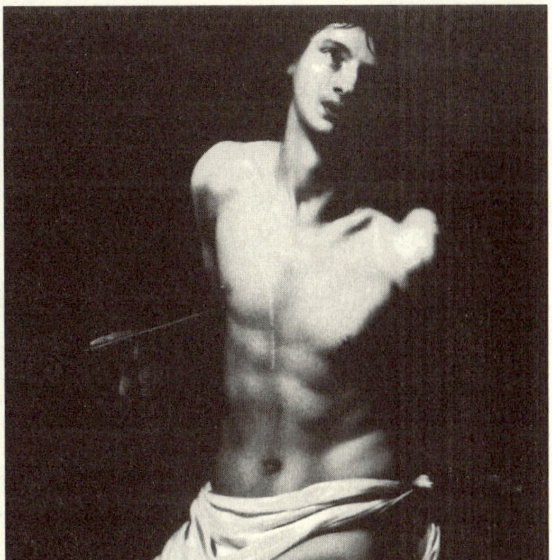

(Renaissance Period)

"Martyrs with the instruments of torture.." Here, St. Sebastian with arrows.

The Virgin Crowned

(Medieval Sculpture)

(The Victoria and Albert Museum, London, England)

"The book, the power converting Paul."

tity. Doctors with books in their hands: virgins, according to the Gospel,[47] with lamps.

16. Paul with a book and a sword: with a book, as a doctor, or with reference to his conversion: with a sword as[48] a soldier. Whence the verse:

The sword denotes the ire of Saul,
The book, the power converting Paul.

17. Generally the effigies of the holy fathers are portrayed on the walls of the church, or on the back panels of the altar, or on vestments, or in other various places, so that we may meditate perpetually, not indiscreetly or uselessly, on their holiness. Whence in Exodus it is commanded by the divine law, that in the breast of Aaron, the breastplate of judgment should be bound[49] with strings: because fleeting thoughts should not occupy the mind of a priest, which should be girt by reason alone. In this breastplate also, according to Gregory, the names of the twelve patriarchs are commanded to be carefully inscribed.

18. To bear the fathers thus imprinted on the breast, is to meditate on the lives of ancient saints without intermission. But then doth the priest walk blamelessly when he gazeth continually on the example of the fathers which have gone before, when he considereth without ceasing the footsteps of the saints, and represseth unholy thoughts, lest he wander beyond the limits of right reason.

19. It is to be noted that the Saviour is always represented as crowned, as if he said, 'Come forth, children of Jerusalem, and behold King Solomon in the diadem with which his mother crowned him.'[50] But Christ was triply crowned. First by His Mother on the day of His conception, with crown of pity: which was a double crown: on account of what He had by nature, and what was given Him: therefore also it is called a diadem, which is a double crown. Secondly, by His step-mother in the day of His Passion, with the crown of misery. Thirdly, by His Father in the day of His Resurrection, with the crown of glory: whence it is written, 'O Lord, Thou hast crowned Him with glory and honour.'[51] Lastly, He shall be crowned by His whole family, in the last day of Revelation, with the crown of power. For He shall come with the judges of the earth to judge the world in righteousness. So also all saints are portrayed as crowned, as if they said: Ye children of Jerusalem, behold the martyrs with the golden crowns wherewith the Lord hath crowned them. And in the book of Wisdom: 'The just shall receive a kingdom of glory, and a beautiful diadem from the hand of their God.'[52]

20. But their crown is made in the fashion of a round shield: because the saints enjoy the divine protection. Whence they sing with joy: 'Lord, Thou hast crowned us with the shield of Thy favour.'[53] But the crown of Christ is represented under the figure of a cross:[54] and is thereby distinguished from that of the saints: because by the banner of His cross He gained for Himself the glorification of His humanity, and for us freedom from our captivity, and the enjoyment of everlasting life. But when any living[55] prelate or saint is portrayed, the glory is not fashioned in the shape of a shield, but four-square: that he may be shown to flourish in the four cardinal virtues: as it is contained in[56] the legend of blessed Gregory.

21. Again, sometimes Paradise is painted in churches, that it may attract the beholders to a following after its rewards: sometimes hell, that it may terrify them by the fear of punishment.[57] Sometimes flowers[58] are portrayed, and trees: to represent the fruits of good works springing from the roots of virtues.

22. Now, the variety of pictures denoteth the diversity of virtues. For 'to one is given by the Spirit the word of wisdom: to another the word of knowledge,' etc.[59] But virtues are represented under the forms of women: because they soothe and nourish. Again, by the ceilings or vaultings, which are for the beauty of the house, the more unlearned servants of Christ are set forth, who adorn the Church, not by their learning, but by their virtues alone.

The carved images which project from the walls, appear as it were to be coming out of it: because when by reiterated custom virtues so pertain to the faithful, that they seem naturally implanted in them, they are exercised in all their various operations. How a synagogue is depicted, shall be said hereafter: as also how the pall of the Roman Pontiff: and the year[60] and the zodiacal signs and its months. But the diverse histories of the Old and New Testaments may be represented after the fancy of the painter. For

Pictoribus atque poetis
Quod libet[61] addendi semper fuit æque potestas.

23. Furthermore, the ornaments of the church consist of three things:—the ornaments of the nave,[62] the choir, and the altar. The ornaments of the nave consist in dorsals, tapestry, mattings, and cushions of silk, purple, and the like. The ornaments of the choir consist in dorsals, tapestry, carpets, and cushions. Dorsals are hangings of cloth at the back of the clergy. Mattings, for their feet. Tapestry is likewise strewed under the feet, par-

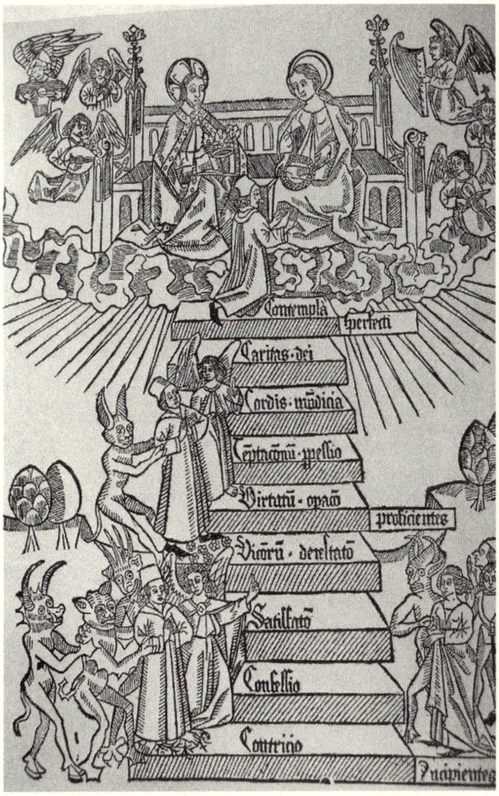

(1480)

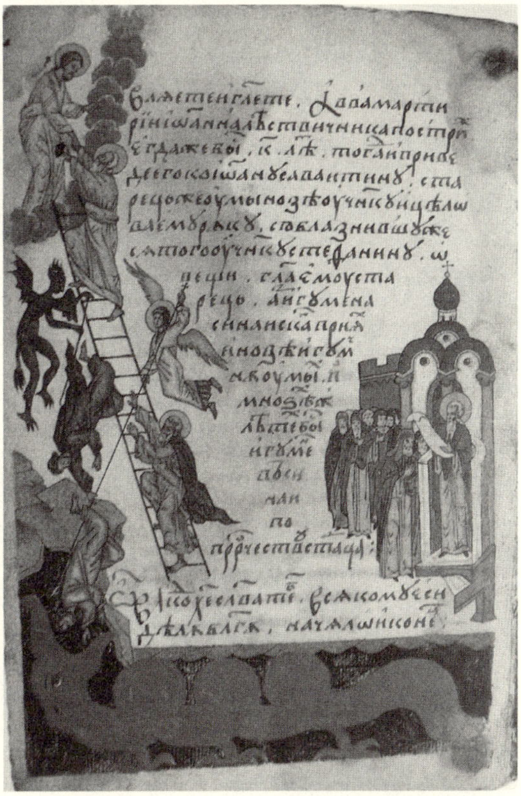

(Russia, 16th Century)

"Sometimes Paradise is painted in churches, that it may attract the beholders to a following after its rewards: sometimes hell that it may terrify them by the fear and punishment."

(1480)

(1480)

(13th Century)

"Sometimes flowers are portrayed, and tress, to represent the fruits of good works springing from the roots of virtues."

A Pyx (13th Century, France)

A Pyx (9th Century C.E., Spain)

(St. Agnes' Convent, Prague)

"...in them some portion of the extremities of the bodies of saints is preserved..."

Reliquaries

Depicting the Virgin and St. John (8th Century)

St. Thomas à Becket's murder (French, 1180))

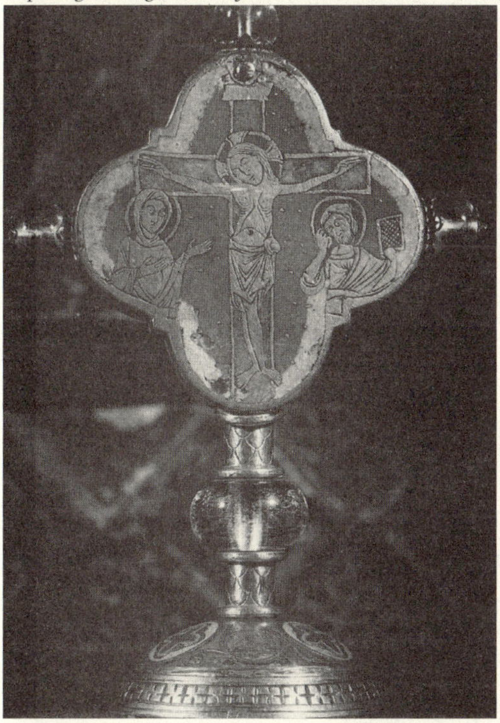

(Saxon, 12th Century)

(France, 1130 C.E.)

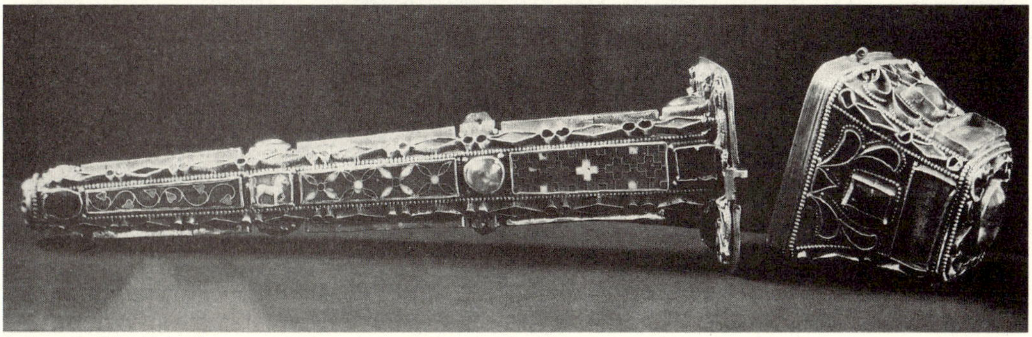

Relic nail of the Holy Cross (Italy, 977 C.E.)

ticularly under the feet of bishops, who ought to trample worldly things under their feet. Cushions are placed on the seats or benches of the choir.

24. But the ornament of the altar consists in portfolios, altar cloths, reliquaries, candlesticks, crosses, an orfray, banners, missals, coverings, and curtains.

25. And notice, that the portfolio in which the consecrated host is kept, signifieth the frame of the blessed Virgin, concerning which it is said in the Psalms, 'Arise, O Lord into Thy resting place.'[63] Which sometimes is of wood: sometimes of white ivory: sometimes of silver: sometimes of gold; sometimes of crystal: and according to the different substances of which it is made, designateth the various dignities of the body of Christ. Again, the pyx which containeth the host, whether consecrated or not consecrated, typifieth the human memory. For a man ought to hold in remembrance continually the benefits of God, as well temporal, which are represented by the unconsecrated, as spiritual, which are set forth by the consecrated host. Which was also set forth by the urn in which God commanded that the manna should be deposited: which, albeit it was temporal, prefigured nevertheless this our spiritual sacrifice, when the Lord commanded that it should be laid up for an everlasting memorial unto future generations. But the pyx, being placed on the altar, which is Christ, signifieth apostles and martyrs. And the altar cloths and coverings are confessors and virgins, or all saints: of whom saith the Prophet to the Lord, 'Thou shalt be clothed with them as with a garment.' And of these we have spoken above.

26. Now there is a difference between *phylacterium* and *phylacteria*. *Phylacterium* is a scroll on which the ten commandments were written: and this kind of scroll the Pharisees used to wear on the front part of their garments, as a sign of devotion. Whence in the Gospel, 'They make broad their phylacteries.'[64] And the word is derived from *philare*, which is to keep, and *teras*, which is *law*. But *phylacteria* (a reliquary) is a vessel of silver or gold, or crystal, or ivory, or some substance of the same kind, in which the ashes and relics of the saints are kept. For when Vigilantius called the faithful *Cinericii*,[65] because they preserved the ashes themselves, to testify contempt of his decision, it was ordered by the Church that they should be honourably preserved in precious vessels. And the name is derived from *philare*, which is to preserve, and *teron*, which is an extremity, because in them some portion of the extremities of the bodies of saints is preserved: such as a tooth or a finger, or somewhat of the like kind. Over the altar in some churches also is placed a shrine: of which we have spoken in our section on the Altar.

27. At the horns of the altar[66] two candlesticks are placed to signify the joy of Jews and Gentiles at the nativity of Christ: which candlesticks, by means of a flint, have their wicks lighted. For the angel saith to the shepherds, 'I bring you good tidings of great joy, which shall be to all people: for to you is born this day the Saviour of the world.'[67] He is the true *Isaac*,[68] which being interpreted, is laughter. Now the light of the candlestick is the faith of the people. For to the Jewish people, saith the Prophet, 'Arise, shine, for thy light is come: and the glory of the Lord is risen upon thee.'[69] But to the Gentiles the Apostle saith, 'Ye were sometimes darkness, but are now light in the Lord.'[70] For before the birth of Christ a new star appeared to the wise men, according to the prophecy of Balaam. 'There shall rise,' saith he, 'a star out of Jacob, and a sceptre out of Israel.'[71] Concerning this we have also spoken in our section of the Altar.

28. The snuffers or scissors for trimming the lamps are the divine words by which men amputate the legal titles of the law, and reveal the shining spirit, according to that saying, 'Ye shall eat old store, and bring forth the old because of the new.'[72] The vessels in the which the wicks, when snuffed, are extinguished, are the hearts of the faithful, which admit the legal observance to the letter.

29. Again, the tongs, by the double tooth of which the fire is arranged, are preachers; who instruct us by the accordant pages of both Testaments, and by their behaviour setting us right, inflame us to the practice of charity.

30. But the scuta, that is cups, of equal size at top and bottom, made for warming water, are those doctors who do not conceal the treasure of their hearts: but 'bring forth out of it things new and old':[73] as a 'candle which is not put under a bushel, but in a candlestick,'[74] that they who are in the house of the Lord may receive the light and the heat of the Holy Ghost.

31. The cross also is to be placed on the altar that the cross-bearers may thence raise it: in which action we commemorate how Simon the Cyrenian took the cross from the shoulders of Christ and bore it. Between the two candlesticks the cross is placed on the altar: because Christ standeth in the church, the Mediator between two peoples. For He is the Cornerstone, 'Who hath made both one':[75] to Whom the shepherds came from Judæa, and the wise men from the East. Concerning this we shall hereafter speak in another sense, when treating of the priest's approach to the altar.

32. Again, the front of the altar is ornamented with an orfray. As it is written: 'Thou shalt make Me an altar, and shalt make a crown in a circle

"'The scissors or snuffers for trimming the lamps are the divine words...' by which men amputate the legal titles of the law and reveal the shining spirit"

(Prague)

"Between the two candlesticks the cross is placed on the altar: because Christ standeth in the Church, the Mediator between two peoples...for he is the cornerstone who has made both One."

"The white cloths wherewith the altar is covered signify the flesh of the Saviour, that is, his Humanity: because it was made white with many toils, as also the flesh of Christ born of earth, that is, of Mary, which attained through many tribulations to the glory of the Resurrection, and the purity and joy of immortality."

"When, therefore, the altar is covered, it signifieth the joining of the soul to an immortal and incorruptible body."

(St. Martin of Tours, Louisville, Kentucky)

(Byzantine 11-12th Century)

A Gospel Book

(Cluny, Paris, France)

about it of four fingers' breadth.'[76] The altar, ye know, sometimes signifieth the heart: in which the sacrifice of true faith must be offered by contrition: and then the orfray signifieth the taking in hand of a good occupation: wherewith we ought to adorn our foreheads, that we may give light to others. Sometimes the altar signifieth Christ: and then by the orfray the ornament of charity is fitly represented. For as gold hath the superiority over all metals, so hath charity over other virtues. Whence the Apostle, in the first to the Corinthians: 'But the greatest of these is charity.'[77] For our faith ought to be adorned with the orfray of charity, that we may be ready to lay down our lives for Christ's sake. Banners are also suspended above the altars: that in the church that triumph of Christ may evermore be held in mind, by which we also hope to triumph over our enemy.

33. The book of the Gospel is fixed on the altar, because the Gospel had Christ for its author, and beareth witness to Him. Which book is therefore adorned on the outside, for the cause that we shall make mention of hereafter. Next, the vessels and utensils in the house of the Lord had their origin from Moses and Solomon: which in the Old Testament were many and divers, as it is written in Exodus, and having divers significations, concerning which, for the sake of brevity, we will not in this place treat.

34. Now all things which pertain to the ornament of a church must be removed or covered over in the season of Lent: which according to some taketh place on Passion Sunday, because after that time the Divinity of Christ was hidden and concealed in Him. For He gave Himself up to be betrayed and scourged, as if He were only man, and had not in Him the virtue of divinity: whence in the Gospel of this day it is written, 'But Jesus hid Himself, and went out of the temple.'[78] Then therefore the crosses are covered, that is, the virtue of His divinity is hidden. Others do this from the first Sunday of Lent: because after that time the Church beginneth to treat of His Passion. Whence in that time the cross must not be borne in procession from the church, except it be covered; and, according to the use of some places, two coverings or curtains are then only retained: of which the one is hung all round the choir, the other is suspended between the altar and the choir: that those things which be within the Holy of Holies may not appear. In that the Sanctuary and Cross are then veiled, we be taught the letter of the Law, that is, its carnal observance, or that the understanding of Holy Scriptures before the Passion of Christ was veiled, hidden, and obscure: and that in that time there was a veil: that is, men had an obscurity before their eyes. It signifieth also the sword which was set before the gate of Paradise: because the carnal observance we have spoken of, and this obscurity, and the sword at the gate of Paradise, were removed by the

Passion of Christ. Therefore the curtains and veils of this kind are removed on Good Friday. But in that in the Old Testament, there were beasts that chewed the cud, and cleft the hoof, as oxen used in ploughing, that is discerning and spiritually perceiving the mysteries of Scripture: therefore in Lent only a few priests, to whom 'it is given to know the mysteries of the Kingdom of God'[79] go behind the veil.

35. Concerning this it is to be noted that there be three kinds of veils which be hung in churches: that which concealeth the mysteries: that which divideth the sanctuary from the clergy: that which divideth the clergy from the laity. The first denoteth the law: the second denoteth our unworthiness, in that we are unworthy, nay unable to behold things celestial. The third is the coercion of our carnal pleasures. The first, namely, the curtain that is hung from each side of the altar, when the priest goeth into the holy place, is typified by that which is written in Exodus, 'Moses put a veil over his face, for the children of Israel could not sustain the brightness of his countenance.'[80] And as the Apostle saith, 'Even to this day is this veil over the hearts of the Jews.'[81] The second, namely the curtain that in the office of the Mass during Lent is suspended before the altar, was set forth by the veil which was hung up in the tabernacle, and divided the Holy of Holies from the holy place, as shall be declared in the proeme to the fourth part: by which the ark was concealed from the people: and it was wrought cunningly, and adorned with a fair variety of devices. This was it that was rent in the Passion of the Lord: and after its pattern, the curtains at this day are cunningly wrought with divers patterns. Concerning the aforesaid veil, and of what sort the curtains ought to be, it is written in Exodus. The third kind of veil deriveth its origin from thence, that the *peribolus* in the primitive Church, or wall which encompasseth the choir, was only raised as far as the elevation of the choir;[82] which even to this day is observed in some churches: which was done that the people seeing the clergy singing psalms, might follow their good example. But at this time as it were a veil or wall is suspended or interposed between the clergy and the laity, that they may not be able to behold each other: as if to say, in very deed, 'turn away mine eyes, lest they behold vanity.'[83]

36. But on Holy Saturday all the curtains are taken away, because on the Passion of the Lord the veil of the temple was rent: and by that thing the spiritual intelligence of the Law was revealed unto us, which till that time lay hid, as is said afore: and the door of the kingdom of heaven is opened, and power was given unto us, that we cannot be overcome of our carnal concupiscence, unless we ourselves do yield. But the veil which separateth the sanctuary from the choir is drawn or lifted up at vespers on

every Saturday of Lent: when the office of the Sunday is begun, that the clergy may be able to look into the sanctuary: because the Sunday commemorateth the Resurrection.

37. This therefore is done on the six Sundays of Lent: because there was no age in which joy, and that joy eternal, was not made in some sort manifest, that joy which is concealed in heaven, as is signified by that veil. Thence is it that we fast not on the Sundays, and this on account of the glory of the Resurrection. For the first Sunday signifieth the joy which our parents enjoyed in the Paradise before the fall. The second Sunday signifieth the joy of the few who were preserved in the ark of Noah, when all else were drowned in the deluge. The third, the gladness of the children of Israel, when in the time of Joseph others were afflicted with famine. The fourth, their joy when they lived with all peace under Solomon.[84] The fifth, their gladness when returning from the Babylonian captivity. The sixth, that of the disciples from the Resurrection to the Ascension: when the bridegroom was with them in presence.

38. In feasts likewise of nine lessons,[85] when they occur in Lent, the before-mentioned veil is raised and lifted up. But this is not of the institution of earliest times, because then no feast was celebrated in Lent. But then on whatever day a feast occurred, commemoration was made of it on the Saturday and Sunday following, according to the canon of Poper Martin; and so in the xiiith book of Burchardus.[86] And all this on account of the sadness of that time. Afterwards the contrary use prevailed: that feasts of nine lessons occurring in Lent should be solemnly observed, and a fast nevertheless kept.

39. Again, on festivals curtains are hung up in churches, for the sake of the ornament they give; and that by visible, we may be led to invisible beauty. These curtains are sometimes tinctured with various hues, as is said afore: so that by the diversity of the colours themselves we may be taught that man, who is the temple of God, should be ordained by the variety and diversity of virtues. A white curtain signifieth pureness of living: a red, charity: a green, contemplation: a black, mortification of the flesh: a livid-coloured, tribulation. Besides this, over white curtains are sometimes suspended hangings of various colours: to signify that our hearts ought to be purged from vices: and that in them should be the curtains of virtues, and the hangings of good works.

40. Moreover, on the Feast of the Nativity of the Lord some churches exhibit no hangings: some poor, and some good. Those which have none, signify our shame; for even if we are filled with the greatest joy at the birth of a Saviour,[87] we ought not, however, to be without shame that such was

our sin that the 'Son of God emptied Himself on our account, and took upon Him the form of a servant.'[88] And on that account also we solemnise His Passion not with joy, but with a severe fast; whereas when we celebrate the passion of other saints we do it with gladness, and indulge ourselves somewhat in meat and drink, as shall be said in the sixth book. But our Lord's Passion is a source of shame to us on account of our sins. The saints, on the other hand, died not for our sins, but suffered for Christ. Those churches which on the Nativity suspend curtains of poor texture thereby typify that Christ did then 'take upon Himself the form of a servant,[89] and was clothed in miserable rags. Those which employ richer hangings, set forth by them the gladness arising from the Birth of a King: and teach what manner of persons we ought to be in our reception of so great a Guest.

41. In some churches, the altar at Easter-tide is decked with precious hangings, and veils of three colours are placed over it: red, pale, and black, which denote three seasons. When the first lesson and its response are finished, the black veil is removed; which signifieth the time before the Law. When the second lesson and its response are finished, the pale veil will be removed: which signifieth the time of the Law. The third being finished, the red is removed, which setteth forth the time of Grace: that is, that by the Passion of Christ an entrance is administered unto us to the Holy of Holies and to eternal glory. But concerning the coverings and cloths of the altars we have spoken in our sections on the same.

42. On high feasts, the treasures of the church are brought forth on three accounts. Firstly, by way of safeguard: that it may be made manifest that he who hath them in charge hath been careful in his care of them. Secondly, for the more reverence of the solemnity. Thirdly, for the memory of their oblation; namely, for the commemoration of them that bestowed them on the church.

But in that the church is gloriously adorned within and not without, it is thereby signified that 'all its glory is from within.'[90] For although its outward appearance be despicable, the soul which is the seat of God is illuminated from within: according to that saying, 'I am black but comely.'[91] And the Lord saith to the Prophet: 'I have a goodly heritage.'[92] Which the Prophet considering in his mind, saith, 'Lord, I have loved the beauty of Thine house':[93] which is spiritually adorned by Faith, Hope, and Charity. Sometimes the church, both material and spiritual, hath need to be cleansed: concerning the seventh book.

In some churches two eggs of ostriches and other things which cause admiration, and which are rarely seen, are accustomed to be suspended:

that by their means the people may be drawn to church, and have their minds the more affected.

43. Again, some say that the ostrich, as being a forgetful bird, 'leaveth her eggs in the dust':[94] and at length, when she beholdeth a certain star, returneth unto them, and cheereth them by her presence. Therefore the eggs[95] of ostriches are hung in churches to signify that man, being left of God on account of his sins, if at length he be illuminated by the Divine Light, remembereth his faults and returneth to Him, Who by looking on him with His Mercy cherisheth him. As it is written in Luke that after Peter had denied Christ, the 'Lord turned and looked upon Peter.'[96] Therefore the aforesaid eggs suspended in churches, this signifying, that man easily forgetteth God, unless being illuminated by a star, that is, by the Influence of the Holy Spirit, he is reminded to return to him by good works.

44. Now in the Primitive Church, the sacrifice was offered in vessels of wood, and common vests: for then were 'chalices of wood, and priests of gold': whereof the contrary is now. But Severinus, Pope, decreed that it should be offered in glass:[97] but because such vessels were easily broken, therefore, Urban, Pope, and the Council[98] of Rheims decreed that gold or silver vessels should be used: or on account of poverty, tin, which rusteth not: but not in wood nor brass. Therefore it might not be in glass on account of the danger of effusion: nor of wood since being porous and spongy, it absorbeth the blood: nor of brass nor of bronze, the rust of which is unseemly.

45. And note that the name of chalice is derived from the Old Testament: whence Jeremiah, 'Babylon is a golden chalice that maketh drunk the nations.'[99] And David: 'In the hand of the Lord is a chalice, and the wine thereof is red.':[100] and in another place, 'I will receive the chalice of salvation, and will call on the name of the Lord.'[101] Again, in the Gospel: 'Are ye able to drink the chalice that I shall drink?'[102] And, again, 'When He had taken the chalice He gave thanks.'[103] A golden chalice signifieth the 'treasures of wisdom that be hid in Christ.'[104] A silver chalice denoteth purity from sin. A chalice of tin denoteth the similitude of sin and punishment, for tin is as it were halfway between silver and lead: and the Humanity of the Christ, albeit it were not lead, that is, sinful, yet was it like to sinful flesh. And therefore not silver: and although impassible for His own sin, passible He was for ours: since 'He thus took our infirmities, and bare our sicknesses.'[105] Concerning the Chalice and the Paten we shall speak hereafter.

46. But if anyone, through cause of his little religion, should say that the Lord commanded Moses to make all the vessels of the Tabernacle for

every use and ceremony whatever, of brass, as it is written in the eight and twentieth chapter of Exodus, and that precious vessels of this sort, 'could be sold for much, and given to the poor,'[106] he is like Judas, and acteth contrarywise to the woman which brought the alabaster box of ointment. This we reply to him: not that God is better pleased with gold than brazen ornaments: but that when men offer to God that which they value, by the worship of the Almighty they vanquish their own avarice. Moreover, these offices of divine peity be moral, and significative of future glory. Whence also under the old law the priest's garments were to be made of gold, and jacinth, and purple, and scarlet twice dyed, and woven linen, and other precious things: that thereby might be made manifest with how great diversity of virtues the priest ought to shine: and it was also commanded that the altar, and the mercy-seat, and the candlestick, and the other vessels and ornaments of the altar should be made of gold and silver. The Tabernacle also was to be made of divers precious materials, as is said in our section concerning the Church. Also the high priest under the Law uses divers precious ornaments, as we have both noted and shall hereafter note.

47. Moreover, it was forbidden in the Council of Orleans,[107] that the divine ornaments should be used for the adorning of nuptials, lest they should be polluted by the touch of the wicked, or by the pomp of secular luxury. By this doubtless it is shown that a chasuble, or any other ornament intended for the divine mysteries, must not be made out of a common person's vest.

48. Stephen, Pope, moreover, forbade that anyone should have the use of the vests of a church, or of those things which be touched by religious men alone, for other purposes: lest that vengeance come upon these transgressors which befel Belshazzar the King.[108]

49. Also Clement, Pope, forbade that the dead should be buried or wrapped or covered, they or their bones, with the altar cloth, or covering for the chalice, or napkin wherewith the priest washeth his hands before consecrating.

50. But when the palls, that is the corporals, and the veils, that is the ornaments of the altar, or the curtains hanging over it shall have become unclean, the deacons with their ministers shall wash them within the sanctuary, and not without. But when the veils, used in the service of the altar, be washed, let there be a new basin. And let the palls, that is the corporals, be washed in another basin. And let the veils for doors, that is, the curtains which are hung up in churches at high feasts, and in Lent, be washed in another. This is it that was decreed by the Council of Lerida:[109] that for washing the corporal, and the altar palls certain vessels be appropriated

and kept within the church: in which nothing else ought to be washed. But according to the afore-mentioned Clement, if the altar pall or covering, or the covering of the seat where the priest sitteth, in his holy vests, or of the candlestick, or the veil, that is the cloth or curtains hanging over the altar be consumed by old age, let them be burnt; and their ashes cast in the baptistery, or on the wall, or in the drains, where there is no treading of passers by. And note that the ecclesiastical ornaments be consecrated: as shall be said under the section of Consecrations and Unctions.

(An ostrich egg such as this one precedes the Christian continuation of an ancient tradition and was found in a tomb in Lachish. 1750 B.C.E.)

(Lachish, 1750 B.C.E.)

(1250 C.E., England)

CHAPTER IV: OF BELLS

1. Bells are brazen vessels, and were first invented in Nola, a city of Campania: wherefore the larger bells are called *Campanæ*, from Campania the district, and the smaller *Nolæ*, from Nola the town.

2. The reason for consecrating and ringing bells is this: that by their sound the faithful may be mutually cheered on towards their reward; that the devotion of faith may be increased in them; that their fruits of the field, their minds and their bodies may be defended; that the hostile legions and all the snares of the Enemy may be repulsed; that the rattling hail, the whirlwinds, and the violence of tempests and lightning may be restrained; the deadly thunder and blasts of wind held off; the spirits of the storm and the powers of the air overthrown; and that such as hear them may flee for refuge to the bosom of our holy Mother the Church, bending every knee before the standard of the sacred rood. These several reasons are given in the office for the blessing of bells.[1]

3. You must know that bells, by the sound of which the people assembleth together to the church to hear, and the clergy to preach, 'in the morning the mercy of God and His power by night'[2] do signify the silver trumpets, by which under the Old Law the people were called together unto sacrifice. (Of these trumpets we shall speak in our sixth book.) For just as the watchmen in a camp rouse one another by trumpets, so do the ministers of the church excite each other by the sound of bells to watch the livelong night against the plots of the devil. Wherefore our brazen bells are more sonorous than the trumpets of the Old Law, because then God was known in Judea only, but now in the whole earth. They be also more durable: for they signify that the preaching of the New Testament will be more lasting than the trumpets and sacrifices of the Old Law, namely, even unto the end of the world.

4. Again bells do signify preachers, who ought after the likeness of a bell to exhort the faithful unto faith: the which was typified in that the Lord commanded Moses to make a vestment for the high priest, having seventy-two bells to sound when the high priest entered into the Holy of Holies.[3] Also the cavity of the bell denoteth the mouth of the preacher, according to the saying of the Apostle, 'I am become as sounding brass or a tinkling cymbal.'[4]

5. The hardness of the metal signifieth fortitude in the mind of the preacher: whence saith the Lord, 'Behold I have made thy face strong against their faces.'[5] The clapper or iron, which by striking on either side

(The Monastery of Our Lady of Gethsemani, Trappist, Kentucky)

"The rope hanging from this, by which the bell is struck, is humility, or the life of the preacher: the same rope also showeth the measure of our own life." "The priest draweth the rope downwards, when he descendeth from contemplation unto active life: but he himself is drawn upward when under the teaching of Scripture he is raised in contemplation. Also he draweth it downwards when he understandeth the Scripture according to the 'letter which killeth'; he is drawn upwards when he expoundeth the same according to the Spirit."

maketh the sound, doth denote the tongue of the teacher, the which with the adornment of learning doth cause both Testaments to resound.

6. Wherefore a prelate which hath not the skill of preaching will be like unto a bell without a clapper: according to that saying of Gregory, 'A priest, if he knoweth not how to preach nor what voice of exhortation he can deliver, is a dumb preacher, and also as a dumb dog which cannot bark.' The striking the bell denoteth that a preacher ought first of all to strike at the vices in himself for correction, and then advance to blame those of others: lest indeed, contrary to the teaching of the Apostle, 'when he hath preached to others, he himself should be a castaway.'[6] Which also the Psalm doth testify, 'But unto the ungodly, saith God: why dost thou preach my laws, and takest my covenant in thy mouth?'[7] Because truly by the example of his own suffering he often gaineth access to those whom by the learning of his discourse he cannot move. The link by which the clapper is joined or bound unto the bell is moderation: by which, namely, by the authority of Scripture, the tongue of the preacher who wisheth to draw men's hearts is ruled.[8]

7. The wood of the frame upon which the bell hangeth, doth signify the wood of our Lord's Cross: which is on this account suspended on high, because the Cross is preached by the ancient Fathers. The pegs by which the wooden frame is joined together or fastened, are the Oracles of the Prophets. The iron clamps by which the bell is joined with the frame, denote charity, by which the preacher being joined indissolubly unto the Cross doth boast and say, 'God forbid that I should glory save in the Cross of our Lord Jesus Christ.'[9] The hammer affixed to the frame by which the bell is struck, signifieth the right mind of the preacher, by which he himself, holding fast to the Divine commands, doth by frequent striking inculcate the same on the ears of the faithful.

8. The rope hanging from this, by which the bell is struck, is humility, or the life of the preacher: the same rope also showeth the measure of our own life. Besides these, since the rope hath its beginning from the wood upon which the bell hangeth, by which is understood our Lord's Cross, it doth thus rightly typify Holy Scripture which doth flow down from the wood of the Holy Cross. As also the rope is composed of three strands, so doth the Scripture consist of a Trinity: namely, of history, allegory, and morality. Whence, the rope coming down from the wooden frame into the hand of the priest is Scripture descending from the mystery of the Cross into the mouth of the preacher. Again, the rope reacheth unto the hands by which it is grasped, because Scripture ought to proceed unto good works. Also the raising and the lowering of the rope in ringing doth denote that

Holy Scripture speaketh sometimes of high matters, sometimes of low: or that the preacher speaketh sometimes lofty things for the sake of some, and sometimes condescendeth for the sake of others: according to that saying of the Apostle: 'Whether we exalt ourselves it is for God, or whether we humble ourselves it is for you.'[10] Again, the priest draweth the rope downwards, when he descendeth from contemplation unto active life: but is himself drawn upward when under the teaching of Scripture he is raised in contemplation. Also he draweth it downwards when he understandeth the Scripture according to the 'letter which killeth'; he is drawn upwards when he expoundeth the same according to the Spirit. Again, according to Gregory, he is drawn downwards and upwards when he measureth himself in Scripture, namely, how much he still lieth in the depths and how much he advanceth in doing good.

Furthermore, when the bell doth sound from the pulling of its rope, the people are gathered in one for the exposition of Holy Scripture, the preacher is heard, and the people are united in the bond of faith and charity. Therefore when a priest acknowledgeth unto himself that he is a debtor unto preaching, he must not withdraw himself from calling men together by his bells, just as also the sons of Aaron did sound their silver trumpets. He therefore moveth the ropes who doth of his office call his brethren or the people together.

The ring (or pulley) in the length of the rope, through which in many places the rope is drawn, is the crown of reward, or perseverance unto the end, or else is Holy Scripture itself. Moreover, Savinianus, Pope, hath commanded that the hours of the day should be struck in churches.

9. And note that bells are commonly rung for the Divine Offices[11] twelve times during the twelve hours of the day: namely, once at prime, and in like manner once at the last hour, because all things come from one God, and God is One, All in All. At tierce they are rung three times, for the second, third, and fourth hours which are then chanted. In like manner three times at sexts, for the fifth, sixth, and seventh hours. Also three times at nones for the three hours. But at vespers, which is the twelfth hour, not one only but many times are they rung, because in the time of grace the preaching of the Apostles was multiplied. Also in the night for matins they are rung often, because we ought often to call out, 'Wake, thou that sleepest, and arise from the dead.'[12]

10. Commonly also they be rung three times at nocturns. First with a *squilla*[13] or hand-bell, which by its sharp sound signifieth Paul preaching acutely. The second ringing signifieth Barnabus joined to his company. The third intimateth that, when the 'Jews put from them the word of God,

(Notre Dame, Paris, France) The Bell Tower (The Monastery of Gesthemani, Kentucky)

Bell Towers (St. Iago de Compostela, Spain)

"The striking the bell denoteth that a preacher ought first of all to strike the vices in himself for correction, and then advance to blame those of others..."

"The link by which the clapper is joined or bound unto the bell is moderation: by which, namely, by the authority of the Scripture, the tongue of the preacher who wisheth to draw men's hearts is ruled."

the Apostles turned themselves to the Gentiles,' whom also they instructed in the faith of the Trinity by the doctrine of the four Evangelists. Whence also some do use *four* peals.

11. And note that there be six kinds of bells which be used in the church; namely, the *squilla*, the *cymbalum*, the *nola*, the *nolula* (or double *campana*), the *signum* [and the *campana*]. The squilla is rung in the *triclinium*, that is, in the refectory; the cymbalum in the cloister; the nola in the choir; the nolula or double campana in the clock, the campana in the campanile, the signum in the tower. Either of these, however, may be called generally a bell. And these be known by diverse names, because the preachers signified thereby be necessary for diverse ends.

12. During the whole Septuagesima, in the which Quadragesima [or Lent] is contained, on common days the bells be not chanted, nor chimed, but tolled, that is rung singly, at the hours of the day, or at matins.[14] In well-ordered churches, they be struck twice at prime; first to call unto prayer, secondly to begin: three times at tierce, according to the number of hours then struck, as was said above; once to call to prayer, twice to assemble them together, thrice to begin. In like manner it is done at sexts and nones. But for matins the same bells are rung and in the same order. For a mass or for vespers only two bells be rung. But in smaller churches they simply ring the bells as aforesaid, and this on the common days. But on Sundays and holy days, they chime them, as at other times. For because preachers who be figured by bells, do the more abound in a season of grace, and 'are instant in season,' therefore on festivals which pertain to grace, the bells do sound more pressingly and are rung for a longer time, to arouse those 'that sleep and be drunken,' lest they sleep beyond measure. But what is signified by the ringing of bells when the Te Deum is chanted we shall speak hereafter.[15]

13. Moreover, the bells ought to be rung when anyone is dying, that the people hearing this may pray for him.[16] For a woman indeed they ring twice, because she first caused the bitterness of death: for she first alienated mankind from God; wherefore the second day had no benediction.[17] But for a man they ring three times, because the Trinity was first shown in man. For Adam was first formed from the earth, then the woman from Adam, afterwards was man created from both, and so there is therein a trinity. But if the dying man be an ecclesiastic, they toll so many times as he hath received orders. And at the last time they ought to chime, that so the people may know for whom they have to pray. The bells ought also to be chimed when the corpse is brought to the church, and when carried out from the church to the grave.

14. Also bells be rung at processions, that the evil spirits may hear them and flee, as shall be said hereafter.[18] For they do fear when the trumpets of the Church Militant, that is the bells, be heard, like as a tyrant doth fear when he heareth on his own land the trumpets of any potent king his foe.

15. And this is the reason also why the Church, when she seeth a tempest to arise, doth ring the bells; namely, that the devils hearing the trumpets of the Eternal King, which be the bells, may flee away through fear and cease from raising the storm; and that the faithful also may be admonished at the ringing of the bells and be provoked to be urgent in prayer for the instant danger.[19]

But for three days before Easter the bells be silent, as shall be said hereafter.[20] Also the bells be silent in time of an interdict, because often for the fault of those put under them the tongue of the preachers is hindered; according to that of the Prophet, 'I will make thy tongue cleave to the roof of thy mouth, for they are a rebellious house';[21] that is, for the people are disobedient.

The Church also hath organs, of which we shall speak hereafter.[22]

(Ireland, 1100 CE)

Reliquary Shrine of St. Patrick in bell form.

CHAPTER V: OF CEMETERIES AND OTHER PLACES, SACRED AND RELIGIOUS

1. Now we will speak of cemeteries and other sacred and religious places. Of consecrated places, some be appropriated to human necessity, others to prayers. Those of the first sort be a *xenodochium* or *xenostorium*, which is the same: a *vasochonium*, a *gerontocomium*, an *orphanotrophium*, a *brephotrophium*. For holy fathers and religious princes have founded places of this kind, where the poor, the pilgrims, old men, orphans, infants, men past work, the halt, the weak, and the wounded should be received and attended. And note that *geronta* in Greek is the same as *senex* in Latin.

But of places appropriated to prayer, there be that are *sacred*, there be that are *holy*, and there be that are *religious*.

2. *Sacred* be they which by the hands of the bishop have duly been sanctified and set apart to the Lord, and which be called by various names, as hath been said in the section on Churches. *Holy* be they which have immunity or privilege: and be set apart for the servitors or ministers of the Church, concerning which, under threat of condign punishment, either by the canon law or by special privilege, it is ordained that no man shall presume to violate them. Such be the courts of churches, and in some places the cloisters, within which be the houses of the canons. To which when criminals of whatever kind betake themselves they have safety. And so according to the statutes of the civil law be the gates and theatres of cities.

3. *Religious* places be they where the entire body of a man, or at least the head is buried: because no man can have two sepulchres. But the body or any member without the head doth not make the place wherein it is buried religious. But according to the civil law the corpse of a Jew, or paynim, or unbaptised infant maketh the place of its sepulchre religious: yet by the Christian religion and the canonical doctrine the body of a Christian alone maketh it so. And note that whatever is *sacred* is *religious*; but the contrary holdeth not. But the afore-named religious place hath divers appellations: such be *cemetery*, *polyandrum*, or *andropolis* (which is the same thing), *sepulchrum*, *mausoleum* (which is also the same), *dormitorium*, *tumulus*, *monumentum*, *ergastulum*, *pyramid*, *sarcophagus*, *bustum*, *urna*, *spelunca*.

4. *Cemetery* hath its name from *cimen* which is *sweet*, and *sterion*, which is a *station*: for there the bones of the departed rest sweetly, and expect the advent of their Saviour. Or because there be therein *cimices*, that is reptiles of intolerable odour.

5. *Poliantrum,* from *pollutum antrum*, on account of the carcases of men therein buried. Or *poliantrum* signifieth a multitude of men, from *polus*, which is a *plurality*, and *andros*, which is a man; and therefore a cemetery is so called on account of the number of men therein buried.[1]

. . . .

11. Cemeteries are said to have their beginning from Abraham, who bought a field from Hebron: in which was a double cave,[2] where he and Sarah were buried: there also Isaac and Jacob were buried: there also Adam and Eve.[3] Therefore there was a double cave there: since they who buried therein were placed side by side, every man and his wife; or the men in the one, and their wives in the other: or because everyone there interred had a double cave, after the fashion of a chair. Whence saith Hierome, Three patriarchs are buried in the city Hebron, with their three wives. But they were buried as it were in a sitting posture: the upper part of the cave held the trunk from the loins: the lower the thighs and legs.

12. But all men ought not to be buried promiscuously in the church: for it seemeth that that place of sepulchre profiteth not. Lucifer was thrown down from Heaven, and Adam cast out of Paradise; and what places be better than these? Also Joab was slain in the Tabernacle, and Job triumphed in the dunghill. Nay rather, it is to his hurt if a man unworthy or a sinner be buried in a church. We read in the 'Dialogues' of Blessed Gregory, book the fourth, chapter the fifty-sixth, that when a certain man of a notorious wickedness[4] had been buried in the church of S. Faustinus at Brescia, in the same night Blessed Faustinus appeared to the warden of the church, saying, Speak unto the bishop that he cast out the body; otherwise he shall die in thirty days. Now the warden feared to tell the thing to the bishop: and the bishop on the thirtieth day suddenly departed out of this life. It is also written in the same book, chapter the fifty-seventh, that another wicked man was buried in a church, and that afterwards his body was found outside the church, the cerecloths remaining in their own place. And Austin says, they who are guilty of notorious sins, if they be buried in the church by their own desire, shall be judged for their presumption; for the sacredness of the place doth not free those whom the accusation of temerity condemns.

No body, therefore, ought to be buried in a church, or near an altar, where the Body and Blood of our Lord are made, except the bodies of holy fathers, who be called patrons, that is defenders, who defend the whole country with their merits, and bishops, and abbots, and worthy presbyters, and laymen of eminent sanctity. But all ought to be buried about the church, or in the court of the cloisters, or in the porch: or in the exedrœ and apses which are joined to the church, or in the cemetery. Some also say that a space of thirty feet round the church ought to be set apart for that purpose. But others say that the space enclosed by the circuit which the bishop makes around the church must suffice for this. S. Augustine saith in his book 'On the Care of the Dead,' towards the end, that to be buried near the tombs of martyrs advantageth the dead in this, that by commending him to the guardianship of the martyrs, the earnestness of our supplication for him may be increased.

13. Of old time men were buried in their own houses: but on account of the stench thereby engendered, it was decreed that they should be buried without the city, and certain places should be set apart by sanctification for that purpose. But noblemen were buried in mountains, both in the middle of them and at the foot: and also under mounds raised of their own expense.[5] But if anyone be slain in besieging a town, where there is no cemetery, let him be buried where he can. But if a merchantman or pilgrim die by sea, and any inhabited land be near, let him be buried in it: but if no port be near, let him be buried in some island. If, however, land cannot be seen, let a little house of timbers (if they can be had) be made for him, and let him be cast into the sea.

14. In a Christian cemetery none may be buried but a baptised Christian: nor yet every such an one neither: one, namely, slain in the act of sin, if it be mortal sin, as if he were slain in adultery, or theft, or some forbidden amusement. And also where a man is found dead, there him be buried, on account of the doubtful cause of his death. But if anyone dieth suddenly in games accustomably used, as the game of ball, he may be buried in the cemetery, because it was not his desire to injure anyone: but because he was occupied in worldly matters, some say that he ought to be buried without psalms and the other obsequies of the dead. But if anyone attacking another in a strife or tumult dieth impenitent, and hath not sought the priest, he ought not, as some say, to be buried in the cemetery: nor yet he who hath committed suicide. But if anyone dieth, not from any manifest cause, but from the visitation of God alone, he can be buried in a cemetery. For the just man, in what hour soever he dieth, is saved. The rather if he were following some lawful occupation. To defenders of justice and those who are engaged in a pious fight, the cemetery and the office of burial are freely conceded: yet they who come to a violent death are not borne into the church, lest the pavement be polluted with blood. But if anyone returning from any place of fornication be slain in the way, or be slain anywhere, where by unforeseen case, he hath tarried, he is not

to be buried in the common cemetery; and this if it can be proved, by evidence sufficient for a court of law, that he had not confessed after the act of fornication nor was contrite: otherwise he ought to be buried.

15. Again, a woman who dieth in child-birth ought not to be carried into the church, as some say, but her obsequies must be said without the church, to which I agree not: otherwise it would be as if she died in fault. Whence she may allowably be borne into the church.

16. But stillborn and unbaptised children are to be buried without the cemetery. Some say, however, that they should be buried with the mother as being a part of her body.

17. A man and wife are to be buried in the same sepulchre, after the example of Abraham and Sarah (unless a wish be specially expressed to the contrary). Whence also Tobias commanded his son, that when his mother had accomplished her days, he should bury her in the same grave with himself.[6] Also everyone is to be buried in the sepulchre of his fathers, unless from a principle of devotion he hath chosen another sepulchre. But it was decreed in the Moguntine Council, that they who have paid the extreme penalty for their crimes, if they have confessed, or have desired to confess and have communicated, may be buried in the cemetery, and the Mass and oblations may be offered for them. How the human body is to be buried, shall be said under the section of the Office for the Dead.

Abraham

Isaac

"Cemeteries are said to have their beginning from Abraham, who bought a field from Hebron: in which there was a double cave, where he and Sarah were buried: there also Isaac and Jacob were buried..."

CHAPTER VI: OF THE DEDICATION OF A CHURCH

1. Twice in the former part of this treatise we have described the material church and the altar; it followeth that we must add something about their dedication: stating,

I. Whence the consecration of churches hath its origin.
II. At whose hands a church is consecrated.
III. For what reason.
IV. In what form; and what is signified, as well by the dedication itself, as by each of the ceremonies observed therein.

Of the offices for the festival of the dedication of a church we shall speak in the seventh book.[1]

2. We have first to state whence the dedication of churches hath had its rise. Upon which, note that under the teaching of the Lord, Moses made the tabernacle, and consecrated it together with its table of show-bread, and altar, and brazen vessels, and utensils for performing the divine worship. And these he not only consecrated with prayers to God, but also anointed, at the command of the Lord, with sacred oil. For[2] we read that the Lord taught Moses to prepare a chrism, with which to anoint the tabernacle and the ark of the testimony at the time of their dedication. Solomon also the son of David, at the command of the Lord, completed the temple and its altar, and consecrated what was still necessary for the performance of the divine worship; as it is written in the third book of Kings.[3] Nebuchadnezzar the king also summoned all his satraps, chief men, and governors to the dedication of the golden image which he had made.[4] The Jews, therefore, as we read in Burchardus,[5] used to have the places in which they sacrificed to the Lord consecrated by divine petitions, nor used they to offer gifts to God in any places but such as were dedicated unto Him. If then they who were in bondage to the shadow of the Law used to do this, how much the more ought we, to whom the truth hath been made manifest—'grace and truth came by Jesus Christ'[6]—to build temples to the Lord, and adorn them as best we may, and devoutly and solemnly consecrate (according to the institution of Pope Felix III)[7] by divine prayers and holy unctions both them and their altars and vessels, and vestments also, and other utensils for fulfilling the divine service?

Again, when once in Syria, in the city of Baruth, the Jews had trampled underfoot an image of the Crucified, and had pierced its side, there soon came forth therefrom blood and water. But the Jews marvelled at this spectacle, and their sick when anointed with this blood were freed from all their infirmities: by reason of which all having received the faith of Christ, were baptised, and proceeded to consecrate their synagogues into churches. And hence hath grown the custom that churches should be consecrated, whereas before this altar alone used to be consecrated. On account of this miracle also the Church ordained that a memorial of the Lord's Passion should be made on the fifth day before the Calends of December: and for the same reason the church was consecrated to the honour of the Saviour, in which a vessel containing some of the blood is preserved, and a solemn festival is celebrated on that day.[8]

3. Secondly, it is to be noted that a bishop alone can dedicate churches and altars: since he beareth the image and figure of the Chief Bishop, Christ, dedicating spiritually, without Whom we can do nothing stable in the Church: whence He hath Himself said, 'Without Me ye can do nothing':[9] and the Psalm saith, 'Unless the Lord build the house their labour is but lost that build it':[10] hence the Council of Carthage prohibiteth a priest from doing this, nor can this office be deputed to anyone of an inferior order.

4. Further, as the Sacred Canons instruct us, a church must not be dedicated, unless it be first endowed, and that from goods lawfully acquired. For we read how when a certain bishop was consecrating a church built out of the fruits of usury and pillage, he saw behind the altar the devil in a pontifical vestment, standing in the bishop's throne: who said unto the bishop, Cease from consecrating the church: for it pertaineth to my jurisdiction, since it is built from the fruits of usuries and robberies. Then the bishop and the clergy having fled thence in fear, immediately the devil destroyed that church, with a great noise.

5. Again, a church which hath been erected from the profit of avarice must not be consecrated; nor one for which a sufficient endowment hath not been assigned; nor one in which a paynim or an infidel hath been buried, until he shall have been cast forth thence, and the church reconciled, the walls and timbers having been first scraped. The case is the same also with respect to an excommunicated person. But if a woman with child be buried there, though she be not removed, the church may be consecrated, even if the child hath not been baptised.

Although certain learned authors have written otherwise the church may also be consecrated on ordinary days as well as on Sundays: and more bishops than one and more altars than one may be consecrated at the same time by the same person in one church.

6. Thirdly, we have to say for what reason a church is dedicated: and indeed there be five reasons. First, that the devil and his power may be

entirely expelled from it. Gregory relateth in a dialogue, in his third book, that when a certain church of the Arians having been restored to the Orthodox was being consecrated, and relics of S. Sebastian and the Blessed Agatha had been conveyed thither, the people there assembled of a sudden perceived a swine to be running to and fro among their feet; the which regaining the doors of the church could be seen of none, and moved all to marvel. Which sign the Lord showed for this cause, that it might be manifest to all that the unclean inhabitant had gone forth from that place. But in the following night a great noise was made on the roof of the same church, as if someone were running confusedly about upon it. The second night the uproar was much greater. On the third night also so vast a noise was heard as if the whole church had been overthrown from its foundations: but it immediately ceased and no further inquietude of the old enemy hath appeared in it. Secondly, that those who fly for refuge to it may be saved, as we read in the Canons of Gregory. And with this view Joab fled into the tabernacle and laid hold of the horns of the altar. Thirdly, that prayers may be heard there. Whence in the prayer of the Mass of Dedication it is said, 'Grant that all who shall meet together here to pray may obtain, whatsoever be their trials, the benefits of the consolation.' Thus also Solomon prayed at the dedication of the Temple, as we read in the eighth chapter of the third book of Kings.[11] Fourthly, that praises may there be offered to God, as has been already mentioned under the head of the Church. Fifthly, that there the sacraments of the Church may be administered. From which the church itself is called a tabernacle, as it were the hostelrie of God, in which the divine sacraments be contained and administered.[12]

7. Fourthly, we have to speak of the manner in which a church is consecrated. All being excluded from the church, a single deacon remaining shut up within, the bishop with his clergy before the doors of the church proceedeth to bless water mixed with salt. In the meanwhile within the building twelve lamps be burning before twelve crosses which be depicted on the walls of the church. Next, the bishop, the clergy and people following him and performing the circuit of the church, sprinkleth from a rod of hyssop the external walls with holy water; and as he arriveth each time at the door of the church he striketh the threshold with his pastoral staff, saying, 'Lift up your heads, O ye gates,' etc. The deacon from within answereth, 'Who is the King of Glory?' To whom the Pontiff, 'The Lord of Hosts,' etc. But the third time, the door being thrown open, the bishop entereth the church with a few of his attendants, the clergy and people remaining without, and saith, 'Peace be to this house'; and then the Litanies. Next on the pavement of the church, let a cross be made of ashes and

sand; upon which the whole alphabet is described in Greek and Latin characters.[13] And then he sanctifieth more water with salt and ashes and wine, and consecrateth the altar. Lastly, he anointeth with chrism the twelve crosses depicted on the wall.

8. In good truth whatsoever things be here done visibly, God by His invisible power worketh the same in the soul which is the temple of the true God: in which Faith layeth the foundation, Hope buildeth up, and Charity perfecteth. For the Catholic Church herself, made one out of many living stones, is the Temple of God, because many temples make one temple, of which the true God is one, and the Faith one. The house, therefore, must be dedicated; the soul sanctified.

9. And it is to be observed that consecration effecteth two things; for it appropriateth the material church itself to God, and doth insinuate our own betrothal, as well namely of the church as of the faithful soul. For a house not consecrated is as a damsel designed for some man, but not furnished with dowry or united in the commerce of wedlock. But in consecration it is endowed, and passeth into the proper spouse of Jesus Christ, which further to violate is sacrilege. For it ceaseth to be the resort of demons, as is evident in the consecration of that temple, which used formerly to be called the Pantheon, or place of all demons.[14]

10. First, however, we have to speak of the benediction of water, concerning which the Lord saith, 'Unless a man be born again of water and of the Spirit, he cannot enter the Kingdom of Heaven.'[15] For water which is designed for washing the body, hath merited to receive from God so great a virtue, that as it washeth the body from impurities, so also it should cleanse the soul from sins. It is manifest indeed that this water, by the aspersion of which a church is consecrated, signifieth baptism, because in some sort the church itself is baptised; and the church itself assuredly denoteth that Church which is contained in it, namely, the multitude of the faithful. Whence also it is called a church because it contains the Church; the thing containing, namely, for the thing contained.

11. But we must inquire wherefore salt is to be mixed with this water, since our Saviour, speaking of baptism, made no mention of salt. For He saith not 'unless a man be born again of salt water or water mixed with salt,' or anything of this sort: but He said 'unless a man be born again of water and of the Holy Spirit,' etc. And the very same inquiry may be made concerning oil and chrism. But we must note that salt in the divine language is often put for wisdom; according to that saying, 'Let your speech be savoured with salt.' And the Lord saith to His disciples, 'Have salt in yourselves and have peace one with another.'[16] And again, 'Ye are the salt

of the earth; but if the salt have lost its savour wherewithal shall it be salted?'[17] Hence also it is that according to the law no victim was offered without salt, but salt was a part of every sacrifice. From all which passages it is clearly shown that salt is put for wisdom. And wisdom indeed is the seasoning of all virtues, as salt is of all meats. Hence therefore it is that no one is baptised before he hath tasted salt; and in order that even infants may have by the symbolical meaning of the sacrament that which they cannot have in fact, the water is not blessed without a mixture of salt. Of the second benediction of water we shall speak in the following treatise.

12. Again, the trine aspersion within and without with hyssop and holy water signifieth the threefold immersion in baptism. And it is done for three reasons. First, to drive away evil spirits. For holy water availeth from its own proper virtue to drive away demons. Whence in the Office for Exorcising the Water we say—'that this water may become exorcised in order to put to flight all the power of the enemy, and may avail to eradicate the enemy himself,' etc. Secondly, for the cleansing and expiation of the church itself. For all earthly things be corrupted and defiled by reason of sin. Hence it is also that in the Law almost everything was cleansed by water. Thirdly, to remove all malediction, and to bring in a blessing instead. For the earth from the beginning received the curse with all its fruits, because that the great deceit was made out of its fruit. But water hath not been under any curse. Hence it is that our Lord ate fish, but we do not read expressly that he ate flesh, unless of the Paschal Lamb; and this on account of the precept of the Law, as an example, namely, sometimes to abstain from lawful things, sometimes to eat the same. Again, the aspersion in going the circuit signifieth that the Lord having a care of His own, sendeth His angel round about them that fear Him.

13. But the three responses which be chanted in the meantime testify the joy of the three ages of men receiving the faith, namely, Noah, Daniel, and Job. And since at this invocation the grace of Faith, Hope, and Charity is poured out as the sprinkling is directed to the foot and middle part, as well as to the upper part of the walls. We will now also speak of the interior aspersion. (Of the virtue of the hyssop, we will speak under the next head.)

14. But the trine circuit, which the bishop maketh while sprinkling, denoteth the thrice-repeated circuit which Christ made for the sanctification of the Church. The first was that by which He came down from heaven to the world: the second in which He descended into hell from the world: the third in which returning from hell and rising again He ascended into heaven. The trine circuit also showeth that that church is dedicated to the

honour of the Trinity. It showeth also the three states of such as shall be saved in the Church, which be the virgins, the continent, the married: which also the arrangement of the material church itself showeth, as hath been said under the head of the Church.

15. Moreover, the trine striking on the lintel of the door signifieth the threefold right which Christ hath in His Church and why it ought to be opened unto Him. For it hath from Him Creation, Redemption, and promise of Glorification. For the bishop representeth Christ, and the rod His power. Again, by the triple striking of the door with the pastoral staff, the preaching of the Gospel is understood. For what else is the pastoral rod than the divine Word? According to that of Esaias, 'He shall smite the earth with the rod,' i.e. the word, 'of His mouth,' etc.[18] Wherefore to strike the door with the rod is to strike the ears of the hearers by the word of preaching. For the ears are the gates by which we bring in the words of holy preachings to the hearts of the hearers. Whence in the Psalm, 'Who liftest me up from the gates of death that I may show all Thy praises within the ports of the daughter of Sion.'[19] For what are the gates of the daughter of Sion but the ears and hearing of the faithful? Thirdly, the trine striking with the staff, and the opening of the gates, signifieth that by the preaching of the pastors the unbelieving shall come to the agreement of the Faith. For by it the gates of justice be opened, and they that enter therein do confess the faith. Whence the Psalm, 'Open unto me the gates of righteousness: I will go into them and I will praise the Lord: this is the gate of the Lord, the righteous shall enter into it.'[20] Wherefore the bishop striketh the lintel, namely, of reason, saying, 'Lift up your heads, ye princes,' that is, ye evil spirits: or rather, 'Lift up, you men,' that is, remove the gates, that is, your ignorances, namely, from your hearts.[21]

16. Again, the question of the deacon shut up within answering in the character of the people, 'Who is the King of glory?' is the ignorance of the people which knoweth not Who He is Who ought to enter.

17. The opening of the doors is the ejection of sin. Rightly, therefore, doth the bishop strike three times, because that number is most known and most sacred; and in any consecration the bishop ought to smite the doors three times, because without the invocation of the Trinity, there can be no sacrament in the Church.

18. The threefold proclamation, 'Lift up your heads,' etc., signifieth the threefold power of Christ, that, namely, which He hath in heaven, and in the earth, and in hell. Whence it is said in the hymn for the Ascension, 'That the threefold frame of things, whether heavenly, earthly, or infernal, may bow the head, having been subdued.'[22]

19. Next the bishop entereth by the open door to denote that if he duly exercise his office, nothing can resist him; according to that saying, 'Lord, who shall resist Thy power?' And he entereth, accompanied by two or three, that in the mouth of two or three witnesses every word of the consecration may stand sure. Or else because the Lord in His Transfiguration, in the presence of a few, prayed for the Church. And the bishop as he entereth saith, 'Peace be to this house and to all them that dwell therein'; because Christ entering the world made peace between God and man; for He came that He might reconcile us to God the Father.

20. After this while the Litany is being said the bishop prostrateth himself and prayeth for the sanctification of the house. For Christ also humbling Himself before His Passion prayed for His disciples and 'them that should believe through His word,' saying, 'Father, sanctify them in Thy name.'[23] But after he hath risen up he prayeth without benediction, since he saith not 'The Lord be with you'; because the Church is not yet, as it were, baptised, and because Catechumens only are not worthy that this mark of approval should be given to them, since they are not yet sanctified: but nevertheless prayer is to be made for them.

21. The clergy praying and chanting the Litany representeth the Apostles who intercede with God for the sanctification of the Church and of souls.

The alphabet is written on the pavement of the church in this manner. A cross made with ashes and sand is described athwart the church, upon which cross of dust the alphabet is written in the shape of a cross in letters of Greek and Latin, but not of Hebrew, because the Jews have departed from the faith; and it is written with the pastoral staff.

22. This alphabet written upon the cross representeth three things. First, the writing made in Greek and Latin characters in the shape of a cross representeth the conjunction or union in faith of both people, namely, the Jews and the Greeks, which is made through the Cross of Christ: according to the saying that Jacob blessed his sons with his hands crossed. But the cross itself or the legend that is described in a direction athwart the church, namely, the one arm from the left corner of the east to the right of the west,[24] signifieth that that people, which was before on the right is now made on the left, and that which was first is now made last, and the converse: and this owing to the power of the Cross. For Christ passing from the east, left the Jews on His left hand, because they were unbelieving, and came to the Gentiles, to whom, though they had been in the west, He grants to be on the right hand: and at length returning from the Gentiles, who are situated at the right hand of the east, He visited the Jews in the left corner of the west; who it is evident are worse than He before

found the Gentiles. But on this account the characters are written obliquely and in the shape of a cross, and not in a straight line, because such an one as doth not receive the mystery of the Cross and doth not believe that he must be saved by the Passion of Christ, is not able to attain to this holy wisdom. Wisdom will not enter into the evil-disposed mind, and where Christ is not the foundation, no edifice can be built upon it.

23. Secondly, the writing of the alphabet representeth the page of both Testaments, because they be fulfilled by the Cross of Christ. For the veil of the temple was rent asunder at His Passion, because then the Scriptures were opened and the Holy of Holies revealed. Whence He Himself said when dying 'IT IS FINISHED.' In these few letters also all knowledge is contained; and the alphabet is written crosswise, because one Testament is contained in the other. For there was a wheel within a wheel.

24. Thirdly, it representeth the articles of faith; for the pavement of the church is the foundation of our faith. The elements written thereon, are the articles of faith, in which ignorant men and neophytes from both peoples be instructed in the Church; who indeed ought to esteem themselves dust and ashes. Just as Abraham saith in the xviii chapter of Genesis, 'Shall I speak to my Lord, who am but dust and ashes?' Wherefore the writing of the alphabet on the pavement is the simple teaching of faith in the human heart.

25. The *sambuca* or staff, with which the alphabet is written showeth the doctrine of the apostles, or the mystery of the teachers, by which the conversion of the Gentiles hath been effected, and the perfidy of the Jews. Afterwards approaching the altar the bishop standeth, and beginneth by saying, 'O God, make speed to save us;' because he is then beginning the principal part of office. And the versicle, 'Glory be to the Father,' etc., is then said.

26. Because this benediction is used to set forth the glory of the Trinity, Alleluia is not then uttered, as will be set forth in the next chapter. Then the bishop consecrateth the altar, for which he blesseth other water, as shall also be declared in the next chapter. With which water also, after that the altar hath been sprinkled seven times, the whole interior of the church is sprinkled three times, as at first without any distinction between greater and smaller stones, since 'there is no respect of persons with God.' For this reason is the interior sprinkled, to signify that an external ablution profiteth nothing without an internal charity. And for this reason *three* times, because, as hath been premised, that aspersion signifieth the aspersion and cleansing of baptism, which is conferred through the invocation of the Trinity, according to the saying, 'Go ye and teach all nations, baptising

them in the name of the Father, and of the Son, and of the Holy Ghost:'[25] for since a church cannot be immersed in water as a man in baptism is immersed, it is on this account sprinkled three times with water, as if in the place of a threefold immersion.

27. Again, the bishop performeth the aspersion proceeding from the east to the west and once through the middle in the form of the cross; because Christ gave instructions to baptise the whole of Judea and all nations in the name of the Trinity, to which baptism He gave efficacy in the ministry of His Passion, beginning from the Jews, from whom He had His birth. And what remains of the water is poured away at the foot of the altar, as shall be mentioned in the next chapter. Some, however, do not bless any fresh water, but perform the whole office with that which was blessed at first. In the meanwhile, however, the choir is chanting the Psalm *Exsurgat Deus* ('let God arise and let His enemies be scattered,' etc.), and the *Qui habitat* ('whoso dwelleth,' etc.), in which mention is made of the church and its consecration, as is plain in that verse, 'He is the God that maketh men to be of one mind in an house.'[26] But the bishop saith, 'My house shall be called an house of prayer,' because it is his duty to cause that the church should bc a house of God, not of merchandise.

28. Next, when the altar hath been anointed with chrism, the twelve crosses painted on the walls of the church are also anointed. But the crosses themselves be painted; first, as a terror to evil spirits, that they, having been driven forth thence, may be terrified when they see the sign of the cross, and may not presume to enter therein again; secondly, as a mark of triumph. For crosses be the banners of Christ, and the signs of his triumph.[27] Crosses therefore are with reason painted there that it may be made manifest that that place hath been subdued to the dominion of Christ.

29. For even in the pomp of an earthly sovereign it is customary when any city hath been yielded, for the imperial standard to be set up within it. And to represent the same thing, Jacob is said to have set up the stone, which he had placed under his head, as a historical, traditional, and triumphal monument.[28]

30. Thirdly, that such as look on them may call to mind the Passion of Christ, by which he hath consecrated His Church, and their belief in His Passion. Whence it is said in the Canticles, 'place me as a signet upon thy arm,' etc.[29] The twelve lights placed before these crosses signify the twelve Apostles who have illumined the whole world by the faith of the Crucified, and whose teaching hath dispersed the darkness: whence Bernard saith, 'All prophecy is verified in the faith of the crucified One;' and the Apostle, 'I determined not to know anything among you except Jesus Christ

and Him crucified.'[30] Wherefore the crosses on the four walls of the church are lighted up and anointed with chrism, because the apostles preaching the mystery of the cross have by the faith of Christ illumined the four quarters of the earth unto knowledge, have lighted them up unto love, have anointed them unto purity of conscience—which is signified by the oil; and unto the savour of a good reputation—which is signified by the balsam. In addition to this, after the anointing of the altar, the altar itself and the church are ornamented; the lamps lighted up; a Mass is said, in which the priest useth different vestments from those which he hath used in the aspersion, as shall be explained in the sequel.

31. Lastly, it is to be noted that a church is said to be consecrated in the blood of someone; whence, according to Pelagius and Pope Nicholas, the Roman Church was consecrated in the martyrdom of the Apostles, Peter and Paul.[31] A church therefore is consecrated in the way just described; and an altar, as will be set forth in the next chapter; and a cemetery and other things, as is declared under the head of its consecration. And although we read in the Old Testament that the Temple was consecrated three times: first in the month of September; secondly, in March under Darius; thirdly, in December by Judas Maccabæus.

32. Yet a church once consecrated, is not to be consecrated again unless it shall have been profaned, which happeneth in three ways. First, if it hath been burnt so as that all the walls or the greater part of them be destroyed. But if only the roof or some part of it hath been burnt, the walls remaining entire, or at least only partially destroyed, it need not be reconsecrated. Secondly, if the whole church or the greater part of it hath fallen to the ground at the same time, and hath been repaired entirely or not with the original stones. For consecration of a church consisteth mainly in the exterior anointings, and in the conjunction and arrangement of the stones. If, however, all the walls shall have fallen in, not at the same time, but in succession, and shall have been repaired, the church is to be considered the same. And so it need not be reconsecrated, but only exorcised with water and reconciled by the solemnisation of a Mass: however, some learned authors have said that it ought to be reconsecrated. Thirdly, a church must be reconsecrated, if it be doubtful whether it ever hath been consecrated, should there remain no writing or painting or inscription to that effect, nor even a single eye-witness, nor yet an ear-witness, who (as some say) would be sufficient.

33. An altar also which hath been once consecrated must not be consecrated again unless it should happen that it become profaned. Which taketh place first if the table, that is the upper surface on which the principal part

of the consecration is bestowed, be moved or changed in its form, or broken beyond measure, for instance above a half. However, a disproportion of this sort may rightly be referred to the decision of the bishop. The same also is especially the case, if the whole structure of the altar hath been moved and repaired. Nevertheless, the church is not to be reconsecrated on account of either the movement or the breaking of the structure of the altar: because the consecration of an altar and of a church be two different things. So conversely if when the church is entirely destroyed the altar be not injured, the church only is to be repaired, and the altar not reconsecrated: although in such case it is fitting that it be washed with exorcised water.

34. Further, when the chief altar hath been consecrated the inferior altars are not the less to be consecrated: although some have said that it is sufficient for the rest to be pointed out with the finger while the former is under consecration.

35. If, however, the altar hath suffered a trifling injury, it is not on this account to be reconsecrated.

Secondly, an altar is reconsecrated, if the *seal* of the altar—that is the little stone by which the sepulchre or cavity in which the relics be deposited is closed or sealed—be moved or broken. And the cavity itself is made sometimes on the top part of the block, and sometimes no other seal is put over it, but the *table*, being placed over it, is considered as the seal. But sometimes it is placed in the hinder part, and sometimes in the front: and in the same cavity the bishop's letters of consecration be generally carefully deposited in testimony of the consecration: containing his own name and that of the other bishops present at the consecration: and declaring in honour of what saint the altar is consecrated, and also the church itself, when both be consecrated at the same time, and the year also and day of consecration.

Thirdly, an altar is reconsecrated, if the junction of the seal to the cavity, or of the *table* to the block, where there is no other seal than this slab, be disturbed; or if any of the stones of the junction of the block, which toucheth either the table or the seal, be either disturbed or broken. For in the conjunction of the seal and cavity, and of the table and block or inferior structure, the consecration is most especially perceived.

Fourthly, an altar is reconsecrated, if to it or to the conjunction of the table with the under structure so great an enlargement be made as that it loseth its original form, since the form giveth the existence to the thing. Yet it doth not become profaned on account of a trifling enlargement: but in that case the sacred part draweth over to itself the part not sanctified: so

Relic of Martyr (St. Martin)

Place in altar surface for a relic

Kneeler containing relic

Since 1901, the skeletal remains of two Christian martyrs—Saint Bonosa and Saint Magnus—have been housed in glass reliquaries in the sanctuary under the two side altars. Saint Bonosa and Saint Magnus were put to death at the hand of Roman Emperor Septimius Severus in 207 C.E. Dressed in maroon robes, white satin slippers and light gauze veils, the relics spent 15 centuries in the catacombs of Rome and another two centuries within the walls of an Agnani, Italy, monastery. The monastery donated the relics to the parish in 1901 after the monastery had been seized by the Italian government. Beside each skeleton is a small poercelain container marked "Vas Sanguinis" that is said to hold congealed traces of the martyr's blood.
St. Martin's of Tours, Louisville, Ky.

The Silver Casket containing the body of St. James situated on the altar of the Cathedral at Santiago de Compostela, Spain. The altar is decorated with a symbol for the Fountain of Immortality and two peacocks drinking therein which represent Paradise.

(Ark, as depicted in 14th Century Spanish manuscript)

(German, 1250)

"Of pictures and images, some are in front of the church, as the ox and the cow, others within, as images, statues, and various kinds of painting and sculpture: and these be represented either in garments, or on walls."

long as the conjunction of the top slab and under structure be not greatly changed.

Fifthly, an altar, just as a church, is reconsecrated in cases of doubt.

Sixthly, a travelling altar, if the stone be removed from the wood in which it is inserted, which in some sort representeth its *seal*, and be replaced again in the same or in other wood, some think should be reconsecrated, but others only reconciled. But although it be often by the command of the bishop transferred from place to place, and carried on a journey (on which account it is called a portable or a travelling altar) yet it is not reconsecrated in consequence of this, nor yet reconciled.

36. But if a consecrated chalice be regilt, is it therefore to be reconsecrated? It seemeth so, since it appeareth to become a new chalice. For he who doth renew the old fashion of a work seemeth to make a new work: and he doth remake, who doth mend a thing already made. And assuredly consecration doth pertain to the outer surface. And hence it is that I have said above that a church, if its walls be stripped of their outer coat, must be reconsecrated.

37. The converse is nevertheless true, that neither on account of whitewashing or painting the walls, nor of any small addition to them, is a church to be reconsecrated; as I have already said. Wherefore, if the shape of the chalice be not changed, it remaineth the same chalice, and is not to be reconsecrated; just as also a church being repaired, since it remaineth the same church, is not to be reconsecrated, as aforesaid. But if the former shape be changed, the case were otherwise, since, as I have said, the shape giveth existence to the thing. Nevertheless, it is decent, as well by reason of its contact with unclean hands as also of the increment of unconsecrated matter, that a chalice, being regilded, should be washed with exorcised water before that the most Holy Body and Blood of the Lord be sacrificed therein. Let us now say something about Reconciliation.

38. Upon this head it is to be noted that the spiritual temple, which is man, is ofttimes polluted. Whence we do read in the twentieth of Leviticus what men be polluted, and how they may not enter the church until they be washed with water and cleansed: as also in the nineteenth of Numbers, 'He that toucheth the dead body of a man shall be unclean...wherefore he shall purify himself and wash his clothes and bathe himself in water and shall be clean.' And the Prophet saith, 'Thou shalt purge me with hyssop and I shall be clean.'[32]

39. The material temple also, which as Pope Gregory doth testify, is the church, is sometimes polluted, as we do read in Leviticus.[33] Whence saith the Prophet, 'Thy holy temple have they defiled and made Jerusalem

an heap of stones.'[34] And the material temple is also washed with water in order to be reconciled.[35] Reconciliation is also effected by the celebration of a Mass, and the aspersion of water duly consecrated with salt, wine, and ashes. For by the salt, is signified discretion; by the water, the people; by the wine, the Divinity; by the ashes, the remembrance of the Passion of Christ; by the wine mixed with water, the union of Godhead and Manhood. These things, therefore, be put together to denote that the people, being cleansed by a discerning remembrance of the Passion of Christ, are made one with Him. Also if the church hath once been consecrated, the reconciliation can be made by a bishop only. And albeit he might devolve upon a fellow-bishop the whole office, namely, both the blessing of the water and the reconciliation; or the benediction of the water only; or even the reconciliation alone with water blessed beforehand by himself; yet can neither be devolved upon a mere priest, unless perchance this be competent to him by a special privilege. But if the church hath not been consecrated, it ought, according to the Constitution of Gregory, to be washed forthwith with exorcised water: the which washing some do affirm may be done by a mere priest, though at the bidding of the bishop: since it hath to be done by exorcised water, which every priest may use. Yet some skilful men of the highest authority have written that it is safer for this also to be done by none but a bishop, and that this may not be devolved by him to a priest; for certain canons do call exorcised water that which is solemnly blessed with wine and ashes: —and this is true indeed in regard of a church which although not consecrated hath been dedicated unto God. For it is otherwise with a mere oratory, which is neither a holy nor a religious place, inasmuch as any man doth order it at his will—at least for prayers, albeit perchance not for celebration without the license of the diocesan—and at his will assigneth the same place to another use.

40. A church then is to be reconsecrated in the aforesaid case: and also if any uncleanness be committed therein, whether by clerk, layman, heretic, or paynim. But albeit some wise men have thought otherwise, we opine that the case is different in regard of unintentional pollution.[36]

41. A church also must be reconciled on account of any homicide, in any way intentionally committed therein, whether with or without the shedding of blood: and also, besides homicide, for any violence or injurious shedding of human blood, whether from a wound or not, or from the nose or the mouth. For we read in the Old Testament, in the fourteenth and fifteenth of Leviticus, how that any man shedding blood, or polluted in divers ways, may not enter the temple. If, however, without violence or injury blood should flow in any natural way whatsoever within the church;

or if any animal should be slain therein, or if anyone should die suddenly, or be killed by a falling stone or timber, or by lightning; for these and the like occasions the church is not reconciled. Nor again, if anyone, having been wounded elsewhere, should flee to a church and die there even with great effusion of blood: since then the homicide is not committed in the church. But conversely, if anyone having been wounded in a church dieth without, or even if blood flow from the wound away from the church, the case is otherwise, even if the blood did not flow at all within the church: since the law regardeth the blow which causeth the wound. But and if blood be shed or other pollutions be caused on the roof of a church, no reconciliation is made, because the deed is committed without the church.

42. But if theft and rapine be committed in a church, it is reconciled by the custom which usually obtaineth in such matters. And some do affirm that the same ought to be done in any case of violence committed therein without the shedding of blood; for example, if anyone having taken refuge therein should be drawn forth with violence. Also if anyone should break into the church or any quarrel should be tumultuously carried on, though without shedding of blood: or if anyone should be grievously beaten therein, so as his bones should be broken, or he be covered with weals and bruises, though without blood; or again, if anyone, being condemned while present in a church either to death or mutilation, be led forth to go to the place of execution. But since these cases be not expressed in the law, it is not necessary for the church to be solemnly reconciled by the bishop. Yet we think it is decent for it to be washed by the priest with exorcised water at the command of the bishop: and the same is to be said, if the church being a long time without roof or doors, should have been open to all impurities, to animals and the natural use of men, as if a common inn: nor perchance would it be amiss for it in such case to be solemnly reconciled by the bishop. Again, if anyone, slain without the church, be shortly borne into the church, and there the murderer or anyone else thinking he will not die should inflict on his yet warm body a blow causing blood to flow, then the church must be reconciled, as well by reason of the horror and abomination, as of the violence and intention of sinning: for though a dead man be not a man, yet is his human blood shed there by violence; and to the corpse itself is violence, horror, and injury offered. But the case is otherwise if anyone, having died a natural death, be, through respect of, and honour to his body, dismembered in the church or disembowelled, that perhaps one part may be buried in one place, and another in another.

43. A church must also be reconciled, in which an infidel, or one publicly excommunicated be buried; and then the walls are to be scraped.

In the aforesaid cases, however, in which a church is to be reconciled, it is requisite that the fact causing the reconciliation should be known at least by report.

44. For this is a scandal to the church, the horror and abomination of baseness and sin and violence committed in a sacred place, or in a church: wherein the pardon for offences is besought, wherein there ought to be a refuge of defence, wherein is offered the saving sacrifice for sins, wherein also those that flee for refuge be saved, and praises be rendered unto God. Furthermore, the intention and design of sinning mortally therein do cause a church to be reconciled. But if this design be hidden, reconciliation is not necessary, since the church itself, being holy, cannot be polluted; nay, the holiness of the place itself doth do away with the infamy: albeit some do think the contrary of this, as that it ought to be reconciled at least privately, so that the delinquents be not exposed.

45. For reconciliation is performed for an example and warning, that all who behold the church, which hath in no wise sinned, washed and purified for the delict of another, may reflect how they themselves must work out the expiation of their own sins.

46. Also a cemetery, in which a paynim, or an infidel or one excommunicated be buried, is to be reconciled; the bones, however, of the paynim, if they can be distinguished from those of the faithful, being interred elsewhere. A cemetery also is reconciled in the above-mentioned cases, in which a church is to be reconciled: for a cemetery enjoyeth the same privileges as doth a church, as we shall say in the chapter of Sacred Unctions; for it is a holy place from the time of its benediction; and it is reconciled by the bishop, just as a church, by the aspersion of water, blessed with wine and ashes.

47. But this is to be noted, that in whatsoever part of the church or the cemetery the violence or pollution be committed, both the church and the cemetery, and also the several parts of either, by reason of their contiguity, are understood to be violated. This first hath of late been set straight by Pope Boniface. For albeit the consecrations of the church, the altar, and the cemetery be diverse, yet is the immunity of them one and the same and is not to be restricted to any one of them separately, nor to any individual part of either. This indeed is true if the church and cemetery be adjacent: but if the one be at a distance from the other, one may well be violated without the other. If therefore when one is violated or polluted, the other be also violated and polluted; by the like reason, if one only be reconciled the other is also taken to be reconciled: since nothing is more natural than that everything should be loosed in the same method as it is bound, and

that the relation of binding and loosing should be the same. Wherefore when the cemetery is violated or polluted, it sufficeth that the church be reconciled. There be nevertheless some who do affirm simply that by the pollution of the one, the other is in no wise polluted, and by consequence that each should be reconciled separately. Yet these doth the authority of the Pontifical oppose, in which is found a special form for the reconciliation of a cemetery. Lastly, if a church or a cemetery, or any such thing, be consecrated or blessed by a bishop under excommunication, these, some affirm, do not require reconciliation, since sacraments administered by such in the form of the Church be valid. But since (as aforesaid) one or more excommunicated persons do profane a cemetery or church, much more indeed do the external sacraments and benedictions, which proceed from the hands and mouth of an excommunicated person, appear so far as pertaineth to their own merits to be contaminated and to stink before God. Wherefore it is decent that we should reconcile them before the faithful use these sacraments; as in truth the reading of the sacred canons doth evidently teach. For the Lord saith by the Prophet, 'I will curse your blessings.'[37]

(13th Century, France)

"Images of the Resurrection"

CHAPTER VII: OF THE CONSECRATION OF AN ALTAR

1. Not only is a church consecrated, but also the altar: and this for three reasons. First, with the sacrament thereon to be offered to God. Noah[1] built an altar to the Lord, and offered a sacrifice upon it, taking some of all clean birds and beasts. But this sacrament is the Body and Blood of Christ which is sacrificed in remembrance of the Lord's Passion, according to the command, 'This do in commemoration of Me.'[2]

2. Secondly, with regard to the invocation in that place of the name of God: whence[3] Abraham built an altar to God who appeared unto him, and called there upon the name of the Lord. But this invocation, which takes place over the altar, is properly called the *Mass*.

3. Thirdly, with regard to chanting: 'He gave him patience against his enemies, and caused singers also to stand before the altar, that by their voices they might make sweet melody.'[4]

4. The consecration of an altar is performed in this method and order. The bishop beginneth, 'O God, make speed to save us.' Afterwards he blesseth the water, and then at the four horns[5] he describeth four crosses with the consecrated water. Next, he goeth round the altar seven times, and sprinkleth the *table*[6] of the altar seven times with holy water, by means of an aspersory of hyssop. The church also is again sprinkled, and the remainder of the water is poured at the foot of the altar: and then four crosses be made with chrism at the four corners of the sepulchre in which the relics are to be deposited: and the relics themselves be placed in a case, together with three grains of frankincense, and so be buried in the sepulchre. Then is placed upon the sepulchre its cover,[7] strengthened in the middle by the sign of the cross: afterwards the stone, which is called the table, is fitted to the top of the altar, and when fitted is anointed with oil in five places, and in the same way is further anointed afterwards with chrism, as hath been said when speaking about oil. The altar also is confirmed in front by the chrism applied in the form of the cross, and incense is burnt upon it in the five places. After this the altar is covered up, and is spread with clean cloths, and then at length the sacrifice is celebrated upon it. Now let us follow out each of the above-mentioned ceremonies in succession.

5. First, then, it is to be noted, that an altar is consecrated by the unction of chrism and act of blessing intervening, and that it is only and entirely of stone. The bishop standing up beginneth, 'O God, make speed to

(Notre Dame, Paris)

"'For the Temple of God is holy, which temple ye are.' Wherefore, if we be the Temple of God, 'we have an altar.' Our altar is our heart; for the heart is in a man what the altar is in a temple. On this altar is made the sacrifice of praise and joy, according to the saying of the Psalmist: 'The sacrifices of God are a broken spirit.' On this altar is made the commemoration of the Body and Blood of Christ. From it do prayers rise to heaven, because God looketh to the heart."

save us,' because the Lord Himself saith, 'Without Me ye can do nothing.'[8]

6. And because this dedication signifieth that those must be baptised, who, after receiving the faith, are preparing themselves to fight, and who are still situated amongst the sighs and struggles of this world; on this account the Alleluia is omitted, since those who be not baptised be not worthy to join in the praises of angels: whence it is written in Tobit, 'And all her streets shall say Alleluia.'[9] But after that the consecration of the church or of the altar is completed, the Alleluia is chanted, because the delusions of devils having been expelled, God shall be praised thereupon. For Christ even when approaching to the altar of the cross in order to manifest the glory of His Eternity, paid the penalty of death: not until after His resurrection sang He Alleluia.

7. Secondly, with respect to the blessing of water, it is to be noted that this kind of exorcising water is performed in order to expel the enemy from it. In which blessing four things be necessary; namely, water, wine, salt, and ashes. And this for three reasons.

8. (i) Because there be four things which expel the enemy. The first is the outpouring of tears, which is denoted by the water: the second is the exultation of the soul, which is denoted by the wine: the third is natural discretion, which by the salt; the fourth, a profound humility, which is signified by the ashes. Wherefore the water is penitence, the wine exaltation of mind, the salt wisdom (as was shown in the preceding chapter), the ashes the humility of penitence. Whence it is said of the Ninevites that their 'king rose up from his throne, and clothed himself with sackcloth, and sat in ashes.'[10] Hence also David saith, 'For I have eaten ashes as it were bread.'[11] Hence also Abraham saith, 'Shall I speak to my Lord, who am but dust and ashes?'[12]

9. (ii) In a second sense water is the people or mankind, because many waters are many peoples; wine is the Deity; salt, the teaching of the divine law which is the salt of the covenant; ashes, that which preserveth the remembrance of the Lord's Passion. Wine mixed with water, is Christ, God and Man. For by means of faith in the Lord's Passion (*ashes*), which is had through the teaching of the Divine Law (*salt*), the people, denoted by the water, is joined through the union of faith, to its Head, God and Man.

10. (iii) In a third method we may say also that this consecrated water signifieth the Holy Spirit, without Whose influence nothing ever is sanctified, and without Whose grace there is no remission of sins. That the Holy Spirit is called water, truth itself showeth when He saith, 'Whosoever

believeth in Me, out of his belly shall flow rivers of living water':[13] which the Evangelist explaining saith, 'This He spake of the Holy Ghost which they should receive who believed upon Him.'

11. And note the order of the sacrament; the church is consecrated outwardly by water, inwardly by the Spirit. For this is what the Lord saith, 'Unless a man shall be born again of water and of the Holy Ghost,' etc.[14] Here is the water: here the Holy Spirit. For in the sacrament of baptism, neither is the water without the Spirit, nor the Spirit without the water: which element indeed the Spirit Himself did sanctify, when in the first creation of the world 'He moved upon the face of the waters.'[15] With this water therefore, both the altar itself and the whole interior of the church is sprinkled, when both it and the altar are dedicated on the same occasion.

12. Although therefore the Spirit and water would suffice for the perfect operation of baptism and the consecration of a church, yet the holy fathers who have made this constitution, wished to satisfy us not only in those particulars which pertain to the efficacy of the sacraments, but in those also which relate to its greater sanctification: and on this account they have added salt, wine, oil, ashes, and chrism. (For Philip, when he baptised the eunuch, had neither oil nor chrism.) Therefore not one of these incredients ought to be wanting; and they ought all to be mixed together, because the people of God, which is the Church, is neither sanctified nor released from sins without the union of these qualities. In this I shall treat also in the chapter on consecrations. With respect to water indeed the case is evident, because 'unless a man be born again,' etc.

13. With respect to the salt also; because without the seasoning of faith, which is typified by the salt, no one shall ever be saved, albeit he be sprinkled by the water of baptism. Also with respect to wine, by means of which the spiritual intelligence of the divine law is denoted. Whence the Lord at the marriage in Cana turned the water into wine. But if anyone shall not have been sprinkled with this, that is shall not have drunk of this or have believed those who offered it to him to drink, he shall not attain to the blessedness of eternal life. The aspersion of ashes also, by which the humility of penitence is understood, is so necessary, that without it there is no remission of sins in adults: for through it they come to baptism, and it is the sole refuge for such as have sinned after baptism. Whence not without reason is baptism called from it: the Lord speaking in the gospel concerning John Baptist 'that he came into the whole region of Galilee, preaching the baptism of repentance for the remission of sins.'[16] Note also that there be four kinds of consecrated water, of which we shall speak in the fourth book, and at the head of 'The aspersion of holy water.'[17]

14. When all these ingredients have been mixed, the bishop maketh four crosses with this water at the four horns of the altar, and one in the middle;[18] the four crosses represent the fourfold charity which they ought to have who approach the altar, viz., love for God, themselves, their friends, and their enemies. Of which four corners of charity it is said in Genesis, 'Thou shalt spread into the east, and the west, and the north, and the south.': and for this reason be the four crosses made at the four corners to show that Christ, by His Cross, hath saved the four quarters of the world. Secondly, they be made to point out that we ought to bear the cross of the Lord in four ways; namely, in our heart by meditation, in our mouth by confession, in our body by mortification of the flesh, in our face by constant impression. The cross in the middle of the altar signifieth the Passion which Christ underwent in the middle of the earth, by which He worked out salvation in the middle of the earth; that is, in Jerusalem.

15. Next, the bishop goeth seven times round the altar. (i) Firstly, to signify that he ought to exercise care for all, and to keep himself vigilant, which is denoted by the act of going round. Whence at that time they chant, 'The watchmen that went about the city found me.'[19] For a bishop ought to watch anxiously over the flocks committed to him: for as Gilbert saith, 'A ridiculous thing it is, a blind watchman, a lame leader, a negligent prelate, an untaught teacher, and a dumb preacher.'

16. (ii) Secondly, the seven circuits of the altar do dignify the seven meditations which we ought to entertain respecting the sevenfold virtue of the humility of Christ, and of which we ought to make frequent circuits in our minds. The first virtue is, that from being rich He became poor; the second, that He was laid in a manger; the third, that he was subject to His parents; the fourth, that He bowed His Head under the hand of a slave; the fifth, that He bore with a thief and a betrayer as a disciple; the sixth, that He stood gentle before an unrighteous judge; the seventh, that He mercifully prayed for them that crucified Him.

17. (iii) Thirdly, by the seven circuits be indicated the seven journeys of Christ. The first was from heaven to the Virgin's womb; the second, thence into the manger; the third, from the manger into the world; the fourth, from the world to the cross; the fifth, from the cross to the sepulchre; the sixth, from the sepulchre to the place of spirits; the seventh, from the place of spirits to heaven.

18. After this, the bishop sprinkleth the altar. But what the altar signifieth in a temple, the Apostle telleth us: 'For the Temple of God is holy, which temple ye are.'[20] Wherefore, if we be the Temple of God, 'we have an altar.'[21] Our altar is our heart: for the heart is in a man what the

altar is in a temple. On this altar is made the sacrifice of praise and joy, according to the saying of the Psalmist: 'The sacrifices of God are a broken spirit,' etc.[22] On this altar is made the commemoration of the Body and Blood of Christ. From it do prayers rise to heaven, because God looketh to the heart. This altar, therefore, is sprinkled with water when the hearts of men, by means of the preaching of the gospel, are cleansed from sin. For preaching is water, according to that saying: 'All ye that thirst, come to the waters.'[23] By this water, therefore, that is, by the preaching of the gospel and the sanctification of the Holy Ghost, both the altar and the whole man are cleansed and sanctified. For the altar of the heart is consecrated by the conception of fear, inviting to good, and by the affection of love, conforming to the better. 'For the fear of the Lord is the beginning of wisdom.'[24]

19. But the altar is sprinkled seven times with water to notify that in baptism the seven gifts of the Holy Spirit be conferred. By this also it is set forth that we ought to have a remembrance of the Lord's Passion. For the seven aspersions of water be the seven outpourings of the Blood of Christ. The first whereof was at circumcision; the second in prayer, when His sweat was as drops of blood; the third, at thc scourging; the fourth, from the crown of thorns; the fifth, from His pierced hands; the sixth, when His feet were nailed to the cross; the seventh, when His side was opened. Some, however, sprinkle three times, because we baptise in the name of the Holy Trinity; or because the church is cleansed from sins of thought, word, and deed; whence also at that time the *Miserere mei* is said.

20. Moreover, these aspersions be made with an aspersory made of hyssop, by which herb, because it is lowly, the lowliness of Christ is conveniently represented: since the above-mentioned effusions of blood were accompanied by the hyssop, of the humility and inextinguishable love of Christ by which the Catholic Church being sprinkled is purified. This herb also groweth naturally upon rock: and lowliness of disposition hath grown upon Christ the rock. For according to the Apostle, 'That rock was Christ.'[25] It is also of a warm nature; and the humility of Christ inflameth cold hearts to the practice of works of love. Its roots also penetrate the rocks; and humility breaketh through the hardest of obstinacy. It availeth for diseases of the breast and against swelling: so doth humility heal the swelling of pride. The former also is born from, and rooted in, the earth: whence by it the whole multitude of the faithful may be understood; and those especially be figured by the hyssop, who, rooted and grounded in Christ, cannot be plucked up or separated from His love. By whom what can we understand better than the bishops and presbyters, because the more

dignity they obtain in the Church, the more firmly ought they to cleave to the faith of Christ. By these assuredly is the water aspersed; by and through these be the faithful of Christ baptised; to these it is given to perfect the sacrament of baptism.

21. But whilst the altar is being sprinkled with water the bishop chanteth, 'My house shall be called an house of Prayer,' etc,[26] and again, 'I will tell out thy name to my brethren.'[27] And because without God no work is perfectly consummated, he prayeth that those who enter therein to seek for blessings may be heard.

Afterwards, when the church and altar are consecrated at the same time, the whole church is sprinkled with that water, as was discussed in the preceding chapter, which being done, the bishop approacheth the altar repeating Psalms, and what remains of the water is poured away at the foot of the altar, as in the old Testament[28] what remained of the blood was poured away at the bottom of the altar; by which it is signified that the remainder in so great a sacrament, which is beyond human power, is given over unto God, Who is the Chief High Priest, Whose part it is to supply the defect of other priests. But the sepulchre or cavity in which relics ought to be deposited, signifieth the golden pot full of manna, which was placed in the ark of the testimony, as hath been explained under the head of the Altar.

22. A sepulchre of this sort, which by some is termed a *confession*, is our heart; and it is consecrated by four crosses made with chrism, because there be four virtues described in the book of wisdom—namely, Prudence, Fortitude, Temperance, and Justice—with which our heart is, as it were, anointed, when it is prepared by the gift of the Holy Spirit to receive the mysteries of the heavenly secrets. But this sepulchre is made sometimes at the upper part of the altar, sometimes in the front side of it.

23. Without the relics of saints, or, where they cannot be had, without the body of Christ,[29] there is no consecration of a fixed altar: but there may be of a travelling or portable one. Relics in truth are, after the example of both Testaments, evidences of the suffering of martyrs and lives of confessors; which things be left to us as examples. These we enclose in a case, because we retain them, in order to imitate them in our heart: but if we hear and understand and do no works, it tendeth rather to damnation than to salvation; because 'not the hearers of the law are just before God, but the doers only';[30] Whence the Apostle saith, 'Be ye imitators of me as I am also of Christ.'[31]

24. But the solemn carrying of relics is in imitation of what is read in the xxv chapter of Exodus. In the ark of the testament there were two golden rings, going through the whole thickness of the wood, and through

these were put the staves of shittim wood overlaid with gold, by which the ark was borne. And before the bishop entereth the church he goeth round it with the relics in order that they may be protectors of that church. We read also in the viii chapter of the third book of Kings that at the dedication of the temple 'there were assembled together all the elders of Israel, with the chiefs of the tribes, and the heads of families to King Solomon in Jerusalem, to carry the ark of the covenant of the Lord into his place, into the oracle of the house, to the most holy place, even under the wings of the cherubims. For the cherubims spread forth their two wings over the place of the ark, and the cherubims covered the ark and the staves thereof above. And King Solomon, and all the congregation of Israel that were assembled unto him, marched with him before the ark.'[32] In remembrance of this event, the prelates, great men, and people[33] of the province meet together, even at this day, for the dedication of churches, and follow in procession him that consecrateth: and relics are solemnly carried by priests under a pavilion or canopy. Afterwards the bishop, before he entereth the church with these, addresseth the people. For Solomon also, after the ark had been carried, 'turned his face about, and blessed all the congregation of Israel,' and prayed for such as should pray in the church. 'For all the congregation of Israel stood, and Solomon said, Blessed be the Lord God of Israel,' etc., as is read in the same place.[34]

25. But the relics of saints are enclosed in a case together with three grains of frankincense, because we ought to retain in our recollection the examples of the saints, together with faith in the Trinity, that is, in the Father, Son, and Holy Ghost. For we ought to believe one God, one faith, one baptism, because 'the just liveth by faith,'[35] without which, as the Apostle hath said, 'It is impossible to please God.'[36] There is placed upon and fitted to the sepulchre itself a certain board fortified by the sign of the cross made with chrism.[37] For by chrism is understood the gift of the Holy Spirit, with which this board, that is charity, is anointed; because our heart is fortified by the grace of the Holy Spirit to observance of the heavenly mysteries. The board therefore fortified by this sign is placed over the relics, because by the example of the saints is inflamed charity, 'which covereth a multitude of sins,'[38] just as also the board covereth the relics. Whence saith the Apostle, 'The love of God is spread abroad in our hearts by the Holy Spirit which is given unto us.'[39] But this slab or stone containeth, or is called, the *seal* of the sepulchre; as saith Pope Alexander III.

After this, however, the stone, which is called the *table* of the altar, is fitted to the top of the altar; by which we may understand the perfection and solidity of the knowledge of God; and it ought to be of stone, not

The Eltenberg Reliquary

(Victoria and Albert Museum, London, England)

"Cherubim spread forth their two wings over the place of the ark, and the cherubim covered the ark and staves thereof above."

"The solemn carrying of relics is in imitation of what is read in the xxv chapter of Exodus. In the Ark of the Testament there were two golden rings, going through the whole thickness of the wood, and in these were put the staves of shittim wood overlaid with gold, by which the ark was born."

because of the hardness, but the solidity of faith. Just as the Lord said unto Peter, 'Thou art Peter, and upon this rock'—that is, upon this firmness of faith—'I will build My Church.'[40]

26. For as this *table* is the completion and finishing of the altar, so is the knowledge of God the confirmation and perfection of all good gifts. Whence in the book of Wisdom it is said unto the Lord, 'For to know Thee is perfect wisdom, and to know Thy justice and Thy virtue is the root of immortality.'[41] The Lord saith by Jeremiah, 'Let him that glorieth glory in this, that he understandeth and knoweth Me.'[42]

27. Or, again, by this stone itself is understood Christ, of Whom the Apostle saith, 'Jesus Christ Himself being the chief corner-stone.'[43] By the stone indeed the humanity of Christ is denoted. Concerning which we read in Daniel that a stone was cut out of the rock without hands—because Christ was born of the Blessed Virgin (who for the excellency of her virtues is called a Mountain), without human agency—and, becoming a huge mountain, filled the whole earth. Concerning which it is said also by the Psalmist, 'The stone which the builders refused hath become the head stone of the corner:'[44] since Christ—Whom the builders, that is the Jews, refused, saying, 'We will not havc this man to reign over us'[45]—hath been made the head of the corner. Because as saith the Apostle, 'God hath exalted Him and given Him,'[46] etc. Or else by this stone, which ought to be great and wide, charity is understood, as was stated before; since the command of charity is wide, extending even unto our enemies; according to that precept of our Lord, 'Love your enemies.'[47]

28. Altars therefore, unless they be of stone, are not anointed, because Christ signified by the altar is the Stone growing into a mountain: as it is said, The mountain itself is fat, 'being anointed with the oil of gladness, above his fellows.'[48] Nevertheless we read in Exodus that the Lord ordered the altars to be made of shittim wood, which does not decay;[49] and the Lateran altar is of wood. Solomon also made an altar of gold, as we read in the eighth chapter of the third book of Kings: but these things were done for a type.[50] And in the county of Provence, in the castle of S. Mary by the Sea, there is also an altar of earth, which Mary Magdalene, and Martha and Mary the mother of James, and Mary the mother of Salome, made there.[51] After this, the altar having been sprinkled and baptised with water, it remaineth for it to be anointed with oil and chrism. The bishop then poureth over it oil and chrism, and chanteth, 'Jacob set up the stone for a memorial, and poured oil upon it.'[52] For that church hath been the memorial of other churches; 'For the law hath gone out from Sion, and the word of the Lord from Jerusalem.'[53]

29. But first he maketh upon it the five crosses, with the oil of the sick, according to the Roman order; but according to the use of some other Churches, with both sorts of oil; one cross in the middle, and four at the corners: afterwards, he maketh the same number of crosses in the same way with chrism. By the oil assuredly is understood the grace of the Holy Ghost, of which saith Esaias the Prophet, 'The yoke shall be destroyed because of the anointing.'[54] For as the bishop poureth oil upon the altar, so Christ, who is the Chief High Priest, poureth His grace upon our altar, which is our heart: for He is the distributor of all graces through the Holy Ghost, as saith the Apostle, 'To one is given the word of wisdom, to another the word of knowledge, to another faith, to another the gift of healing,' etc.[55] And just as the bishop, by means of oil, cleanseth the *table* of the altar, so also doth the Holy Ghost purify our heart from all vices and sins.

30. Christ also was anointed with oil, not with visible oil indeed, but with invisible; that is with the grace of the Holy Ghost. Whence David, 'The Lord thy God hath anointed thee with the oil of gladness above thy fellows';[56] that is above all the saints who have been partakers of His Grace, that is, Christ. Whence unction more expressedly agreeth with Christ (the Anointed One) than with others, because God hath anointed Him above all others to have the fulness of good things, and therefore his name is interpreted 'The Anointed'. Unction also with oil signifieth mercy, according to that saying of the Evangelist, 'Anoint thy head with oil, and wash thy face':[57] because as oil is among fluids, so is mercy superior among good works. For whatever liquid you pour upon oil, yet it always swimmeth at the top. Of mercy it is written, 'The Lord is loving unto every man, and His mercy is over all His works,'[58] and 'Mercy rejoiceth against judgment.'[59] With this oil, therefore, is the altar of our heart anointed, that being always mindful of mercy, we may never lose the effect of the aspersion of water, and of regeneration and of baptism.

31. The five crosses made with the oil signify that we ought always to have a remembrance of the five wounds of Christ, which He suffered for our sakes upon the Cross. For He suffered five wounds; namely, in His hands, His feet, and in His side.

32. They denote further the five feelings of pity which be necessary for us. For it is necessary for a man to pity Christ, by sympathising in His Passion: whence Job, in the person of Christ, saith, 'Pity me, pity me,' etc.[60] A man must also pity his neighbours whose calamities he seeth; whence in Ecclesiasticus, 'The pity of a man towards his neighbour.'[61] And a man must pity himself: and this in three ways; namely, for the sins

of commission, by bewailing them; whence Jeremiah, 'There is no one who hath penitence for his sin, saying, What have I done?'[62]—for his sins of omission: whence Isaiah, 'Woe is me, for I have held my peace,'[63] that is, for I have not spoken; as if he should say, For I have omitted the good that I might have done:—and for good deeds done for less pure motives; whence S. Luke saith, 'When we have done all good deeds, we must say that we are unprofitable servants,' etc.;[64] as if we should say, We have done good, but not well, not purely, and therefore we have done it unprofitably; just as anyone giving alms for vain glory doth good indeed, but not well and not purely. Of this threefold compassion it is said in Ecclesiasticus, 'Have pity on thy soul and please God;'[65] because true compassion of mind ought to co-exist with the exhibition of good works. Wherefore the crosses be twice made: the first time of oil, the second of chrism: whence the Psalm, 'A good man is merciful and lendeth';[66] that is, pitieth in mind, and lendeth in deed. And since it sufficeth not to have compassion in mind together with the exhibition of good deeds, without the savour of a good report, according to that saying of the gospel, 'Let your light so shine before men that they may glorify God';[67] therefore the crosses be made with chrism, which consisteth of balsam and oil.

33. Balsam indeed, on account of its good odour, signifieth good report; oil, on account of its brightness, signifieth the clearness of conscience which we ought to have: according to the saying of the Apostle, 'Our rejoicing is this, the testimony of our conscience.'[68] Again, balsam is properly conjoined with oil, because good report is added to mercifulness.

34. Again, by the five crosses made of oil and of chrism the five senses of our body be understood, which are doubled and made into ten, because by properly using the senses of our body, we both keep ourselves, and confirm others by our example and teaching in well-doing. Whence that good trader boasted, saying, 'Behold I have gained five more talents.'[69] But whilst these anointings are going on, they chant, 'The Lord thy God hath anointed thee,'[70] which was said of Christ.

The altar therefore is anointed three times; twice with oil, and once with chrism; because the Church is marked by Faith, Hope, and Charity, which last is greater than the others. And while the chrism is used they chant, 'See the smell of my son is as the smell of a field.'[71] This field is the Church, which is verdant with flowers, which shineth in virtues, which is fragrant with good works; and wherein be the roses of martyrs, the lilies of virgins, the violets of confessors, and the verdure of beginners in the faith. After the unction there is incense burnt, which signifieth the devotion of prayer. For he that hath the seven gifts of the Holy Ghost, and is made like unto God, is able to offer unto Him devout prayer, of which he hath this similitude.

35. It is burnt in five places, namely, at the four corners and in the middle, because we ought so to exercise the five senses of the body that the report of our good works may extend to our neighbours. Of which saith the Apostle, 'We are the sweet savour of Christ in every place.'[72] And in the Gospel, 'Let your light so shine before men,' etc. Besides this, the frequent use of incense is the continual mediation of Christ the Priest, and our High Priest, for us unto God the Father.

36. To describe a cross with the incense, is to exhibit His Passion to the Father and Him interceding for us. The burning incense plenteously in the middle and at the corners is to multiply prayers through Jerusalem and in the Catholic Church.

37. Next to this the bishop confirmeth the altar with the sign of the cross, saying, 'Confirm this altar, O Lord,' etc. And this confirmation performed by the bishop with chrism on the front of the stone, signifieth the confirmation which is performed daily by the Holy Spirit, through charity, upon the altar of the heart, so that no tribulation should avail to separate our heart from the love of God: whence saith the Apostle, 'Who shall separate us from the love of Christ? Shall tribulation?' etc.[73] Then there is added the *Gloria Patri* in praise of the Trinity.

38. The last benediction of the altar signifieth that final benediction when it shall be said, 'Come, ye blessed of my Father,' etc.[74] Afterwards the altar is wiped over with a white linen cloth, to notify that we ought to cleanse our heart by chastity of life. Then the vessels, vestments, and linen cloths, devoted to the divine worship are blessed. For Moses also during the forty days was instructed by the Lord to provide linen cloths and the ornaments necessary for the Temple.

39. Assuredly, thus to bless the utensils is to refer all our works unto the Lord. After this, the altar is covered with white and clean cloths: concerning which ceremony we have spoken under the head of the Altar. Lastly, the church is ornamented and the lamps are lighted: for then shall the works of the just shine forth, 'Then shall the just shine, as sparks run swiftly among the stubble.'[75] And then upon the altar, consecrated after this order, the Mass is celebrated and the sacrifice offered unto the Most Highest: that sacrifice, namely, of which the Prophet speaketh, 'The sacrifices of God are a broken spirit; a broken and a contrite heart, O God, Thou wilt not despise':[76] as shall be declared in the introduction to the fourth book.[77] For consecration ought not to be performed without a Mass, according to

Pope Gelasius,[78] because then there is revealed a sacrament, which hath been hidden from the angels even from the beginning.

And observe, that in the aspersion of the church the bishop useth only the linen and inferior vestments: but at the Mass he is adorned with pontifical and precious vestments, because the high priest in the law used to expiate the sanctuary in a linen ephod, and afterwards used to offer the ram for the burnt offering being washed and arrayed in the high priest's vestments. But because he used to send forth the scapegoat after the expiation being clothed in the same linen ephod, on this account some, in the consecration of fonts and immersion of the catechumens where their sins are transferred, do use the simple linen vestments.

"The High Priest, adorned with these Vestments, did represent as in a picture the whole of Creation. The four Vestments of the lesser Priest, and the four of the greater, represented by their number the four parts of Man, the Microcosm, and the four parts of Nature, the Macrocosm, to wit, the four Temperaments, and the four Elements."

CHAPTER VIII: OF CONSECRATION AND UNCTIONS

1. We read that the Lord commanded Moses[1] to make a chrism, with which unguent to anoint the tabernacle at the time of the dedication, and the ark of the testimony, and the table, together with the vessels; and with which also the priests and kings should be anointed. Yet Moses himself is not said to have been anointed, except with a spiritual unction, as also was Christ.

2. Christ hath willed that we should be anointed with a material unction in order that we may by it obtain the spiritual unction: and on this account our loving Mother, the Church, provideth different sorts of unction. Upon which let us here touch lightly, saying—

- I. What unctions of this sort signify.
- II. Of what they be made.
- III. Of the unction before baptism.
- IV. Of the unction after baptism, which is performed by the bishop on the forehead.
- V. Of the unction in ordination.
- VI. Of the unction in consecrating bishops and princes.
- VII. Of the unction of a church, altar, chalice, and other ecclesiastical instruments.
- VIII. Of extreme unction.
- IX. Of the consecration and benediction of a cemetery, vestments, and other ecclesiastical ornaments.
- X. Of the consecration and benediction of virgins.

2. Firstly; with respect to the first, then it is to be noted that there be two kinds of unction: an *external*, which is material or corporeal, and visible; and an *internal*, which is spiritual and invisible. The body is anointed visibly with the external unction; the heart invisibly by the internal. Of the first, the Apostle S. James saith, 'Is any sick among you? Let him call for the elders of the Church; and let them pray over him, anointing him with oil in the name of the Lord; and the prayer of faith shall save the sick.'[2] Of the second the Apostle S. John saith, 'But the anointing which ye have received of Him abideth in you, and ye need not that any man teach you: but the same anointing teacheth you of all things.'[3] The external unction is a sign of the internal. But the internal is not only a sign, that is a thing signified, but a sacrament also; because if it be worthily received, it either effecteth, or without doubt increaseth, that which it doth

signify—for instance, healing: according to the saying, 'They shall lay their hands upon the sick, and they shall be healed.'[4]

3. Secondly; with respect to the second point, you must know that in making use of the external and visible unction, two sorts of oil are consecrated: namely, holy oil, or the oil of the catechumens, with which catechumens are anointed; and the oil of the sick, with which the sick are anointed. Of which kind of unction the authority of S. James quoted above doth speak, 'Is any sick among you,' etc.

But in what way the benediction of these two sorts of oil and of chrism is performed will be declared in the sixth book in the chapter upon the Fifth Day of the Holy Week.[5]

4. But is it asked why the sick and the catechumens are anointed with oil? I answer, in order that the invisible benefits may be more easily received through the visible signs: for as oil by expelling weakness refresheth the wearied limbs, and as it from its own natural qualities affordeth light, so it is to be believed that unction with consecrated oil, the which is a type of faith expelling sin, doth impart health to the soul and doth afford it light. Herein the visible oil is in the outward sign, the invisible oil in the inward sacrament; and the spiritual oil is within. For the oil of the sick we have received authority from the apostles; for the oil of the catechumens from apostolical men.

5. And although God can grant the spiritual oil without the material, yet because the apostles have used this rite in the case of the sick, and apostolical men in the case of catechumens, this practice which their authority hath consecrated cannot be omitted without sin (as hath been said in the chapter upon the Altar): just as anciently the just pleased God without circumcision; but after it had been enjoined them to be circumcised, such as omitted this rite were subjected to sin.

Thirdly; we have to speak of the unction before baptism. And indeed in the New Testament not only kings and priests be anointed, as hath been already said, but also—(because Christ by His Blood hath made us kings and priests, that is, royal priests, unto our God, as the Apostle S. Peter saith,[6] 'Ye are a chosen generation,' that is, chosen out from the tribes of men, 'a royal priesthood,' that is, governing yourselves well)—also, I say, all Christians be anointed twice before their baptism with consecrated oil—first, on the breast: secondly, between the shoulders: and twice after their baptism, with holy chrism—first, on the crown of the head; and secondly, by the bishop on the forehead.

6. And, according to Augustine, the first three unctions have been introduced rather by use than by any written authority. The candidate for

(France, 13th Century)

(France, 13th Century)

(St. Mark's Cathedral, Venice, Italy)

Oil at St. Martins

(St. Martins of Tours, Louisville, Kentucky)

(Sienna, Italy)

(St. Mark's Cathedral, Venice, Italy)

"…there be two kinds of unction: an external, which is material or corporeal, and visible; and an internal, which is spiritual and invisible. The body is anointed visibly with the external unction; the heart invisibly by the internal." "Apostle S. John saith, 'But the anointing which ye have received of Him abideth in you, and ye need not that any man teach you: but the same anointing teacheth you of all things."

baptism is anointed with oil—first, on the breast, in which is the locality of the heart; first, in order that by the gift of the Holy Ghost he may cast away error and ignorance and embrace a right faith; because 'the just liveth by faith,'[7] and 'with the heart we believe unto justification.'[8] But he is anointed between the shoulders, in order that he may, by the grace of the Holy Ghost, shake off indifference and sloth, and practise good works (because 'faith without works is dead'),[9] so that by means of sacraments of faith there may result a purity of thoughts. On the breast, again, that by the practising of good works there may arise a boldness of labour: between the shoulders, to the end that 'faith (according to the Apostle) may work by love.'[10] The oil therefore is carried over from the heart to the shoulders, since faith, which is conceived in the mind, is perfected in works (because, that is, faith consisteth in making our *deeds* like our *words*.)[11] But the person after baptism is anointed by the priest on the head with chrism, that 'he may be ready always to give an answer to every man that asketh him a reason for the faith that is in him,'[12] because by the head is understood the mind: as it is written, 'The eyes,' that is, the understanding, 'of the wise are in his head,'[13] that is, his mind; of which mind, the superior part is reason and the inferior sensuality. Hence, by the crown, which is the upper part of the head, is well represented reason, which is the superior part of the mind. Of this we shall speak in the sixth book also, under the head of Easter Eve, in which confirmation is treated of.[14] But this is the reason that before baptism one is anointed with consecrated oil, and after baptism with holy chrism; because chrism is competent to a Christian alone.

7. For Christ is so named from *chrism*, or rather *chrism* is so called from Christ, not according to the form of the name only, but according to the rational order of faith. For *Christians* are called from Christ, as *the anointed* would be derived from the Anointed One, namely, Christ; so that all may unite in the odour of that unguent, namely, Christ, Whose name is as oil poured out: but according to the power of the word, *Christians* are called so from *chrism*, according to Isidorus.[15] This subject is treated in the introduction to the second book.[16]

8. Again, according to Augustine, the first unction with oil showeth us to be prepared fully to hear the faith, and called to the sweet odour of Christ, and warned to renounce the devil. The second unction, according to Rabanus, is upon the breast and between the shoulders, that we may be fortified on both sides by faith, and confirmed by the grace of God for the performance of good works. For by the breast is rightly understood the virtue of faith: but by the shoulders—upon which any burden is borne—the strength and working of a man: according to that saying, 'They bind

heavy burdens and lay them on the shoulders of men,' etc.[17] A man is anointed therefore on the breast and between the shoulders, that both in thought and deed he may relinquish the works of the devil, and become capable of understanding the Word of God, and strong enough to bear its yoke and the burden of the law.

9. But the unction upon the crown, that is the top part of the head over the brain, is performed according to the same authority in order that he who is so anointed may become a partaker of the heavenly kingdom: and because the soul of the baptised person is espoused unto the Head, that is Christ, therefore this unction is made with chrism, compounded of oil and balsam, in order that we may know that the Holy Ghost, Who worketh invisibly, is given unto him: for oil, as we said above, cherisheth the wearied limbs and affordeth light. But balsam giveth it a sweet odour. If so be the limbs of the soul be wearied, when it repenteth of having acted in opposition to God, the Holy Ghost cometh to it, giving light to its understanding and showing it that its sins are, or may be, forgiven, and bestowing on it good works which breathe out a sweet odour amongst others: all which is denoted by the fragrant balsam. Also because the seat of high-mindedness, which according to the name is always seeking higher things, appears to exist in the head, therefore the unction on this part is rightly performed in the form of the cross and in token of humility.

10. Pope Sylvester appointed that this unction might be administered by priests upon occasion of death: whence it is likely that before his time[18] the anointing both of the crown of the head and of the forehead was reserved for the bishop. For when the bosom of the Church was extended, and bishops could no longer be at hand for each individual in confirmation, he then ordered, lest any should perish without the unction of chrism, that all should be anointed on the crown of the head over the brain, which is the seat of wisdom, at the hands of a priest, for the increasing of strength and grace. Whence if afterwards they should have died, saith Richard (of Cremona), they shall receive an increase of grace and glory.

11. Yet nevertheless we believe that a man may be saved by baptism alone even without the unction, and that the Holy Ghost is given without the laying on of hands to such as God may will, as we read in the Acts of the Apostles.

12. Yet the faithless heretics, The Arnaldistæ,[19] assert that men never receive the Holy Ghost through the baptism of water; and that Samaritans who were baptised did not receive Him until they received the laying on of hands. Both these unctions are administered, according to Rabanus, in the form of the cross, that the devil, whose vessel the person is, recognising

the sign of his own discomfiture, the sign of the Holy Cross, may know that from that moment the vessel is Another's, being alienated from him.

13. According to the same writer the unction on the breast is afterwards administered with invocation of the Trinity, in order that no remains of the hidden enemy may abide therein, but the mind be comforted in the faith of the Holy Trinity, and receive and understand the commandments of God. Therefore each of the faithful is anointed first twice with oil, next in like manner twice with chrism. First in baptism on the crown of the head: secondly after baptism, namely at confirmation, on his forehead: because to the apostles also was the Holy Ghost twice given, as will be set forth in the sixth book on Holy Saturday.[20]

Fourthly; in the fourth place we were to speak of the unction which is administered by the bishop on the forehead of such as have been baptised: but of this we shall speak in the same place.[21]

14. Fifthly; in the fifth place, with respect to the unction of ordination, it is to be noted that the hands of the priest are anointed by the bishop, that he may know that he in this sacrament doth receive by the Holy Ghost the power and grace of consecrating. Whence the bishop, whilst anointing them, saith: 'Deign, O Lord, by means of this unction and our benediction to consecrate and sanctify these hands, that whatsoever they consecrate may be consecrated, and whatsoever they bless may be blessed in the name of the Lord.' And for this cause devout men kiss the hands of priests immediately after their ordination, believing by this to become partakers of their prayers and blessings. And the anointing is with holy oil, because they ought to work with their hands the works of mercy with all their might towards all men: for the works are denoted by the hands; mercy by the oil. Whence the good Samaritan coming near to the wounded man poured wine and oil into his wounds. The hands are anointed with oil also that they may be supple for offering the host unto God for the sins of men, and that they may be open to all acts of piety and not be kept dry and clenched. For both these things, namely the grace of healing and the charity of loving, are denoted by the oil. Wherefore further the laying on of hands, together with oil upon the heads of such as be ordained, is done because by the hands the operation, by the fingers the gifts, of the Holy Ghost, and by the head the mind, be understood. The hand then is laid on because it is sent forth imbued with the gifts of the Holy Ghost to perform the works of Christ.

15. Sixthly, with respect to the unction of bishops and of temporal princes, it is to be known that the former hath derived its origin from the Old Testament. For in the 21st chapter of Leviticus the high priest is said to

be he 'upon whose head the anointing oil is poured,'[22] and whose hands were consecrated in priesthood. A bishop, however, is anointed with chrism, which (as we said before) is composed of oil and balsam; and he is anointed therewith both outwardly, and inwardly in his heart, in order that by the inward oil he have a clear conscience towards God, and by the outward oil may have the odour of good report towards his neighbour: which is denoted by the balsam. The Apostle saith of a clear conscience, 'For our rejoicing is this the testimony of our conscience.'[23] 'For the king's daughter is all glorious within,'[24] that is, her glory proceedeth from within. Concerning the odour of a good report the same Apostle saith, 'For in every place we are unto God a sweet savour of Christ,' that is, an example and imitation, and, 'to some we are the savour of life unto life,' etc.,'[25] as if he had said, we are an example of love and a good opinion leading unto eternal life, 'and to others a savour of death unto death,' that is, of hatred and evil opinion leading unto eternal death.

16. For a bishop ought to have in himself 'a good report' both of them which are within and 'them which are without';[26] so that one curtain, that is, the faithful, may draw on the other curtain, that is, the unbeliever, namely, unto belief;[27] and 'he that heareth,' namely, by learning and believing, 'say, come,'[28] namely, by preaching and teaching. With this unguent be the head and hands of a bishop consecrated: for by the head is understood the mind, as the gospel saith, 'anoint,'[29] that is, humble, 'thy head and wash thy face,' that is, thy conscience, namely, with tears: by the hands be denoted good works, as is said in the Canticles, 'my hands,' that is, my good works, 'dropped with myrrh,' that is, gave to others a good example.[30]

17. The head, therefore, is anointed with the balsam of charity. (i) That the bishop may love God with his whole heart and with his whole mind and whole soul, and also, after the example of Christ, 'love his neighbours as,' that is, as much as, 'himself.' For according to Gregory, oil on the head is charity in the soul. (ii) Secondly, the head is anointed by reason of authority and dignity; since not only bishops but also kings are consecrated. (iii) Thirdly, to show that a bishop representeth the person of Christ, as being his vicar, of whom it is said by the Prophet, 'it is like the precious ointment upon the head.'[31] For the head of man is Christ, the head of Christ is God: Who saith of Himself, 'the Spirit of the Lord is upon Me, because He hath anointed Me to preach the gospel to the poor.'[32] For Christ, our Head, was anointed with the invisible oil. He intercedeth for the Church Universal, a bishop for that Church committed unto him.

18. But his *hands* also are anointed, on account of his mystery and office; and for the anointing of these, which do signify works, is employed

oil, that is, the chrism of piety and mercy. (i) First, in order that the bishop may 'do good unto all men, and especially unto them that are of the household of faith,'[33] his hands should be closed to none, but be open to all; according to the saying, 'He hath opened his hands to the poor, and extended his arm to the destitute.'[34] A hand that is dried up, that is avaricious, that is tenaciously held clenched, cannot be opened: therefore his hands are anointed, in order that they may be healed and opened, and may bestow alms on the indigent. (ii) Secondly, to show that he hath received the power of blessing and consecrating. Whence the consecrating bishop, when he anointeth them, saith, 'Deign, O Lord, to consecrate and sanctify these hands,' and so forth, as we quoted above. (iii) That they may be clean for offering sacrifices for sins. And note, that although a bishop's hands were anointed with oil beforehand when he was ordained a priest, yet they be again anointed with chrism when he is consecrated a bishop. Herein by the hands are typified good works; by the oil, the abundance of the Holy Ghost of grace; by the balsam, which is mixed with the oil in making the chrism, the savour of good report; as in Ecclesiasticus, 'My sweet odour is as myrrh unmixed.'[35] Wherefore because in the works of bishops and other superiors there ought to appear more than in their inferiors the gifts of the Holy Ghost and the savour of good report; according to that saying, 'For we are unto God a sweet savour of Christ';[36] for even in the heavenly hierarchy the superior angels excel the inferior in blessings and grace; hence, therefore, at their consecration as bishops their hands, already anointed with oil, are with reason again anointed with chrism.

19. The thumb also is fortified with chrism, that the laying on of the thumb may profit all men for salvation.

20. Further, in the Old Testament, not only was a priest anointed, but also a king and prophet: as we find in the books of Kings. Whence the Lord enjoined Elias, 'Go return on thy way to the wilderness of Damascus: and when thou comest, anoint Hazael to be king over Syria; and Jehu the son of Nimshi shalt thou anoint to be king over Israel; and Elisha the son of Shaphat of Abel-Meholah shalt thou anoint to be prophet in thy room.'[37] Samuel also anointed David to be king. But after that Jesus of Nazareth, 'Whom (as we read in the Acts of the Apostles) God anointed with the Holy Ghost, was anointed with oil above his fellows,'[38] Who is (according to the Apostle) 'the Head of the Church, which is also His body';[39] after this the anointing of a sovereign was transferred from the head to the arm: whence princes since the time of Christ are not anointed on the head but on the arm, or on the shoulder; by which parts of the body kingly power is aptly represented, as we read, 'and the government was

laid upon his shoulder':[40] to signify the same, Samuel caused the shoulder to be laid before Saul, when he placed him at the head of the table before those who had been bidden.[41] But in the case of a bishop the sacramental anointing is applied to the head, because in his episcopal office he representeth the Head of the Church, that is, Christ.

21. There is this difference, then, between the anointing of a bishop and a prince, that the head of the bishop is consecrated with chrism, while the arm of the prince is anointed with oil: to show, namely, how great a difference there is between the authority of a bishop and the power of a prince. And observe that, as we read in the gospel,[42] a certain man called his servants and gave unto them ten talents. Herein the calling of a servant is the canonical election of a bishop, which taketh place according to the calling of the Lord Who called Aaron. A talent is given to him, when he who hath laid his hands upon him giveth him the text of the gospel, saying, 'Go and preach.' And the bishop himself, according to the use of some churches, when first he entereth his see, carrieth the gospels in his bosom, showing his talent as if to trade with it. In some churches also when the archbishop giveth the bishop his pastoral staff, he saith, 'Go and preach,' and he immediately blesseth the people: by which is represented that Moses was sent into Egypt with a rod.

22. Furthermore, bishops on the day of their consecration have been wont to ride on horses covered with white robes; to represent that which we read in the Apocalypse, 'The armies which are in heaven follow him riding on white horses.'[43] The armies which are in heaven are good and just men and prelates, who as these heavenly riders do daily follow God in all good works: who for this reason are said to be in heaven, because they love and seek after heavenly things alone; whence the Apostle saith, 'Our conversation is in heaven.'[44] These armies, that is good and just men and prelates, follow Jesus, whensoever they vanquish vices in themselves by discipline, in their neighbours by admonition. Whence S. James saith, 'He which converteth the sinner from the error of his way shall save a soul from death, and shall hide a multitude of sins.'[45] These armies have white horses and chaste bodies.

23. The bodies of good men are also called horses, because, just as horses are governed by the will of the rider, so are the bodies of the just ruled according to the will of Christ. These horses ought to be chaste and pure. For if they be not pure they cannot follow Christ: And S. Peter saith, 'Christ also suffered for us, leaving us an example that we should follow His steps, who did not sin, neither was guile found in his mouth.'[46] Further, the clergy of the holy Roman Church, by the grant of the Emperor

Constantine, do ride upon horses adorned with trappings of the most snowy white. On what day a bishop ought to be consecrated, and why a copy of the gospels is put upon his shoulders in consecration, shall be declared in the second book, under the chapter upon Bishops.[47] Seventhly, we have to speak of the unction of altars, chalices, and other instruments of the church; which according to the rule are anointed at their dedication; and this not only from the command of the divine law, but also because Moses 'sprinkled with blood the tabernacle and all the vessels of the ministry, and almost all things are by the law cleansed with blood;'[48] and also again after the example of S. Sylvester, who when he consecrated an altar used to anoint it with chrism. For the Lord commanded Moses to make oil of unction with which to anoint the tabernacle of the testimony, the table, the ark of the covenant, the candlestick, and other furniture as aforesaid. Which unctions are performed on things that have not been anointed, to show greater reverence to them and to bestow more grace upon them. And of these unctions we have spoken and shall again speak in their right places. But the sacrament of unction hath indeed some further effect and meaning both in the Old and New Testament: whence the Church doth not Judaize, when she observeth the unctions in her sacraments, as some old writers, who know neither the Scripture nor the power of God, do falsely say. Of the unctions of the church and altar we have spoken under their own heads.

24. Further the paten is consecrated and anointed for the administration of the body of Christ, who willed to be sacrificed on the altar of the cross for the salvation of all men. Almighty God also did order the flour to be brought to His Altar scattered on golden and silver patens. The chalice also is consecrated and anointed, that by the grace of the Holy Ghost it may be made a new sepulchre of the body and blood of Christ, and then He, Himself, may deign to make it overflow with his virtue, as He made the cup of Melchizedech, His servant, to flow over.

25. Eighthly; in the eighth place we have to speak of extreme unction, which from the institution of Pope Felix the Fourth, and from the command of the Apostle S. James, is administered unto such as are at the point to die. Concerning which some say that it is not so properly a sacrament as the anointing of the forehead or any other part with chrism, because (as they assert) it may be repeated and since there is offered a prayer over the man; a circumstance which is not a condition of a sacrament. This unction also may be administered by a single priest if more cannot be present: and by it venial sins are remitted, according to S. James, 'If any rich among you,' etc., as before, 'and if he have committed sins they shall be forgiven him.'[49] And this unction is applied to divers parts of the body or the limbs,

for reasons which may be gathered from the prayers then used; and especially on those parts in which the five senses chiefly reside, that whatever sins the rich man may have committed by means of these may be abolished by virtue of this unction. Concerning some other rules we ordinarily read, that the party to be anointed must be at the least eighteen years of age, and that he ought to be anointed in sickness once only during a year, though he may be sick many times, and that on one must be anointed, unless, being in his senses, he shall have first demanded it either by words or signs:—and besides this, that the shoulders ought not to be anointed, because they were anointed in baptism, and that a confirmed person ought not to be anointed on his forehead but on his temples, and a priest's hands ought to be anointed on the backs and not inside, because they were anointed on the inside at his ordination:—and that one who hath been once anointed by a bishop ought not in respect to him to be further anointed by a priest:—and that if a sick man who hath been anointed should recover, the anointed places should be washed, and the water used be thrown into the fire; but should he depart, his body ought not to be washed because of the recent unction. Besides this, some penitents, and dying men, put on sackcloth and lay themselves down on ashes as we shall explain in the sixth book, when we speak of Ash Wednesday.[50]

26. Ninthly, a cemetery, which enjoyeth the same privileges as a church, is also consecrated and blessed; just as the Lord blessed by the hands of His servants Abraham, Isaac, and Jacob, the land bought for a burial ground from the sons of Ephron. It is blessed also in order that it may cease from that time forward to be the abode of unclean spirits, and that the bodies of the faithful may therein rest in peace until the day of judgment; unless the bodies of paynims or infidels, or even of excommunicate persons should be buried there, until they shall be cast out thence.

27. This also is to be noted, that the palls of the altar, the priestly vestments, and ecclesiastical ornaments of this kind are to be blessed. For we have already read that Moses, by command of the Lord, consecrated the tabernacle with divine prayers, together with the table and altar, and vessels and utensils for performing the divine worship. If therefore the Jews, who served the 'shadow of the Law and of good things to come,'[51] did this, how much the more ought we to do it to whom the truth hath been made known by Christ! Whence we read in the last chapter but one of Exodus, 'Moses blessed all the vessels of the ministry.'[52] And should an additional piece or a fringe be attached to it, it is proved by the testimony of right that the blessing need not on this account be repeated. But the reason why these things and other like things are consecrated is evidently gathered

from the forms of blessing them. Of the sacred vestments we shall speak in the introduction to the third book.[53] And observe: That the blessing or consecration of a church, and of vestments, and of ecclesiastical ornaments is not performed as if they were capable of receiving grace, for they are inanimate: but this practice is introduced, because as men are, so also are these things, by the act of blessing and consecration rendered suitable and fit for divine worship, and are made of greater holiness. Whereas on *persons* greater grace is bestowed by unction and benediction. But some in the benediction of ornaments, let fall their hands, of which we shall speak in the second book under the head of the Deacon.[54]

Tenthly, we were to speak of the consecration of Virgins, but of this we shall treat in the preface to the second book.[55]

Font (St. Anstell, Cornwall, England)

Font (Early Medieval)

"For in the sacrament of baptism, neither is the water without the Spirit, nor the Spirit without the water: which element indeed the Spirit Himself did sanctify, when in the first creation of the world 'He moved upon the face of the waters.'"

Chalice and Paten Tray

Chalice and Paten Tray

CHAPTER IX: OF THE SACRAMENTS OF THE CHURCH

1. With respect to the sacraments of the Church, it is to be noted that, according to Gregory, there is a *sacrament* in any celebration when an outward act is so performed as that we receive inwardly some degree of the thing signified; the which is to be received holily and worthily. Also a *mystery* is that which the Holy Ghost worketh secretly, and invisibly, so as to sanctify by His operation, and bless by His sanctification. A mystery is said to exist in sacraments; a ministry only in ornaments.

2. But, according to Augustine, a sacrament is a visible sign of an invisible grace. Again, a sacrifice is visible; a sacrament invisible. Again, the same sign is a thing which bringeth under cognisance some thing different from itself over and above the outward appearance which it presenteth to the senses.

3. A sacrament is said also to be a sign of a sacred thing, or a sacred concealment of a thing. Of this we shall further speak in the fourth book, under the seventh part of the Canon of the Mass, upon the word 'the mystery of faith,' and under the head of the Oblation.[1]

4. Some of the sacraments be of necessity only; some of dignity and necessity; some of order and necessity; some of dignity and choice; and some of choice only. The sacrament of necessity only is baptism, which when administered by anyone, so it be in the form of the Church, in the greatest extremity profiteth unto salvation. And it is said to be 'of necessity,' because without it no one can be saved, if it be neglected through contempt. Of this sacrament we shall speak in the sixth book, under the head of Holy Saturday.[2] The sacrament of dignity and necessity is confirmation: of dignity, because it is conferred by the bishop alone; of necessity, because he who neglecteth it through contempt of it, cannot be saved. Of this also we shall speak under the head just specified.

5. The sacraments of order and dignity are Penance, the Eucharist, and Extreme Unction. Of order; because they ought only to be administered by such as are rightly ordained according to the Church's power of the keys; except in necessity, in which one may *confess* even unto a layman: of necessity; since such as neglect them through contempt of them cannot be saved. About penance, see the sixth book, upon the fifth day of Holy Week, the *Cœna Domini*:[3] about the Eucharist, we shall speak in the fourth book, upon the Canon;[4] about Extreme Unction we have spoken in the preceding chapter.

6. But the sacrament of dignity and choice is Orders: of dignity; because conferred by bishops alone, and because no one is admitted thereunto save a worthy person and in a worthy way: of choice; because anyone may be saved without it. Of this we shall speak in the preface to the second book.[5]

7. The sacrament of choice only is matrimony; and it is said to be of choice, because anyone may be saved without it. Indeed a man seeking to marry is not inclined to tend towards the kingdom of heaven.

With respect to this it is to be remarked that, according to the canons, the solemnity of marriage ought not to be celebrated from Septuagesima Sunday, because it is a season of sorrow, until the octave of Easter, nor in the three weeks before the Feast of S. John.[6] But according to the custom of the Catholic Church, marriages may be solemnised in the church from the morrow of Low Sunday, namely, from the octave of Easter, until the first Rogation Day. And from the morning of the first Rogation Day this rite is prohibited until the octave of Whitsuntide inclusively: and so saith Pope Clement in his Decretal. Again, marriages ought not to be celebrated from the First Sunday in Advent until the Epiphany: nor should they have been allowed until the octave of the Epiphany had not the Lord honoured a marriage with His presence, and even with a miracle.[7] Whence they then chant, 'To-day the Church is united to her Heavenly Spouse.' Some, however, say that it is more holy to extend this prohibition unto the octave of the Epiphany.

In the aforesaid times, therefore, marriages are not to be contracted; because these seasons are set apart for prayer.

8. But although the solemnising of marriages is prohibited in these intervals, yet a contract of marriage holds good at whatever time it may have been duly made. But in that it is ordered by the canons that weddings should not be celebrated in the three weeks before the Festival of S. John Baptist, the rule was made that men might be more at leisure for prayer. For the Church had formerly appointed two periods of forty days, besides the great one of Lent:—the one preceding the nativity, usually called S. Martin's , and lasting from his day to the nativity;[8] the other, forty days before the Feast of S. John Baptist:—in which men should give especial heed unto prayers, alms, and fastings. But in regard of the frailty of man, these two seasons have been reduced to one, and that one again divided into the three weeks of advent, and three before the nativity of S. John: at which times men ought to fast and abstain from marriage.

9. According to S. Isidore (of Seville), women wear veils, when they are married, so that they may know that they must always be subject to

their husbands: and because Rebecca, when she saw Isaac, veiled herself. The same saith also that married persons after the benediction are coupled by a fillet, to show that they must not break the tie, that is the fidelity, of conjugal unity. And the same fillet is both white and purple mixed; because the white signifieth purity of life, and purple their lawful raising of offspring: so that by this symbol, their continuance and mutual 'defrauding one another for a time is signified, as well as their coming together again'[9] and return afterwards to conjugal duties.

10. Also in that at the beginning of the ceremony the husband giveth a ring to the bride, this is done as a sign of mutual love, or rather in order that their hearts may be united by the same pledge. And the same ring is put on the fourth finger, because (as some say) a certain vein runneth through it which reacheth to the heart. Also one Protheus is said to have first made a ring of iron as a pledge of love, and to have enclosed an adamant therein: and from this he founded the custom of betrothing brides, because as iron subdueth all things, so doth love conquer all things, since nothing is more violent than its ardour.

11. And as an adamant cannot be broken, so love cannot be overcome: for love is as strong as death. Therefore also he founded the custom of putting the ring on the ring-finger through which a vein passeth to the heart. Afterwards, however, golden rings were substituted for iron, and were set with gems, instead of adamant, because as gold excelleth other metals, so doth love excel all other blessings. And as gold is set off by the gems, so is conjugal love by other virtues. But the word *nuptials* (marriage) is so called according to Ambrose, *a nubendo* (from covering the head). For brides are wont to veil the head and abstain from speaking. Whence also Rebecca, when she saw Isaac to whom she was about to be espoused, began to veil her face. For bashfulness ought to precede marriage, inasmuch as bashfulness more highly commendeth wedlock itself: and the bride should appear rather to be sought by the hsuband, than herself to have sought after him.

12. We have further to note that a three fold spiritual sacrament is signified by the consummation of marriage. The first sacrament is the spiritual union of the soul to God, through faith, love, and charity; or the union of will, namely charity which consisteth in the spirit, between God and a just soul. Whence saith the Apostle, 'but he that is joined unto the Lord is one spirit.'[10] This sacrament is signified by the union of soul which takes place at the first betrothal in carnal matrimony. The second is the union of the human nature with the divine, which took place in the incarnation of the Word of God; or the conformity of nature, which existeth in the flesh,

between Christ and His Holy Church. To which that saying referreth, 'The Word was made flesh, and dwelt among us.'[11] The third sacrament is the unity of the Church, gathered out of all nations and subjected to one spouse, namely Christ. This sacrament is typified in the case of such as, having had one wife and her a virgin, have afterwards been admitted into holy orders.

13. But when anyone yieldeth to a second marriage, he giveth up this unity, and the signification of this third sacrament does not hold in his case: wherefore marriage should not advance beyond one, because such advance cannot signify unity. Besides, by a second marriage he departeth from the union of his former marriage: but the Church ever since she hath united herself to Christ, hath never departed from Him, neither hath Christ ever departed from her. Wherefore one who hath twice married cannot signify such an unity. Whence also deservedly from the defect of this sacramental signification marriage cannot be repeated.

14. Note also this, that according to the statute of the Council of Carthage the bridegroom and bride are to be presented by the parents or bridesmen unto the priest in order to be blessed. And having received the blessing, out of reverence to it, they do not consummate the marriage until the next day.

15. Again by the appointment of Pope Evaristus marriages are to be blessed by the priest not without prayers and offerings. However, a man and woman who contract a second marriage must not be blessed by the priest, since, they having been already blessed, the ceremony may not be repeated. Nor ought marriages to be blessed unless both parties are still unmarried, for the reason given in the preface to the second book.[12] And any priest who shall have given the blessing in such a second marriage is to be suspended from his office and benefice and to be sent to the apostolical see; a custom this, introduced as an incitement to continence. According to the custom of some places, if any contracts a second marriage with an unmarried woman the benediction is repeated: but this does not avail unless our Lord the Pope know of it and approve it. Some also say that if any unmarried persons were not blessed when they contracted marriages, they may when marrying a second time receive the benediction; but if they were blessed at first, it cannot be repeated at a second marriage even though the first were never consummated. Of the benediction of virgins we shall speak in the preface and the second book.

16. But it is to be noted that one sacrament may be more worthy than another in four ways: namely, in efficacy, as baptism; in sanctity, as the

eucharist; in significancy, as marriage (though some do not admit this way); in the dignity of the administrator, as confirmation and orders.

17. But is it asked why sacraments are appointed, when without them God could have given eternal life and His Grace unto mankind? I answer, for three reasons. First, for our humiliation; in order that when man reverently humbleth himself by the command of God unto insensible and inferior things, he may from this obedience become more acceptable unto Him. Secondly, for our instruction; that by that which is seen objectively in a visible form, our mind may be instructed in that invisible virtue, which is to be perceived within. Thirdly, for our exercising: in order that, since man ought not to be idle, there may be set before him a useful and healthy exercise in the sacraments; so that he may avoid vain and hurtful occupation. According to that saying, 'Always be doing some good work, that the devil may find you occupied.' Wherefore, as we said in the foregoing chapter, they must never be neglected.

END OF THE FIRST BOOK

(Italy, 1345)

Saint Lawrence with the grill, the instrument of his martyrdom.

EPILOGUE TO THE WHOLE WORK[1]

Let none imagine that in the foregoing work the Divine Offices be sufficiently set forth, lest by extolling that which is human, he rashly depreciate that which is divine. For in the Divine Offices of the Mass, so many and so great be the mysteries involved, that none, unless he be taught of the spirit, is sufficient to explain them. 'For who knoweth the ordinances of heaven, or can explain the reasons of them upon earth?'[2] For he that prieth into their Majesty is overwhelmed by their glory. But I, who cannot from the weakness of mine eyes behold the sun in his brightness, have looked on these mysteries, as through a glass, darkly: and, not penetrating into the interior of the palace, but sitting at the door, have done diligently, as I could, not sufficiently, as I would. For on account of the innumerable and inevitable business of the Apostolic See,[3] pressing on me daily, like a flood, and holding down the mind of him that would diligently rise to a contemplation of heavenly things: I, perplexed as it were, and entangled in the knots of various employments, could not have the lcisurc that I wished for, and could scarcely either dictate what I had composed, or compose what I had conceived. For the mind that is divided in several trains of thought hath less power in each. Wherefore I not only ask pardon of the courteous reader, but implore the assistance of a friendly corrector. For I cannot deny that many things are inserted in this book which may be blamed, and that justly and without temerity. But if anything worthy be found in it, let the praise thereof be ascribed entirely to Divine Grace: for 'every good gift, and every perfect gift is from above, and cometh down from the Father of Light.'[4] But let that which is unworthy, be set down to human insufficiency, 'for the corruptible body presseth down the soul, and the earthly tabernacle weigheth down the mind that museth upon many things.'[5] That which is worthy hath been taken from the sayings of others, whose words I have introduced, rather by way of recital[6] after than of approval. I have collected from diverse books, the manner of the honey making bee, not without profit, of those things which divine grace hath held forth to me: and this doctrine, flowing with sweetness like the honeycomb, I offer, trusting in God's help, to those who desire to meditate on the Divine Offices: expecting this reward alone of my great toil among men, that they will pray earnestly to the merciful Judge for the pardon of my transgressions.

GULIELMI DURANDI, *Epi Mimatensis Liber de ecclesiis et ornamentis ecclesiasticis explicit feliciter.*

APPENDICES

APPENDIX A: CHANCELS

'The temple of old was divided into two parts by a veil hung in the middle thereof. The first part was called the Holy Place, but the inner part the Holy of Holies. Whatever part then of the office of the Mass cometh before the secret[1] is performed as it were in the outer place: but the secret itself within the Holy of Holies. There were in the Holy of Holies the altar of incense, the ark of the testimony, the mercy-seat above the ark, and over this two cherubims of glory with their faces looking towards each other. Herein the high priest entered alone once in the year, having the names of the patriarchs written upon the breastplate of judgment and the shoulderplates, and bearing a censer of burning coals and blood, and incense, which with prayer he placed in the thurible until the cloud of incense covered him.[2] Afterwards he sprinkled the mercy-seat and the altar with blood, and then he went out to the people, and washed his vestments in the evening. These were types of old, but they have ceased since the things signified thereby have come. But thus the former temple doth denote the present church; the Holy of Holies, heaven; the high priest, Christ; the blood, His Passion; the coals, His love; the thurible, His flesh; the burning incense, prayers of sweet savour; the altar, the hosts of heaven; the ark, Christ in His humanity; the mercy-seat, God the Father; the two cherubims, the twain Testaments, the which do look towards each other because the two do agree; the vestments which be washed, mankind. Wherefore consider what things were done of old, and what things Christ hath done, and then see how the minister of the Church doth represent the same in the office of the Mass. By the ark also is signified the humility of Christ, from which through his mercy all good hath come unto us' (Durandus, Book IV, Preface 13, 14).

In the next section the same subject is further illustrated, though without reference to the immediate subject of this appendix, the necessity of the division of every church into a chancel and a nave.

The reader may consult a most interesting series of chapters in Hugo de Sancto Victore (Tituli ii-viii, Ex. Misc. II, Lib. IV) upon this subject: the passages are far too long for insertion here.

The *absolute necessity* of this twofold division is a point which it is more than painful at this time to have to prove. It is only within the last two centuries that our own or any branch of the Church Catholic has dared to depart from a usage which, if any, has universality, antiquity, and consent on its side, and of whose authority was never any doubt in the Church.

For some of the arguments which have been adduced in the present controversy we must refer to the publications of the Cambridge Camden Society, and particularly the *Ecclesiologist.* There is nothing more wanted than a careful treatise on the subject which shall in a compendious form put this and several points depending upon it, such as orientation itself, and praying towards the east, in a clear light.

APPENDIX B: ORIENTATION

'Furthermore albeit God is everywhere, yet ought the priest at the altar and in the offices to pray towards the east: according to the constitutions of Vigilius, Pope. Whence in churches which have the doors at the west, he that celebrateth turneth in the salutations to the people: but in churches which have the entrance at the east,[1] as at Rome, there is no need in the salutations for turning round, because the priest always turneth to the people. The temple also of Solomon, and the tabernacle of Moses had their entrance from the east. Pray we therefore towards the east, being mindful, firstly, that He, Who is the splendour of eternal light, hath illuminated 'them that sit in darkness and the shadow of death,[2] rising with healing in his wings':[3] of whom it is said, 'Behold the man, whose name is the East.'[4] For the which cause he saith in the book of Wisdom,[5] 'We ought to pray eastward, where the light ariseth.' Not because the Divine Majesty is locally in the east: which is potentially and essentially in all places; as it is written, 'Do not I fill heaven and earth';[6] and in like manner speaketh the Prophet, 'If I ascend into heaven, Thou art there: if I go down to hell, Thou art there also':[7] but because to those 'who fear His name shall the sun of righteousness arise,'[8] 'which lighteth every man that cometh into the world.'[9]

Secondly, that our souls be thereby taught to turn themselves to the things that are more desirable.

Thirdly, because they who praise God ought not to turn their backs on Him.

Fourthly, according to Joannes Damascenus (who giveth also the three following reasons),[10] to show that we seek our country.

Fifthly, that we may look upon Christ crucified, Who is the True East.

Sixthly, that we may prove that we expect Him to come to be our Judge. For Damascenus saith in that place, 'God planted a garden eastward';[11] whence man's sin made him an exile, and instead of Paradise made him to dwell in the west: therefore, looking to our ancient home, we pray towards the east.

Seventhly, because our Lord, at His Crucifixion, looked towards the east: and also when he ascended into heaven, He ascended towards the east: and thus the apostles adored Him: and thus 'He shall come again in like manner as they saw Him go into heaven.'[12]

Eighthly, Daniel likewise in the Jewish captivity prayed towards the temple.

Yet Augustine saith that 'no Scripture hath taught us to pray towards the east.' [He, however, says also, 'Though I find not a thing on record in Scripture, yet I receive it as proceeding from the apostles if the Universal Church embrace it'][13] (Durandus V, ii, 57).

S. Isidore has a curious passage about orientation. A place, he says, designed so as to face the east was called templum, from contemplating. Of which there were four parts; the front facing the east, the back the west, the right hand the south, and the left hand the north: whence also when they builded temples, they took their east at the equinox, so that lines drawn from east to west would make the sections of the sky on the right and left hands equal, in order that he who prayed might look at the direct east (Orig. XV, iv).

APPENDIX C: ON THE DESIGN OF THE ANALOGIUM, AMBO OR ROOD LOFT, AND THE READING OF THE GOSPEL FROM IT

1. We have noted afore, that the priest, in the celebration of Mass, when it is not High Mass, himself readeth the gospel. But when a bishop or priest celebrateth High Mass with the highest solemnity, then, in some churches, as at Rome, the deacon having kissed the right hand of the bishop, taketh the book of the gospel from the altar, and giveth it to the sub-deacon to bear, and asketh and receiveth the bishop's or priest's blessing before he taketh the book. The benediction having been bestowed, the deacon proceedeth along the south side[1] of the choir to the rood loft, and before him goeth the sub-deacon with the volume of the gospel, and before him the incense-bearer with lighted tapers, and before him in some churches the banner of the cross: and thus they ascend the rood loft. And the deacon readeth the gospel: the which being finished, they return to the priest or bishop together. Which things we will more particularly go through. It is also to be noted, that in some churches, the deacon, when about to go to the rood loft, beginneth the antiphon which followeth benedictus in the nocturns, and while he is going thither, it is taken up, and finished by the chorus, to set forth charity: and it is sung without instruments, to denote that God commandeth us to have love alone. And now is the figure changed: for the deacon, who before represented S. John Baptist, now setteth forth

(France, 1480)

"The benediction having been bestowed, the deacon proceedeth along the south side of the choir to the rood loft."

(Italy, 12th Century)

(Ravenna)

(Italy, 12th Century)

"Now 'ambo' meaneth the pulpit, whence the gospel is read, so called from 'ambio' (to surround) because that place is surrounded with steps. In some churches also there be two ascents, one left, namely towards the east, where the deacon ascendeth; one to the right, namely towards the west, where he descendeth."

S. John Evangelist: because 'the law and the Prophets were until John:[2] and after the kingdom of heaven is preached.

2. And the word *evangelium* meaneth good tidings; from εὐ, well, and Ωγγελος, a messenger. For the preaching of Christ and His apostles is indeed a gospel, as proclaiming Life after death, Rest after labour, a Kingdom after slavery.

3. And ye are to wit, that as the head hath pre-eminence over the other members of the body, and as the other members obey it: so the gospel is the principal thing of all that are said in the office of the Mass, and hath the pre-eminence, and whatever things be there read, or sung, they consent to it, as may well be perceived.

4. The deacon therefore first kisseth the hand of the bishop in silence, because the preacher must proclaim the gospel for the sake of eternal glory, as saith the spouse in the Canticles, 'His right hand shall embrace me.'[3] Also because the angel which came to announce the glory of Christ's Resurrection did sit on the right hand, clothed in white.[4] In other churches, however, he doth not kiss, but only bowing asketh for a blessing. But the sub-deacon or deacon doth not kiss the hands, but the feet, of the Roman Pontiff, that he may exhibit the greatest reverence to the greatest bishop, and show that he is his Vicar, Whose feet the woman that was a sinner kissed.[5] For his footstool is to be adored because it is holy. Whose feet also, when He had risen from the dead, the woman held and adored. Generally, none ought to kiss the hand of the Roman Pontiff, unless when he receiveth something from his hands, or giveth something to them: to show that we ought on both accounts to give thanks unto Him, Who giveth to all of His own, and receiveth from none.

5. The deacon incontinently thereafter taketh the book of the gospel from the altar, because the 'Law shall go forth out of Sion, and the Word of the Lord from Jerusalem':[6] not the Mosaic Law which went forth of Sinai, but the Gospel Law, of which the Prophet saith, 'Behold the days come, saith the Lord, that I will make a new covenant with the house of Jacob and with the house of Israel.'[7] The book is also taken from the altar, because the apostles received the gospel from the altar, when they went about preaching the Passion of Christ. Or the altar in this place signifieth the Jews, from whom the kingdom of God is taken, and given unto a nation that will do its fruits: and from this, that the gospel is taken from the altar, we learn, that it is the Word of God, which is signified by the altar, according to that saying, 'An altar of earth shall ye make unto me.'[8]

6. But he taketh it, according to some, from the right side of the altar: because the Church of the Jews, whence our Church springeth, was situate

in the east: and placeth it on the left, as it is written, 'His left hand is under my head, and his right hand doth embrace me':[9] and that for a threefold cause. Firstly, the gospel teacheth that things celestial, which be signified by the right, be preferred to things terrestrial, which the left hand setteth forth. Secondly, the book is inclined on the left shoulder, to signify that the preaching of Christ shall pass from the Gentiles, as it is written: 'In those days Israel shall be saved.'[10] Thirdly, because in temporal life, which is set forth by that side, needful is it that Christ should be preached: and the book of the gospel is in some churches adorned on the outside with gold and gems. But the book remaineth on the altar, from the time that the priest goeth there, till the gospel be read, because it, in this respect, signifieth Jerusalem: since the gospel was first preached in Jerusalem, and remained there from the advent of the Lord till it was published to the Gentiles. As he saith, 'From Sion shall go forth the laws.'[11] For Jerusalem was the place of the Passion, which is also set forth by the altar.

7. Thereafter he seeketh the benediction: because none must preach unless he be sent. According to that saying, 'How shall they preach, except they be sent?'[12] And the Lord saith to His disciples, 'Pray ye therefore the Lord of the harvest that He may send forth labourers into His harvest.'[13] But Esaias, when he had heard the voice of the Lord, saying, 'Whom shall I send, and who will go for us?'[14] made answer and said, 'Here am I, send me.' And the Lord said, 'Go and tell this people,' etc.

8. Again, Moses prefigured this kind of blessing: who, when he had ascended unto the mountain, received the tables of the law and the blessing, and gave the commandment to the people. And the Lord also Himself blessed the order of deacons, and gave it the Holy Spirit and sent it to preach through the whole world. The bishop, therefore, or the priest, visibly blesseth the deacon who is about to read the gospel, which he did not do to the sub-deacon when about to read the epistle, because Christ sent the law and the Prophets, which be signified by the epistle, while he remained hidden from the world: but after that he had visited it, and conversed with men He sent forth His apostles and evangelists, and taught them, saying, 'Go and teach, saying, the kingdom of heaven is at hand.'[15] 'And they went through the villages, evangelising, and doing cures everywhere.' And he sendeth him to read the gospel, to note that Christ sent the apostles to preach the kingdom of God.

9. But the deacon, laying up in his heart the things which were said in the benediction, must study to show himself pure in heart, clean in words, chaste in deed, that he may be able to set forth the gospel worthily, because the fountain of living waters, that is, the gospel, doth not flow freely, ex-

cept from Libanus, that is, from a chaste heart, and a pure mouth. For praise is not seemly in the mouth of a sinner; nay rather of the sinner saith God, 'What hast thou to do to set forth My ordinances, and take My covenant into thy mouth.'[16] And therefore he is fortified by the sign of the cross, and then having received license and benediction, as is aforesaid, and having made the sign of the cross, that the may walk in safety, proceedeth to the rood loft in silence, with his eyes fixed on the ground: bearing, according to the custom of some churches, nothing in his hand, as the Lord commanded the apostles whom He sent to preach the kingdom of God. 'Take,' saith He, 'nothing for the journey, and salute no one.'[17] But in other churches the deacon beareth a book, as shall be said hereafter. But when he cometh to the rood loft, he saluteth it, as entering into a house to which he offereth peace, and passeth from the right side of the choir to the left, as he had before transferred the book from the right to the left side. For when the Jews had refused the Word of God, it was preached to the Gentiles, who are understood by the left side.

10. In the Roman Church, and in certain others, the sub-deacon ascendeth the rood loft one way,[18] and the deacon another: because the one proceedeth to an increase of knowledge by teaching, the other by learning: and because the minister by the merit of his works, and the preacher by the merit of his words, proceedeth to an increase of righteousness. Whence the Psalmist: 'Thy righteousness standeth like the mountains of God':[19] but they both return to the bishop by the same way, because by final perserverance they attain their reward, as the Lord testifieth, saying: 'He that endureth to the end, the same shall be saved.'[20] And that preaching sufficeth not without good deeds. For 'Jesus began both to do and to teach.'[21] Therefore the preacher returneth by the same way by the which the minister had gone up. Moreover, he that is about to read the gospel goeth and ascendeth by one way, and returneth by another, according to that saying, 'They returned into their own country another way':[22] because the apostles did first preach to the Jews and then to the Gentiles: as it is written, 'Since ye have cast from you the Word of God,'[23] and the rest.

11. The sub-deacon precedeth the deacon (because John and his preaching preceded Christ and His preaching), carrying in some churches a cushion; which he may place under the book. By the cushion, on which the book resteth, be set forth the temporal things of life, as it is written: 'If we have sown spiritual things, is it a great matter if we reap your temporal things?'[24] For according to the Apostle, 'They which serve the altar, eat of the altar.'[25] For 'the labourer is worthy of his hire.'[26] And the Lord taught us the law, 'Thou shalt not muzzle the ox when it treadeth out the corn.'[27]

Again, a cushion is placed under the book to denote that which the Lord saith, 'My yoke is easy, and My burden light.'[28] Austin saith, 'To this yoke whosoever is subject, hath all things subject to him.'

The cushion therefore denoteth the sweetness and pleasure that ariseth from the commands of God. Whence the Prophet, 'Thou, O God, hast of Thy goodness prepared for the poor.'[29] And again, 'O how sweet are Thy words unto my taste.'[30] Yet in the Roman Church, the deacon goeth first, as the teacher: sub-deacon followeth as the learner: the one precedeth, that he may preach, the other followeth, that he may minister. But after the reading of the Gospel, the sub-deacon, as being now sufficiently instructed, returneth first, having in his hand the gospel, as bringing back the gospel as the fruit of his ministrations: according to that which the Lord promised: 'He that receiveth a prophet in the name of a prophet shall receive a prophet's reward.'[31] Whom therefore the deacon sendeth aforehand to the bishop, to show that he is bringing back the fruit of his preaching: concerning which the Lord commanded, 'I have called you that ye should go and bring forth fruit, and that your fruit should remain.'[32] Moreover, the deacon, bearing back the cushion and gospel, signifieth that the preacher ought, by his good works, to offer his life to God. Whence the Apostle, 'Whatsoever you do in word and deed, do all in the name of our Lord Jesus Christ.'[33]

12. The deacon also sendeth aforehand the thurible with incense, because the works of Christ preceded His doctrine. As it is written, 'Jesus began to do, and to teach.' But the thurible with incense signifieth prayer with devotion, which the faithful then chiefly ought to employ when they hear the word of God. Again, he doth it, because the preacher must send forth the sweet odour of good works: according to that saying of the Apostle: 'We are a sweet savour of Christ in every place.'[34] He whose life is despised needs is it that His preaching also is contemned.

. . . . . .

The cross precedeth the gospel in token that the preacher must follow the Crucified. Whence the Lord saith to Peter, 'Follow Me.' After this, the deacon ascendeth the *ambo* [the rood loft].

17. Now *ambo* meaneth the pulpit, whence the gospel is read, so called from *ambio* [to surround] because that place is surrounded with steps. In some churches also there be two ascents, one left, namely towards the east, where the deacon ascendeth; one to the right, namely towards the west, where he descendeth.

. . . .

(Germany, 1159 C.E.)

"The book of Gospel is also taken from the altar, because apostles received the gospel from the altar, when they went about preaching the Passion of Christ."

Lindisfarne Gospel Page (Ireland)

(France, 13th Century)

Eagle Lecturn (Notre Dame of Hal, Belgium, 15th Century)

Eagle Lecturn (made in Maastricht, ca 1500 C.E.)

"Also, the gospel is read from an eagle, according to the saying, 'He came flying upon the wings of the winds.'"

(Norwich Cathedral, England)

Eagle Lecturn with Lion Base

(13th Century)

"The sign of the cross is to be made with three fingers, in honour of the Trinity."

18. He ascendeth that he may read the gospel with a loud and clear voice: as that which is to be heard of all, according to that saying of the Prophet, 'O thou that evangelist to Sion, get thee up into the high mountain.'[35]

. . . . . .

Also that we may imitate our Lord, Who went up into a mountain,[36] that He might preach the gospel. The gospel is also read in a lofty and eminent place, because it hath been preached throughout all the world: as it is written: 'Their sound is gone out unto all lands.'[37] But the epistle is read in a lower place, as typifying the law, which was confined to Judea alone, as it is written: 'In Jewry is God known.'[38]

. . . . . .

19. But in a Mass of requiem the gospel is not read in that exalted place, but at the altar, to signify that preaching profiteth not the departed.

. . . . . .

20. Also the gospel is read from an eagle, according to that saying, 'He came flying upon the wings of the winds.'[39] And the eagle itself is covered with a covering of cloth or silk, on certain feasts, to signify the softness of the heart: as he saith, 'I will take away the stony heart out of your flesh, and will give you a heart of flesh.'[40]

. . . . . .

21. But he that readeth the gospel passeth to the left side: and setteth his face to the north, that the saying may be fulfilled, which is written, 'I will say to the north give up, and to the south keep not back'[41] (Durandus, Book IV, chap. xxiv).

APPENDIX D: ON THE SIGN OF THE CROSS

In the second chapter of his fifth book Durandus enters at great length into this subject. The reason for making the sign is to drive away evil spirits, who, as S. Chrysostome says, 'always flee when they see the sign of the cross, as fearing that staff by which they have been wounded.' The pole on which the brazen serpent was raised, the crossing of Jacob's hands when blessing Joseph's children, the mark *tau* (Ezekiel ix, 4) on the forehead, and the seal on the forehead in the Apocalypse, are some of the representations of the cross here alleged. The cross is to be made with three fingers, in honour of the Trinity. The Jacobites and Eutychians use only one finger. Next the different methods of crossing are discussed. The sign ought to be made at the end of the gospel, the creeds, the Lord's Prayer, the *Gloria in excelsis*, the *Sanctus*, the *Agnus Dei*, the *Benedictus*, *Magnificat*, *Nunc dimittis*, at the beginning of the hours, the end of the Mass, when the priest gives the benediction, and whenever mention is made of the Cross of the Crucified. See also our author in his sixth book *De die Parasceue*.

APPENDIX E: ON THE FOUR COLOURS USED IN CHURCH HANGINGS, ETC.

1. There be four principal colours, by which, according to the diversity of days, the Church distinguisheth her vestments: to wit, white, red, black, and green. For we read that in the garments of the law there were four colours, fine linen, purple, jacinth, scarlet. The Roman Church also useth violet and saffron, as shall be said below.

2. White vestments be used in the festivals of holy confessors, and virgins which be not martyrs, on account of their integrity and innocence. For it is written, 'Her Nazarites were whiter than snow.'[1] And again: 'They shall walk with Me in white:[2] for they are virgins: and follow the Lamb whithersoever He goeth.' On account of the same thing white is used on the festivals of angels; concerning whom the Lord saith to Lucifer:[3] 'Where wast thou ... when the morning stars sang together?' Also in all the festivals of the Holy Mother of God. In the feast of All Saints: yet some then use red. In the principal festival of S. John Evangelist.[4] In the conversion of S. Paul. In the cathedra of S. Peter.[5] Also from the vigil of the nativity of our Lord to the octave of the Epiphany: both inclusive; excepting the festivals of the martyrs included in that period.[6] In the nativity of our Lord, and also of His Forerunner, because each was born pure. 'For the Lord rode upon a light cloud,'[7] that is, took unto Himself sinless humanity, 'and entered Egypt,' that is, came into the world: as saith the angel to the virgin, 'The Holy Ghost shall come upon thee, and the power of the Highest shall overshadow thee.'[8] But John, although he were born in sin, was sanctified from the womb: according to that saying, 'Before thou camest forth from the womb I sanctified thee.'[9] And the angel saith to Zecharias, 'He shall be filled with the Holy Ghost from his mother's womb.'[10] Also white is used in the Epiphany, on account of the splendour of that star which led the wise men, as saith the Prophet, 'and the Gentiles shall come to thy light, and kings to the brightness of thy rising.'[11] In the purification also, on account of the purity of the Virgin Mary: which, according to Simeon, gave birth to 'a light to lighten the Gentiles, and the glory of Thy people Israel.'[12] On Maundy Thursday, to set forth the anointing, which is consecrated to the purification of the soul. For the gospel on that day principally setteth forth purity; 'He that is washed needeth not save to wash his feet, but is clean every whit': and again, 'If I wash thee not, thou hast no part with me.'[13] It is also used with the office of the Mass from Easter Eve until the octave of the Ascension inclusive: except on the roga-

tion days and intervening festivals of martyrs. On Easter Day, on account of the angel who brought the tidings of the Resurrection, who appeared in white garments: concerning whom Matthew testifieth, saying, 'His countenance was as lightning, and his garment white as snow.':[14] and also because children, when baptised, are clothed in white. So also on the Ascension, because of the bright cloud in which Christ ascended. 'For two men stood by them in white garments, which also said, Ye men of Galilee,'[15] etc.

3. And this is to be noted, that albeit in the consecration of bishops, the vestments be of the colour suitable for the day, at the dedication of a church they be ever white, on what day soever the ceremony be celebrated: since in the consecration of a bishop the Mass of the day is sung, but in the dedication of a church, the Mass of dedication is sung. For the Church is called by the title of a virgin: according to that saying of the Apostle, 'For I have betrothed you to one man, that I may present you as a chaste virgin to Christ.'[16] Concerning which saith the bridegroom in the Canticles: 'Thou art altogether fair, my love, and there is no spot in thee.'[17] But this vestment ought to be white, to signify that her garments must at all times be pure, that is, her life must be spotless. Also in the octaves, the white colour is used.

4. Scarlet vestments are used on the festivals of the apostles, evangelists, and martyrs, on account of the blood of their passion, which they poured out for Christ. For 'these be they which came out of great tribulation.'[18] Except on the feast of the innocents, as shall be said below. Also on the feast of the Cross, because Christ on the cross poured out His blood for us. Whence the Prophet, 'Wherefore is thine apparel red, as one that treadeth out the wine vat?'[19] But according to others, we then use white vestments: because it is not the feast of the passion, but of the invention, or exaltations.[20] Also from the vigil of Pentecost to Trinity Sunday inclusively: and this on account of the fervour of the Holy Ghost, which appeared in fiery tongues on the apostles. 'For there appeared unto them divers tongues as of fire.'[21] Whence the Prophet: 'He sent a fire in their bones.' Although in the martyrdom of SS. Peter and Paul both red and white be used: and in the nativity of S. John Baptist, white: but in his decollation, red.

5. But when her festivity is celebrated, who was both a virgin and martyr, the martyrdom taketh precedence of the virginity; because it is a sign of the most perfect love: according as the Truth saith, 'Greater love hath no man than this, that a man lay down his life for his friends.'[22] Wherefore on the commemoration of All Saints, some use scarlet: but others,

and among them the Roman Church, white: at which time the Church saith, 'They shall walk in the sight of the Lamb with white garments: and palms in their hands.'[23] Whence the spouse saith in the Canticles: 'My beloved is white and ruddy:' white in His confessors and virgins, ruddy in His apostles and martyrs. For these are the flowers of roses, and the lilies of the valley. Again they who use scarlet on the feast of All Saints, do it with that intent because that feast was first instituted in honour of All Martyrs.[24] But answer may be made that it was also in honour of the blessed Virgin: and that at the present time, after the decree of S. Gregory VII, the Church keepeth that day holy to the memory of confessors and virgins. Also, the octaves of these days follow the colour of the feasts themselves.

6. Black is used on Good Friday: and on days of abstinence and affliction: and also in rogations. Moreover, in those processions which the Roman Pontiff maketh with bare feet: and in Masses of requiem, and Septuagesima to Easter Eve. For the spouse saith in the Canticles, 'I am black but comely,'[25] etc. But on the feast of the Innocents, some use black on account of sadness, some scarlet. The former allege the text, 'In Rama was a voice heard,'[26] etc. And for the same cause canticles of joy are omitted: and the mitre is brought without the orfrey, on account of the martyrdoms to which the Church hath principally an eye, when she saith, 'I saw beneath the throne of souls,'[27] etc.

(So also on Sunday Lætare[28] Jerusalem, the Roman Pontiff beareth a mitre, beautified with the orfrey, on account of the joy which the golden[29] rose signifieth, but on account of the time being one of sadness, he weareth black vestments.) But the Roman Church, when the festival falleth on a week-day, useth violet, but on the octave, red.

7. In fine, on common days green vestments be employed: because green is the middle colour between black, white and red; and specially between the octave of Epiphany and Septuagesima: and between Pentecost and Advent, in the Sunday office, this colour is used.

8. As he saith, 'Cypress and nard, nard and crocus.'[30] To these four colours be the others referred; to wit, the scarlet to the red,[31] the violet to the black, the fine linen to the white, the saffron to the green. But some refer the roses to martyrs, the saffron to confessors, the lilies to virgins.

9. It is not unmeet to use the violet on those days for which black is appointed. Whence the Roman Church useth it from the first Sunday in Advent, to the Mass of the vigil of the nativity, inclusive: and from Septuagesima to Easter Eve exclusive. But on the feasts of Saints on Septuagesima and Advent, violet or black is not to be used. And note that on Easter Eve in the whole office before Mass violet is used, except that

the deacon who blesseth the taper, and the sub-deacon who ministereth, wear a white dalmatic and tunic, respectively: because that benediction pertaineth to the Resurrection, as doth also the Mass. But the benediction being finished, the deacon putteth off the dalmatic, and putteth on a violet chasuble: the sub-deacon, however, changeth not his vestments. Some also use white in the procession on Palm Sunday: and in the blessing of the boughs, and while the hymn *Gloria, laus, et honor*, is sung, on account of the joy of that festivity. But the Roman Church useth violet: as it doth also in the procession on Candlemas Day; because that office treateth of the anxious expectation of Simeon, and savoureth of the Old Testament.

10. It also useth that colour in the September ember days, and on the vigils of saints, when the Mass is of the vigil: and on the rogation days, and in Mass on S. Mark's Day.[32] For when we fast, then we bring under our flesh, that it may be conformed to that of Christ, 'By the lividness of whose stripes we be healed.'[33]

The which to express we use violet, which is a pale, and as it were, a livid colour (Durandus, Book III, 18).

APPENDIX F: OF BELLS BEING NOT RUNG FOR THREE DAYS BEFORE EASTER

'On these three days the bells be silent, because the apostles and preachers and others who be understood by bells were then silenced. For the sound of bells doth signify the sound of preaching: of which it is said, "Their sound hath gone out into all lands." For at that time they no longer went round the towns and villages preaching the gospel, but "after they had sung an hymn they went out with Jesus to the Mount of Olives." To whom when the Lord had said, "Behold he is at hand that doth betray Me," they slumbered for sadness, and ceased from praises. Whence also from compline, or vespers, when our Lord was betrayed beginneth the silence of the bells. Others, however, do not sound their bells during prime of this fifth day of passion week' (Durandus, Book VI, 72, 73).

APPENDIX G: THE DEDICATION FESTIVAL

The authority for the dedication festival is our Lord's observing the feast of the dedication of the Temple. This festival has an octave: as also had the Jewish feast, though the Passover and feast of Tabernacles had not.

'But this festival specially denoteth that eternal dedication, in which that other church, the holy soul, shall be so dedicated and united to God that it shall never be transferred to other uses: which will take place in the octave of the Resurrection.' The Psalms for the office of the festival are the Domini *est terra, Judica me Domine, Deus noster refugium, Magnus*

Dominus, Quam dilecta, Fundamenta ejus, and *Domine Deus* (Durandus, Book VII, 48).

APPENDIX H: ON THE DEDICATION OF A CHURCH

The following particulars are extracted and condensed from Martene's invaluable work: and as his account is not easily accessible, and somewhat long, it has been thought well to subjoin them here.

Churches were often, in the primitive ages, dedicated by more than one bishop. Constantine having completed a magnificent church at Jerusalem, invited the prelates, then assembled in council at Tyre, to assist in its consecration (Euseb. *Vit. Const.* iv, 43; Sozomen. i, 46).

Constantius his son, having finished a church erected by his father at Antioch, Eusebius of Nicomedia, the intruding patriarch of Constantinople, summoned a council under pretence of consecrating the church, however much in reality to decide against the Catholic doctrine of Consubstantiality. Ninety-seven bishops were present (Sozomen. iii, 5).

So it was also in the Western Church. This is proved by the Preface to the Fourth Council of Arles, holden in 524: which begins, 'When the priests of the Lord had assembled in the will of God to the dedication of the church of S. Mary at Arles.'

In the time of S. Louis, Pope Pascal I consecrated the church of S. Vincent, with the Sacred College of Bishops and Cardinals. About the year 1015, the crypt of the monastery of S. Michael was consecrated by S. Bernard of Hildersheim and two other bishops; and three years afterwards, the church being finished, it was consecrated by the same S. Bernard with three other bishops (*Vita S. Bernardi*, cap. xxxix, xl).

All these bishops took an actual part in the service. In the consecration of the church of Mans, in 1120, the high altar was consecrated by Gilbert, Archbishop of Mans: S. Julians by Galfred of Rouen: Hildebert of Mans consecrated S. Mary's; Reginald of Angiers that of the Holy Cross. There is a fine passage to the same point in Suger's book on the dedication of the church of S. Denis: 'Right early in the morning,' saith he, 'archbishops and bishops, archdeacons and abbots, and other venerable persons, who had lived of their proper expense, bore themselves right bishopfully; and took their places on the platform raised for the consecration of the water, and placed between the sepulchres of the holy martyrs and S. Saviour's altar. Then might ye have seen, and they who stood by saw, and that with great devotion, such a band of so venerable bishops, arrayed in their white robes, sparkling in their pontifical robes and precious orfreys, grasp their pastoral staves, call on God in holy exorcism, pace around the consecrated enclosure, and perform the nuptials of the Great King with such care, that it seemed as though the ceremony were performed by a chorus of angels, not a band of men. The crowd, in overwhelming magnitude, rolled around to the door; and while the aforesaid episcopal band were sprinkling the walls with hyssop, the king and his nobles drive them back, repress them, guard the portals.'

Yet the principal actor on the occasion was the bishop of the diocese. The thirty-sixth canon of the second Council of Arles decrees, 'If a bishop be minded to build a church in another diocese, let its dedication be reserved for the diocesan.' S. Columbanus, being only a priest, dedicated the church of S. Aurelia (Walfrid. Strabo. *Vita S. Gallo*, cap. vi).

The preceding night was spent either in the church or in neighbouring churches in a solemn vigil. S. Ambrose testifies that this was done on occasions of the dedication of the Ambrosian church (*Epist.* 22, *ad Marcellina*). So S. Gregory of Mans, in his dedication of the church of S. Julian, removed the relics of that saint into the church of S. Martin, and there kept vigil *(De Glor. Mart.* ii, 34).

Relics were considered indispensably necessary: so S. Paulinus (Epist. xxii, ad Sever). This church was dedicated in the name of Christ, the Saint of saints, the Martyr of martyrs, the Lord of lords, and was honoured with the relics of the blessed apostles. See also the beautiful epistle of S. Ambrose, translated in 'The Church of the Fathers.' The phrase was, *Consecrare ecclesiam de reliquiis Beati n.*

Yet some churches were consecrated without relics. The second Nicene Council decreed that in this case they should be supplied. Those portions of the consecrated elements were placed with these: to which perhaps that expression of S. Chrysostom is to be referred—'What is the altar by nature but a stone? But it is made holy, when it hath once received the body of Christ.'

These relics occupied different positions. In the church of S. Benedict, consecrated by Pope Alexander II, there were relics in the chapel-apse of S. John, in the bases of the piers, in the four angles of the bell tower, in the cross on the western gable, in the cross of the tower (*Chron. Cass*, iii, 30).

Ashes were sprinkled on the floor, and the bishop with his pastoral staff wrote on them the alphabet, sometimes in Latin alone, sometimes in Greek also.

The whole ceremony concluded with the endowment of the church: or, as it was termed, presenting its dowry.

By way of setting before our readers as clearly as possible the ancient form of dedication, we have chosen, among ten forms preserved by Martene, that of S. Dunstan.

Here beginneth the order of the dedication of a church. The bishops and other ministers of the church advance singing the antiphon, 'Zaccheus, make haste and come down,' etc.

Prevent us, O Lord, in all our, etc.

Then twelve candles are to be lighted, and placed round the church, with the antiphon, three from the east, three from the west, three from the north, three from the south.

God, which by the preaching of Thine apostles, didst open to Thy Church the Kingdom of Heaven, and didst call them the Lights of the world, grant, we beseech Thee, that being assisted by their prayers, by whose teaching we are guided, and splendour illuminated, we may make these our actions pleasing to Thy Divine Majesty.

Here followeth the Litany: the priests going thrice round the church, and beginning from that door at which they be after to enter, namely, the south door.

O Christ, hear us, etc.

Prevent us, O Lord, with Thy tender mercy, and by the intercession of Thy saints, receive our prayers graciously.

Let our prayers, O Lord, come up before Thee, and expel all wickedness from Thy Church.

God, which rulest heaven and earth, graciously give us the aid of Thy defence.

Then one of the deacons entering the church, and shutting the door standeth before it, the other remaining without: and the bishop striking it with his staff, saith:

Lift up your heads, O ye gates, and be ye lift up, ye everlasting doors, and the King of Glory shall come in.

The deacon within answereth, and saith: Who is the King of Glory?

The Bishop. Lift up, etc.

The Deacon. Who is, etc.

The Bishop. Lift up, etc.

The Deacon. Who is, etc.

Chorus. The Lord of Hosts, He is the King of Glory.

The bishop again striking the door it is opened: and he entereth: the chorus singing after him, Lift up your heads, etc., *to the end of the Psalm.*

The Bishop. The Lord be with you.

Response. And with thy spirit.

The Bishop. Let us pray:

We beseech Thee, O Lord, of Thy mercy, to enter Thy house, and to make for Thyself an habitation in the hearts of the faithful. Through, etc.

Then the bishop entereth the choir, saying:

Peace be to this house, and to all that are in it; peace to them that come in, and to them that go out.

Bless, O Lord, this house, which the sons of men have built for Thee: hear those which shall come up to this place: hear their prayers in the lofty throne of Thy glory.

The clerks begin the Litany; the bishop, with certain priests and deacons, remaining prostrate at the altar.

Lord have mercy upon us, etc.

As soon as Agnus Dei *is said, the bishop rising, saith*:

Let us pray.

Be Thou exalted, Lord, in Thine own strength, etc.

Then the bishop shall write the alphabet along the pavement[1] *, first from east to west, then from north to south, the chorus saying the Psalm,* Fundamenta ejus.

The Bishop. O God, make speed, etc.

Response. O Lord, make haste, etc.

The Bishop. Glory be, etc.

Response. As it, etc.

Then followeth the exorcism of the salt, and the water, and the ashes.

Then the bishop maketh the sign of the cross at the four corners of the altar, with hyssop, going round it seven times. The chorus sing the Psalm, Miserere mei Deus. *Then the bishop sprinkleth the water three times round the church: the chorus singing* Deus noster refugium. *Then the bishop sprinkleth the water over the altar: the chorus singing* Qui habitat. *Then the bishop sprinkleth the whole church inside with the water thrice: to signify the Church's inward faith in the Trinity: and once outside, to signify the one baptism. The chorus sing* Fundamenta ejus*; and while the priests are ascending the turrets,* Jacob beheld a ladder*, etc., and the Psalm* Deus noster refugium.

Then the bishop entereth the church: and sprinkleth water on the pavement in the form of a cross: the chorus singing Benedicite, omnia opera.

The Bishop. Lift up your hearts.

Response. We lift, etc.

The Bishop. Let us give thanks, etc.

Response. It is meet, etc.

Then the bishop goeth to the altar, and poureth the remainder of the water at its base.

Then he blesseth the altar-stone, the altar clothes, the sacerdotal vestments, the corporal, the paten, the chalice, the thurible.

Here followeth the Mass of Dedication.

The post communion ended, the Bishop saith:

Incline, O Lord, Thine ears unto me, and hear me: Look down, O Christ, from heaven, on thy flock and thy sheep: stretch Thine hand over them: bless their bodies and their souls: that in the communion of the saints they may receive celestial benediction, light angelical, the Holy Ghost, the Paraclete. Amen.

They who be regenerate of water and the Holy Ghost who be redeemed on earth by Thy precious blood, who have received Thy sign on their foreheads, grant them to be Thine on the day of judgment. Amen.

And as Thou didst bless patriarchs and Prophets and apostles, martyrs and confessors, virgins and priests, so bless this flock, who are assembled to-day in Thy name in this church. Amen.

And as by Thine angel Thou didst free the three children from the burning fiery furnace, so free this flock from everlasting death and the power of the devil, and from earthly lusts and all manner of weaknesses. Amen.

Spare their faults, remit their sins, and present them pure and undefiled in the day of judgment: as Thou didst receive Enoch and Elias into the kingdom of heaven. Amen.

God Almighty bless and keep you, and make this house to shine with the glory of His presence, and open the eyes of His pity upon it day and night. Amen.

And grant of His mercy, that all, who have assembled together at this dedication, by the intercession of Blessed N., and all other saints whose relics rest here, may obtain the remission of their sins. Amen.

That ye may be made a holy temple in the spirit, where the Holy Trinity may ever deign to dwell; and after this short life ye may attain to everlasting felicity. Amen.

Which He grant, Who liveth and reigneth, world without end. Amen.

APPENDIX I: ADDENDA

Page xxx.—But how great is the admiration, etc. Compare S. Hildebert's hymn, *Extra portam*, towards the conclusion:

Quantum tui gratulentur,
Quam festive conviventur
Quis affectus eos stringat,
Et quæ gemma muros pingat,
Quis chalcedon, quis jacintus,
Norunt isti, quis sunt intus !

The last line has the same beautiful turn with the expression of Hugh of S. Victor.

Page 9.—'The lattice work of the windows.' Wrongly translated in Lewis, 'the screens before the windows.' (ch I, note 41)

Page 10.—This passage proves that in the time and country of Durandus seats or chairs except in the choir were unknown. Though in England Early English or Early Decorated open seats do occur, as in Clapton-in-Gordan, Somersetshire, they are very rare, and take up much less of the church than is the case in later examples. See 'Hist. of Pews,' 3rd ed., pp. 19, 20, 79. (ch I, note 49)

Page 18.—The reader is aware that the words *in medio* of the early Christian altars gave rise to the warmest disputes between the Puritans and the Catholics of the 17th century. The Puritans insisted that they meant in the body of the church: the Catholics generally, and more particularly that most able defender of altars, Dr Laurence, insisted that when the fathers spoke of an altar *in medio*, they only meant one so placed as to be where all might see it. The words undoubtedly may bear this meaning: yet perhaps it is better to understand them, as they must be understood in this passage of Durandus, of an altar placed in the chord of the segment of a circle formed by the apse. See *Ecclesiologist*, vol. ii, p. 13.

Page 22, note 20.—This is a mistake. The fresco alluded to represents a priest repeating the Pater Noster (which is written in his open book) at the N. W. angle of an altar. Upon the altar are two candlesticks and a ciborium: rising out of the latter is the figure of our Blessed Lord. There can be no doubt of the objectionable nature of such a representation.

Page 26.—The nimbus of the Saviour, it is perhaps needless to observe in explanation, is always inlaid, as it were, with a cross: at least the exceptions are excessively rare.

Page 26.—These 'carved figures' probably signify the corbels.

Page 26, note 54.—There is a valuable article on the nimbus by M. Didron from the *Revue Générale de l'Architecture* in the *Literary Gazette* for Dec. 1842. An example is there given of the square nimbus in the case of Pope Nicholas, as represented in a contemporary MS. The whole is well worth reading.

Page 53.—Dedication crosses. We have seen a valuable example of these in the church of Moorlinch, Somersetshire. There are four circles containing crosses pattées on the north and south sides of the chancel; and two at the east end, in all ten: the other two have disappeared.

Page 80.—The bodies of good men called horses. The same idea is worked out at great length in S. Chrysostom's earlier homilies on the Statues.

Page 92.—Most of the following practices are observed to this day in the Metropolitical Church of Seville. There are two ambos, but no rood loft: the sub-deacon chants the epistle by himself, in the southern ambo; the deacon, preceded by a taper, chants the gospel from the northern.

Page 94.—So S. Bernard in his commentary on that verse of the 90th Psalm, 'A thousand shall fall at thy side, and ten thousand at thy right hand.'

THE

SACRED VESTMENTS

AN ENGLISH RENDERING OF THE THIRD BOOK OF THE 'RATIONALE DIVINORUM OFFICIORUM' OF DURANDUS, BISHOP OF MENDE

WITH NOTES

BY THE

REV. T.H. PASSMORE, M.A.
LONDON

Translated from The Venice Folio, 1491.

St. Dunstan's House
1899

(St. Clement, 11th Century)

"For the Priestly Vestments do mean virtues, wherewith Priests ought to be adorned: according unto that of the Prophet, LET THY PRIESTS BE CLOTHED WITH RIGHTEOUSNESS, AND LET THY SAINTS SING WITH JOYFULNESS." "Wherefore the Priest, willing to celebrate Mass, must adorn himself with apparel which agreeth unto his order, and the beauty of his life must beseem his vesture's splendour."

THE SACRED VESTMENTS

FOREWORD

With the exception of Neale and Webb's 'Symbolism,' which is an edited translation of its first Book 'Of the Church and its Parts,' the eight books of the *Rationale Divinorum Officiorum* of Durandus have not, so far as I know, been rendered into English. This means that the greatest and most beautiful, perhaps, of ancient works on the worship of the Catholic Church is inaccessible to any but readers of the Latin tongue.

What herein follows is an attempt in part to supply this defect. In making it I have felt that should the work fail to find readers (which would appear unlikely in days when the mind of all England is strained upon matters liturgical) the blame will attach to the inefficient interpreter, not to the pious and gifted author, of an illustrious book.

For the Catholic Revival, under God, in our English Church has not yet brought us to that degree of liturgical perfection, that we can afford to turn a deaf ear to those great voices of the past which being dead yet speak to us of 'the sacred mysteries, and the virtues which they signify.' The lore of the sanctuary and the cunning of holy rite can hardly be called strong points with the English clergy, concede to them what we will of piety and reverence in heart. Nor is the cause far to seek, when we consider how sadly deficient is the ordinary course of English clerical training as regards that most necessary instruction in the externals of worship, without which it is impossible to enter with fitness upon the holiest of callings. The present writer may recall, without any invidious feeling whatever, the utter ignorance of the details of the offering of the Holy Sacrifice, in which he entered upon his ministry in the Church, after having received excellent instruction in both doctrinal and pastoral theology both at Cambridge and at one of the best of our Theological Colleges.

One has heard it put forth indeed almost as a boast by many a good priest, that he is 'no ritualist.' Yet it may be thought strange that a craftsman should arrogate to himself either ignorance or inefficiency in any department of his craft, however subordinate, as a thing to be vaunted. If 'Priestcraft,' which is the craft or common business of a Priest, were less anathematised and more studied, the Church would be a gainer at large. Surely it is the solemn duty of every Priest to be a 'Ritualist', in so far as touches the competent and careful discharge of his dread office in the sanctuary. There is a tendency even in Catholic minds, especially in times of

'Crisis'—which seem perennial—to think and speak of Ritual a little slightingly, as though it were the rival of interior or practical piety, rather than its correlative and helpmeet. We are reminded of words uttered by a dignitary of the Church some few years ago, '*We want happy homes, not frequent services*.' But why not both? Shall we the better proclaim the precepts or shepherd the lambs of God, by attending, with sloven attitude and scanty shift of service, His awful courts of praise? Shall we take the spikenard, due to Him, of the beauty that He loves, and sell it for three hundred pence? Nay, let us bestow all our goods to feed the poor; but never rob the sacred treasuries of Him Who said, 'Ye shall reverence My Sanctuary: I am the Lord.' 'For this ought ye to have done, and not to have left the other undone.' The great motive assigned by Almighty God to the ancient Pontiff for the reverent offering of the shadowy sacrifices of the Law was this, '*that he die not*.' What shall we say of the Oblation of the Lamb that taketh away the sin of the world?

Yet by God's grace the picture has a brighter side. And now that the Sacred Vestments of the Church, in common with many other features of Christian ceremonial, are by His goodness so widely revived amongst us (*et attendat studiose sacerdos ut signum sine significato non ferat*) it may surely be supposed that many, both clergy and laity, will be glad to hear their story and learn their symbolism, from one of the greatest and holiest Ritualists that ever lived. The works of Durandus are always rare and expensive, and are for the most part ancient editions printed in Gothic letter, which with its blackness and frequent abbreviation is dazzling to the eye, and ill-adapted to a hurrying age.

The mediaeval mysticism of Durandus is not calculated to be acceptable to all. It has indeed been objected that he sets out with the deliberate intention of 'finding a meaning for everything.' But is not this a laudable intention? Has not the poet immortalised the spirit which

'Finds tongues in trees, books in the running brooks,
Sermons in stones, and good in everything'?

I will add here, as Shakespeare adds,

'I would not change it.'

Such a mind at least compares favourably with the spirit—alas! all too prevalent even among the pious—which is content to take all things on trust; which can look unmoved upon earthly and heavenly mysteries, and ask no question, feel no 'Divine curiosity,' as to their birth or message; which can accept with grateful calm the immense heritage of the Faith, but never cares to scrutinise the golden coins that bear the superscription of the King. Unfortunate were that owner of a vast and beautiful estate, who should fulfil punctiliously the duties of the manor's lord, but never open a book in his library, nor muse before a picture on his gallery-walls, nor gaze with thoughtful wonder into the chalice of a single flower in his bright and wide parterres.

Quite true it is, that many a rite and instrument of worship has been born of utility and new-born of symbolism. The very word 'Use,' in liturgical phrase, testifies to this. Candles were burnt for their light, before ever men saw in them the emblem of the Light of Light. A maniple was employed for the meanest of uses, before ever it suggested the righteous '*portantes manipulos suos*.' But this is no argument against symbolism. It is rather a witness to its heavenly character. For if men devise a rite with a definitely symbolic purpose in the first instance, the charge of human invention will have an air of plausibility. But if, passing into it imperceptibly and naturally for its usefulness' sake, they realise afterwards that it is big with heavenly meaning, then all who behold it will be fain to cry out, '*A Domino factum est istud, et est mirabile in oculis nostris*.'

All along the range of religious experience the principle holds good. It is often not until later life that men begin to trace an ordered design in the seemingly fortuitous happenings of earlier days. A common stone served Jacob for pillar at Luz, before ever he saw in it Beth-El, the House of God. It was a natural thing that One should ride into Jerusalem on an ass; so natural, that His disciples, paying little heed, 'understood not these things at the first; but when Jesus was glorified, then remembered they.' So the innumberable things and uses which were prest quite naturally into the service of the early Church were like obscure seeds cast into the ground; but it was holy ground, and sanctified the germs it nourished; and these sprang up in God's hour into beautiful flowers, brightening all the soil and sweetening all the air around the Tree of Life. '*For lo, the winter*' of obscurity '*is past, the rain*' of persecution '*is over and gone, and the flowers appear on the earth*.' But men perceived neither fragrance nor beauty, until the '*north wind awoke, and the south came, and blew upon My garden, that the spices thereof might flow out*'; and then they discerned that the thing was from the Lord.

Yet it is not true of our Bishop, that he is doggedly determined 'to find or invent a meaning for everything.' He is willing to leave much unexplained but by the primary principle of utility. 'It must carefully be noted,' he says in his general Proeme, 'that in the divine offices there be many customary rites which have, from their institution, respect neither unto a moral nor a mystical meaning. Of these, some are known to have arisen of necessity; some of congruity; some of the difference of the Old and New Testaments; some of convenience; and some for the more honour and reverence of the offices themselves; whence saith blessed Austin, "so many things are varied without number by the divers customs of divers places, that seldom or never can those causes be found out, which men followed in ordaining them."' His principle of finding symbolic reasons for long-established usages he justifies as follows: 'The professors of the arts liberal, and of all arts beside, if there be aught baldly and unadornedly set forth therein, do give diligence to clothe, support, and adorn it with causes and with reasons. Painters moreover, and artificers and handicraftsmen of what sort soever, do study in all the divers branches of their works to render and to have at hand probable reasons thereof. So also it is unseemly for the magistrate to be unknowing of this world's laws, and for the advocate to know nought of that law, wherein his daily work standeth.' For his right to a certain freedom of exposition, and for his manner of using it, he makes this plea: 'As none are prohibited (in the law) from using divers grounds of exception and manners of defence, so neither are they forbidden to use divers expositions in the praise of God, provided only that the Faith be kept whole.' And for aught blameworthy in the book, which may have arisen from lack of strength or wisdom or leisure, the Epilogue which will be found inserted at the end of this work makes ample and humble amends; leaving the most 'sober' critic surely fain to admire the reverential devoutness, the prevailing Scriptual tenor, the humility and dignity tempered together, and above all things the sanctified common-sense, of the work wherein the good Bishop brings out of Holy Church's treasure 'things new and old.'

In the Notes I have aimed to keep a diversity of readers in view. References to some authorities are given for the sake of those who may have a special interest in the subject; while extracts are in most cases translated, and elementary details are briefly explained, for the benefit of the less erudite. It has not been thought necessary to give various readings in every instance where they occur. In such cases I have usually employed the variant which seemed to me clearest, using as a basis the very satisfactory text of my own edition, a Venice folio of 1491, and unknown to Hain and Panzer. This I have corrected by other editions in the Bodleian where necessary.

The translation is as close as seems consistent with English idiom. The quotations from Holy Scripture, where the Vulgate permits, are in the words of the Authorised Version, except in the case of the Psalms, where they are given in the more familiar language of the Prayer-Book. The reader who desiderates that controversial treatment (as regards 'Roman claims' and so forth) which so often creeps into editions of works of this kind, will be under the necessity of supplying it for himself. 'Anglicanism' is not paraded, and 'Romanism' is not tiraded. 'Though I understand all mysteries, and have not charity, I am nothing.' Moreover, the book is a book of Ritual, and to that theme the notes are as far as possible confined. I may add that I have another and a more extensive Book of the *Rationale* in preparation, which I hope to produce should the present work prove acceptable.

It remains but to commend the latter to the all-wise and all-glorious Father of lights, in Whose Name and Whose honour alone our earthly service is offered, and without Whose acceptance and blessing no worship is holy, no sacrifice pure. '*Who hath seen Him, that he might tell us? and who can magnify Him as He is? There are hid yet greater things than these be, for we have seen but a few of His works. For the Lord hath made all things; and to the godly hath He given wisdom.*'

T. H. P.
London:
Feast of St. Dunstan,
1899.

"Therefore the Bishop must take earnest thought, and the Priest give careful heed, that he bear not the sign without the thing signified: that is, that he wear the Vestment without its virtue..."

CHAPTER I: PROEME

Here beginneth the Book of the Vestments or Ornaments of the Church, as worn by Priests and Bishops, and other Ministers.

1. It behoveth not to wear the Sacred Vestments in the use of everyday.[1] Whereby we mark, that even as we make change of vesture according unto the letter, so we must do also according unto the spirit. We may not enter therefore into the Holy of Holies with garments tainted by the use of common life; but with a pure conscience and with clean and holy raiment must we handle the holy things of God. Wherefore Stephen,[2] Pope, did order that the Sacred Vestments should not be used, save in the rites of the Church, and in service meet for God; as saith Ezekiel in the forty-fourth chapter,[3] *THEY SHALL NOT SANCTIFY THE PEOPLE WITH THEIR GARMENTS.* One raiment therefore hath Divine religion, for the Church's Offices; and another hath man for common use, to deliver the lesson of good conversation unto all Christian folk: to the end that they, being washed from their former foulness, may be made new men in Christ. For at such a time the Priest doth doff the old man with his doings, and putteth on the new man, made in the image of God. By the Vestments, moreover, as worn only in sacred services, we do understand that not all holy things are to be unfolded unto the people. Note also that in the days of the Emperor Ludovic,[4] the son of Charlemagne, the Bishops and clergy laid aside their girdles wove with gold, and their exquisite garments and other trappings of this world.

2. Now the Sacred Vestments seem to have been taken from the Law of old. For the Lord gave commandment unto Moses that he should make for Aaron the High Priest and for his sons *HOLY GARMENTS FOR GLORY AND FOR BEAUTY,*[5] that being washed and clad in sacred vesture they might discharge their office in the sanctuary. For by the space of forty days the Lord did teach Moses to make pontifical and priestly vestments for His Priests and for the sons of Levi, yea, ornaments and robes of linen; moreover, Miriam[6] wove and wrought them unto the use of the ministry of the Tabernacle of the Covenant. And so it is said in the forty-seventh chapter of Ecclesiasticus,[7] *HE BEAUTIFIED THEIR FEASTS.* There be certain Vestments, on the other hand, which are taken from the Apostles: but both these and those do signify virtues, and express the ministry[8] of the Incarnation.

3. The Bishop, of a truth, when about to celebrate, doth put off his clothes of everyday, and arrayeth himself in garments pure and holy.

And first, he must put on the Sandals, that he may be mindful of the Incarnation of the Lord.

Secondly, he placeth upon himself the Amice, that he may restrain his motions and his thoughts, his lips and tongue, that he may have a clean heart, receiving a right spirit renewed within him.

Thirdly, the Albe, which reacheth to his feet; that he may have enduring purity in his flesh.

Fourthly, the Girdle, that he may rein in the impulse of desire.

In the fifth place, the Stole, for token of obedience.

In the sixth place, the Tunic, which is of blue, signifying heavenly conversation.

In the seventh place, he doth put on the Dalmatic, which is holy piety, and the mortifying of the flesh.

In the eighth place, the Gloves, that he refuse vainglory.

In the ninth place, the Ring, that he love his Bride, the Church, even as himself.

In the tenth place, the Chasuble, which is Charity.

In the eleventh place, the Napkin, that he wipe away with penance whereinsoever, through frailty or ignorance, he is a sinner.

In the twelfth place, he putteth on the Pall, to shew himself that the imitateth Christ, Who bare our sicknesses.[9]

In the thirteenth place, the Mitre, that he so live as to be worthy of receiving an eternal crown.

In the fourteenth place, he taketh the Staff, which is the authority of power and doctrine.

And after this he goeth upon carpets,[10] that he may learn to despise the earth, and to be in love with heavenly things. And with all these foregoing Vestments he is clad by his Ministers; for the angels do minister unto him, that he may array himself in the garments of the Spirit: or because he is Vicegerent of Christ, unto Whom angels minister, and Whom all things serve.

The Bishop, then, looking toward the north—or toward the east, or the Altar, he may look, if it be more convenient—like a rescuer, a warrior about to fight with a long-standing foe, doth put on the Sacred Vestments as one accoutreth himself with arms, according to the Apostle, as I shall presently set forth.

4. First, the Sandals hath he for greaves of war, lest aught of the stain or dust of this world's affections cleave unto him. Secondly, with the Amice, as with an helm, he covereth his head. Thirdly, with the Albe, as with a breast-plate, he enveloppeth his whole body. Fourthly, he taketh the Girdle,

to a bow, and the Undergirdle[11] to a quiver; now the Undergirdle is that which hangeth down from the Girdle, and wherewith the Bishop's stole is fastened into the same. In the fifth place, with the Stole he surroundeth his neck, as one that brandisheth a spear in the face of his enemy. In the sixth place, he taketh the Maniple, as who wieldeth a club. Lastly, with the Chasuble he covereth himself as it were with a shield; and with a Book he armeth his hand, as with a sword. Of all the which I will speak singly in different wise hereafter.

And so these are the accoutrements wherewith the Bishop or the Priest ought to arm himself, willing to do battle against ghostly wickedness. For thus saith the Apostle:[12] *THE WEAPONS OF OUR WARFARE ARE NOT CARNAL; BUT MIGHTY TO THE PULLING DOWN OF STRONG-HOLDS.* And in another Epistle, that unto the Ephesians, in the sixth chapter:[13]—*PUT YE ON*, saith he, *THE ARMOUR OF GOD, THAT YE MAY BE ABLE TO STAND AGAINST THE WILES OF THE DEVIL. STAND THEREFORE HAVING YOUR LOINS GIRT ABOUT WITH TRUTH ON THE BREASTPLATE OF RIGHTEOUSNESS*, And *YOUR FEET SHOD WITH THE PREPARATION OF THE GOSPEL OF PEACE; ABOVE ALL TAKING THE SHIELD OF FAITH, WHEREWITH YE SHALL BE ABLE TO QUENCH ALL THE FIERY DARTS OF THE WICKED*: And *TAKE THE HELMET OF SALVATION, AND THE SWORD OF THE SPIRIT, WHICH IS THE WORD OF GOD.* Which armour is the foregoing sevenfold priestly vesture, signifying the sevenfold virtue of the Priest; and representing moreover the raiment of Christ wherewith He was arrayed at the time of His Passion, as shall be said anon.

5. Therefore the Bishop must take earnest thought, and the Priest give careful heed, that he bear not the sign without the thing signified: that is, that he wear the Vestment without its virtue; lest perchance he be as a sepulchre, whited without, *BUT WITHIN FULL OF ALL UNCLEANNESS.*[14] For what Priest soever adorneth himself with vestments, and putteth not on good manners, the more worthy of respect he seem unto men, so much the more unworthy doth he become in the sight of God. Wherefore the glory[15] of the Episcopate is not approved by the splendour of garments, but by brightness of souls: since those very adornments which did once delight the eyes of the flesh did call the rather for those virtues which were to be understood by their mean; that whatsoever those vestments with the gleam of their gold, the sheen of their jewels, and the variety of all kinds of broidery, did signify, might in these latter days shine out in the conduct and deed of the wearer. For even amongst the ancients the form did win reverence for its meaning, and in our own days the experience of deeds is

surer than the riddle of symbols; whereof, with other matters, we read in the Pontifical, where it treateth of the consecration of the Bishop.

6. So accoutred, then, for his conflict *AGAINST SPIRITUAL WICKEDNESS IN HIGH PLACES*, and for the allaying of the Judge's anger against His subjects, he proceedeth to the Altar, and by the Confession doth renounce the dominion of the devil, and accuseth himself; and upon ordinary days the folk, as about to pray for their champion, do prostrate themselves upon the ground. When he uttereth the Collects and other devotions, he doth fight as it were with all his might against the devil. When the Deacon before the Gospel upon Fast-days foldeth back the Chasuble[16] over his shoulder, he brandisheth as it were a sword against the foe. When the Epistle is read, it is the edicts of the Emperor that are being proclaimed by the voice of the herald. The chants are the trumpeters, the precentors ruling the choir are the generals of the host marshaling it unto battle, and as they lead the onset, others come to their aid; and the strains of the Sequence are the plaudits and the praise of victory. When the Gospel is read, the foe is as it were wounded with the sword, or scattered forces after victory are gathered into line. The Bishop, the while he preacheth, is the Emperor, lauding the conquerors; the Oblations are the spoils, which the victors share; and the strains of the Offertory are the triumph, due to the Emperor. The Pax[17] at the end is given unto the people, as a token of their quiet now that the foe is overthrown. And at the last the folk, after leave granted unto them in the *Ite missa est*,[18] depart again unto their own with gladness, for that victory and peace be won.

Wherefore the Priest, willing to celebrate Mass, must adorn himself with apparel which agreeth unto his order, and the beauty of his life must beseem his vesture's splendour.

7. Now in this matter it must be noted, that there be six Vestments[19] common unto both Bishop and Priest, for that there be six matters wherein standeth such power as belongeth alike to both. Yet are there nine ornaments peculiar to the Bishop, because there are nine points wherein standeth such power as belongeth unto the Bishop alone. By this reckoning, then, of Vestments common and peculiar, are signified the functions common to both Bishop and Priest, and those peculiar to the former alone. Of such appointment, moreover, we read both in the Old and in the New Testament; for we are told that the High Priest, beside those garments which he had in common with the Priests, had also certain peculiar to himself. But in the Old Testament there were four common, and four peculiar, as shall be set forth in the chapter of the Vestments of the Law; and this, indeed, was demanded by mystic truth, for those Vestments were given unto car-

nal and worldly men. For unto the flesh the number four doth well agree, by reason of the four Humours; and unto the world, by reason of the four Elements. But these other are assigned unto them that are spiritual and perfect.

8. For the number six, which is a perfect number, in that it is made up of its own parts added together, doth agree unto perfect things. This is the reason that on the sixth day God finished the heavens and the earth, *AND ALL THE HOST OF THEM*; and furthermore, being come in the fulness of time, in the sixth age, on the sixth day, at the sixth hour, He redeemed the sons of men. This number, I say, then, is perfect, because it is made up exactly, if one count it in the order of its parts. For when we add one, two, and three, the number six is fulfilled. For it is divided into three parts, to wit, one-sixth, one-third, and a half, that is one, two, and three. The number nine also doth fit with spiritual things, because there are nine orders of angels, which according to the prophet are signified by nine kinds of precious stones.[20]

9. Wherefore there are in all fifteen ornaments of the Bishop; and these by their number do signify fifteen degrees of virtues, which the Psalmist did mark out by as many Songs of Degrees.[21] For the Priestly Vestments do mean virtues, wherewith Priests ought to be adorned: according unto that of the Prophet,[22] *LET THY PRIESTS BE CLOTHED WITH RIGHTEOUSNESS, AND LET THY SAINTS SING WITH JOYFULNESS.* And they are called *talares*, that is, reaching unto the feet, because the foot is the end of the body; by which it is set forth that to begin a good work sufficeth not, save thou give attention to fulfil it with perseverance even unto the end; but of this more in the chapter of the Tunic.

Thou seest, then, how that our Bishop putteth on more than eight Vestments; whereas Aaron had but eight, which have their counterparts to-day; and this is to say that our *RIGHTEOUSNESS MUST EXCEED THE RIGHTEOUSNESS OF THE SCRIBES AND PHARISEES, if we would ENTER INTO THE KINGDOM OF HEAVEN.*[23] On the other hand it may also be said that our Bishop hath eight from head to feet, if we except the ornaments of his feet and hands; to wit, the Amice, the Albe, the Girdle, the Stole, the two Tunics, the Chasuble, and the Pall. For the vesting of the feet doth the rather pertain unto our Pontiff than unto Aaron, since unto the former it hath been said, *GO YE AND TEACH ALL NATIONS.*[24]

Lastly, beside the foregoing Vestments appointed unto Holy Orders and Ministers, there remaineth yet another Vestment of linen, called the Surplice, which those ought to wear over their common dress, who have time that they can give to any of the services of the Altar and Sanctuary; as shall be shown in the following chapter.

10. The Surplice, by reason that it is white, doth point out the cleanness and purity of chastity; as it is written, *LET THY GARMENTS BE ALWAYS WHITE.*[25]

11. And on account of its name it is a figure of the mortification of the flesh, being called *superpellicium*, surplice, because of old it was wont to be worn *super pellicias tunicas*, over tunics of skin,[26] made of the hide of dead animals; which thing is observed in some churches to this day, and figureth how Adam was clad in such skins after his fall.

In the third place it denoteth innocence; and therefore is it often put on before all other sacred Vestments,[27] because they that are appointed unto the ministry of Divine worship ought to count innocency of life the first of all acts of virtue; according unto that of the Psalmist,[28] *THE INNOCENT AND JUST HAVE CLOVEN UNTO ME.*

12. In the fourth place, by its fulness,[29] it doth meetly express charity, wherefore it is put on over profane and common garments, to mark that *CHARITY COVERETH THE MULTITUDE OF SINS.*[30] Lastly by its shape—for it is wrought in the form of a cross—it representeth our Lord's Passion, and that they who wear it ought to crucify the flesh, with its vices and lusts.[31]

(Notre Dame, Paris, France)

"The surplice, by reason that it is white, doth point out the cleanliness and purity of chastity; as it is written, LET THY GARMENTS BE ALWAYS WHITE."
"...White vestments to some degree lead us to understand the beauty of our souls, which is to say the glory of our immortality which is not openly manifest to us."

CHAPTER II: OF THE AMICE.

1. First I must speak of the six Vestments common to both Bishop and Priest, according to the foregoing.

The Priest or Bishop who is about to celebrate, having washed his hands, taketh the Amice, and covereth his head[1] with it; and this he hath in the stead of the Ephod or Superhumeral, or of the Breastplate of Judgment;[2] nay, even now it may be called the Superhumeral. This signifieth salvation, which is granted through faith; whereof also the Apostle speaketh, saying unto the Ephesians,[3] *PUT ON THE HELMET OF SALVATION.* It figureth also chastity of heart and body, because it goeth round his reins and breast, and covereth them; and though it be put on beneath all other sacred Vestments,[4] yet it is supreme over all, for that chastity ought both to dwell within the heart, and in practice to shine out abroad. Wherefore it is drawn tight over the reins, for there desire doth hold his chief sway. Moreover, by the Amice is signified that a man should be strong in good works, for it spreadeth over the shoulders every way:[5] and it is the shoulders that be strong unto the carrying-out of labour, even as the patriarch Jacob saith, *HE BOWED HIS SHOULDER TO BEAR, AND BECAME A SERVANT UNTO TRIBUTE.*[6]

There be two strings wherewith the Amice is tied across the breast; these are the intention wherewith, and the end whereunto, our works must be informed, that they be not done in the leaven of malice and wickedness, but in the unleavened bread of sincerity and truth.[7] Thus ought not the Priest to live in idleness, but to labour in good works, according to that of the Apostle unto Timothy,[8] *LABOUR AS A GOOD SOLDIER OF JESUS CHRIST.* In certain places a praiseworthy custom holdeth, that a white shift of linen, or a surplice, should be put on over the common dress before the Amice;[9] whereby faith is understood, which ought to be had before all things. Again, the Amice goeth round the mouth of the Chasuble; but of this I will treat in the chapter of the Chasuble.

2. The Amice is drawn tightly round the neck: and by this is symbolised the subjection of the voice, for the neck, wherein is the voice,[10] doth express the act of speaking; it is therefore held bound, as it were, lest falsehood pass unto the tongue therefrom. Yet over the breast and throat it is drawn but loosely, as shall be expounded in the chapter of the Girdle. With the Amice also we cover the head, lest,if we cast the eyes freely every way, we should ponder unlawful things. And the breast and heart are covered with it, for the mind of the Priest ought to be all intent on those

(painting by Bellini, Italy)

Amice/Vestment

"There be two strings wherewith the Amice is tied across the breast; these are the intention wherewith, and the end whereunto, our works must be informed, that they be not done in the leaven of malice and wickedness, but in the unleavened bread of sincerity and truth."

"The Amice is drawn tightly round the neck: and by this is symbolized the subjection of the voice, for the neck, wherein is the voice, doth express the act of speaking; it is therefore held bound, as it were, lest falsehood pass unto the tongue therefrom."

"With the Amice also we cover the head, lest, if we cast the eyes freely every way, we should ponder unlawful things. And the breast and heart are covered with it, for the mind of the Priest ought to be all intent on those things which lie upon him; nor may he in that hour relax his heart unto vanities, or to unrestrained meditation of any worldly thing."

things which lie upon him; nor may he in that hour relax his heart unto vanities, or to the unrestrained meditation of any worldly thing.

3. Further, as touching that which agreeth unto the Head, even Christ, the Amice, which overshadoweth the Priest's head, doth represent that which is described in the Apocalypse,[11] *AND I SAW A MIGHTY ANGEL COME DOWN FROM HEAVEN, CLOTHED WITH A CLOUD*; and in Esaias,[12] *BEHOLD, THE LORD RIDETH UPON A SWIFT CLOUD*. And the world's Saviour, the Son of God, the Angel of Great Counsel, coming to save the world, was veiled as with a cloud, when He hid away His Godhead in Flesh. For *THE HEAD OF EVERY MAN IS CHRIST; AND THE HEAD OF CHRIST IS GOD.*[13]

The Priest's Amice, then, doth symbolise this hiding in Flesh; but it is more particularly set forth by that Veil[14] which the Holy Father draweth over his head, and of which I will speak in the chapter of the Undergirdle. And it is a comely thought that this very thing, which is typified by the shoes of the feet, is also expressed by the veiling of the head—namely, the lying-hid of the Godhead in Flesh, and Its revelation through it. For when *HE WAS KNOWN IN JEWRY, AND HIS NAME WAS GREAT IN ISRAEL*;[15] then *OVER EDOM DID HE CAST OUT HIS SHOE*,[16] and *HIS RIGHTEOUSNESS DID HE OPENLY SHOW IN THE SIGHT OF THE HEATHEN.*[17]

The Amice doth also represent the fold wherewith the Jews veiled the Face of Christ, saying in the twenty-sixth chapter of Matthew,[18] *PROPHESY UNTO US, THOU CHRIST, WHO IS HE THAT SMOTE THEE*?

CHAPTER III: OF THE ALBE

1. After the Amice the Priest putteth on him a shift called the Albe; and this, being exactly fitted to all the limbs of the body, doth show that there must be nought of excess or looseness in the life of the Priest, or in his members. By its whiteness it doth represent purity; for it is written, *LET THY GARMENTS BE ALWAYS WHITE*;[1] and it is made of byssus, or fine linen, for it is written that *FINE LINEN IS THE RIGHTEOUSNESS OF SAINTS*.[2]

2. Now byssus is Egyptian linen. And even as linen, or byssus, doth win by cunning, being beaten with many blows, that whiteness which by nature it hath not; so also man's flesh, being lashed with many stripes[3] in the exercise of good works, hath by grace that pureness allotted unto it which by nature it cannot have. The Priest therefore, according unto the Apostle,[4] must *BUFFET HIS BODY, AND BRING IT INTO SUBJECTION, LEST THAT BY ANY MEANS, WHEN HE HATH PREACHED TO OTHERS, HIMSELF SHOULD BE A CASTAWAY.*

3. The Albe hath also an hood,[5] the profession of chastity; and a lappet, signifying the priestly tongue, which bindeth the forward, and looseth the penitent. Again, this Vestment, which in the ancient priesthood was called a linen coat, and in Greek ποδήρης, or the garment which reacheth unto the feet, is said of old to have been closely-fitting, which pointeth unto the Jews' *SPIRIT OF BONDAGE TO FEAR*.[6] But in the new Priesthood it is ample, according to the spirit of adoption, in that *LIBERTY WHEREWITH CHRIST HATH MADE US FREE*.[7] It hath also golden broidery and devices[8] for ornament wrought with varied work in divers parts, which hinteth of that which the Prophet saith in the Psalms,[9] *UPON THY RIGHT HAND DID STAND THE QUEEN IN A VESTURE OF GOLD, WROUGHT ABOUT WITH DIVERS COLOURS.*

4. The Albe is also drawn tight with a girdle, and this meaneth the strangling of all carnal pleasure, as the Lord saith, *LET YOUR LOINS BE GIRT*.[10]

5. And the sleeves of the Albe, as also of the Tunicle, ought to be tight enow, not too loose, lest they slip away and leave the arms bare; and having apparels at the edges, representing the golden bracelets which by a miracle did enclose in seemly wise the bare arms of Saint Martin[11] while he celebrated Mass. By the Albe also, which covereth the body from above downwards, is typified that hope which cometh unto the Church from above through grace, and through her own merits below. Of this the Apostle

saith,[12] *WE ARE SAVED BY HOPE.* And in that it reacheth unto the feet, it pointeth to perseverance, as was mentioned near the end of the Proeme of this Book.

6. But as touching that which agreeth unto Christ, Which is the Head; the Albe being a linen vestment, and widely differing from the clokes made of the skins of dead animals, wherewith Adam was clad after his fall, doth picture that newness of life which Christ both had and taught, and doth give in Baptism unto us. And concerning this the Apostle[13] saith, *PUT OFF THE OLD MAN WITH HIS DEEDS, AND PUT ON THE NEW MAN, WHICH IS CREATED AFTER GOD.* For in the Transfiguration *HIS FACE DID SHINE AS THE SUN, AND HIS RAIMENT WAS WHITE AS SNOW*;[14] nay, the garments of Christ were ever white and clean, forasmuch as *HE DID NO SIN, NEITHER WAS GUILE FOUND IN HIS MOUTH.*[15]

This Vestment representeth also the white robe,[16] which Herod put on Christ to mock Him.

"By the Albe also, which covereth the body from above downwards, is typified that hope which cometh unto the Church from above through grace, and through her own merits below. Of this the Apostle saith, "WE ARE SAVED BY HOPE." And in that it reacheth unto the feet, it pointeth to perseverance, as was mentioned near the end of the Proeme of this Book."

CHAPTER IV: OF THE ZONE, OR GIRDLE

1. Now the Albe must be girded around the loins of the Priest or Bishop with a Zone or Girdle, called in the Law and by the Greeks *balteus*,[1] lest it flow down and hinder his steps; that no motives may provoke him to relax his chasteness, whereof the Albe is a type. For Girdle doth signify continence, as it is written, *LET YOUR LOINS BE GIRDED ABOUT, AND YOUR LAMPS BURNING IN YOUR HANDS*;[2] for that in the loins lust reigneth, as the Lord sheweth, speaking of the devil, *HIS STRENGTH IS IN HIS LOINS, AND HIS FORCE IS IN THE NAVEL OF HIS BELLY.*[3]

2. On the left side of the Bishop there hangeth down from the Girdle a two-fold Undergirdle,[4] because there be two things whereby Chastity is made strong, and without which it is hardly preserved, to wit, Prayer and Fasting. Thus the Lord saith, *THIS KIND GOETH NOT OUT, BUT BY PRAYER AND FASTING.*[5]

3. With Continence, therefore, ought the loins to be girded, and under-girded with Abstinence; wherefore the Apostle,[6] *STAND HAVING YOUR LOINS GIRT ABOUT WITH TRUTH.* But the Undergirdle, which is called otherwise Perizona or Succingulum, was not found among the Vestments of the Law. For though the Priests of the Law, being girded, must not come at their wives in the time of sacrifice, yet at other times they were free in this matter. But nowadays one girdle is added, for the ministers of to-day must needs have continence, and therefore they must be not only girded, but also under-girded.

4. Wherefore the Undergirdle is twofold, to denote a two-fold chastity: namely, of the mind, as the Girdle, and of the body, as the Undergirdle signifieth. And this latter hangeth, as I have said, from the left side; for as the right is mightier than the left, so is chastity of mind more potent than chastity of body. Wherefore Saint Gregory saith, 'We gird our loins, when we restrain the lust of the flesh through continence.'

5. The Girdle doth also fitly designate temperance. (Of the Undergirdle I have spoken also in the Proeme[7] of this Book.) And mark that (as hath been already said) the breast and throat are but loosely held bound by the Amice, because their motions are not under our power. Elias did sooner shut up heaven when he prayed that it might not rain, than his own wrath, when he desired vengeance for the death of the Prophets.[8] The tongue, too, dwelleth in moisture and dampness, and is made easily to slip, even as the Prince of the Apostles did at the word of a damsel deny his Master. But

by the Girdle the reins are bound strongly and tightly, that we may buffet the body and bring it into servitude, and may bridle the motions of lust.[9]

6. As touching that which agreeth unto the Head, even Christ, the priestly Girdle is a figure of that whereof the Apostle John[10] speaketh: *AND I TURNED, AND SAW ONE LIKE UNTO THE SON OF MAN, GIRT ABOUT THE PAPS WITH A GOLDEN GIRDLE*. By a 'golden girdle' is intended the perfect love of Christ, called by the Apostle[11] the *LOVE OF CHRIST WHICH PASSETH KNOWLEDGE*, burning within the heart, and shining forth in works. And its Undergirdle doth represent that which Esaias[12] did prophesy, speaking of Christ, *AND RIGHTEOUSNESS SHALL BE THE GIRDLE OF HIS LOINS, AND FAITHFULNESS THE GIRDLE OF HIS REINS*. For again, *THE RIGHTEOUS LORD LOVETH RIGHTEOUSNESS: HIS COUNTENANCE WILL BEHOLD THE THING THAT IS JUST.*[13] And, *THE LORD IS RIGHTEOUS IN ALL HIS WORKS.*[14] The two ends of it are the two natural precepts of the righteousness which Christ wrought and taught, to wit, 'Do not unto others as ye would not have them do unto you, but as ye would that men should do unto you, do ye also unto them.'[15] It doth therefore represent Righteousness, having two arms joined tightly together, that is, to refuse evil and to do good.

The Girdle signifieth also the scourge, with which Pilate did scourge Jesus.[16]

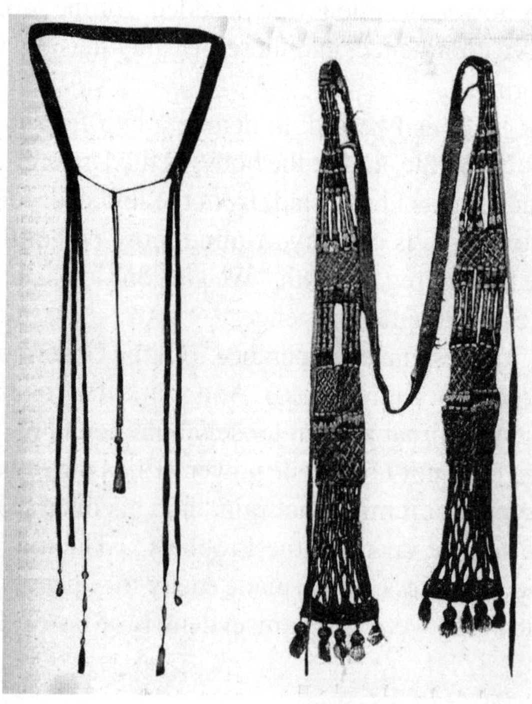

"And its Undergirdle doth represent that which Esaias did prophesy, speaking of Christ, 'AND RIGHTEOUSNESS SHALL BE THE GIRDLE OF HIS LOINS, AND FAITHFULNESS THE GIRDLE OF HIS REINS.'"

CHAPTER V: OF THE STOLE

1. After the Girdle the Priest doth put upon his neck the Orarium,[1] or Stole, which is a type of the light yoke of Christ, or of the yoke of His precepts, to show that he hath taken the Lord's yoke upon him. This he doth kiss in putting it on and off, to mark the consent and desire wherewith he submitteth himself to that yoke. And it falleth down from the neck before, adorning both the right side and the left; for *BY THE ARMOUR OF RIGHTEOUSNESS ON THE RIGHT HAND AND ON THE LEFT,*[2] that is, in weal and woe, the Priest ought to be armed, that he be neither broken by misfortunes nor lifted up by well-being. Wherefore when the Priest receiveth the Stole in Holy Order, the Bishop saith[3] unto him, 'Receive the yoke of God, *FOR HIS YOKE IS SWEET, AND HIS BURTHEN IS LIGHT;*' that is, sweet in well-being,and in misfortune light.

2. The Stole reacheth down to the knees, which are bent by us as showing that we must be humble and gentle of heart. It signifieth also patience, whereof it is written, *YE HAVE NEED OF PATIENCE, THAT YE MIGHT RECEIVE THE PROMISE;*[4] and again, *IN YOUR PATIENCE YE SHALL POSSESS YOUR SOULS.*[5] Hence it ariseth that the Stole is tied in certain knots on the right and on the left, with the Zone or Girdle, for virtue doth company with virtue and succoureth it, lest by some impulse temptation be stirred up; which showeth also that both in things good and in things evil the yoke of Christ ought patiently to be borne, in the bond of charity.[6] But unto the foregoing some Bishops do add these words, 'May the Lord clothe thee with the Stole of innocence';[7] and this hath respect unto the Stole in its olden shape,[8] which was typical of innocence.

3. Again, the Stole is crossed[9] over from the left shoulder of the Priest unto his right side, while he is ordained, for obedience, taking its beginning from the active life through the love of his neighbour, doth pass over into the contemplative life through the love of God. The length of the Stole meaneth perseverance, and its two ends hanging down are prudence and temperance; thus the Apostle saith unto Titus,[10] *LET US LIVE SOBERLY, RIGHTEOUSLY, AND GODLY, IN THIS PRESENT WORLD.* But according to a decree of the Council of Braga,[11] the Priest ought with one and the same Stole, disposing it equally round his neck and both his shoulders, to trace and make ready[12] on his breast the sign of the Cross, as one who is bidden to live between good and evil fortunes, yet is not dismayed; that men may ever mark him surrounded with the adornment of virtue upon either shoulder. And whoso shall do otherwise, saith the decree, he

"The Stole is a type of the light yoke of Christ, or the yoke of His precepts, to show that he hath taken the Lord's yoke upon him. This he doth kiss in putting it on and off, to mark the consent and desire wherewith he submitteth himself to that yoke."

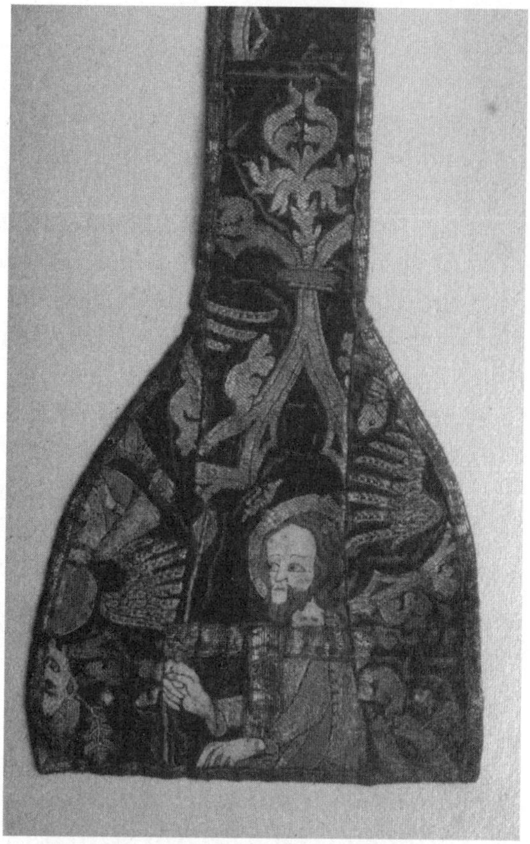

St. Cuthbert's Maniple (10th Century)

St. Cuthbert's Maniple (10th Century)

"As an example of the high standard attained in Anglo-Saxon needlecraft we may take the celebrated stole and maniple, over a thousand years old, found in the coffin of St. Cuthbert (died 687) at Durham in 1827."

shall be duly liable to excommunication. Unless indeed one might deem this decree to have been repealed by the general custom of the Church to the contrary;[13] for it is not everywhere that the two arms of the Stole are thus disposed upon the breast in the form of a cross. He beareth, then, the Cross on his breast, the while in his heart he taketh pattern by the Passion of Christ, Whose servant he is.

4. The Stole, as I have said, is at once a yoke and a burthen. It is a yoke, that is, unto the Priest, and a burthen unto the Deacon; and by reason of this the Priest weareth it around his neck, but the Deacon over his left shoulder. For on the neck a yoke is worn, but a burthen is carried upon the shoulder. And if thou read in Leviticus, thou wilt see that the Levites only were appointed unto the bearing of the burthens. Unto the Deacon the Stole signifieth also a yoke, as I have shewn in another Book.[14] And it is placed upon his left shoulder, because it is meet that temporal things should be subject unto things spiritual; or else because it behoveth the right shoulder of the Deacon to be unencumbered, to the end that he may go hither and thither the more freely in the service of the Priest; whereof also I have already treated, in that place aforesaid.

5. It is girt round at the loins, that the Priest may be strong and active against the onslaughts of lust. But sometimes its forepart is folded over the left arm only; and this is drawn from the Priests of the Law, who while they sacrificed used to turn back the ends of the girdle over their shoulders.[15] But upon the Bishop or Priest it falleth down before on either side evenly, because Christ, Whose likeness they bear, and Who kept an even mind in weal and woe—which are denoted by right and left—did desire to lead the dwellers of the earth unto heavenly things, and did ever bear this thought before the eyes of His mind.

6. The Stole is also called Orarium, the Praying-Vestment;[16] because, whereas it is lawful to baptise, to confirm, and to do many other things which stand in prayer, without the other Vestments, yet without the Stole it is lawful to do none of these things, save when driven by urgent need. At the Council of Tribur[17] it was appointed that Priests should not walk, save when vested with the Stole.

It is to be noted, that the Stole was originally a white garment flowing down to the feet, such as the Patriarchs wore before the Law. This was put on by firstborn sons when they received their father's blessing; on which occasions they offered victims unto God, as though they had been priests. But when the Albe began to be worn, the Stole was altared into the form of a collar. For by the first Stole was understood innocence, which was the estate of the first man. But when he lost his innocence through sin, it needed that he should recover it as it were through the Fatted Calf. It remaineth, then, that we, who fell through disobedience, should by obedience rise up again; wherefore we do rightly bow our necks unto the collar of obedience, that we may win back the robe of innocence.[18] For by the Stole which now we wear, we do accept the obedience of the Gospel of the Crucified.

7. As touching that which agreeth unto the Head, even Christ, the Stole, as lying over the Amice on the Priest's neck, doth signify that obedience and servitude which the Lord of all things underwent in order to the salvation of His own. For He, *BEING IN THE FORM OF GOD, THOUGHT IT NOT ROBBERY TO BE EQUAL WITH GOD; BUT MADE HIMSELF OF NO REPUTATION, AND TOOK UPON HIM THE FORM OF A SERVANT, AND BECAME OBEDIENT UNTO DEATH, EVEN THE DEATH OF THE CROSS.*[19] Yet did He neither inherit originally, nor commit actually, aught worthy of death.

The Stole is also a figure of the band, wherewith Jesus was tied to the column.

8. It hath been appointed[20] in the Canons, that Subdeacons, Readers, and Singing-Men may not wear Stoles.

Winchester Cathedral Bible (1160 - 1175 C.E.,)

CHAPTER VI: OF THE MANIPLE[1]

1. Forasmuch as there is a weariness which often creepeth upon minds well disposed and had in hand for Divine Worship, rendering them slumberous with a kind of sluggishness, as saith the Psalmist,[2] *MY SOUL MELTETH AWAY FOR VERY HEAVINESS*; therefore in the left hand of the minister who approacheth unto the service of the Altar is placed a Maniple, which is also called a Sudarium; as that he may wipe away the sweats of his mind and shake off his heart's heaviness, keeping the watch of good works and driving weariness and slumber from him. For the Maniple is a figure of good works and watchfulness, whereof the Lord saith, *WATCH, FOR YE KNOW NOT THE HOUR WHEREIN THE SON OF MAN COMETH;*[3] and Spouse in the Canticles,[4] *I SLEEP, BUT MINE HEART WAKETH.* As a Sudarium it also denoteth penitence, wherewith the stain of daily indulgence and the weariness of worldly life are wiped away; as it is said, *MY SOUL MELTETH AWAY FOR VERY HEAVINESS;*[5] for the knowledge of sins, and the weakness of the flesh, are a weariness unto the soul.

The Maniple signifieth also the reward of future blessings. Thus in certain places they wear this Vestment, whose name signifieth also a sheaf,[6] on Festivals whensoever Albes are used, to show that in that life each one shall receive his due reward; for *THEY SHALL COME AGAIN WITH JOY, BRINGING THEIR SHEAVES WITH THEM.*[7]

The Sudarium of the Subdeacon is made greater than that of the Priest, for where there is greater transgression, there is required more fruit of repentance.[8] But of the Sudarium I will speak again.

2. The Ministers wear the Maniple upon the left arm, to show that they must be bound up as touching earthly things, but untrammelled unto heavenly. They of old were not thus bound, for they served God, not only for spiritual, but also for temporal ends. But we in this life, whereof the left hand is a type, do undergo the irksomeness as it were of much sweating, that is, of pleasure, and other excesses of the mind. The Maniple, hanging upon the left arm, denoteth also the faith, which in this life we must have.

3. The use of the Maniple was not taken from Aaron, but from the ancient Fathers of the Church; as it is written in the Martyrology of Bede, that Arsenius[9] did ever bear a kerchief in his bosom or his hand, to wipe away the abundance of his tears. The holy Fathers also, while they handled the sacred things and celebrated the Sacraments, had little napkins or hand-

Bishop Johannes

(Lubeck, 1350 C.E.)

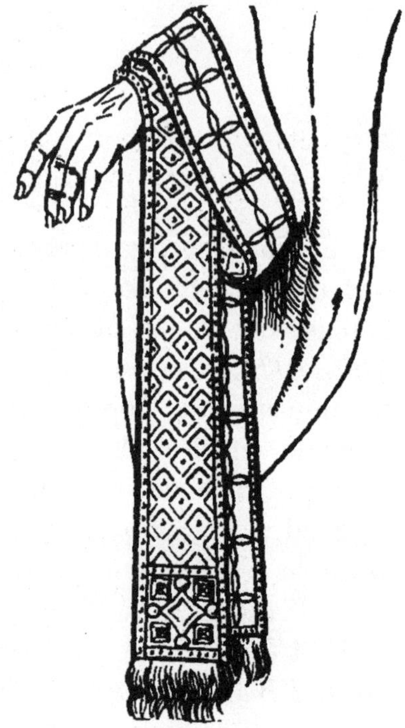

"The ministers wear the Maniple upon the left arm, to show that they must be bound up as touching earthly things, but untrammeled unto heavenly."

"For the maniple is a figure of good works and watchfulness, whereof the Lord saith, 'WATCH, FOR YE KNOW NOT THE HOUR WHEREIN THE SON OF MAN COMETH,' and Spouse in the Canticles, 'I SLEEP, BUT MINE HEART WAKETH.' As a Sudarium, it also denoteth pentinence, wherewith the stain of daily indulgence and the weariness of worldly life are wiped away..."

kerchiefs on their hands, sometimes to wipe their hands, and sometimes for covering or reverently handling the things of God.

4. As touching that which agreeth unto the Head,[10] even Christ, the wearing of the Maniple on the left hand denoteth this, that Christ won His Prize while in the way; for, as I have said, the Maniple signifieth a prize, as in that Scripture, *THEY SHALL COME AGAIN WITH JOY, BRINGING THEIR SHEAVES WITH THEM*; and the left hand is this present life, as it is written, *HIS LEFT HAND IS UNDER MY HEAD, AND HIS RIGHT HAND DOTH EMBRACE ME.*[11] For Christ did enjoy His reward at one and the same time that He was earning it; He enjoyed it in His own land, and did merit it on His way thither, compassing His prize the while he ran His course, in that He was at once in His native land and on the way to it: as he said, *NO MAN HATH ASCENDED UP TO HEAVEN, BUT HE THAT CAME DOWN FROM HEAVEN, EVEN THE SON OF MAN WHICH IS IN HEAVEN.*[12]

5. The Maniple is also a figure of the rope with which Jesus was bound, after that He was taken by the Jews, as saith Saint John,[13] *THEY TOOK HIM, AND BOUND HIM.*

This Vestment is wont to be put upon the Holy Father after the Chasuble,[14] and there be many Bishops beside, who observe this.

6. It is to be noted, that the Deacon and Subdeacon, in assisting the Bishop to put on the Sacred Vestments, wear not the Maniple; first, that they may do their parts with the more ease and freedom; and secondly because in the discharge of such a duty they ought not to look for temporal guerdon; which latter is one of the meanings of the Maniple, as I have shown from that of the Psalmist, *THEY SHALL COME AGAIN WITH JOY, BRINGING THEIR SHEAVES WITH THEM.* And while the Bishop putteth the Vestments on and off, the Deacon standeth at his right, and the Subdeacon at his left; for the Deacon, by virtue of his Order, taketh that mightier and higher place than the Subdeacon, which is signified by the right hand.

CHAPTER VII: OF THE CHASUBLE

1. Lastly, over all the Vestments the Priest putteth on the Chasuble,[1] which is being interpreted a 'little cottage.' It is called by the Greeks the Planet, from *Plane*, a wandering, for that its border wandereth[2] wide as it is raised over the arms, signifying Charity, without which the Priest is as a *SOUNDING BRASS, OR AS A TINKLING CYMBAL.*[3] For as Charity covereth *THE MULTITUDE OF SINS,*[4] and containeth all the commandments of the Law and the Prophets, and is called by the Apostle,[5] *THE FULFILLING OF THE LAW*; so also this Vestment wandereth over all, and doth enclose and contain all other Vestments within itself.[6]

2. Of charity also the Apostle saith,[7] *YET SHOW I UNTO YOU A MORE EXCELLENT WAY. THOUGH I SPEAK WITH THE TONGUES OF MEN AND OF ANGELS, AND HAVE NOT CHARITY, I AM NOTHING.* And again, *THOUGH I HAVE ALL FAITH, SO THAT I COULD REMOVE MOUNTAINS, AND HAVE NOT CHARITY, I AM NOTHING.*[8] The Chasuble, moreover, is the Wedding-Garment spoken of by the Lord in the Gospel,[9] *FRIEND, HOW CAMEST THOU IN HITHER, NOT HAVING ON A WEDDING-GARMENT*? Without this, the Priest may never discharge his office, for it beseemeth him ever to abide in the bond of charity.

The Amice goeth round the mouth of the Chasuble, which meaneth that good works ought always to have charity for their source and end.[10] For *THE END OF THE COMMANDMENT IS CHARITY OUT OF A PURE HEART, AND OF A GOOD CONSCIENCE, AND OF FAITH UNFEIGNED.*[11] And the dividing of the Chasuble into two parts, back and fore, when the Priest extendeth his hands, signifieth the two arms of charity, wherewith it reacheth unto God, and to his neighbour, as in that Scripture,[12] *THOU SHALT LOVE THE LORD THY GOD, AND THY NEIGHBOUR AS THYSELF; ON THESE TWO COMMANDMENTS HANG ALL THE LAW AND THE PROPHETS.* Again, the wideness of the Chasuble is a figure of the breadth of Charity, which reacheth even as far as our enemies; whence it is written, *THY COMMANDMENT IS EXCEEDING BROAD.*[13]

3. The Chasuble hath two folds, right and left;[14] these be the two precepts of charity, the love of God, and the love of his neighbour. Also it is folded double across the breast,[15] which meaneth the heart, and between the shoulders, which are good works; in these parts, I say, the Chasuble is made to double upon itself, for we ought so to show good deeds unto our

neighbour outwardly, that we may keep the same within, whole in the heart before God. For we need to have charity in our heart, and in our work; both within and without. It is doubled before the breast, again, because by charity are gotten goodwill and holy thought; and between the shoulders, because by charity are borne untoward dealings of neighbours and adversaries. And it is lifted up at the arms, as when we work the good works of love: at the right arm, as when we *DO GOOD UNTO THEM WHO ARE OF THE HOUSEHOLD OF FAITH*;[16] and at the left, as when our righteous dealings reach even unto our enemies.

4. Furthermore, over the arms it maketh three folds;[17] on the right arm, as when we succour the faithful, monks, clergy, and laity; and on the left, as when we minister to the needs of unbelievers, that is, bad Christians, Jews, and paynim. For well are works of righteousness symbolised by the Chasuble, according unto this Scripture,[18] *LET THY PRIESTS BE CLOTHED WITH RIGHTEOUSNESS.* The Priest may not put off his Chasuble while he performeth his office; for the Lord commandeth in the twenty-first chapter of Leviticus,[19] that *HE SHALL NOT GO OUT OF THE SANCTUARY,* that is, out of holy things or commandments.

Further, as touching that which agreeth unto the Head, even Christ, the Chasuble of the Great Priest is the Catholic Church, concerning which the Apostle[20] saith, *AS MANY OF YOU AS HAVE BEEN BAPTISED INTO CHRIST HAVE PUT ON CHRIST.* This is that Vestment of Aaron, unto whose skirt the ointment ran down: *IT RAN DOWN FROM HIS HEAD UNTO HIS BEARD, AND FROM HIS BEARD UNTO THE SKIRTS OF HIS CLOTHING IT RAN DOWN.*[21] For *OF THE FULNESS OF HIS SPIRIT HAVE WE ALL RECEIVED,*[22] first the Apostles, then they that are come after them.

5. The Chasuble is of one piece, and whole, and is hemmed on every side, which signifieth the unity and wholeness of the Faith. Yet when the Priest spreadeth out his hands, it is in a manner divided in two parts, back and fore; and this denoteth the ancient Church, which went before the Passion of Christ, and the new which followeth it; for *THE MULTITUDES THAT WENT BEFORE, AND THAT FOLLOWED, CRIED, SAYING, HOSANNA TO THE SON OF DAVID: BLESSED IS HE THAT COMETH IN THE NAME OF THE LORD.*[23]

This Vestment representeth also the purple robe with which the soldiers encompassed Christ, as saith John in the nineteenth chapter.[24]

(Augustinian priory at Ivychrurch, Wiltshire, 1160 C.E.)

Orphery embroidered with rich gold design and sometimes set with precious stones, used to decorate vestments with the exception of the amice.

Vicar in full vestments (1300's)

Chasuble (Venice, 15th Century)

Medieval Chasuble

Medieval Chasuble

Medieval Chasuble

"For as Charity covereth THE MULTITUDE OF SINS, and containeth all the commandments of the Law and the Prophets, and is called by the Apostle, THE FULFILLING OF THE LAW; so also this Vestment wandereth over all, and doth enclose and contain all other Vestments within itself."

Chasuble (The Far East, 1780)

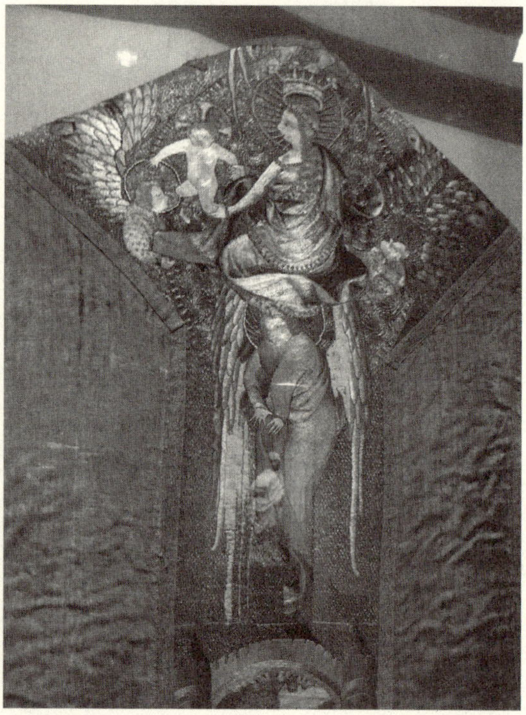
Chasuble (Venice, 15th Century)

Chasuble and Dalmatic (Peru, 19th Century)

"The Chasuble, morever, is the Wedding-Garment spoken of by the Lord in the Gospel, FRIEND, HOW CAMEST THOU IN HITHER, NOT HAVING ON A WEDDING-GARMENT? Without this, the Priest may never discharge his office, for it beseemth him ever to abide in the bond of charity."

"Again, the wideness of the Chasuble is a figure of the breadth of Charity, which reacheth even as far as our enemies; whence it is written, THY COMMANDMENT IS EXCEEDING BROAD."

CHAPTER VIII: OF THE BUSKINS AND SANDALS

1. In the foregoing we have spoken of the six Vestments common to both Bishops and Priests. It now remaineth to treat of the nine that are peculiar to the Bishop. And first let us consider the Buskins and Sandals.

The vesting of the feet taketh not its beginning from Aaron's line of Priests, for they lived in Jewry, and therefore had no need thereof; but from the Apostles, unto whom it was said, *GO YE AND TEACH ALL NATIONS.*[1] Unless indeed one might say that the Buskins and Sandals take the place of the breeches of the ancient Priest.

2. The Bishop, then, being about to celebrate, while the five appointed Psalms[2] are said, putteth on the Buskins and Sandals, the *PREPARATION OF THE GOSPEL OF PEACE.*[3] These are they which for beauty the Prophet did laud, saying, *HOW BEAUTIFUL ARE THE FEET OF THEM THAT BRING GOOD TIDINGS OF PEACE, THAT PUBLISH GOOD TIDINGS OF GOOD!*[4] And the Apostle, saying unto the Ephesians, *HAVING YOUR FEET SHOD WITH THE PREPARATION OF THE GOSPEL OF PEACE.*[5] And in the Gospel we read that the Lord sent His disciples forth shod with sandals[6]—shod indeed, that is, with the *PREPARATION OF THE GOSPEL OF PEACE*; for if they had not been thus shod, how could they have trodden upon serpents and scorpions?[7]

3. Let Bishops take thought, therefore, why they are thus shod, and let them copy the example of those, whose sandals they copy. For the feet are a fit type of the affections; wherefore they ought to have sandals, so to speak, upon their affections and desires, that they be not stained with the dust of things earthly or temporal.

4. By these Sandals we do also meetly understand a check, put upon the feet, lest they hasten unto forbidden things. And whereas a man's affections become more readily tainted and marred in time of prosperity, which is signified by the right hand, than in time of adversity, which is exprest by the left, the Bishop doth put the sandal on his right foot first, to show that one ought to run the quicker, to meet the greater danger.

But before the Sandals are put on the feet, they are clad in Buskins,[8] reaching so far as the knee and there girt round, for that the preacher ought to *MAKE STRAIGHT PATHS FOR HIS FEET, AND CONFIRM THE FEEBLE KNEES;*[9] for *HE THAT SHALL DO AND TEACH THESE COMMANDMENTS, THE SAME SHALL BE CALLED THE GREATEST IN THE KINGDOM OF HEAVEN.*[10] And the Buskins, being of blue,[11] the colour of the firmament, denote that his feet—that is, his affections—must be heavenly, and strong, that he halt not; but that he may *SAY TO THEM THAT ARE OF A FEARFUL HEART, BE STRONG.*[12]

5. After these, his feet are vested in the Sandals,[13] which are so called from the plant of that name, or from sandarach,[14] wherewith they are coloured. Now these have an entire sole underneath, but on the top there is latticed hide; because the steps of the Preacher ought to be guarded from beneath, lest they be defiled with earthly things, as saith the Lord, *SHAKE OFF THE DUST OF YOUR FEET*;[15] but they must be open above, that they may be unveiled unto the knowledge of heavenly mysteries, according unto that of the Psalmist,[16] *OPEN THOU MINE EYES, THAT I MAY SEE THE WONDROUS THINGS OF THY LAW.* They are open on the top, again, because we ought to have hearts ever uplifted unto God, and our minds' eyes open unto those things which be above: and solid beneath, because we must keep a mind impervious amid earthly things, and seek the blessing, not of Esau, which is earthly, but of Jacob, which is in the heavens.

6. The Sandals again, being open in certain places and closed in others, signify that the preaching of the Gospel ought neither to be revealed unto all, nor hid from all, as it is written, *UNTO YOU IT IS GIVEN TO KNOW THE MYSTERIES OF THE KINGDOM OF GOD, BUT UNTO OTHERS IN PARABLES.*[17] And *GIVE NOT THAT WHICH IS HOLY UNTO THE DOGS, NEITHER CAST YE YOUR PEARLS BEFORE SWINE.*[18]

7. The inner part of the Sandals is sometimes made of white leather, for it needeth to have a clean intention, and a conscience pure before God; and without there is a dark appearance, because the life of the preacher seemeth dark and mean in worldly eyes, by reason of the trials of this world. Sometimes too they are red, to signify the spirit of martyrdom; and at other times they are variegated with divers colours, the manifold virtues wherewith we need to be adorned.

8. A latchet, which is separate from the leather, goeth up over the foot, and figureth the tongues of those who bear good testimony unto the preacher, but who are nevertheless separate in a manner from the conversation of spiritual men. In the second place, this latchet is itself the tongue of the spiritual, which did induct the preacher into the office of preaching. Thirdly, it denoteth also the tongue of the preacher himself. The line which runneth from this latchet through the midst of the Sandal unto the end thereof, is Evangelical Perfection; and the lines which come forth from either side, and which at the end of the Sandal run into that middle line and there have an end, are a figure of the Law and the Prophets, which be ratified in the Gospel, and there find the end of their being. The upper part

of the Sandal, into which the foot is placed, is joined together with divers strings, that its two sides slip not away nor be parted, coming unfastened the one from the other; and this is to show that the Preacher ought to bind himself with divers virtues, or truths of Scripture, that his inner part may not be disjoined from that which shineth without, in the sight of the Most High. Also the very fastening of the Sandals signifieth that the prelate, who hath to go hither and thither, ought to make sure his mind's steps, the while he goeth to and fro amid the throng.

9. The drawing of the thongs this way and that with the hands, in binding and making fast the Sandals, signifieth that the Priest ought to walk with so firm a step, that he may be a burden unto none nor faint in the way of his ministry. For it is in vain if he run fast who fainteth or ever he reacheth the goal; inasmuch as the Sandals do mystically represent the race of the Preacher. But sometimes they are not fastened, for that Christ's Incarnation is in some measure open unto human understanding, as we may understand the being wrapt in garments, or placed in an enclosure. Sometimes, again, the cost of the thongs is over and above that of the Sandals, as it is written, *WHATSOEVER THOU SPENDEST MORE, WHEN I COME AGAIN I WILL REPAY THEE.*[19]

It may also be said that the Buskins are a type of that washing, of which the Lord said, *HE THAT IS BATHED NEEDETH NOT SAVE TO WASH HIS FEET.*[20] But, for that cleanness of heart sufficeth not without patience in persecution, they have also stripes of red,[21] which are a type of martyrdom. Thus he that hath cleanness in his heart, and patience, an it so needeth, in his will, shall come secure unto the office of preaching, which the apostolic Sandals signify.

10. Further, as touching that which agreeth unto the Head, even Christ, the Sandals have another meaning. The Bishop, who in the service of the Altar representeth the Person of Christ his Head, Whose member he is; the while he putteth the Sandals on his feet, doth suggest the Lord putting on those Sandals of the Incarnation, whereof He saith in the Psalms,[22] *OVER EDOM WILL I CAST OUT MY SHOE*, that is, 'among the nations will I make known my Incarnation.' For the Godhead came unto us as it were sandaled, that for us the Son of God might discharge the Priestly office. And by the latchets wherewith the Sandals are fastened upon the feet, we do understand that same mystery which John the Baptist saw in the sandal-strings, when he said, *WHOSE SHOE'S LATCHET I AM NOT WORTHY TO UNLOOSE:*[23] that is, the unspeakable union and indissoluble bond of flesh whereby the Godhead of the Word did join itself with humnanity of ours. Moreover, the feet are united with the Sandals by the mediation of

the Buskins, which are worn between; and this pictureth the union of the Human Soul with the Godhead, through the mean of Flesh. For as the foot beareth up the body, even so the Godhead governeth the world.[24] Thus the Psalmist[25] saith, *FALL DOWN BEFORE HIS FOOTSTOOL, FOR HE IS HOLY.*

11. According to a decree of Gregory,[26] Deacons may not wear 'compagi,' that is, Sandals, nor 'maniples,' that is, episcopal shoes, without special license of the Apostolic See. Formerly they did wear these, because it was their duty to go hither and thither in attendance. But nowadays neither Deacons nor Priests wear these Vestments, but Bishops only, that by this diversity of their Sandals the distinction of their office may be marked; and beside, they have to go abroad amongst the people, whereas it is the duty of the Priest to offer the sacrifices of the Lord. Yet the clerics of the Roman Church by the indulgence of Constantine, Emperor, might wear shoes with socks[27] of white linen.

(English, 1200)

(11th Century)

(12th Century)

(13th Century)

"By these Sandals we do also meetly understand a check, put upon the feet, lest they hasten unto forbidden things."

CHAPTER IX: OF THE UNDERGIRDLE AND VEIL

1. As touching the Undergirdle, I will add nought further to such as I have already said in the treating of the Zone or Girdle, in the Proeme[1] of this Book.

The Bishop of Rome after the Albe and Girdle putteth on the Orale,[2] a Vestment of fine stuff, which after the manner of a veil he placeth upon his head, and foldeth it over his shoulders and before his breast; following the use of the Priest of the Law, who after the broidered coat and girdle did put on the ephod or superhumeral, whose place the Amice doth now take.

2. The aforesaid Bishop putteth on also a certain Cross,[3] fastened to a fine chain, which he hangeth around his neck, disposing the Cross before his breast. For the High Priest of the Law did wear a golden plate upon his forehead,[4] in the stead of which this High Priest, the Bishop, doth wear the Cross upon his breast; and so the golden plate yieldeth place unto the Sign of the Cross. For the mystery[5] which the golden plate enshrined in its Four Letters, hath been set forth in four arms by the Sign of the Cross; as saith the Apostle,[6] *THAT YE MAY BE ABLE TO COMPREHEND WITH ALL SAINTS WHAT IS THE BREADTH, AND LENGTH, AND DEPTH, AND HEIGHT.* Wherefore that holy thing which he then did bear in the plate upon his brow, his successor doth now hide within his heart; for *WITH THE HEART MAN BELIEVETH UNTO RIGHTEOUSNESS, AND WITH THE MOUTH CONFESSION IS MADE UNTO SALVATION.*[7] And according to Hierome, 'the Blood of the Gospel is more precious than the gold of the Law.' He placeth the Cross before his breast, again, for the shewing forth of that which the Apostle saith, *GLORIFY GOD AND BEAR HIM IN YOUR BODY.*[8] And when he putteth the Cross on himself, and when he taketh it off, he kisseth it, for that he doth believe and confess Christ's Passion, whereof it is the sign, and unto whose representation in the Office of the Math he maketh him ready.

CHAPTER X: OF THE TUNIC

1. After the Stole put on, the Bishop is arrayed in the Tunic, which is otherwise called Subtile,[1] and in the Law, Poderes, that is, the garment which reacheth unto the feet. And this signifieth Perseverance. Thus Joseph is described as having worn such a garment amongst his brethren.[2] For when the other virtues run in the race, Perseverance only receiveth the prize, as it is written, *HE THAT PERSEVERETH UNTO THE END, THE SAME SHALL BE SAVED*;[3] and One teacheth, *BE THOU FAITHFUL UNTO DEATH, AND I WILL GIVE THEE A CROWN OF LIFE*.[4] Again, he putteth on the Tunic after the Albe, because by the Albe is figured the chastening of the flesh, while the Tunic is the symbol of those inner virtues, which the perfect need alway to have. The Tunic is not girded, because by reason of its shape it hindereth not the steps: so also the virtues that are set forth by it afford a free walk in the contemplation of God. Yet is the Albe girded, as I have said in the chapter which treateth of the Girdle.

2. In the Old Testament there were two tunics, the tunic of fine linen, and the blue tunic.[5] And at this day also certain Bishops use two Tunics,[6] to show that it beseemeth them to have knowledge of both Testaments, that they may know how to bring out of the Lord's treasure things new and old;[7] or that they may shew themselves that they are both Deacons and Priests. Besides, each of the Tunics doth bear his own proper signification. The white Tunic,[8] which is of fine linen, signifieth Chastity, as may be gathered from what hath been said in the chapter of the Albe.[9] This former Tunic, too, if it be of silk, denoteth Chastity and Humility; for silk taketh its beginning from worms, which are created without intercourse.

3. The second Tunic ought to be blue, as in olden days it was of the colour of the jacinth, which followeth in its hue the sereneness of the sky; wherefore it is a figure of the Saints with their heavenly thoughts and lives, and of celestial thought and conversation. For as that precious stone, the jacinth, doth change his colour with the changes of the sky, being bright when the firmament is bright, and pale beneath a darkling heaven; even so in spiritual figure ought the Bishop to *REJOICE WITH THEM THAT DO REJOICE, AND WEEP WITH THEM THAT WEEP*.[10] Yet if the Tunic be of any other colour, it beareth accordingly some other meaning.

4. And the Bishop weareth the one Tunic beneath the other, to shew that as that which is hid may not be seen of the people, but is known to the clergy alone, so also that measure of lofty virtues pictured by it, which the

perfect man ought ever to possess, may not be open to the eyes of all, but only unto the higher orders, and unto them that are perfect.

5. Furthermore, as touching that which agreeth unto the Head, even Christ, this Vestment in the ancient Priesthood was of blue, and had for its fringe pomegranates and golden bells hanging from its lower hem, that the High Priest might walk all in music;[11] as shall be said in the chapter of the Vestments of the Law.[12] And this giveth an hint of the heavenly doctrine of the Christ, Whereof all have taken knowledge; unto Whom it was said by the Prophet,[13] *O THOU WHO TELLEST GOOD TIDINGS TO SION, GET THEE UP INTO THE HIGH MOUNTAIN.* More than all, however, had the Weaver of the doctrine of the Gospel this Tunic, the Wisdom of God, Jesus Christ, and gave it unto His Apostles; For *ALL THINGS,* said He, *WHICH I HAVE HEARD OF MY FATHER, I HAVE MADE KNOWN UNTO YOU.*[14] This also was the signification of that Tunic of the Lord, which the soldiers would not rend, for that it was *WITHOUT SEAM, WOVEN FROM THE TOP THROUGHOUT*[15]—as though they thought the Lord's loss would be great; the which sheweth how great a loss they cause who strive to rend with their heresies the doctrines of the Gospel.

The Subdeacon, also, weareth the Tunic, as shall be shewn in the following chapter.

(12th Century)

"Again, he putteth on the Tunic after the Albe, because the Albe is figured the chastening of the flesh, while the Tunic is the symbol of those inner virtues, which the perfect need always to have."

CHAPTER XI: OF THE DALMATIC

1. The Bishop, immediately after the Tunic, vesteth him in the Dalmatic, according to the institution of Silvester, Pope.[1] This is believed to have been borrowed from the Lord's seamless coat, and from the Colobium of the Apostles. Now the Colobium[2] is a dress without sleeves, such as is now seen in the cowl[3] of a monk. But Pope Silvester changed it into the Dalmatic, by adding broad sleeves, and ordered it to be worn at the Sacrifice of the Altar.[4]

2. Now the Dalmatic is so called, because it was devised[5] in Dalmatia, after all other priestly Vestments. By its shape it signifieth liberality, for it hath large sleeves and long. For according to the Apostle[6] it beseemeth that a Bishop should be *NOT GREEDY OF FILTHY LUCRE, BUT GIVEN TO HOSPITALITY*; wherefore he must not have a hand closed from giving and stretch out to receive; but must do that which the Prophet doth advise, *BREAK THY BREAD UNTO THE HUNGRY, AND BRING THE POOR THAT ARE CAST OUT TO THINE HOUSE.*[7] And it is on this account, doubtless, that Deacons in especial do wear Dalmatics, for that they chiefly were appointed by the Apostles unto the office of serving tables.

3. Further, the Deacon's Dalmatic hath fuller sleeves than the Tunicle of the Subdeacon, because he himself ought to have a charity ampler than the other, by reason of his greater gift. But the Dalmatic of the Bishop hath wider sleeves than that of the Deacon, to shew that the former is more unhindered, and hath nought that may hold back his hand; for upon heavenly things he must lavish all, and his charity must reach even unto his adversaries. But the Tunicle of the Subdeacon, the Dalmatic of the Deacon, and the Chasuble of the Priest, do all follow in the stead of the blue Tunic, which was of the colour of the heaven; in token that all the ministers of the Altar ought to live an heavenly life, according unto higher or lower rank, which are marked by the breadth or straitness of the sleeves of the Dalmatic and Tunicle respectively, as hath been said before.

4. The Priest, because he ought to be the least hindered as touching heavenly things, weareth not these Vestments, nor indeed aught else whereby the arms may be straitened. But the Bishop weareth at once the Dalmatic, and the Tunic, and the Vestments of all Orders, to shew that he containeth all Orders in himself perfectly, as who bestoweth them all upon other. These the lesser ministers bestow not, and therefore wear not the Vestments that figure them, but for them one sufficeth, to signify the heavenly life. Beside, the Bishop, both in his ornaments and in his Office,

The Medieval Dalmatic

"By its shape it signifieth liberality, for it hath large sleeves and long. For according to the Apostle it beseemeth that a Bishop should be NOT GREEDY OF FILTHY LUCRE, BUT GIVEN TO HOSPITALITY...Moreover, the Dalmatic maketh the form of a cross, wherein it is a token of Christ's Passion, and so is worn in the Office of the Mass, in which that Passion is shown forth. It signifieth holy religion, and mortification of the flesh, and the spirit or supernal things..As touching that which agreeth unto the Head, which is Christ, the Dalmatic by its breadth and largeness is significant of His mercy, which Himself more than all others both taught and used...".

beareth in more special wise the likeness of the Saviour than doth the simple Priest, and the significations of the Vestments do pertain more aptly unto him; wherefore he weareth the more.

5. The Dalmatic ought to have two scarlet orfreys[8] reaching all its length from top to bottom back and fore, that the Bishop may shew himself to have, both in weal and woe, fervent charity unto God and his neighbour; and this agreeth unto the commandment of both the Old and the New Testament, to wit, *THOU SHALT LOVE THE LORD THY GOD WITH ALL THINE HEART, AND THY NEIGHBOUR AS THYSELF.*[9] Thus also John,[10] *BELOVED, NO NEW COMMANDMENT WRITE I UNTO YOU, BUT AN OLD COMMANDMENT, WHICH YE HAD FROM THE BEGINNING*; and again, *A NEW COMMANDMENT I WRITE UNTO YOU.* And sometimes the purple stripes be significant of faith in the Blood of Christ, so necessary unto either people. Upon the left side the Dalmatic is wont to have a fringe, for emblem of the cares of the active life, which the Bishop must have for his flock, agreeably unto the word of the Apostle,[11] which saith, *BESIDE THOSE THINGS THAT ARE WITHOUT, THAT WHICH COMETH UPON ME DAILY, THE CARE OF ALL THE CHURCHES.* The right side, lacking the fringe, is a token of the contemplation of heavenly things, which lacketh care, and is unmolested by the multitude of troubles.

6. Furthermore, certain Dalmatics have fringes fifteen-fold before and behind, because fifteen psalms[12] in the Old Testament, like fifteen branches or steps, do issue forth from the path of charity, and fifteen likewise in the New Testament do grow out of her work: to wit, *CHARITY SUFFERETH LONG, CHARITY IS KIND*, and so forth unto the words *CHARITY NEVER FAILETH.*[13] But others have a fringe of twenty-eight before, and as many behind; wherein the sevenfold Spirit is represented eight times over, Who filleth eight orders of them that praise God, that is, *KINGS AND PEOPLE, PRINCES AND JUDGES, YOUNG MEN AND MAIDENS, OLD MEN AND CHILDREN.*[14] Again, in the Dalmatic is diversity without division, because divers works of religion are done in the sight of God, yet in prayer is no difference at all. And at the sides it is open beneath the armpits, putting him who weareth it in mind to follow in Christ's steps, Who was stabbed in the side with a spear.

7. Moreover, the Dalmatic maketh the form of a cross, wherein it is a token of Christ's Passion, and so is worn in the Office of the Mass, in which that Passion is shown forth. It signifieth also holy religion, and mortification of the flesh, and the spirit of supernal things. If white, it standeth for a holy and spotless life; if red, for a martyr; but the white

Dalmatic wrought about with divers colours denoteth purity together with the variety of virtues, and is adorned with an orfrey, as it is written, *AT THY RIGHT HAND DID STAND THE QUEEN IN A VESTURE OF GOLD, WROUGHT ABOUT WITH DIVERS COLOURS.*[15]

8. As touching that which agreeth unto the Head, which is Christ, the Dalmatic by its breadth and largeness is significant of His mercy, which Himself more than all others both taught and used; *BE YE MERCIFUL,* said He, *EVEN AS YOUR FATHER IS MERCIFUL.*[16] And *BLESSED ARE THE MERCIFUL, FOR THEY SHALL OBTAIN MERCY.*[17] He is that Samaritan, our Neighbour, Who wrought mercifully with us, pouring into our wounds wine and oil:[18] *THROUGH THE TENDER MERCY OF OUR GOD THE DAYSPRING FROM ON HIGH HATH VISITED US;*[19] *NOT BY WORKS OF RIGHTEOUSNESS WHICH WE HAVE DONE, BUT ACCORDING TO HIS MERCY HE SAVED US,*[20] coming for sinners' sakes, that He might grant them pardon for their sins; Who said, *I WILL HAVE MERCY AND NOT SACRIFICE.*[21]

We read in a Canon of Gregory[22] that in the primitive Church neither Bishops nor Deacons might wear the Dalmatic, save by special licence of the Apostolic see.

9. The Deacons leave off their Dalmatics[23] at the time of our Lord's Advent. For when some measure of the splendour of holy service is laid aside for a time, it seemeth to the minds of the faithful to shine out the more brightly when it is resumed, and is taken again with the more gladness; because the more uncommon a thing is, the more we weary after it.[24] Another reason wherefore the Deacon weareth not his Dalmatic in Advent, nor the Subdeacon his Tunicle, is this: that the Law (for which the Subdeacon standeth) did lack the beauty of the Gospel, and the Gospel's charity (which the Deacon signifieth) was not yet made manifest, before the Incarnation of the Lord. Or it is for this, if thou wilt, that He Who should put upon us the robe of innocence and immortality was not yet come; wherefore at this time the Vestments of gladness be laid aside. Yet Chasubles are worn in Advent; whereof somewhat hath been said by me in another book of the 'Rationale.'[25] Nevertheless upon the Fasts in the Octave of Pentecost,[26] the Deacon may wear his Dalmatic.

(12th Century)

(12th Century)

"Wherefore the hands be sometimes covered with the Gloves, and sometimes bared, because good works be sometimes hidden for the avoiding of vainglory, and sometimes made manifest to the edification of his neighbour."

CHAPTER XII: OF THE GLOVES

1. Because by vain men-pleasing full many spoil the good works they do; immediately after the Dalmatic put on, the Bishop according unto the Apostolic rite covereth his hands with the Gloves,[1] that his left hand may not know what his right hand doeth.[2] For by the Glove is meetly figured caution, which doeth her work before the eyes of men, yet hideth her plans in secret none the less. For albeit the Lord said, *LET YOUR LIGHT SO SHINE BEFORE MEN, THAT THEY MAY SEE YOUR GOOD WORKS, AND GLORIFY YOUR FATHER WHICH IS IN HEAVEN,*[3] in type whereof the Glove hath a golden circlet upon it; yet the same Lord gave this precept, *TAKE HEED THAT YE DO NOT YOUR ALMS BEFORE MEN, TO BE SEEN OF THEM; OTHERWISE YE HAVE NO REWARD OF YOUR FATHER WHICH IS IN HEAVEN.*[4]

2. Wherefore the hands be sometimes covered with the Gloves, and sometimes bared, because good works be sometimes hidden for the avoiding of vainglory, and sometimes made manifest to the edification of his neighbour.

3. They are without seam, for the actions of the Bishop ought to be in right agreement with his faith. As worn upon the hands, also, they are a type of the examples of the Saints, which are held fast by him in all his works; which works must be cleansed from all pollution, lest the *LITTLE LEAVEN LEAVEN THE WHOLE LUMP.*[5] And by the Gloves themselves, as being white,[6] we understand chastity and purity, that his hands, that is, his works, may be clean, and innocent of all stain.

4. As touching that which agreeth unto the Head, even Christ, the Gloves are made of the skins of kids, such as Rebekah put on the hands of Jacob, that their hairiness might set forth the likeness of his elder brother. And the skin of the kid is the likeness of sin, with which likeness Mother Rebekah—that is, the grace of the Holy Spirit—did array the hands of the true Jacob,[7] that is, the works of Christ; to the end that He, the Second Adam, might bear the likeness of the elder, that is, the first Adam. For Christ did without sin take upon Himself the likeness of sin, that the mystery of the Incarnation might be concealed from the devil;[8] and did hunger and thirst, suffered and was affrighted, slept and toiled, after the similitude of sinners. Unto Whom when He had *FASTED FORTY DAYS AND FORTY NIGHTS, AND WAS AFTERWARD AN HUNGRED,*[9] the devil came in the likeness of the first Adam, and did essay to tempt Him; yet he who had after the same manner conquered the first, was by the Second vanquisht.

CHAPTER XIII: OF THE MITRE

1. Having put on the Chasuble, the Bishop placeth on his head the Mitre,[1] in the stead of the ancient Mitre or priestly bonnet; according unto the words, *THOU HAST CROWNED HIM, O LORD, WITH GLORY AND HONOUR.*[2] The Lord Pope hath moreover the Crown, the Imperial Tiara and Pall, the Purple Cloak and Blue Tunic, according to the Donation of Constantine, Emperor.[3]

2. Now the Mitre betokeneth the knowledge of both Testaments; for its two horns[4] are these same, the fore horn the New, the after horn the Old; and both these the Bishop ought to know by heart,[5] and with them, as with a twofold horn, to smite the enemies of the Faith. Thus ought he to appear horned unto his flock, as did Moses in the eyes of Aaron and of the children of Israel from his companying with the Word of God, when bearing the two Tables of the Testimony he came down from Mount Sinai;[6] as it is said in the thirty-fourth chapter of Exodus. Yet do certain heretics condemn the Mitre with its horns, and the Bishop wearing it; who allege unto the fostering of their error the words of John in the Apocalypse,[7] *I BEHELD ANOTHER BEAST COMING UP OUT OF THE EARTH, AND HE HAD TWO HORNS LIKE A LAMB, AND HE SPAKE AS A DRAGON.*

3. The two fringed bands[8] that hang from behind the Mitre are the spirit and the letter; by which bands, or little tongues, it is set forth that the Bishop ought to be ready both in the mystical and in the historical interpretation of Holy Scripture. At their ends are fringes of red, denoting that he is prepared to defend the Faith and the Holy Scriptures, yea, even unto blood. And these hang down over his shoulders, in token that he should shew forth in his deeds that which he preacheth with his lips; for that there is no part more eminent than the shoulders for might to labour, or for bearing of burdens; wherefore by them works be meetly understood.

4. The golden circlet which embraceth the after and fore parts of the Mitre, sheweth that *EVERY SCRIBE WHICH IS INSTRUCTED UNTO THE KINGDOM OF HEAVEN IS LIKE UNTO AN HOUSEHOLDER WHICH BRINGETH FORTH OUT OF HIS TREASURES THINGS NEW AND OLD.*[9] Let the Bishop therefore take earnest heed that he desire not to be a master or ever he know how to be a disciple, lest if the *BLIND LEAD THE BLIND, THEY BOTH FALL INTO THE DITCH;*[10] for it is written in the Prophet, *BECAUSE THOU HAST REJECTED KNOWLEDGE, I WILL ALSO REJECT THEE, THAT THOU SHALT BE NO PRIEST TO ME.*[11] Moreover, it well befitteth that the Mitre, whose shape

(St. Agnes' Convent, Prague)

(13th Century)

"The two fringed bands that hang from behind the Mitre are the spirit and the letter; by which bands, or little tongues, it is set forth that the Bishop ought to be ready both in the mystical and in the historical interpretation of Holy Scripture."

(15th Century)

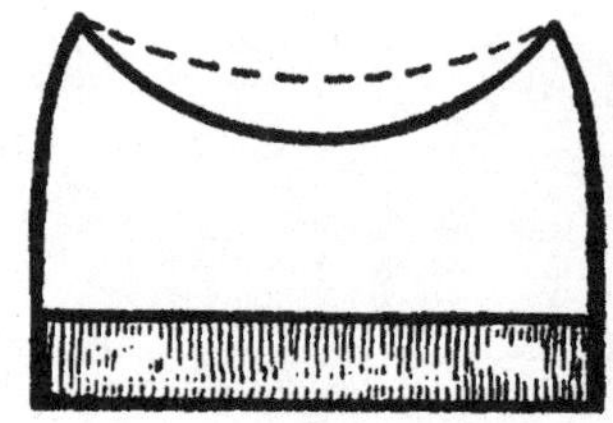

(12th Century)

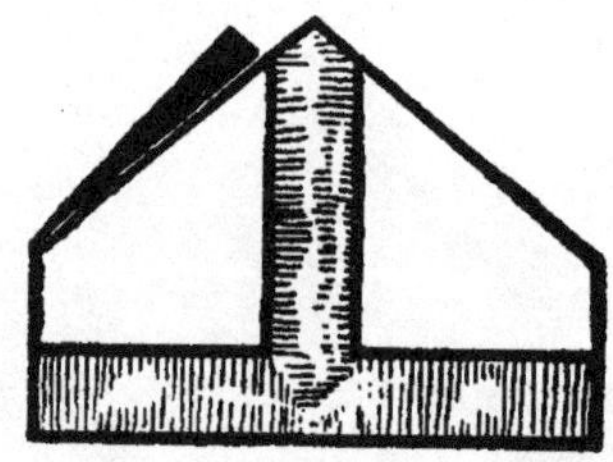

(13th Century)

(Jeweled Mitre)

(The Mitra Pretiosa)

(Mitre of St. Thomas)

"The seventh and last Vestment was that of the head, the Mitre or Tiara, which the High Priest put on last of all, and which signified humility; whereof the Lord said, WHOSOEVER EXALTETH HIMSELF SHALL BE ABASED, AND HE THAT HUMBLETH HIMSELF SHALL BE EXALTED. *This he wore on his head, to show that the High Priest ought to bear humility in his mind; after the example of our Head, who saith,* LEARN OF ME, FOR I AM MEEK AND LOWLY IN HEART. *For by the head do we understand the mind, as it is written,* ANOINT THINE HEAD, AND WASH THY FACE. *Again, the Mitre, as worn by the lesser Priests, signified Continence in the five senses; but as worn by the higher Contemplation, whereunto they ought to be given."*

goeth up into an height,[12] should stand for the loftiness of wisdom, for the Bishop ought so to excel in knowledge those who are subject uto him, that in their relation to him they may worthily be called his flock.

The two bands which hang from the hinder part of the Mitre denote a twofold mindfulness. The former is the mindfulness of the Divine acts; lest in celebrating he make little reckoning thereof, and be punished: and for a like reason even in the Old Testament he that would offer sacrifice was wont to walk amid the sound of bells, that thereby he might be received as worthy or be rejected as unworthy, by the Angel who was placed to guard the Temple. And the second band is the mindfulness of his sins, that he have contrition of them.

5. The Mitre, being sometimes of white linen, signifieth the whiteness and cleanness of Chastity; wherefore this Vestment is very necessary unto the head, in which the body's five senses have their seat of life;[13] for Chastity is easily violated, if thou corrupt these.

Also there be some who affirm that the Bishop's Mitre is a type of the Crown of Thorns. And hence it cometh that in the Office of the Mass, wherein the Bishop representeth Christ in His Passion, it is the Deacon who putteth him the Mitre on and off; for that it is the Deacon's office to read the Gospel, in the which it is written concerning Christ crowned with thorns. And the two horns are the two precepts of Charity; wherefore the Bishop taketh the Mitre in understanding that he ought to guard his five senses against the allurements of the world, so as to keep the laws of the two Testaments; and to fulfil the two precepts of Charity, that he may be counted worthy to receive an eternal crown.

But the others, Priests and clergy, cover not in general their heads with any ornament,[14] albeit upon Festivals they be vested in every other part of the body. And this is in part because our joy is not yet full, for we joy not in the possession of things present, but in the hope of things to come; and in part because we be journeying unto that estate, wherein we shall behold God with open face.

6. Now the Orfreyed Mitre[15] is to be used from Easter unto Advent and from the Lord's Nativity unto Septuagesima, and upon all Doubles, and upon Feasts having nine Lessons throughout the year, save upon the Feast of the Holy Innocents, as shall be said in the chapter of the Colours;[16] and upon the Sundays of the aforesaid seasons, and in general whenever *Gloria in Excelcis* and *Te Deum* shall be said. For when these are said upon Feasts, wherein we have in mind generally or specially the excellence of the Head of the joy of the members, we do rightly use the Orfreyed Mitre; for the brightness of gold and jewels representeth joy. But upon

Fasts it is not to be used, as followeth, because these have been ordained for the blotting-out of sins, which upon them are to be brought to remembrance; and therefore nought is then to be wrought or worn which signifieth joy, but rather all that may mark affliction and humility.

7. At other times the Orfreyed Mitre is ruled not to be used, but the Simple: namely, from Advent unto the Nativity (save that the Lord Pope weareth the Orfreyed upon Gaudete Sunday) and from Septuagesima unto Easter (save of the Pope upon Laetare[17] Sunday, Maundy Thursday at Mass only, and Holy Saturday at Mass). Also upon Feasts of three Lessons occurring within these seasons, upon all Vigils whereon a Feast is kept, at the Four Seasons,[18] and upon Rogation days (save that the Lord Pope weareth the Orfreyed upon the Feast of St. Mark at Mass only); also in the Offices of the departed.[19]

8. This also is to be noted, that the Bishop of Rome weareth the Regnum,[20] that is, the Imperial Crown, in token of Imperial sway, and the Mitre in token of High Priesthood; but he weareth the Mitre everywhere and always, yet not everywhere and always the Regnum, because Pontifical authority hath priority of Imperial power, and is of more dignity and extent.[21] For the Priesthood took precedence of the Kinghood amongst the people of God; for Aaron the first High Priest was before Saul the first King, and Noe was before Nimrod, as it is written,[22] *THE BEGINNING OF THE KINGDOM OF NIMROD WAS BABYLON*; but Noe *BUILDED AN ALTAR UNTO THE Lord, AND OFFERED BURNT OFFERINGS ON THE ALTAR.*[23] Wherefore the Lord Pope doth not wear the Regnum, save on certain days and in certain places, nor anywhere within the Church, but without it.

9. As touching that which agreeth unto the Head, even Christ, the Bishop's Mitre betokeneth that which the Prophet,[24] speaking of the Son, saith unto the Father, *THOU HAST CROWNED HIM WITH GLORY AND HONOUR*: *THOU MADEST HIM TO HAVE DOMINION OVER THE WORKS OF THINE HANDS.* It is the Name *WHICH IS ABOVE EVERY NAME, THAT AT THE NAME OF JESUS EVERY KNEE SHOULD BOW, OF THINGS IN HEAVEN, AND THINGS IN EARTH, AND THINGS UNDER THE EARTH.*[25] For upon the golden plate[26] of the High Priest's Mitre was graven the Four-Lettered Name[27] of the Lord, whose mystery we shall set forth in the chapter of the Vestments of the Law.[28] Thus by the Christian Mitre we understand that supreme glorifying of the Head or Person of Christ, which by reason of His Godhead we owe unto His Manhood, even as His Footstool is adored by reason of His Feet; for it is written, *FALL DOWN BEFORE HIS FOOTSTOOL, FOR HE IS HOLY.*[29]

CHAPTER XIV: OF THE RING

1. The Ring[1] is the sign of plighted faith, wherewith Christ hath espoused His Bride Holy Church, that she may have authority to say concerning herself, *The Lord Jesus Christ hath espoused me with His Ring, Whose watchmen and teachers are the Bishops and Prelates, who bear rings as a figure and token of this very thing;* those watchmen whereof saith the Spouse in the Canticles,[2] *THE WATCHMEN THAT GO ABOUT THE CITY FOUND ME.* This is the Ring that was given by the Father unto his son returning, according to that of the Gospel,[3] *PUT A RING ON HIS HAND*; and from this place of the Gospel it is thought that the use of the Ring hath been derived.

2. The Bishop's Ring therefore signifieth the integrity of plighted troth, namely, that he should love the Church, God's Spouse, committed unto him, even as himself, and should keep her pure and chaste for her Heavenly Bridegroom; as in that of Paul,[4] *I HAVE ESPOUSED YOU TO ONE HUSBAND, THAT I MAY PRESENT YOU AS A CHASTE VIRGIN TO CHRIST*; and that he may be mindful that he himself is not a master, but a pastor. Of this Bridegroom and Bride John Evangelist saith,[5] He *THAT HATH THE BRIDE IS THE BRIDEGROOM*; *BUT THE FRIEND OF THE BRIDEGROOM, WHICH STANDETH AND HEARETH HIM, REJOICETH GREATLY BECAUSE OF THE BRIDEGROOM'S VOICE.* The Bishop, therefore, is the Vicar and Friend of the Bridegroom; and being His Vicar, is himself also the Bridegroom in certain wise.

3. Again, with a Ring of old they were wont to seal letters; wherefore the Bishop weareth a Ring, for that he should seal up the mysteries of Scripture and the holy things of the Church from the faithless, and reveal them unto the humble.

And as touching that which agreeth unto the Head, even Christ, the Ring on the finger is a type of the gift of the Holy Ghost; for the finger, which is a part jointed and distinct, giveth an hint of the Holy Ghost, according unto that scripture, *THE MAGICIANS SAID, THIS IS THE FINGER OF GOD*;[6] and in another place, *IF I WITH THE FINGER OF GOD CAST OUT DEVILS, BY WHOM DO YOUR SONS CAST THEM OUT*?[7]

4. Also the Ring, being golden and round, representeth the perfection of the Spirit's gifts, which Christ hath received without measure,[8] for that in Him dwelleth *ALL THE FULNESS OF THE GODHEAD BODILY.*[9] For He *THAT COMETH FROM HEAVEN IS ABOVE ALL*,[10] unto Whom *GOD GAVE NOT THE SPIRIT BY MEASURE*, saying, *UPON WHOM THOU*

SHALT SEE THE SPIRIT DESCENDING, AND REMAINING ON HIM, THE SAME IS HE THAT BAPTISETH.[11] For *THE SPIRIT OF WISDOM AND UNDERSTANDING SHALL REST UPON HIM.*[12] And He of His fulness distributeth in divers gifts, giving unto one, as saith the Apostle, *THE WORD OF KNOWLEDGE, TO ANOTHER THE GIFT OF HEALING, TO ANOTHER THE WORKING OF MIRACLES,*[13] and so forth; and this the visible Bishop imitateth, making in the Church some Priests, some Deacons, others Subdeacons, and the rest. Wherefore it is not amiss that the jewelled Ring gleameth upon the finger of the Bishop; for by Him, of Whom it is the mystic symbol, are given the bright gifts of grace.

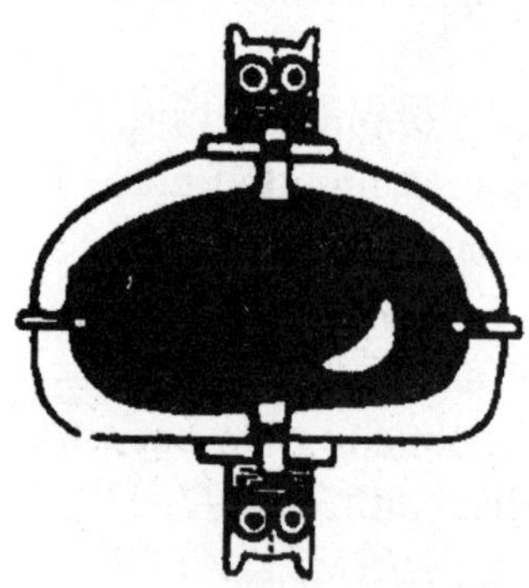

The Episcopal Ring (12th Century)

(12th Century)

(13th Century)

"The Ring, being golden and round, representeth the perfection of the Spirit's gifts, which Christ hath received without measure."

(14th Century)

The Ecclesiastical Ring (15th Century)

Bishop's Ring (15th Century)

"The Bishop's Ring therefore signifieth the integrity of plighted troth, namely, that he should love the Church, God's Spouse, committed unto him, even as himself, and should keep her pure and chaste for her Heavenly Bridegroom."

CHAPTER XV: OF THE PASTORAL STAFF

1. The Pastoral Staff[1] signifieth Pastoral Correction, according unto that which is said by the Consecrator unto him that is consecrated, '*Receive the Staff of the Pastoral Office, that in the chastising of vices thou mayest be angry, and sin not.*'[2] And hereof also the Apostle,[3] *SHALL I COME TO YOU WITH A ROD*? By the Pastoral Staff therefore we do understand the priestly power, which Christ did confer upon His Apostles, when sending them out to preach He charged them that they should bear staves. And Moses also was sent into Egypt with a rod.

2. Thus the Staff is derived from both the Law and the Gospel, being called both the Pastoral Staff, and the Crosier, and the Crook, and the Rod. For Moses had a Rod by the commandment of God, which wrought terrible things in sea and sky, bringing food from heaven, and water from the rock; and drave his flock unto the *LAND FLOWING WITH MILK AND HONEY*.[4] Further, the Staff is Doctrinal Authority. For by it the weak are sustained, the restless rallied, and the erring drawn to repentance; whence it is called Pedum, the Crook, which is the name of the curved wooden staff wherewith shepherds draw back their herds by the feet.

3. Now the Staff is for the most part made of ivory and wood,[5] which are joined together by a knop[6] of crystal and gilt; the ivory above is crooked, and the wood below hath an iron point, but not much of the end is hidden therein.[7] The ivory is the severity of the Law, the wood the Gospel's gentleness; and these twain are joined with the knop, as it were by the Divinity of Jesus Christ. Or, if thou wilt, the ivory is the Bishop's severity, and the wood his gentleness, both the which in his judgments he combineth with the BOND OF CHARITY; for either sternness or mildness lacketh exceedingly, if the one be held to without the other; and to this end the iron is blunt, for that justice is tempered with mercy. The Staff is crooked, to signify the recalling of the contrite into penance. Sometimes the curve maketh the shape of an head, because eternal life is promised unto them that turn to God; and sometimes round the curved part is written,

> CVM . IRATVS . FVERIS . MISERICORDIAE .
> RECORDABERIS,

which is, being interpreted, *In wrath remember mercy*;[8] lest by reason of the backslidings of his flock the shepherd's wrath should becloud the eyes of his reason. Sometimes upon the knop is inscribed HOMO, that the Bishop may remember himself to be but man, nor be puffed up with the power committed unto him; sometimes also hard by the point is written PARCE, that in his discipline he may spare those subject unto him, and being merciful may for his mercy obtain mercy.

4. The Staff is sharp at the end, straight in the midst, and crooked at the top; this meaneth that the Bishop ought to goad on the idle, to direct the feeble with his own rightness, and to gather the wanderers together; hence the verse,

> COLLIGE . SVSTENTA . STIMVLA . VAGA .
> MORBIDA . LENTA,

which being interpreted is,

> Gather, and guide, and goad unto the goal
> The stray, the ailing, and the tarrying soul;

wherein if thou refer word to his word, thou wilt find that all the foregoing are contained. Or it may be thus,

> ATTRAHE . PER . PRIMVM . MEDIO . REGE .
> PVNGE . PER . IMVM,

which is

> The Top, to draw into the road:
> The Midst, to rule: the End, to goad.[9]

5. But the Bishop of Rome useth not the Pastoral Staff, partly for an historical, and in part for a mystical reason. The historical reason is as follows. The Blessed Apostle Peter sent Martial his disciple (whom the Lord made to be His follower when He said, *EXCEPT YE BECOME AS THIS LITTLE CHILD, YE SHALL NOT ENTER INTO THE KINGDOM OF HEAVEN*[10]) with certain others to preach unto the Germans. When they had gone a twenty-days' journey, Martial's colleague, Frontus, died, and Martial returned to tell this to Peter; whereupon Peter said unto him, 'Take this Staff and touch him with it, and say, *In the Name of the Lord arise and preach.'* This Martial did, touching him on the fortieth day after his death; and he arose, and did preach. And it was thus that Saint Peter put away his Staff from him and gave it unto his flock; nor did he recover it again. But on the other hand, Innocent the Third, Pope, wrote in the *Speculum Ecclesiae* that Blessed Peter sent his Staff unto Eucherius,[11] first Bishop of Trèves, whom he appointed, together with Valerius and Maternus, to preach the Gospel unto the Teutonic people; and to him Maternus succeeded as Bishop, who had been raised up from death by Peter's Staff.[12] And this Staff is preserved by the Church of Trèves with great veneration

Font cast in brass: Moses parting the waters of the Red Sea (Hildesheim, Germany, c. 1220)

Moses (Venice Bible, 1490)

Moses (Hortus Deliciarum, 12th Century)

"The Staff is derived from both the Law and the Gospel, being called the Pastoral Staff, and the Crosier, and the Crook, and the Rod. For Moses had a Rod by the commandment of God, which wrought terrible things in sea and sky, bringing food from Heaven, and water from the rock; and drave his flock unto the LAND FLOWING WITH MILK AND HONEY."

The Charles Bridge (Prague)

(Belgium, 1225-50 C.E.)

(Cluny Museum, Paris, France)

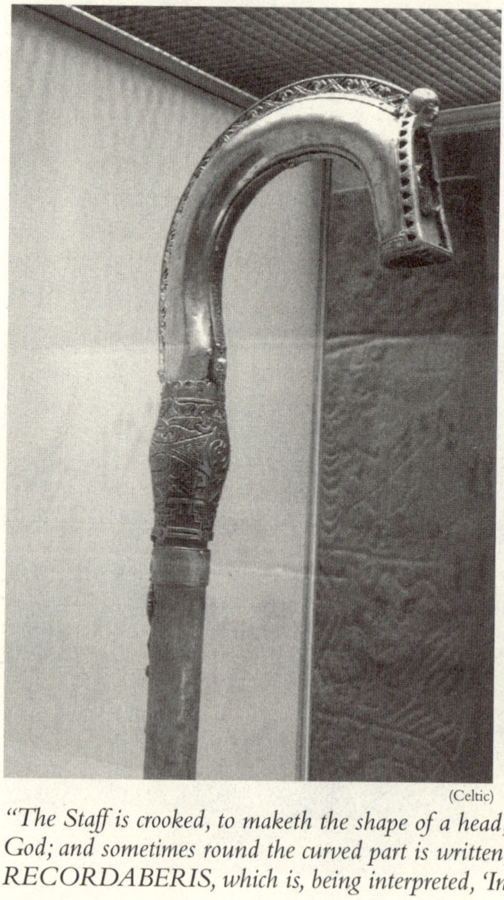

(Celtic)

(Constance, 1351)

"The Staff is crooked, to maketh the shape of a head, because eternal life is promised unto them that turn to God; and sometimes round the curved part is written, CVM. IRATVS. FVERIS. MISERICORDIAE. RECORDABERIS, which is, being interpreted, 'In wrath remember mercy.'"

(Dublin, Ireland, 1100)

(Dublin, Ireland)

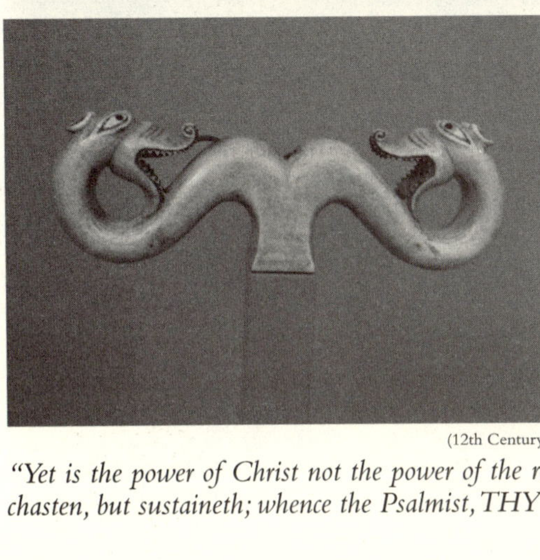

(12th Century)

(Prague)

"Yet is the power of Christ not the power of the rod alone, but the power of the Staff, for it doth not only chasten, but sustaineth; whence the Psalmist, THY ROD AND THY STAFF COMFORT ME.*"*

even unto this day;[13] wherefore the Pope useth the Staff in that diocese, and none other.[14]

6. But the mystical reason is this, that the drawing-in of wanderers, as symbolised by the crookedness of the top of the Staff, is not needed in the case of the Bishop of Rome; for that none can altogether turn away from him.[15] Moreover the Staff is a type of that constraining power, which the other Bishops receive at the hand of men, and therefore do they receive and hold their Staves from those set over them. But the Pope, because he receiveth his power from God alone, hath not the Staff.

7. Lastly, as touching that which agreeth unto the Head, even Christ, the Bishop's Staff signifieth the power of Christ, whereof the Psalmist saith, *THE ROD OF THY KINGDOM IS A RIGHT SCEPTRE*, that is, a sceptre of direction, *FOR THOU HAST LOVED RIGHTEOUSNESS, AND HATED INIQUITY;*[16] and elsewhere, *THOU SHALT RULE THEM WITH A ROD OF IRON.*[17] The hardness of the iron signifieth the might of rightness, with which Christ *SHALL BREAK THE UNRIGHTEOUS IN PIECES LIKE A POTTER'S VESSEL.*[18]

Yet is the power of Christ not the power of the rod alone, but the power also of the Staff, for it doth not only chasten, but sustaineth; whence the Psalmist,[19] *THY ROD AND THY STAFF COMFORT ME.*

(Victoria and Albert Museum, London, England)

(Victoria and Albert Museum, London, England)

CHAPTER XVI: OF THE SUDARIUM

1. And now, having done with the Nine Vestments peculiar to the Bishop, let us for a space consider certain others: whereof the first shall be the Sudarium. This is a linen cloth, which he that serveth the Bishop hath alway ready, wherewith the latter may wipe away from himself all the sweat and unnecessary moistness of the body; and it signifieth the care we must have to wipe away all this life's human defilements through the examples of the holy Fathers, by the which we are confirmed unto patience. For as sweat in the body, so is that weariness in the soul, whensoever it doth bedew as it were the brow of the conscience through the consciousness of sin.

2. Let us have, then, as it were a Napkin of linen, chastened and cleansed by many blows, with which to wipe off the affections of this world; and with David[1] and Job[2] laying aside sadness, let us wipe away all that may oppress us.

In some Churches the Deacon hath a Sudarium, and layeth it down on the right side of the Altar, that if aught foul should chance to come near he may wipe it away, and so may keep the Priest's Sudarium clean every whit.

The meaning of the Sudarium is almost the same as that of the Maniple; whereof I have spoken above.

Bishop with Martyr Saint Sebastian

CHAPTER XVII: OF THE PALL

1. Now in due course we shall subjoin somewhat concerning the Pall.[1] This Vestment pertaineth unto Patriarchs, Primates, and Metropolitans, to distinguish them from the rest of the Bishops, for that unto these is committed a special dignity of privilege; wherefore I have in no wise mentioned it under the heads of the foregoing Vestments common or peculiar.

In the Pall, then, we find at once both the Ephod and the Breastplate of the Priest in the Law. For it may be called Superhumeral, in that it falleth over both the Bishop's shoulders, and Rationale or Breastplate, in that it falleth thence upon his breast, and is fastened there; for the ancient High Priest had both Ephod and Breastplate joined together by chains of gold. Some there be, however, who hold that the Breastplate hath to-day no Vestment to represent it; concerning which matter I will speak in the last chapter of the Book.[2] Others say that the Pall was instituted in the stead of the Golden Plate; though it seem more likely that the Orfreyed Mitre representeth the Plate.

2. Now the Pall as worn by these greater ones signifieth the authority wherewith they ought to rule and restrain, not only those submitted unto them, but also themselves; for by this means is won that golden chain which those receive who strive lawfully, of which Solomon speaketh in the Proverbs,[3] saying, *MY SON, HEAR THE INSTRUCTION OF THY FATHER, AND FORSAKE NOW THE LAW OF THY MOTHER*: *FOR THEY SHALL BE AN ORNAMENT OF GRACE UNTO THY HEAD, AND CHAINS ABOUT THY NECK*. But even as the chain or prize was not wont to be given, save unto them that strove lawfully, according unto the word of the Apostle, *MANY RUN, BUT ONE RECEIVETH THE PRIZE*,[4] so also none shall make his way unto the honour of the Pall, save that he have first laboured lawfully in each degree of office ecclesiastical. For even as touching the offices of this world they confer not the highest place upon them that are but just entered upon the threshold of their labours, but upon such as have been approved in their passage through many degrees; and that degree excelleth the rest, whereunto more protracted labour and longer service have given the precedence.

The Pall, then, is worn over all Vestments,[5] that the other Ministers when they see it may be exhorted unto lawful striving. And the Bishop, when he putteth it on and off,[6] doth kiss it, to show his own great desire of contending lawfully, and of deserving the prize.

3. It is woven of white wool,[7] having a circular part confining the shoulders, and two strips hanging down before and behind; on the left it is double, on the right single; and it hath four purple crosses, one before, one behind, one on the right, and one on the left; there be also three pins fastened therein. Some things there be, which may not be done by the Metropolitan without the Pall, nor is it lawful to wear it save upon fixt days. And all these things are tinged with spiritual mysteries and big with heavenly meaning, for as the Scripture witnesseth, *THE PARABLES OF KNOWLEDGE ARE IN THE TREASURES OF WISDOM.*[8] In the wool of the Pall we see asperity; in its whiteness, kindness: for the Church's discipline useth towards the rebellious and froward, severity, but gentleness towards the contrite and humble. Wherefore the Pall is made not of the wool of any and every animal, but only of the sheep, which is a gentle creature; the Prophet[9] saith, *HE WAS LED AS A SHEEP TO THE SLAUGHTER, AND LIKE A LAMB DUMB BEFORE HIS SHEARER, SO OPENED HE NOT HIS MOUTH.* Hereunto agreeth the word we are told concerning that man half-dead with wounds, whom the Samaritan led into the inn and applied unto him wine and oil,[10] that the wine might eat into his wounds, and the oil foment them; even so he who hath the chief part in the healing of wounds must apply the bite of severity, as wine, and the gentleness of love, as it were oil. Which also is well shewn by the Ark of the Tabernacle, wherein were contained, with the Tables, the Rod and the Manna; for in the mind of him that ruleth there ought to be, together with the knowledge of Scripture, both the Rod of guidance, and the Manna of kindness, that his severity be neither unduly severe, nor his love more indulgent than is meet. Again, the wool is of little price, whereof the Pall is made, that it may be precious not in itself, but in that which in itself it portrayeth, and may be meet to be looked upon, not with the eyes, but with the mind; in understanding that it is worn for its meaning, rather than for its beauty.

4. The circular part of the Pall, which confineth the shoulders, is that fear of the Lord by which works are wrought, so as neither to decline unto lawlessness, nor relax unto excess. For discipline must restrain the left hand from that which is unlawful, through fear of punishment, while it tempereth the right hand from extravagance, by the love of right; wherefore blessed is the man who feareth alway. For according to the word of Solomon,[11] *THE FEAR OF THE LORD DRIVETH AWAY SIN; BUT HE THAT LIVETH WITHOUT FEAR SHALL NOT BE JUSTIFIED.* Wherefore this circle of the Pall doth confine the shoulders below the neck, to denote that he who weareth it ought to be one in word and deed.

(Cape of Charlemagne, late 8th Century)

(late 12th Century)

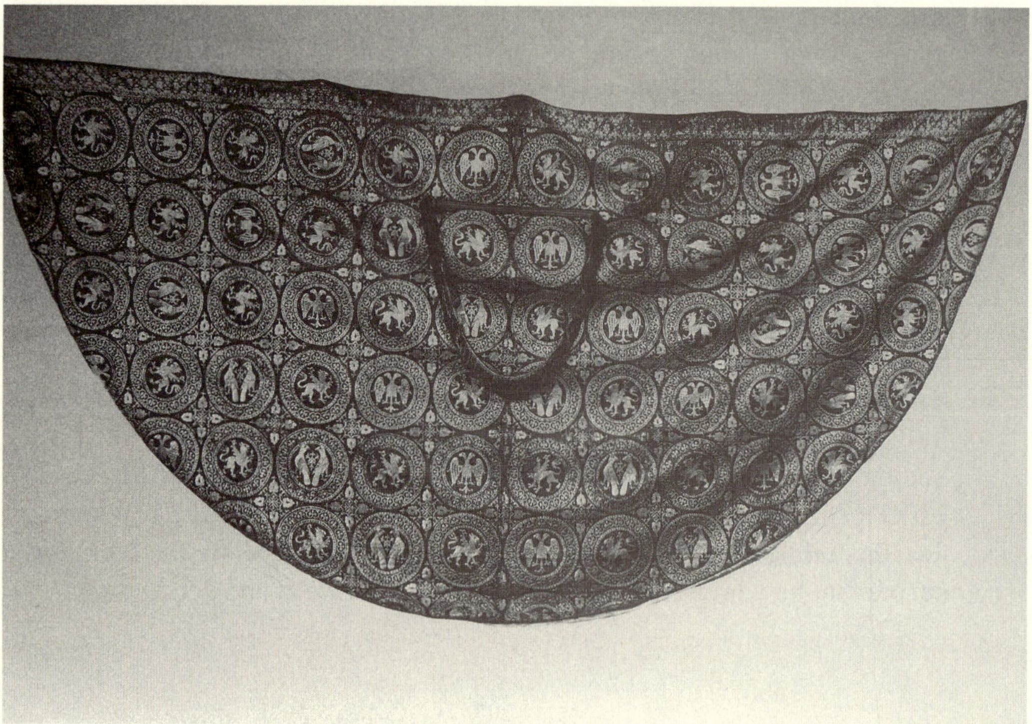

(Byzantine, 12th Century)

"The Pall worn by these greater ones signifieth the authority wherewith they ought to rule and restrain, not only those submitted unto them, but also themselves... The Pall, then, is worn over all Vestments."

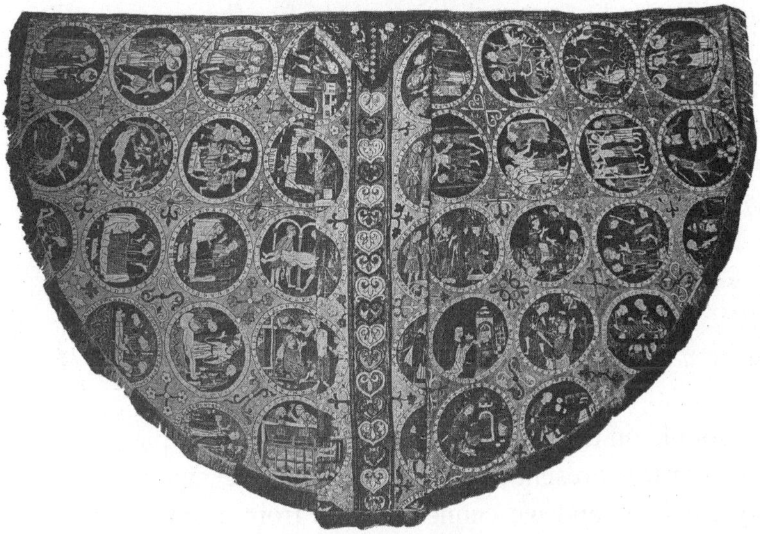

"This circle of the Pall doth confine the shoulders below the neck, to denote that he who wear it ought to be one in word and deed."

"The pins must be of gold, the end sharp, and the head round, with a precious stone set in it: because of a truth the good pastor, in caring for his sheep, is afflicted on earth, but shall be crowned in Heaven; where he shall have that precious pearl spoken of by the Lord in the Gospel."

5. The two strips, the one extending behind the back and the other before the breast of the Bishop, we hold to be a sign of the cares and anxieties of this life; which do too often on this wise cumber and weigh down the heart and shoulders of the Bishop, causing him to stoop from that erectness which should be his, so that he must bear in mind and body the burden of vain and transitory things. For this reason the Pall is fitted on from right and left before and behind, before the breast and over the shoulders, this signifying, that casting such things behind him[12] he shall often restore himself to himself.

Hereby are also signified the life active and the life contemplative; which the Prelate ought to live in such wise, that after the example of Moses he may now climb up into the Mount and there hold parleyings of wisdom with the Lord, and now may go down into the camp, to take thought for the needs of his people. For he must be very ready to have a care that though he devote himself unto others, he restore himself sometimes unto himself; being with Martha duly busied about his constant ministry, the while with Mary he hearkeneth unto the words of the Saviour. And by either strip he is weighed down, because *THE CORRUPTIBLE BODY PRESSETH DOWN THE SOUL, AND THE EARTHLY TABERNACLE WEIGHETH DOWN THE MIND THAT MUSETH UPON MANY THINGS.*[13]

6. The Pall is double on the left side, as was also the Breastplate, but single on the right. For this present life, which the left side signifieth, is subject unto many troubles, and we cannot be free from a double state therein; being now puffed up with well-being, now broken with adversity; now seeking the things of earth, now cleaving unto heavenly things; serving now the flesh, now the spirit. But the life to come, which is signified by the right side, is gathered up into one endless rest; as the Very Truth declareth, when He saith, *MARTHA, MARTHA, THOU ART CAREFUL AND TROUBLED ABOUT MANY THINGS, BUT ONE THING IS NEEDFUL; AND MARY HATH CHOSEN THAT GOOD PART, WHICH SHALL NOT BE TAKEN AWAY FROM HER.*[14]

7. Again, the Pall is double on the left side, that the Prelate may in his day be strong to bear the troubles of this present life; but single on the right, that with his whole heart he may sigh to win the tranquillity of the life to come. Whereof the Psalmist,[15] *ONE THING HAVE I DESIRED OF THE LORD WHICH I WILL REQUIRE: EVEN THAT I MAY DWELL IN THE HOUSE OF THE LORD ALL THE DAYS OF MY LIFE, TO BEHOLD THE FAIR BEAUTY OF THE LORD, AND TO VISIT HIS TEMPLE.*

For There is neither doubleness nor wrinkle, but prosperity without adversity, and joy without sadness, and felicity without grief.

8. The four purple crosses be the Four Cardinal Virtues, to wit Justice, Fortitude, Temperance, and Prudence; and these do usurp the name of virtue falsely unto themselves, nor lead unto true blessing or glory, except they be made purple in the Blood of Christ's Cross. Wherefore the Lord said unto His Apostles, *EXCEPT YOUR RIGHTEOUSNESS SHALL EXCEED THE RIGHTEOUSNESS OF THE SCRIBES AND PHARISEES, YE SHALL IN NO CASE ENTER INTO THE KINGDOM OF HEAVEN.*[16] This is that *KING'S PURPLE DYED WITH STRIPES,*[17] whereof Solomon speaketh in the Song of Songs. He therefore that is adorned with the honour of the Pall, if he wish to be that which is exprest in the forepart, ought to have Justice, that he may render unto every man his own; for the after part he ought to have Prudence, that he may beware of that which is harmful unto any; for the left, Fortitude, that ills cast him not down; and for the right, Temperance, that he be not puffed up with prosperity.

9. The three pins which are fastened in the Pall, one before the breast, one over the left shoulder, and one behind the back, are not made for piercing—that is to say, not for the piercings of this life—but to fasten the Pall and the Chasuble together; and some little rings were fixt of old in the Chasuble, into which the pins were inserted, making both Pall and Chasuble fast, so that the former should not move out of his place. In these three pins we may discern Faith, Hope, and Charity, without which the Pall cannot fitly be had by the Bishop. They denote also compassion for his neighbour, the administration of his office, and the discrimination of his judgment; whereof the first with sorrow, the second with labour, and the third with fear, pricketh his soul. With the first of these the Apostle was prickt, when he said[18] *WHO IS WEAK, AND I AM NOT WEAK*? *WHO IS OFFENDED, AND I BURN NOT*? and with the second, when he said,[19] *BESIDE THOSE THINGS THAT ARE WITHOUT, THAT WHICH COMETH UPON ME DAILY, THE CARE OF ALL THE CHURCHES.* With the third Job was prickt, saying,[20] *IF THE RIGHTEOUS SCARCELY BE SAVED, WHERE SHALL THE UNGODLY AND THE SINNER APPEAR*? Upon the right shoulder there is no pin fastened, for that our everlasting rest hath no prick of affliction nor sting of sorrow. For *GOD SHALL WIPE AWAY ALL TEARS FROM THE EYES OF THE SAINTS, AND AT THAT TIME THERE SHALL BE NO MORE EITHER SORROW OR CRYING, NEITHER SHALL THERE BE ANY MORE PAIN*; *FOR THE FORMER THINGS ARE PASSED AWAY.*[21]

10. The pins must be of gold, the end sharp, and the head round, with a precious stone set in it; because of a truth the good pastor, in caring for his sheep, is afflicted on earth, but shall be crowned in Heaven; where he shall have that precious pearl spoken of by the Lord in the Gospel,[22] *THE KINGDOM OF HEAVEN IS LIKE UNTO A MAN SEEKING GOODLY PEARLS; WHO WHEN HE HAD FOUND ONE PEARL OF GREAT PRICE, WENT AND SOLD ALL THAT HE HAD, AND BOUGHT IT.*

11. In and with the Pall is conferred[23] the plenitude of the Episcopal Office. Hence it cometh that the Metropolitan may neither call a council, nor consecrate the Chrism, nor ordain clergy in his province, nor consecrate Bishops, nor dedicate Churches, nor take unto himself the title of Archbishop,[24] until he have been honoured therewith; although there be some who say that if he be invited outside his own province, he might confer Holy Order as a simple Bishop, without the Pall. Some there be, again, who affirm that a Bishop, even though he be such an one as may use the Pall, may not grant permission to an Archbishop of another province to wear the Pall in his diocese, unless the said Palled Bishop be an exempt; and that even an Archbishop may not do the like in his province, unless the Archbishop invited have special privilege of wearing the Pall outside his own province if he be so invited. But these be points rather of rigorous order than of courtesy; nor, save thou look upon the matter curiously, does the case of an exempt Palled Bishop seem to differ greatly from one not exempt.[25]

12. But one Metropolitan may not officiate with the Pall of another, nor by the same count may he be buried therein, but only in his own; nevertheless he who hath been Palled, if he have been translated unto another Church, is buried with the Pall granted unto him in his second place.[26] Nor may he who hath been Palled, if he be translated unto another Church, make use of the Pall he was invested in his former Church; for the Pall is granted, not in respect of persons only, but of place as well. Hence it followeth that he may not wear it outside the province assigned unto him. Moreover, if anyone resign the Archbishoprick, he may no longer wear the Pall, save in Church, and at the Church's offices; thus if it should fall to his lot to go out of Church in procession, or to preach, or for any the like purpose, he shall not go out with the Pall.

13. The use of the Pall is forbidden by rule, save upon solemn Feasts, and such occasions as may be contained among the privileges of each several Church. And the Festivals are as followeth:—

The Nativity of our Lord.
Saint Stephen.

Saint John.
The Circumcision.
The Epiphany.
Palm Sunday.
Maundy Thursday.
Holy Saturday.
The Three Days of the Resurrection.[27]
The Ascension.
Pentecost.
The Feast of Saint John Baptist.
The Feast of All Apostles.[28]
The Four Festivals of Blessed Mary.[29]
Saint Michael.
All Saints.
Saint Martin, Peer of the Apostles.[30]

Also[31] upon the principal Feasts of the Church honoured with the Pall;[32] and at

The Dedication of Churches.
The Consecration of Bishops.[33]
The Ordination of Clergy; and upon
The Anniversaries of the consecration of him that weareth the Pall.

By some are added the Sundays after Easter; but this latter is not the common use. I may also mention that wherever in his province there resteth the body of any Saint, upon the Feast of that Saint, and even upon the principal Festival of any place in his province, the Metropolitan may visit that place and may there wear the Pall and the Sandals. But at the Burial of the Dead, and at the Solemnisation of Matrimony, these may not be worn, unless there be contained in a Privilege the express permission to do so. The Bishop of Ostia,[34] who consecrateth the Pope, weareth the Pall, as ordained by Marcus, Pope; and there be certain Bishops beside, who do so by special privilege.

14. Lastly it is to be noted, that the Roman Pontiffs who were before Blessed Silvester are depicted as having linen Palls wrapt around their shoulders (for the Priest of the Law, too, when he sacrificed, turned back the ends of the Girdle over his shoulders). And this signifieth that the jurisdiction and authority of those said Popes, as set forth by the Pall, were involved and straitened, being not free. But Silvester, and they that came after him, have had power free and untrammelled; wherefore the stripes of their Palls are represented as hanging open and outspread behind and be-

fore. Another reason why these stripes, which denote cares and anxieties (as is aforesaid) do hang down without fold since the days of Pope Silvester, may be this—because the temporalities have been granted unto him and to his successors, which may not be had without anxiety and carefulness.

It hath been said by Bruno, that the Sovereign Pontiff weareth, beside the Vestments afore mentioned, the Regnum and Purple; and this not for any mystical reason, but because the Emperor Constantine did hand over to Blessed Silvester all the insignia of the Roman Empire. Wherefore in great processions all that pomp, which used to be made in honour of the Emperors, is displayed in the person of the Roman Pontiff; and the Pope himself is crowned with the Imperial diadem.

The Blessed Virgin and Child (14th Century)

CHAPTER XVIII: OF THE FOUR COLOURS WHICH THE CHURCH USETH IN HER VESTMENTS

1. There be four principal colours, wherewith the Church doth make distinction in her Sacred Vestments according to the propers of the seasons: namely, white, red, black, and green. For in the Vestments of the Law, too, we read that four colours were used, fine linen, purple, blue, and scarlet; of the which I purpose to treat in the following chapter. The Roman Church useth also violet and yellow, as shall be noted hereafter.

2. White Vestments are to be used at the times following:—

Upon the Feasts of Holy Confessors, and Virgins who are not Martyrs, by reason of their integrity and innocence. For *HER NAZARITES WERE WHITER THAN SNOW*;[1] and *THEY SHALL WALK WITH ME IN WHITE,*[2] *FOR THEY ARE VIRGINS, AND SHALL FOLLOW THE LAMB WHITHERSOEVER HE GOETH.*[3]

For the same reason white is to be used upon the Festivals of the Angels, of whose brightness the Lord saith unto Lucifer,[4] *WHERE WAST THOU WHEN THE MORNING STARS SHOUTED FOR JOY*?

Upon all Feasts of Mary, Holy Mother of God.

Upon the Feast of All Saints (although there be some who use red at this time, as shall be further noted below).

Upon the principal Feast of S. John, Evangelist.[5]

Upon the Conversion of S. Paul.

Upon the Enthronement of S. Peter,[6] whereof I will speak again.

From the Vigil of our Lord's Nativity to the Octave of Epiphany inclusively, save only upon such Feasts of Martyrs as occur between.[7]

Upon the Nativity of our Saviour, and also of His Forerunner, for that both were born pure, that is, without original sin. For *THE LORD RIDETH UPON A SWIFT CLOUD,*[8] which is to say that He took Flesh unspotted of sin, and *COMETH INTO EGYPT,*[9] that is, into the world; according to that which the Angel spake unto the Virgin, *THE HOLY GHOST SHALL COME UPON THEE, AND THE POWER OF THE HIGHEST SHALL OVERSHADOW THEE.*[10] And John, even if thou hold him to have been conceived in sin, was nevertheless sanctified in the womb, as saith the Prophet, *BEFORE THOU CAMEST FORTH OUT OF THE WOMB I SANCTIFIED THEE*;[11] and the Angel spake unto Zachary concerning him, *HE SHALL BE FILLED WITH THE HOLY GHOST EVEN FROM HIS MOTHER'S WOMB.*[12]

White is used, again, in the Epiphany, by reason of the brightness of the star which led the Magi, as saith the Prophet,[13] *THE GENTILES SHALL COME TO THY LIGHT, AND KINGS TO THE BRIGHTNESS OF THY RISING.*

At Hypapante,[14] in honour of the purity of Mary, who at that time according to the song of Symeon did offer a *LIGHT TO LIGHTEN THE GENTILES.*[15]

Upon Maundy Thursday, by reason of the consecration of the Chrism,[16] for the soul's cleansing; for cleanness is commanded in especial by the Gospel read upon that day, wherein the Lord saith, *HE THAT IS BATHED NEEDETH NOT SAVE TO WASH HIS FEET, BUT IS CLEAN EVERY WHIT.*[17] And again, *IF I WASH THEE NOT, THOU HAST NO PART WITH ME.*[18]

Upon Holy Saturday, in the Office of the Mass, and from thence unto the Octave of the Ascension inclusively, at all Offices of the season; save only upon Rogation Days, and upon such Feasts of Martyrs as occur between, whereof I will speak anon.

Upon the Feast of the Resurrection, because of the Angel, the witness of the Resurrection, the herald, who appeared *CLOTHED IN A LONG WHITE GARMENT*;[19] of whom saith Matthew, that *HIS COUNTENANCE WAS LIKE LIGHTNING, AND HIS RAIMENT WHITE AS SNOW.*[20] Also because children, who receive the New Birth at that time, are arrayed in white garments.[21]

Upon the Feast of the Ascension, by reason of the bright cloud in which Christ ascended; for *TWO MEN STOOD BY THEM IN WHITE APPAREL, WHICH ALSO SAID, YE MEN OF GALILEE, WHY STAND YE GASING UP INTO HEAVEN?*[22]

3. At the Dedication of a Church. For note, that although at the consecration of a Bishop the colour of Vestments shall be such as agreeth unto the proper of the day, yet at the Dedication of a Church white Vestments be always used, whatever be the day of its solemnisation. The reason hereof is, that at the Consecration of a Bishop the Mass of the day is sung, but at the Dedication of a Basilica, the Mass of Dedication. For the Church is named with the name of a Virgin, according to that of the Apostle, *I HAVE ESPOUSED YOU TO ONE HUSBAND, THAT I MAY PRESENT YOU AS A CHASTE VIRGIN TO CHRIST.*[23] And of her the Bridegroom saith in the Canticles, *THOU ART ALL FAIR, MY LOVE; THERE IS NO SPOT IN THEE.*[24] Yet the Bishop himself who is consecrated weareth white Vestments, to denote that at all times *HIS GARMENTS* (that is, his life) *MUST BE WHITE*[25] (that is, without stain).

And, lastly, white Vestments are used throughout the Octaves of such of the Feasts aforesaid as have Octaves, at all Offices wherein such Octaves are kept.

4. Red Vestments are used at the following times:—

Upon the Festivals of Apostles, Evangelists, and of Martyrs, by reason of the blood of suffering which they shed for Christ; for *THESE ARE THEY WHICH CAME OUT OF GREAT TRIBULATION*;[26] save only upon the Feast of the Holy Innocents, as shall be presently set forth.

Upon the Feast of that Holy Cross, whereon Christ shed His Blood for us; as saith the Prophet, *WHEREFORE ART THOU RED IN THINE APPAREL, LIKE HIM THAT TREADETH IN THE WINEFAT*?[27] But others say it is better to use white on that day, since it is the Feast, not of the Passion, but of the Invention[28] or Exaltation[29] of the Cross.

At Mass from the Vigil of Pentecost until the Sabbath following, inclusively; because of the burning fire of the Holy Spirit, Who appeared upon the Apostles in tongues of fire; for *THERE APPEARED UNTO THEM CLOVEN TONGUES LIKE AS OF FIRE, AND IT SAT UPON EACH OF THEM*.[30] And according to the Prophet, *FROM ABOVE HATH HE SENT A FIRE IN MY BONES*.[31] But although upon the Feast of the Martyrdom of the Apostles Peter and Paul red be used, yet upon the Conversion of Saint Paul, and upon the Enthronement of Saint Peter, we wear white. And though upon the Nativity of Saint John Baptist white be worn, yet is read used upon his Decollation.

5. And upon the Feast of a Saint who is both Martyr and Virgin, the Martyrdom hath the preference, for it is the sign of love in perfection; as saith the Truth, *GREATER LOVE HATH NO MAN THAN THIS, THAT A MAN LAY DOWN HIS LIFE FOR HIS FRIENDS*.[32]

For this reason there be some who use red Vestments in the Commemoration of All Saints, but others use white, as doth the Roman Church, for that not only on that day, but concerning it, the Church saith that the Saints, as according to John in the Apocalypse, will stand *BEFORE THE LAMB, CLOTHED WITH WHITE ROBES, AND PALMS IN THEIR HANDS*.[33] The Bride saith also in the Canticles, *MY BELOVED IS WHITE AND RUDDY, THE CHIEFEST AMONG TEN THOUSAND*;[34] that is, He is white, in His Confessors and Virgins, and red, in His Martyrs and Apostles; for these are the roses, those the lilies of the valley. They, on the other hand, who wear red on All Hallows' Day, are prompted by the thought that this Feast was first instituted in honour of Martyrs only.[35] But unto this it may be answered, that it was instituted in honour of the Blessed Virgin also; and that nowadays the Church holdeth festival on that day on behalf not of Martyrs only, but of Confessors and Virgins also, according to the institution of Gregory.

And lastly, Red is used throughout the Octave of such of the Festivals foregoing as have Octaves, whensoever the Office shall be of the Octave.

6. Black is worn upon the following:—

Upon Good Friday.

Upon days of affliction[36] and fasting for sin, and upon Rogation Days.

In barefoot processions which the Lord Pope maketh.

In Masses for the dead.

From Advent Sunday unto the Vigil of the Nativity.

From Septuagesima unto Holy Saturday. For the bride saith in the Canticles,[37] *I AM BLACK BUT COMELY, O YE DAUGHTERS OF JERUSALEM, AS THE TENTS OF KEDAR, AS THE CURTAINS OF SOLOMON; LOOK NOT UPON ME BECAUSE I AM BLACK, BECAUSE THE SUN HATH LOOKED UPON ME.*

Upon the Feast of the Holy Innocents some do contend that black, some that red, Vestments should be used. They who favour black, allege the sadness of the day, how that *IN RAMA WAS THERE A VOICE HEARD, LAMENTATION, AND WEEPING, AND GREAT MOURNING, RACHEL WEEPING FOR HER CHILDREN, AND WOULD NOT BE COMFORTED, BECAUSE THEY ARE NOT*;[38] and how for the same cause the joyous hymns upon that day are hushed,[39] and the Mitre without orfrey is brought. They on the other hand who contend for red, affirm that it is a day of martyrdom, in commemoration principally whereof the Church saith, 'All the Saints cry out beneath the Throne of God, Avenge our blood which is poured forth, O Lord our God.'[40] (So also upon Laetare Sunday, for the joy which the Golden Rose[41] bespeaketh, the Bishop of Rome hath a Mitre adorned with the orfrey, but black Vestments, by reason of the Lenten Fast.) But the Roman Church useth violet Vestments upon Holy Innocents' Day, when it falleth upon other than Sunday;[42] and upon its Octave, always red.

7. The colour that remaineth is Green, and this is used at the following times:—

Upon ferial and common days, because this colour is a kind of mean betwixt white, black, and red.

And especially between the Octave of Epiphany and Septuagesima, and between Pentecost and Advent, whensoever the Office shall be of the Sunday. For this colour is exprest in the words, *CAMPHIRE WITH SPIKENARD, SPIKENARD AND SAFFRON.*[43]

8. And unto these four colours thou mayest refer all the others: namely, unto red, scarlet; unto black, violet; unto white, fine linen; and unto green,

yellow.[44] Nevertheless according to some the rose belongeth unto Martyrs, the yellow crocus to Confessors, and the lily unto Virgins. And of colours I will treat also at the end of the following chapter.

9. It is not unmeet to use Violet at those seasons whereunto black belongeth. Thus the Roman Church useth violet from the first Sunday of Advent unto Mass on the Vigil of the Nativity inclusively, and from Septuagesima unto Mass on Easter Eve exclusively of the latter,[45] whensoever the Office is of the season; except upon Maundy Thursday[46] and Good Friday.[47] But upon the Saints' Days as occur in Lent and Advent neither black nor violet is to be worn. And be it understood that upon Holy Saturday violet is to be worn at every office[48] which hath place before Mass; with this exception, that the Deacon who blesseth the Paschal Candle, and the Subdeacon[49] who serveth him, are vested respectively in a Dalmatic and Tunicle of white, for that such Blessing of the Candle, as also the Mass itself, hath respect unto the Resurrection. But after the Blessing be done, the Deacon layeth aside his Dalmatic, and putting on a violet folded-chasuble keepeth the same even until the beginning of Mass. But the Subdeacon changeth not his Vestments.

Some, again, wear white Vestments upon Palm Sunday in the Procession and at the Blessing of Palm-branches, and during the singing of the Gospel and of the *Gloria laus et honor*, by reason of the gladness of the honour offered unto Christ, which is commemorated in those parts of the Office. But the Roman Church useth always violet at those times; as also in the Procession before Mass on the Feast of the Purification, because that Office bringeth to mind the anxious expectation of Symeon, and savoureth of the Old Testament.

10. The Roman Church useth Violet also upon the Ember Days of September, and upon such Vigils of Saints' Days as are Fasts, when Mass shall be of the Vigil. Also upon Rogation Days, and at the Mass of Litanies upon the Feast of Saint Mark.[50] For when we fast, we do buffet and crucify the flesh, that being livid with stripes it may be conformed unto the stripes which Christ suffered, *WITH WHOSE STRIPES WE ARE HEALED*;[51] and in token hereof we do at times of fasting use violet, which is pale, and as it were of the hue of stripes.

It may be noted that at the Feast of Easter there are Veils[52] of three colours placed upon the Altar.

CHAPTER XIX: OF THE VESTMENTS OF THE LAW, OR OF THE OLD TESTAMENT[1]

1. Now seeing that human weakness comprehendeth the meaning of things the less fully, if it be ignorant essentially of the things themselves; we will say a few words upon the Vestments of the Law, unto the dispelling of this blind ignorance whereof I speak. And let us treat them, first, according to history;[2] secondly, according to allegory; and thirdly, according to parable.

First, then, as speaking historically, thou must know that according to the Mosaic Law there were four Vestments common both to the lesser Priests and to the High Priest himself; and of these we read in the twenty-eighth chapter of Exodus.[3]

The first was called *Manascasim*,[4] that is, linen Breeches, wove of fine twined linen, worn for that purpose whereof we read in the twentieth chapter of Exodus,[5] *THOU SHALT NOT GO UP BY STEPS UNTO MINE ALTAR, THAT THY NAKEDNESS BE NOT DISCOVERED THEREON.*

The second was the *Cathemone*,[6] or the Linen Coat, which we call the Subuncula,[7] or Albe; but Moses calleth it *Abaneth*;[8] and the Hebrews, when they departed from Babylon, called it *Emissanea*. This was of fine linen, and twofold.

The third was Balteus, that is, the Zone or Girdle; this was about four fingers in breadth, and was netlike, so as to resemble a viper's skin; and it was wove of fine linen, scarlet, purple, and blue, which were symbols of the four elements.

The fourth was the Tiara, which the Hebrews named *Mamphie*, and which we call Bonnet,[9] or Mitre; this, in the case of the lesser Priests, differed for the most part from the High Priest's Mitre, resembling in shape a round helm.

2. Over and above these four common Vestments, there were four worn by the High Priest, peculiar to him.

The first was the blue Robe, called in Hebrew *Vethit*,[10] in Greek *Poderes*, in Latin *Talaris*, that is, the garment that reacheth unto the feet; it had for its fringes pomegranates and eighty golden bells disposed altarnately, that the sound of the latter might be heard when the High Priest entered into the sanctuary, 'that he die not.'[11]

3. The second was the Ephod, or Superhumeral.[12] This was wove of the four colours aforesaid, with gold; it was sleeveless,[13] after the manner of an undergarment, having an opening in the breast of a span square,

wherein was fastened the Breastplate, being of the same size. And upon the upper part of the Ephod, that is, upon its shoulders, were set in golden ouches[14] two onyx-stones, whereon were graven the names of the twelve sons of Israel, six on the one, and six on the other. We read that Samuel and David[15] were clad with an ephod; but this was of linen, and was properly called *Ephotar*.

4. The third, called in Hebrew *Heen*, in Greek *Logion*, and in Latin *Rationale*,[16] or Breastplate, was worn by the High Priest upon his breast. It was called the Breastplate of Judgment; for there was a stone[17] therein, by whose brightness[18] he knew that God was favourable to him. Now the Breastplate was four-square, being doubled, a span broad and long; it was fashioned of the four colours foregoing, with gold. And it had twelve stones,[19] even four rows of stones. In the first row were a sardius, a topaz, and an emerald. In the second row, a carbuncle, a sapphire, and a jasper. In the third, a ligure, an agate, and an amethyst. In the fourth, a chrysolite, an onyx, and a berylstone. And upon these were graven the names of the twelve sons of Israel, every one with his name, according unto the order of their birth; and upon the Breastplate were inscribed also these two words, *URIM, THUMMIM*,[20] that is, Doctrine and Truth. And the Breastplate was made fast at[21] its upper part unto the Ephod by two rings, unto which were attached two golden chains, the other ends of the chains being fastened into two ouches which were fixt beneath the aforesaid onyx-stones to the Ephod; and at its lower part also it was joined unto the Ephod by the means of two other golden rings, into which were fastened two strings or laces of blue.

5. The fourth and last Vestment was that of the head, to wit, the Tiara or Mitre;[22] this did end in a point, and had a golden circlet, with pomegranates and flowers; and from it there did hang down upon the brow a Plate of gold,[23] in the shape of an half-moon, whereon was written *Anoth Adonai*, to wit, the Holy Name of the Lord, the Tetragrammaton or Four-lettered Name, whereof again below. And this Plate, lest it should move when the High Priest moved, was bound with a blue lace or ribband, plain to see, having its ends flowing loosely behind.

Now our own Bishop hath,—

In the stead of the Breeches, the Sandals.
For the Linen Coat he hath the Albe.
For the Girdle, the Girdle.

For the Robe of the Ephod, the Tunic.
For the Ephod, the Amice, or the Stole.
For the Breastplate, the Pall.
For the ancient Mitre or tiara, the Mitre.
For the Golden Plate, the Cross.

And of these Vestments certain have a different shape from those, but each hath the same notion as that other which it representeth.

6. Secondly, let us speak of the meaning of the aforesaid Vestments of the Law, according to allegory.

The High Priest, adorned with these Vestments, did represent as in a picture the whole of Creation. For the Breeches of fine linen did meetly signify the earth,[24] because fine linen cometh form the earth. The Girdle, with its laces and strings, denoted the ocean that windeth round it. The blue Tunic, by its hue, was the firmament; the Bells, the sound of the thunder; the Pomegranates, the gleam of the lightnings. The four Vestments of the lesser Priest, and the four of the greater, represented by their number the four parts of Man, the Microcosm,[25] and the four parts of Nature, the Macrocosm,[26] to wit, the four Temperaments, and the four Elements. The Ephod, with its many hues, was a picture of the starry heaven; the gold interwove with the colours, the warmth of life which penetrateth all things; and the two onyx-stones were the sun and moon, or the two hemispheres. The twelve pectoral jewels in the Breastplate represented the twelve signs of the zodiac; and the Breastplate itself, or Rationale, being in the midst, did shew forth that *Ratio*[27] or Law whereof all things on earth are full, whereby they cleave in obedience unto things in the heavens; yea, the law of the life of earth, and of the seasons of heat and cold and the temperate periods between them both, which cometh down from the law of the courses of the heavenly bodies. The rings and chains and ouches signified the linking together of the elements, and temperaments, and seasons. The Mitre shadowed forth the vast vault of heaven; the Golden Plate upon it represented God presiding over all things. And all this allegory is confirmed by the authority of the eighteenth chapter of the Book of Wisdom,[28] wherein it is written, *FOR IN THE LONG GARMENT, WHICH HE HAD, WAS THE WHOLE WORLD, AND IN THE FOUR ROWS OF THE STONES WAS THE GLORY OF THE FATHERS GRAVEN, AND THY MAJESTY UPON THE DIADEM OF HIS HEAD*.

7. In the third place must be added the explication of the Vestments of the Law according to parable.

Now the following was the order wherein the Priest of the Law was wont to array himself in the Vestments.

Having first washed his hands and feet, he put on the Breeches, in token that the Priest, having cleansed his affections and works with the tears of penance, ought to put on Continence, that he might offer a sacrifice without spot, sacred, acceptable unto God.[29] But our own Bishop, for that he ought to have continence alway, putteth not on the breeches for sacrifice, but Sandals, as though one might say, *HE THAT IS BATHED[30] NEEDETH NOT SAVE TO WASH HIS FEET, BUT IS CLEAN EVERY WHIT*. For by the hands are signified works, according to that Scripture,[31] *BLESSED BE THE LORD MY STRENGTH, WHO TEACHETH MY HANDS TO WAR, AND MY FINGERS TO FIGHT*; and by the feet the affections, as it is written, *SHAKE OFF THE DUST OF YOUR FEET*.[32] And it is to be noted, that the Priest did himself put on him the Breeches, which were a type of virginal continence: these, I say, for that virginity is a matter of counsel, not of commandment, he did put on with his own hand, in agreement with that of Paul to the Corinthians,[33] *NOW CONCERNING VIRGINS I HAVE NO COMMANDMENT OF THE LORD; BUT I GIVE MY JUDGMENT*. And the Lord in the Gospel saith Himself, *HE THAT IS ABLE TO RECEIVE IT, LET HIM RECEIVE IT*.[34] Also the Priests were wont to put on this Vestment by turns,[35] because they were not held bound to perpetual virginity, as are the ministers of the New Testament; and for this reason, according to some, there is no Vestment nowadays answering thereto.

8. Next, he put on the Linen Coat, in token that the Priest ought to put on innocence, that he do not unto others that which he would not have them do unto him. For linen by its whiteness doth signify innocence, as it is written, *LET THY GARMENTS BE ALWAYS WHITE*.[36]

9. In the third place he girded him with the Girdle, the type of Chastity, wherewith he must be girt around the loins, that he might keep in subjection the concupiscence of the flesh; as saith the Truth, *LET YOU LOINS BE GIRDED ABOUT, AND YOUR LIGHTS BURNING IN YOUR HANDS*.[37] This Girdle, being woven of four colours, as is aforesaid, did betoken that he ought to bridle all motions that should arise from the four temperaments, or from the four elements; as it is said in the last chapter of the Proverbs,[38] *A VIRTUOUS WOMAN DELIVERETH GIRDLES UNTO THE MERCHANT*; and in the eleventh chapter of Esaias,[39] *RIGHTEOUSNESS SHALL BE THE GIRDLE OF HIS LOINS*. For it is by righteousness that all such animal motions are restrained. The Girdle also did hang

down even unto the feet, for that he must be clean, yea, even unto the end of his life.

10. The fourth Vestment he put on was the Robe, which reached unto the heel, meaning that he must put on Perseverance; for *HE THAT ENDURETH UNTO THE END SHALL BE SAVED.*[40] For by the heel, which is the end of the body, we understand Perseverance, as it is written, *IT SHALL BRUISE THY HEAD, AND THOU SHALT BRUISE HIS HEEL.*[41] For a fringe, too, there hung from the Robe pomegranates with golden bells; now the pomegranate signifieth work, and the golden bells, preaching: which two things must be combined in the Priest, that *HE DIE NOT*, entering in without them into the sanctuary before the Lord. For Jesus Himself *BEGAN BOTH TO DO AND TEACH,*[42] leaving unto Priests *AN EXAMPLE, THAT THEY SHOULD FOLLOW HIS STEPS*; *WHO DID NO SIN*, that righteousness might be found in their lives, *NEITHER WAS GUILE FOUND IN HIS MOUTH,*[43] that in their preaching truth might be found.

By the bells, again, we understand the preacher's voice, that the Priest provoke not by his silence the judgment of Him, Who being above seeth all things; and the pomegranates are the pattern of a good life, or the spirit of martyrdom, because by fruit of this kind the sick are refreshed. According to Gregory,[44] the Priest must die, if on going in or out his sound be not heard; which is to say, that he bringeth upon himself the wrath of Him that judgeth in secret, if he walk without the sound of preaching: and with this it agreeth well that he should have bells, as we read, fastened unto his Vestments. Moreover, what are we to understand by the Priest's Vestments, save righteous works, according unto that of the Prophet, *LET THY PRIESTS BE CLOTHED WITH RIGHTEOUSNESS*? wherefore the bells cleave unto his Vestments, that his very works may proclaim, as it were with tongues, his life's way. And the bells are joined with pomegranates, because these latter signify the unity of the Faith; for as in the pomegranate many seeds within are united together beneath one rind without, so the innumerable peoples of Holy Church are all overspread with the Unity of the One Faith, albeit they have a diversity of merit within.

11. The fifth Vestment he put on was the Ephod, which he placed over his shoulders, to shew that the High Priest ought to put on patience, that *IN HIS PATIENCE HE MIGHT POSSESS HIS SOUL;*[45] for it is upon the shoulders that we carry burthens, as it is written, *HE BOWED HIS SHOULDER TO BEAR, AND BECAME A SERVANT UNTO TRIBUTE.*[46] And it had the two shoulder-pieces thereof joined at the two edges thereof, signifying that the High Priest ought to have the *ARMOUR OF RIGHTEOUSNESS ON THE RIGHT HAND AND ON THE LEFT,*[47] that he be not puffed

up with well-being, nor cast down with reverses. Also were there two onyx-stones fastened into the shoulders thereof, whereon were graven the twelve names of the children of Israel, six on the one, and six on the other; and by these two stones were represented Truth and Singleness—Truth, by their brightness, and Singleness by their solidity; and the names of the children of Israel were holy desires and works of righteousness, as it is written, 'Cursed is the man that hath not left seed in Israel.' The number six also doth denote perfection, for that on the sixth day God *FINISHED THE HEAVENS AND THE EARTH, AND ALL THE HOST OF THEM.*[48] Thus the graving of the six names of the children of Israel on the one stone, land six on the other, was a sign that the desires and works of the Priest ought not to stand in the *LEAVEN OF MALICE AND WICKEDNESS, BUT IN THE UNLEAVENED BREAD OF SINCERITY AND TRUTH;*[49] that his intention be informed with Singleness, and his end with Truth.

Gregory, in his Pastoral Letter,[50] saith that they were bidden to make the Ephod of gold, and blue, and purple, and twice-dyed scarlet, and fine twined linen, for the shewing forth that great diversity of virtues, wherewith the life of the Priest should shine. And in his garments it is gold that gleameth forth above all things, in token that in his life the understanding of wisdom must shine out before all. And to this is added blue, which gleameth in the hue of heaven, that all things through which he maketh way by his understanding may not minister unto earthly men-pleasing, but may soar up into the love of heavenly things; lest while he is unwisely taken up with the praises of himself, he himself become void of the understanding of truth. With the gold and the blue there is also purple mingled, that the heart of the Priest, while it hath hope concerning those lofty things which he preacheth, may repress in itself the suggestions of evil, and may as it were by a royal authority refute them. Again, to the gold and the blue, the fine linen and the purple, was added scarlet twice-dyed, that before the eyes of Him Who judgeth the hearts the excellencies of all his virtues might be adorned with the ornaments of Charity; and that all those merits in him which glitter before the eyes of men, might be kindled in the sight of the Secret Judge with the flame of an inner love. For this Charity, that a man should love both God and his neighbour, doth gleam as it were with a double tinge. But when the mind inclineth unto the precepts of Charity, it remaineth that one buffet the flesh by Abstinence; wherefore unto the twice-dyed scarlet fine twined linen is added. For fine linen cometh from the earth, with its radiant whiteness; what meaneth it, therefore, but the body's chastity, so white with her comely pureness? And it is also twisted, ere it be inwoven with the beauty of the Ephod; because it is when the flesh is wearied with fasting, that Chastity is brought unto her whiteness clean and perfect. For when amongst the other virtues the body's discipline flourisheth, it is as though, admidst the varied beauty of the Ephod, the fine twined linen shewed its gleam.[51]

12. The sixth Vestment was the Breastplate or Rationale, which was to say that the High Priest must put on discretion, whereby he may distinguish between light and darkness, between the right hand and the left; for light hath no fellowship with darkness, neither *CHRIST WITH BELIAL.*[52] This Breastplate also was four-square, shewing that he must make distinction between four things, namely, between truth and falsehood, that he swerve not in believing; and between good and evil, that he swerve not in doing. Double also it was, for that there were two on whose behalf he must see clearly, to wit, on his own behalf, and on his people's; lest, the blind leading the blind, both should fall into the ditch. And it had four rows of precious stones, because he must have four Cardinal Virtues, namely, Justice, Fortitude, Prudence, and Temperance; and in each row it had three stones, for that he should have, first, Faith, Hope, and Charity; secondly, Modesty, Gentleness, and Kindness; thirdly, Peace, Mercy, and Liberality; and fourthly, Vigilance, Carefulness, and Long-suffering. For precious stones are virtues, according to that scripture, that one buildeth *GOLD, SILVER, AND PRECIOUS STONES.*[53]

13. Two chains also it had of purest gold, attached thereto each in his place, and themselves fastened into two ouches, signifying that the High Priest ought to have two affections of love, that is, unto God and his neighbour; whereof we are taught, *THOU SHALT LOVE THE LORD THY GOD WITH ALL THY HEART, AND THY NEIGHBOUR AS THYSELF.*[54] For as gold taketh above all metals the pre-eminence, so Charity excelleth all virtues, as saith the Apostle[55] concerning it, *THE GREATEST OF THESE IS CHARITY.* The two ouches, into which the chains were fastened, were Intention and Consummation, that he should love God and his neighbour *OUT OF A PURE HEART, AND OF A GOOD CONSCIENCE, AND OF FAITH UNFEIGNED,*[56] and also for the sake of blessedness; loving God for his own sake, and his neighbour for God's. And this Breastplate of Judgment which Aaron wore, and whereon were inscribed the names of the twelve Patriarchs, was, as Gregory[57] saith, rightly called by this name; because a ruler ought ever with subtle discrimination to judge betwixt good and evil: determining what things are meet to be diligently observed, and by whom, and at what time, and after what manner; and not to seek his own, but to deem that the good of others agreeth best unto his own weal.

Thus in the Book of Exodus[58] it is written, *AND THOU SHALT PUT IN THE BREASTPLATE OF JUDGMENT THE URIM AND THE THUMMIM; AND THEY SHALL BE UPON AARON'S HEART, WHEN HE GOETH IN BEFORE THE LORD: AND AARON SHALL BEAR THE JUDGMENT OF THE CHILDREN OF ISRAEL UPON HIS HEART BEFORE THE LORD CONTINUALLY.* Now, if a Priest 'bear the judgment of the children of Israel upon his heart before the Lord,' it is to say that he pleadeth the cause of his flock before that Judge alone, Who seeth the hearts of men.

14. Some, however, have said that there is no Vestment to-day which answereth to the Breastplate, because there is amongst us no plenty of precious stones. Yet it is after the fashion of the Breastplate that the Bishop, at his consecration, beareth the Text of the Gospels[59] before his breast in the sight of all the people; for in the Text Doctrine and Truth are put in writing; and also ought the Bishop to have in his heart the Truth of the Gospel, and in his mouth its Doctrine as pertaineth to the setting forth thereof. And this, it may chance, is the reason why in certain Churches the covers of the script of the Gospels are embellished with gold, and silver, and precious stones;[60] and there is also another reason, for that in the Gospel there gleameth the gold of wisdom, the silver of eloquence, and the precious stones of wondrous works; these are the Bride's *BORDERS OF GOLD, WITH STUDS OF SILVER.*[61]

15. The seventh and last Vestment was that of the head, the Mitre or Tiara, which the High Priest put on last of all, and which signified humility; whereof the Lord said, *WHOSOEVER EXALTETH HIMSELF SHALL BE ABASED, AND HE THAT HUMBLETH HIMSELF SHALL BE EXALTED.*[62] This he wore on his head, to shew that the High Priest ought to bear humility in his mind; after the example of our Head, Who saith, *LEARN OF ME, FOR I AM MEEK AND LOWLY IN HEART.*[63] For by the head we do understand the mind, as it is written, *ANOINT THINE HEAD, AND WASH THY FACE.*[64] Again, the Mitre, as worn by the lesser Priests, signified Continence in the five senses; but as worn by the higher, Contemplation, whereunto they ought to be given.

16. From the front of the Mitre there hung down the Golden Plate, which was a figure of wisdom; or, if thou wilt, it foreshadowed the Sign of the Cross, which is made in the Office of Confirmation.[65] And upon this was graven the Tetragrammaton, that is, the Four-lettered Name of the Lord; and the letters were Yod, He, Vav, He, that is, The Beginning of the Life of Passion. Or, if one should speak more plainly, Christ, in Whose Name that High Priest did act, is the Beginning or Author of the Life of

Passion, which is to say the Life that hath been restored through His Passion; for *BY HIS DEATH HE HATH DESTROYED OUR DEATH, AND BY HIS RISING TO LIFE AGAIN HATH RESTORED TO US EVERLASTING LIFE.*[66]

17. Now all these Vestments were for the more part wove with work of varied colours, symbolising the variety of the virtues; whereof saith the Psalmist,[67] *UPON THY RIGHT HAND DID STAND THE QUEEN IN A VESTURE OF GOLD, WROUGHT ABOUT WITH DIVERS COLOURS.* And of four precious colours were they wove, namely, purple, scarlet, fine linen, and blue. The purple, the hue of kingly dignity, was the High-Priestly power; which needs must walk a royal way, that it deviate neither to the right hand nor to the left, that it bind not the worthy, nor loose the unworthy. The purple also signified water, because the worms that wrought it dwelt in shells of the sea. The scarlet, being of the colour of fire, signifieth the doctrine of the High Priest, which must gleam and burn like fire; wherefore also it is said to have been twice-dyed. For it must gleam, in promise, as that everyone who shall have left *HOUSE, OR FATHER, OR MOTHER, FOR HIS NAME'S SAKE, SHALL RECEIVE AN HUNDREDFOLD, AND SHALL INHERIT EVERLASTING LIFE:*[68] and it must burn, in threatening, as that *EVERY TREE WHICH BRINGETH NOT FORTH GOOD FRUIT SHALL BE HEWN DOWN, AND CAST INTO THE FIRE.*[69]

18. Hence it cometh that the Sovereign Pontiff is ever seen to be clad with a red robe without, while he weareth white garments within. For within he must be white with yet another whiteness, that is, Innocency and Charity; and without he must be red as in token of compassion, that is, that he may shew himself every ready to lay down his life for his sheep: for that he is Vice-gerent of Him Who made red His garments for all this world's sheep.

19. But by indulgence of Constantine,[70] Emperor, he may wear a purple cloak and a scarlet tunic, and all the robes of empire, the sceptre, the insignia, and ornaments. And whithersoever he goeth the Cross is borne in front of him, to shew that this Sign agreeth unto him more than unto all other; as it is written by the Apostle, *GOD FORBID THAT I SHOULD GLORY, SAVE IN THE CROSS OF OUR LORD JESUS CHRIST;*[71] that he may know it to be his duty to imitate the Crucified. Again, the scarlet twice-dyed in the High Priest's Vestments is Charity, which is as it were twice dyed, being coloured with the love of God, and the love of his neighbour.

By the fine linen, being of excellent whiteness, is signified the excellence of a good report; and it must be twined, that the High Priest might have a good report both of them that are within, and of them that are without, as the Apostle hinteth.

And lastly, the blue, being of the colour of the firmament, signified that serenity of conscience which the High Priest must have within himself, according to that word of the Apostle,[72] *FOR OUR REJOICING IS THIS, THE TESTIMONY OF OUR CONSCIENCE.*

HERE ENDETH THE BOOK OF THE VESTMENTS OF THE CHURCH.

The Pelican feeding its young from its own blood symbolizes Jesus' sacrifice for His followers.

Chi Rho Monogram

(Spain, 5th-6th Century)

ON THE MASS

EIGHT CHAPTERS
FROM THE FOURTH BOOK OF
THE RATIONALE DIVINORUM OFFICIORUM

TRANSLATED BY
THE REVEREND FATHER RAMA COOMARASWAMY
2005

RATIONAL
OU
MANUEL DES DIVINS OFFICES
DE
GUILLAUME DURAND
Évèque de Mende au treizième siècle
ou
RAISONS MYSTIQUES ET HISTORIQUES
DE LA LITURGIE CATHOLIQUE;
TRADUIT POUR LA PREMIÈRE FOIS, DE LATIN EN FRANÇAIS
Par M. CHARLES BARTHÉLEMY (de Paris),
Membre de la Société des Antiguaires de Picaardie,
Correspondant du Ministère de l'instruction publique
pour les Travaux historiques
PRÉCÈDÉ
D'UNE NOTICE HISTORIQUE SUR LA VIE
ET SUR LES ÉCRITS DE DURAND DE MENDE.
SUIVI
D'UNE BIBLIOGRAPHIE CHRONOLOGIQUE
DES PRINCIPAUX OUVRAGES QUI TRAITENT DE LA LITURGIE
CATHOLIQUE, AVEC UN GRAND NOMBER DE NOTES A LA SUITE
DE CHAQUE VOLUME.

Litttera enim occidit, spiritus aulem vivificat.
La letter tue, c'est l'espirit seul qui vivifie.
(S. Paul, II ad Cor., III, 6.)

PARIS
1854

(Notre Dame, Paris, France)

ON THE MASS

CHAPTER I: CONCERNING THE MASS AND ALL THAT TAKES PLACE DURING THE MASS

1. Of all the mysteries (*sacramenta*) of the Church, all are in agreement that the most important is the Mass celebrated on the most holy altar. This mystery represents the feast of the Church for which the Father killed the fatted calf in order to celebrate the return of His Son, and wherein He offered Him the bread of life and the wine mixed with his wisdom.

2. Now, it is Christ Himself who instituted this office when He concluded the New Testament, sharing his kingdom with His inheritors, as His Father had done with Him, in order that they could eat and drink with Him in Heaven. For, after He had eaten, Jesus took the bread, and giving thanks, he blessed and broke the bread and gave it to his disciples saying "accept and eat, this is My Body which is given up for you; do this in memory of me." Subsequently the Apostles, formed by this teaching, began to frequently offer this most holy mystery for the same reasons that Christ had indicated, expressly preserving the same form of the words and the same matter or species (*in rebus*), as St. Paul stated to the Corinthians when he said: "For I have received of the Lord that which also I delivered unto you, that the Lord Jesus, the same night in which he was betrayed, took bread, and giving thanks, broke, and said: Take ye, and eat *etc*." It follows that the office of the Mass is the most sacred and solemn of all Church rites. This is why we should discuss this mystery before any of the others in this fourth part. We shall also consult the *Speculum* of Pope Innocent III with regard to certain mysteries and some of the points which heretics have attacked.

3. Certainly, Our Lord Jesus, priest according to the order of Melchisedech, instituted the Mass when He transformed (*transmutavit*) the bread and the wine into His Body and Blood, saying "This is My Body... this is My Blood" adding "Do this in memory of me."

4. And the Apostles have added to this Mass, by not only saying these very words, but by joining to them the Lord's prayer.

5. And so it is that the blessed Peter, the premier Apostle, after the passion of Our Lord, celebrated this Mass in the eastern lands, where for a period of four years he sat upon the sacradotal chair. Subsequently, when he took the chair in Antioch, he added three prayers to the Mass. It is clear then that at the beginning, the Mass was said differently than it is today, as

is explained in greater detail in the sixth part dealing with Good Friday and Holy Saturday; for originally the Mass on these days consisted only of reading the Epistle and Gospel.

6. Later, Pope Celestine established the practice of chanting the Introit before Mass, as is explained in the chapter on the *Introit.* Studies show that in the course of time as the Christian faith spread, other additions were made to the Mass by different popes such as Galasius, Celestine, and Gregory, and this to enhance the beauty of the rite. This will also be discussed in the introduction to the sixth part.

7. Historical studies show that James the Less, the brother of Our Lord and Bishop of Jerusalem,[1] and Basil, the Bishop of Caesarea have provided us in their writings with the manner in which Mass was said in their day. It is also documented that James, the son of Alpheus, after the Ascension of Our Lord, was the first among the Apostles to celebrate the Mass in Jerusalem. This honor was given to him by the other Apostles because of his eminent sanctity, and this perhaps before he was consecrated as Bishop—though others say that he first celebrated dressed in Bishop's robes, as was the case of Peter after him in Antioch and Mark in Alexandria.

8. But certain perfidious heretics would have us believe that in the Mass we only read the Gospel of which different parts are taken and patched together, and that apart from the Lord's Prayer, we have added various phrases to the primitive Mass. And they point out that it is written that "if anyone should add anything to what is written in the Scriptures, God will punish him with terrible penalties." They also accuse us of adding to the New Testament, as well as to the precepts of the Apostles, establishing further rules new teachings of the theologians, and practices that go against what Christ said: "Truly, you have rendered the commandment of God to preserve your traditions useless." And again "Every institution which has not been instituted by my Father who is in heaven will be rooted up." So too the Apostle: "Do not let yourselves be seduced by diverse and strange doctrines." And again: "No one should offer any other foundation than that which has been established, which is Christ."

9. They further claim that the Church of Christ never chanted either the Mass or Matins, that neither Christ nor the Apostles instituted this practice, that no one practiced this in the time of the Apostles, that there is no evidence that anyone in those times spoke of a Mass, and that there is no written evidence to support the existence of a Mass as we now understand it. They claim that what we now call a Mass was called a Supper by the Apostles. In the early Church and among the Apostles there was no chanting, no use of the organ, nor the practice of singing in high and low voices.

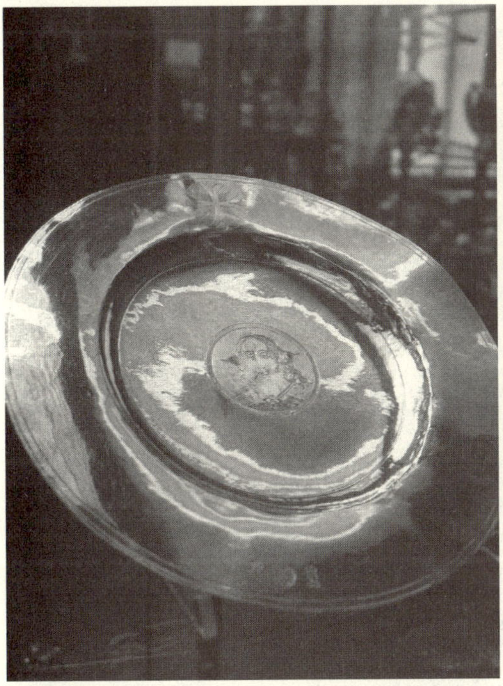

Paten Tray

Chalice

Chalice

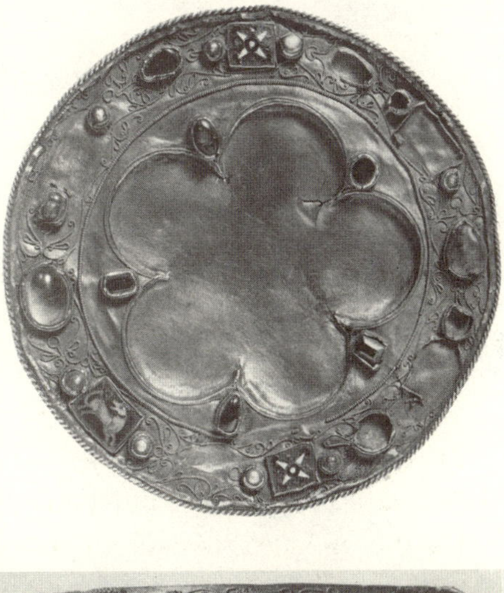

(Cathedral of Nancy, France, 10th Century)

(Notre Dame, Paris, France)

"On the altar of the body, the flesh is immolated by contrition; in the censor of the heart, devotion is fire that burns the incense; in the propitiation of God the Father the blood is offered by way of redemption."

We are accused of doing these things, and of saying nocturnes and the other canonical hours, and that in doing so we are going against the words of the prophet Amos who said "You have changed your feasts into mournings and all your songs into lamentations." Again they point to the words of the prophet Ezekhiel: "They listen to the words but do not practice them, because they change them into a song which they speak with their tongue while their heart follows after its own lusts, and this they do while they sing songs that are soft and pleasing."

10. However, their error is easily confuted and turned against them as will be shown in the preface to the fifth part. Beyond this, in the early Church, the divine mysteries were celebrated in Hebrew; but in the time of the Emperor Adrian I, they began in the eastern churches to be celebrated in Greek.

11. We see with certainty that the office of the Mass was established in a most providential manner. The greater part of it is based on what Christ did, from the moment when he descended from heaven until he mounted on high again, and these things he represented in an admirable manner both by words and by signs.

12. This Office can be divided into four categories, namely persons, works, words and things. There are three orders of persons, namely the celebrants, ministers or aids, and assistants. There are three kinds of works, namely gestures, acts and movements. There are also three kinds of words, namely prayers, modulations of voice, and lessons or readings. Similarly, there are three kinds of things, namely, ornaments, instruments and elements; for all these things are full of divine mysteries as we have previously pointed out in the preface to this work.

13. Actually, in former times the temple was divided into two parts separated by a veil. The first part was called the holy or the sanctified, and the second (or inner) part the Holy of Holies or the sanctified of the sanctified. Now, everything that takes place during the Mass before the *Secret* is in many ways similar to what occurred in the first and outer part of the temple, while what occurs during the *Secret* and thereafter pertains to what occurred in the inner part of the temple. Now inside the Holy of Holies was placed the altar of incense, the Ark of the Covenant and the table over the Ark, as was explained in the first part of this work in the chapters dealing with the Church, the Altar, and as is set forth in *Exodus*; and on the table are the two cherubim of glory looking at one another. Only the High Priest entered into this inner sanctuary, and this but once a year. He had, on this occasion, the names of the fathers or patriarchs written on the breastplate and subhumeral. He carried with him the blood and the coals, which

he placed in the censer with sweet scents while praying until the smoke rose and enveloped him like a cloud. Then he sprinkled the blood on the and the table. He then came out before the people and washed his vestments, for he was not considered to be pure until the evening when the red cow was immolated.

14. Formerly these things were signs; but they fell into disuse when that which they signified became physically manifest. For the first part of the sacred edifice signified the present Church, the Holy of Holies, Heaven, and the High Priest Christ; the blood His passion, the coals the charity of Christ, the censer His own flesh, the incense burnt the sweet scent of prayers, the altar the heavenly hosts, the Ark the human nature of Christ, the table God the Father, the two cherubim the two testaments which look on each other with mutual envy because they are in complete accord with each other; the vestments which one washes signify man and the evening the aging of man. Compare all this with all that Christ did, and carefully consider how the minister of the Church represents and reproduces these things during the office of the Mass. We will also speak about the significance of these things during the Canon of the Mass, at the start of one of its parts. The Ark is also a symbol of the humility of Christ from which, through His mercy we have received so many good things.

15. And further note that, as we read in Exodus (chaps. 25 and 37), placed over the Ark was the golden table of propitiation —that is to say, a golden table that had the same breadth and width as the Ark and which completely covered it. One called this the oracle (*oraculum*), because the Lord gave His responses to those who beseeched *(orantibus*) Him from this place. It was also called the table of propitiation because, when the Lord spoke from this place, he was being propitious to His people, or because on the day of propitiation one always saw the glory of the Lord descend on this place. And this is why in our days the tabernacle is placed on the posterior part of the altar, for in the tabernacle Christ, our propitiation, which is to say the consecrated Host, is kept. Now in one or the other part of the oracle, namely in one of the two frontal angles, were placed the two golden cherubim, which are, according to Josephus, two winged animals figured in a manner which no man has ever seen. Moses tells us that they appeared like the figures carved on the throne of God. One cherubim looks at the other; their faces however are turned towards the propitiatory. Now the propitiatory represents our incarnate Savior, for as Saint John says: "He is the propitiation for our sins." The two cherubim are the two Testaments. And just as these two Testaments in no way disagree, but both recount the mystery of the Incarnation of Christ, the one by prophecy and

(1731 depiction of the Ark and Cherubim)

The true cherub is composed of man, ox, lion, and eagle, and is thus a tetramorph

the other by witnessing, they direct their eyes and intention towards the propitiatory and gaze upon it together.

16. There are three sacrifices of the Church symbolized in the Old Testament by the propitiatory, the incense and the altar; namely the sacrifice of penitence, of justice and the Eucharist. With regard to the first, it is said: "A spirit broken with suffering is a sacrifice worthy of God. You will not scorn, O God, a contrite and humble heart." With regard to the second: "Then you will receive the sacrifice of justice." With regard to the third: "I will offer you a sacrifice of praise." On the altar of the body, the flesh is immolated by contrition; in the censer of the heart, devotion is fire that burns the incense; in the propitiation of God the Father the blood is offered by way of redemption. Now the priest offers these three sacrifices during the Mass: the first in the *Confiteor*, the second in the *Preface* and the third in the *Act of Grace* (or *Consecration*).[2] For these are the three things which the Prophet says God requires of man and regards with favor in man: to cherish mercy, to do justice and to walk attentively with God. For he greatly desires mercy who offers up the sacrifice of penitence. And he practices justice in so far as he offers up the sacrifice of justice. And he walks attentively with God who offers up the sacrifice of the Eucharist.

17. This is why the blessed Bernard said: "My brothers, in immolating the host of glory, we join the Word to words, meaning to meaning, affection to affection, loftiness to loftiness, perfection to perfection, humility to humility and liberty to liberty." Thus it is that he who offers the Mass to the Almighty should have the attitude which the Psalmist describes: "A broken and contrite heart is a sacrifice worthy of God" and more, "Sacrifice to God a sacrifice of praise." And the Apostle: "offer yourselves as a living sacrifice, holy, acceptable to God, that your service might be reasonable; mortify then, on the altar of your heart, your members, which are prone to worldly impurity, debauchery, evil concupiscence and avarice, in order that you can sacrifice yourselves to God with a pure heart and a chaste body."

18. Now in the sacrament of the Body of Christ, according to St. Augustine, "the priest perfects nothing, neither good nor bad, but remains with the others in the Ark and observes the form revealed by the dove, because it is not by the merit of the priest, but by the word of the Creator that the Sacrament is consummated." For gold is gold, whether it be in the hands of a thief or in the treasury of the king. And so it is that the High Priest Caiaphas, prosecutor of the true High Priest (though he was not sincere himself) gave counsel that was true; but he did not give this on his own, but it was from God. And a similar thing occurs in the Church, for the

iniquity of the priest in no way affects the sacrament, any more than the illness of the physician impedes the strength of the medicine he prescribes. Even though the *opus operans* (he who performs) is sometimes impure, the *opus operatum* (the work performed) is always pure. And even as all is pure for those who are pure, so also everything is impure for those who are impure. Thus when an evil person receives life, he incurs death. So also when a good person dies, he receives life. For he who unworthily receives the Body of Christ does so to his own judgment. But, with regard to such individuals, the Prophet says: "I curse your blessings," and St. Gregory: "Their blessings turn into curses, and their prayers into sins." Such men are cut off from the Church, for the Church cannot suffer them or others like them whose blessings, even if they be bishops, are equivalent to curses, because, as St. Augustine says, "to that degree that evil is in them, they sully the sacrament, while the sacrament itself remains pure; for the good shall be recompensed and the reprobates shall be judged." And again, "if the power of the sacrament is spiritual, it is received as a pure light by those who should be illuminated by the sacrament for their salvation; but in passing through the hands of impure ministers, which is like passing through a conduit, it is not soiled."

19. However, the perfidious and heretical followers of Arnauld claim that Christ in no way gave to the impure and luxurious ministers left to guard His Church, His bride, the power to celebrate the sacred mysteries. Nor did he give them the power of the keys to bind or to loose, because, as St. Gregory said, "only those who are upright in their lives, those that guard with their life the faith and doctrines of the Apostles, have, like the Apostles, the power to bind and to loose." Hence it follows, they claim, that the sacraments given by the impure have no power and do not avail for salvation, for it is said in the book of Numbers: "Everything that an impure man touches is rendered impure", and Christ Himself said, "a bad tree cannot give forth good fruit." Indeed, God asked the sinner David: "Why do you speak of my justice and let words of praise pass your lips?" And the Apostle: "Everything is pure for those who are pure; but nothing is pure for those who are defiled and who are unbelievers." Again, St. Gregory (*In Pastorali*, 1.I, cap., x and xcix, dist. 1): "When a person who is unpleasant is sent to intercede, the soul of the person is incensed and he is greatly provoked... (l.III.cap.xii) It is necessary that such a one's hands be pure if he is to wash those who are defiled, for fear lest being themselves unclean, they might defile all that they touch."

20. Now one celebrates Mass at the third, the sixth and the ninth hours: at the third hour because, according the St. Mark, Christ was elevated on

the Cross as a result of the cries of the Jews who clamored out "Crucify him," and because it was at this hour that the Holy Spirit descended on the Apostles in tongues of fire[3]; at the sixth hour because it was at this hour that, St. Matthew says, Christ was truly crucified and sacrificed. At the ninth hour because Christ, suspended on the cross, gave up the Spirit. Pope Telesphore decreed that Mass should not be said before the third hour, meaning public and popular Masses, for as St. Augustine said, "these things should not be done in public for fear lest the people should fail to attend those public Masses said at the third hour." Now the Mass is sung on Sunday, on feasts, and on vigils of feasts at the third hour; at the sixth hour during Lent; at the ninth hour on fast days, and also, following the decree of Pope Pelagius and others, on fast days, but not on all of them. But, on Saturdays in Quarter time, it can be celebrated late (*sero*) because of the sacred orders celebrated on the following Sunday. And, since Mass should be said while fasting, this is why, so that the length of the fast not be reduced, one begins to fast after vespers, for in this way the fast is prolonged until night. This is further discussed in the sixth section dealing with the Easter Saturday. That sometimes Mass is celebrated very early in the morning one must conclude that such is dictated by custom and not by decree. However Pope Leo would say Mass at daybreak, and I cannot say whether this was by necessity or by obligation, or whether he was taking advantage of his apostolic authority, or perhaps that this was for some particular reason. But those who because of necessity start before the third hour, or who offer the Holy Sacrifice after the sixth or ninth hour, for the love of God, lest the day pass without offering the sacrifice, can be excused as were those disciples who gathered up corn on the Sabbath, and with David who ate the showbreads. For in the Mass one makes present the passion, death, burial, resurrection, and ascension of Our Lord. And hence it is that Mass was said at different times, at the third hour, in memory of the passion and ascension; at the sixth hour in memory of the burial; early in the morning perhaps in memory of the resurrection. And there are those who hold that Our Lord was crucified at noon. And so it is that Mass is said at a variety of different times.

22. No one can celebrate two Masses with a single sacrifice, or a single Mass with two sacrifices. But one can within the same Canon, consecrate innumerable hosts, for the priest should always have a host ready for the Viaticum.

23. A priest can celebrate a single Mass with the sacrifice, and another one as a "dry Mass".[4] It is called "dry" because, if the priest cannot consecrate because perhaps he has already celebrated, or for some other cause,

he can, after putting on a stole, say the Epistle, Gospel, Lord's Prayer, and then give the blessing. In addition, out of devotion and not superstition, if he wishes say the whole office of the Mass without offering up the sacrifice, he may wear all the priestly vestments and celebrate the Mass in its order up to the end of the *Offertory*, passing over the *Secret* which pertains to the sacrifice. He can say the Preface in which one calls upon and makes present the angels in anticipation of the consecration of the Body and Blood of Christ. But he is not to say anything of the *Canon* with the exception of the Our Father, saying nothing that follows, which would normally be said in a low voice. He may have neither chalice or Host and say nothing that would be said over the chalice or Eucharist. He can then say, "May the peace of the Lord always be with you (*Pax Domini sit semper vobiscum*)." After that he can say the remaining prayers of the Mass in the ordinary manner, though it is better to omit the remainder.

24. The priest who has started the daily Mass can proceed to the *Offertory*; then he can start another Mass and say it up to the same place. Indeed, he can do this several times if he wishes, and after having commenced the Mass of the living, he can start to say the Mass of the dead, again stopping at the same place. And then, proceeding from there, he can also say the *Secrets*, but he can only say the *Canon* once and only consecrate one time; and after the Canon he can continue with the other prayers for the various Masses he started. But this is not approved and is detestable.

25. However the priest can sometimes celebrate several masses on a single day, Especially on Christmas as is explained in the sixth part where this feast is discussed; secondly, when the situation demands such, as for example if someone dies. However, the Council of Carthage laid down that if a Bishop or someone else died after the third hour, the commemoration should only be made by prayers and without the celebration of Mass. Thirdly, for courtesy or honor should some grand personage suddenly arrive and wish to hear Mass. Fourthly, according to some, for any useful reason such as the arrival of pilgrims or strangers, for travelers or for the sick, for those engaged; again because of the paucity of clerics or the poverty of churches; fifthly because as Richard, Bishop of Cremona says: "When two festivals concur one can also celebrate three times, as happens licitly at Christmas, or because the Passion of Christ is tripartite or divided into three parts. For he suffered from the tongues of those who insulted him, the hands of those who struck him and the nails by which they crucified him. He was also immolated by the patriarchs through their actions,[5] sacrificed by the Prophets through their words, and really offered by His

Father and Himself. Sixth, for the same reason, if a solemn feast coincides with a fast day, the priest can celebrate a Mass of the feast and another for the fast, providing no other priest can be found for this purpose.

26. One reads that Pope Leo often celebrated Mass seven, and even nine times on the same day. However, a priest who has to celebrate a second Mass on the same day only perfuses his fingers at the last Mass, because, if he does so at the first, he would no longer be fasting, and thus would be hindered from celebrating again; but elsewhere, every time he celebrates, he takes the Body of Christ and perfuses his fingers.

27. But can he consecrate after eating? I respond thus: It is permitted, but it should not be done. In effect, the fast is not absolutely necessary, as St. Augustine clearly testifies in the canon *D.c.*; for if so, Our Lord could not have consecrated. However, Master Hugh (of St. Victor) holds a contrary opinion.

28. In ancient times when heresies multiplied and attacked the Trinity, at the instigation of Alcuin, the teacher of Charlemagne, Boniface, archbishop of Mayence instituted the custom of saying the Mass of the Trinity on Sunday, Wisdom on Monday, the Holy Spirit on Tuesday, Charity on Wednesday, the angels on Thursday, the Cross on Friday, and the Blessed Virgin on Saturday. But when this was no longer a problem, this practice ceased, and the office of Sunday having been settled, it was established that Sunday should have its own office, namely that of the Trinity, and Monday that of the Angels because they were created on this day, first of all in the possession of gratuitous gifts; next light was separated from darkness, which is to say the good angels from the bad, because the bad angels fell but the good ones were established and confirmed.

29. On the first day, the angels were created before the good things of nature. Also, a Mass for the dead is said on the second day [Monday], for we apply to them the merits of the angels, and because in the opinion of some, the souls in Purgatory are relieved of their suffering on the first day, and on the second return to their pains and labors.

30. And this is why we come to their aid in relieving their suffering on the second day. On the third day Mass is said for sinners; on the fourth, for peace; on the fifth, for those undergoing trials; on the third day the Introit of the previous Sunday should be repeated. The fourth day (Wednesday) is also a fast day, and similarly on this day one should say the Mass of Sunday unless some other feast takes precedence. On the fourth day, the *Introit*, *Epistle* and *Gospel* from the Sunday office should be repeated, because it is held that Thursday (*dies Jovis*) is the cousin of Sunday (*cognata diei Dominicae*) as is said in the chapter regarding the Entry of a Pontiff to the

altar. On the fifth day (Friday), the Mass of the Cross; for this day in fact belongs especially to Christ and His cross as He wished to be crucified and to die on this day for the salvation of the human race.

31. On the seventh day (Saturday) is said the Mass of the Blessed Virgin, which practice originated in a church in Constantinople where there was an image of the Blessed Virgin before which was suspended a veil that completely covered it; but this veil or curtain, without being touched by human hands, would, through the grace of God, be lifted on Friday after Vespers, exposing the image as if descending from heaven, to the view of the people. And after the celebration of Vespers on Saturday the veil would once again descend and obscure the image and remain there till the next Friday evening. As a result of this miracle, the Mass of the Blessed Virgin was always said on this day.

32. There is another reason, for when the Savior was crucified and died, His disciples fled away and despaired of the resurrection, and she alone retained the faith on this Saturday, for she knew how she had carried Him without fatigue and gave birth, and this is why she was certain that He was the Son of God and that He would rise again on the third day from among the dead. And this is the reason why the day of Saturday, more than any other day, is dedicated to Blessed Mary.

33. The third reason is that Saturday is the door and entry to Sunday. Thus it is that on Saturday, we are near to Sunday. Now the day of our Lord is the day of rest, which symbolizes eternal life. It follows then that when we are in the grace of our Lord, we are in a certain way before the gate of paradise. And as our Blessed Virgin is herself the gate which conducts us to the realm of heaven, symbolized by Sunday, this is why we solemnize the memory of the seventh day which comes before Sunday.

34. A fourth reason is that the feast of the Mother should be followed by that of the Son. And a fifth, because a feast should take place on the day when God is resting from all work.

35. Now it is important to note that in the office of Mass where the passion of Christ is represented, we utilize three different languages, namely Greek, Hebrew and Latin—to recall the title on the Cross of Christ which was written in three languages (St. John, 19), and to signify that every language which is implied in this triple usage should give praise and confess God, because Our Lord Jesus Christ is in the glory of God the Father; because, while there are all sorts of languages, these three are the most important ones. Hebrew because of the ancient law and because it is the mother of the others. Greek because of its use in philosophy (*sapientiam*). And Latin because of its noble character and the domination of the Roman

(Germany, 12th Century)

"On the fifth day (Friday), the Mass of the Cross; for, in effect, this day especially belongs to Christ and His Cross as He wished to be crucified and to die on this day for the salvation of the human race."

(14th Century)

"On the seventh day (Saturday), one says the Mass of the Blessed Virgin, which practice originated in a church in Constantinople. As our Blessed Virgin is herself the gate which conducts us to the realm of heaven, which is symbolized by Sunday, this is why we solemnize the memory of the seventh day which comes before Sunday."

(14th Century)

Angel at the Throne of Divine Mercy (14th Century)

"One should also piously believe, and this is approved by certain authorites, that the angels of God assist as companions those who pray and hold close to them. According to the word of the Prophet: "I chant praises to you in the presence of angels." And the Angel said to Tobias, "when you pray with tears, I present your prayer to the Lord." But in the very canon of the Mass we find these words: "We beg and pray you, God the most powerful, that You order that these things be carried by the hands of your holy angel to the most high altar." Moreover, every man has his guardian angel appointed to him, for as our Lord said in the Gospel, speaking of little infants: "Their Angels always see the face of my Father." And so we always have them as participants in prayer who are co-associates in eternal glory."

Depictions of John the Baptist (Italy, 1225)

Cathedral Door St. Zeno, Verona, Italy, 1135-1140)

(12th Century France)

"The Introit is related to the choir of Prophets, because, according to St. Augustine, "Moses was the minister of the Ancient Testament, and the Prophets which lived shortly before the coming of the Lord, such as Zacharius, and John the Baptist, his son."

empire. Latin words are used for the epistles, gospels, prayers and canticles. Greek is used with the *Kyrie Eleison, Christe Eleison.* Hebrew provides the *Alleluia, amen, Sabaoth* and *Hosanna.* And so it follows that in the principle solemnities of the Pontifical Roman Mass, the gospels and the epistles are not only read in Latin, but also in Greek, to show the complete union of both peoples in one and the same faith, and to show that the Church does not just consist of Latins, but also of Greeks which will be seen in the sixth part in the chapter on Easter and Holy Friday.

36. The question arises as to whether a priest should celebrate Mass in the presence of less than two people. It seems that the answer is no because Pope Soter has also established that no one should think of solemnly celebrating unless two people are present, having also with them a third who can also give the responses. In effect, when the priest says "*Dominus vobiscum*", and at the *Secret* "*Orate pro me*", it is appropriate that several voices should reply to his greeting and invitation. But there is another point of view, which is that of necessity, in which case one can celebrate in the presence of a single person, and in yet another situation, which is that of the contempt of religion.

37. One should also piously believe, and this is approved by certain authorities, that the angels of God assist as companions those who pray and stand before them. According to the word of the Prophet: "I chant praises to you in the presence of the angels." And the Angel said to Tobias, "when you pray with tears, I present your prayer to the Lord." But in the very *Canon* of the Mass we find these words: "We beg and pray you, God most powerful, that You order that these things be carried by the hands of your holy angel to the most high altar." Moreover, every man has his guardian angel appointed to him, for as Our Lord said in the Gospel, speaking of little children: "Their angels always see the face of my Father." And so we always have them as participants in prayer who are co-associates in eternal glory. However the priest cannot celebrate the divine office alone, without the help of a minister or server, as is shown in the Constitution of Alexander. Canon XII (quest. 1) of the Council of Toledo again established this, namely: when there is a shortage of priests, and one offers the holy Sacrifice, he should have behind him the aid of a helper, lest if by chance he should mount the altar to celebrate the divine offices and should fall to the ground either ill or wounded, there be no one behind him to take his place. If, however, the Mass is said in a time of peace, and there is no war going on, if the Church is rich with the number of clergy, one may act in a different manner.

38. But generally, one should say that it is the ordinary Mass at which priests assist, to which one makes responses, at which one offers and communicates, such that the composition of the prayers themselves demonstrate this by a manifest rule.

39. The Introit is related to the choir of Prophets because, according to St. Augustine, "Moses was the minister of the Ancient Testament, and the Prophets are the ministers of the New." *Kyrie eleison* is connected with the Prophets who lived shortly before the coming of the Lord, such as Zacharius and John the Baptist, his son. The *Gloria in excelsis* pertained to heaven, which announced to the shepherds the joy that the angels felt for the nativity of Our Lord. The first *Collect* is connected with what Our Lord did around the age of twelve, namely when He went to Jerusalem and was sitting among the doctors both listening and asking. The *Epistle* is connected with the teaching of St. John. The responses related to the good will of the Apostles, namely how they were called by Our Lord, and how they responded in following Him. Their *Alleluia* was a reflection of the joy in their souls which they felt on hearing His promises and seeing His miracles and being able to perform miracles in His Name. The *Gospel* deals with the time of His preaching up to the time of His predicted death. And that which takes place next during the office of the Mass is connected with what happed since the Sunday when the children of the Jews went before Him until the day of His Ascension and Pentecost. The prayer which we call the *Secret* up to the *Nobis quoque peccatoribus* is designated as that prayer which Jesus said on the Mount of Olives. And what follows after signifies the time that Our Lord spent lying in the sepulcher. When one puts the host in the wine, it shows that the soul of God returned to His body. The greeting which follows signifies the graces which Christ gave to His disciples. The breaking of the bread (*oblatae*) represents the breaking of the bread by Our Lord with the disciples at Emmaus. These things will be mentioned more completely in their proper place. In the seventh section we will speak of the Requiem Mass and its special prayers.

40. Up to the present time Mass could only be said—apart from some true necessity—in places consecrated to God, which is to say in sanctuaries consecrated by prayers addressed to God by bishops. It follows that the Mass could not be said in profane locations without the permission of a bishop, for it is more saintly to not say or attend Mass in such places. This is why it is said, "See that you do not offer holocausts in every place that you find yourself; but in every place where the Lord, your God, chooses." This is spoken of in the fifth part. But necessity may arise, as for example on a boat, or among soldiers under a pavillion, or under the sky if a pavillion

(St. Domingo of Silos, Spain, 1100's) Entombment (St. Agnes' Convent, Prague, 13th Century)

(St. Domingo of Silos, Spain)

"The prayer which we call the Secret up to the Nobis quoque peccatoribus is designated as that prayer which Jesus said on the Mount of Olives. And what follows after signifies the time that Our Lord spent lying in the sepulcher. When one puts the host in the wine, it shows that the soul of God returned to His body."

Pentecost

is not available. But even then on a table or portable altar. And the priest should not celebrate Mass without the permission of the bishop, or on an altar that the bishop has used on the same day.

41. Formerly Pope Sixtus established the rule that Mass could not be celebrated except on an altar. Pope Felix I established the practice of celebrating Mass on the tombs or elevated monuments built in memory of the martyrs. Pope Boniface II established the practice of separating clerks from the laity during Mass. Pope Martin established the practice of saying Mass aloud. Pope Vigilius established the practice of saying Mass with the altar oriented towards the East.

42. It is also noteworthy that during the Mass the combat and victory of the priest over the ancient enemy is represented. We will speak of the progress of this combat in the chapter dealing with the Entry of the Bishop on the altar at the end. In the preface of the third part, we show what the arms of the priest are in this battle.

43. The Mass also imitates to some degree a judgment. This is why the *Canon* is also called an action. Now, an action is a cause brought forward in justice: word for word, it is as if we were before the bar. In effect, during the Mass we plead our cause; the sanctuary is the law court, God is the judge, the devil the accusor, the ministers or servers the witnesses, the priest the advocate and defender. Moses carried the pleas of the people before the Lord. As a result of his action falsehood and hypocrisy were confounded and our innocence entirely proven. We were absolved, the anger of the judge was appeased, the fault forgiven through His mercy. Beyond this thc Mass is called a mystery because it is it is beyond us, and a sacrifice because it is offered before everyone and for everyone.

44. The Mass is divided into two parts, namely the Mass of the Catechumen and the Mass of the Faithful.

45. The Mass of the Catechumens runs from the Introit to the *Offertory*. This Mass derives its name from the dismissal and exclusion of the Catechumens when the priest begins to consecrate the Eucharist. This is the source of the ancient custom of the Deacon crying out in a loud voice from the pulpit after the reading of the Gospel: "If there are any catechumens here, they should leave," as is explained in the sixth section in the paragraph dealing with the Fourth Feria (Wednesday) of the Fourth Week in Lent. This is because the Catechumens, being instructed in the faith have not as yet received a second birth through Baptism, and hence are, like the Jews and Gentiles, not members of the body of the Church. This is why they should not assist at the sacred mysteries of the altar which are only shared with the baptized faithful—for one should never expose the

treasures of the Church to her enemies. "For Jesus had no confidence in them, for He knew what was in man." From this again comes what is said in a canon from the Council of Carthage (*De consecratione*, distinct, I, *Episcopus*) that "one should prevent the gentile, heretic and Jew from entering the Church and hearing the word of God up to the end of the Mass of the Catechumens, and also the incestuous" (XXXV, dist. iii, *De incest.*, et cap. seq.).

46. But the Mass of the Faithful runs from the *Offertory* to the *Postcommunion* prayers, and this Mass gets its name from the word *dimittere* (*missa*), to dismiss, because when it is completed the faithful are dismissed to their dwelling places.

47. Or again, the phrase *missa est* is a collective name, because whether one refers to the Mass as occurring from the Introit to the *Offertory*, or from the Introit until the priest says *Ita missa est* (Go, the Mass has been said), and this is certainly true because the sacrifice has been completed and the victim consumed. Sometimes, which is quite appropriate, the Mass is considered to include the entire office from the Introit to the *Ita missa est*, or the invocation of the name of Our Lord which the priest invokes at the altar, which is in some way transmitted much like the faithful transmit their prayers, supplications and vows to the Most High through the sacred ministry of the priest who fulfills the role of mediator between men and God, namely Christ. Sometimes, however, this name signifies the office which one says in a low voice, and sometimes just the words used to consecrate the Body of Our Lord.

48. Sometimes the word Mass (*missa*) is a proper name because it signifies the Christ who was sent to the world by the Father. Or again the angel who was sent (*mittitur*) in order to bring by his hands the sacrifice which is offered, to the sublime altar of the Lord in heaven. Or the sacrifice itself, which is to say the host is called *mass* (*misse*), because, if one wishes, it is transmitted (*transmissa*); first by the Father to us, that it can live with and in us; then by us to the Father, that it in turn might intercede for us with Him. It is also transmitted, first of all to us, by God the Father by the incarnation of Christ, His Son, who was sent from heaven, and then to the Father by us through His passion. So also, in the Sacrament of the altar, it is transmitted to us, first of all by the Father as a result of its sanctified presence with us, and then to the Father by us with the oblation through which it intercedes for us with the Father. This legation or mission is in itself sufficient and capable of removing the enmity and obliterating the offences which exist between God and men. When then the deacon at the end of Mass says *Ita missa est*, it is the same thing as if he said, "Return

(Prague, 1360)

(Prague, 1360)

(Notre Dame, Paris, France)

"Reading of the Gospel."

home," or "Follow Christ," for the Mass that is offered is the sacrifice of salvation placed between our hands in order to appease God the Father.

49. In another way, the Mass can also be divided into four parts, as did the Apostle in the second chapter of the *Letter to Timothy*. The canons of the Council of Toledo also has the Mass consist of and include supplications, prayers, requests and praises or thanksgivings, as is explained in discussing the various formulas used in the fifth section of this work, in the article dealing with Terce. The first part extends from the Introit to the *Offertory*, which is labeled the section of supplication, which is to say the preaching that occurs before the blessing of the sacred species. The second up to the completion of the *Lord's Prayer*, namely when one says at this point: *Libera nos, quaesumus, Domine*, etc. (Deliver us, O Lord). The third up to the time of *Communion*, namely as Augustine says, up to that time when the Bishop says the *Postcommunion* prayers. The forth part from this point to the end, namely, according to Augustine, when, after the *Ite missa est* or *Benedicamus Domino* (Let us bless the Lord), the people respond *Deo gratias*. But others divide it differently, with the first part from the Introit up to the *Te igitur*, the second from this point to *Oremus praeceptis salutaibus*, etc; the third up the time of the *Collects*; the fourth, to the *Ita Missa est*. Again, because Christ has poured forth His blood from His body's five wounds, this is why the Mass is divided into five parts: the first up to *Pridie*, the second up to the *Momento*, the third up the *Praeceptis*, the fourth part up to the *Embolisms*,[6] and the fifth up to the *Collects*.

Portable Altar (1118 C.E.)

CHAPTER II: THE FIVE PSALMS THAT THE PONTIFF SAYS BEFORE CELEBRATING THE HOLY MYSTERIES

1. Before celebrating Mass the Pontiff says certain psalms and prayers in obedience to the rule established by Pope Celestine I. He says them before putting on his shoes and sandals in order to be in conformity with the exhortation of the Psalmist: "Let us hasten to present ourselves before Him in order to celebrate praises and songs on the musical instruments." These psalms are five in number, namely: *Quam dilecta tabernacula tua, Benedixisti, Inclina, Credidi* and *De Profundis*. He recites them in order to wash away by the prayer of the five psalms all the stains which his soul has contracted through the disobedience of the five senses. These psalms contain in effect certain things which are perfectly fitting for those who celebrate the mystery of the altar and the sacrament of the Eucharist. Now these prayers that the Pontiff says clearly have as their purpose the obtaining of virtue and purity of heart and body. He then says the psalm *Quam dilecta tabernacula* and the others to make it clear that the fullness of the virtues resides in Christ, of whom he is a figure.

2. It should be noted that any religious who goes barefoot according to the rule of his order, must put on shoes when he says the Mass in accordance of the precept of the Apostle writing to the Ephesians: "Place shoes on your feet in order that you may be disposed to follow the Gospel of peace." In effect with shoes (*calciamenta*) made of the skins of dead animals, the earth is trampled with the feet (*calcant*), and they are closed below and opened above to signify that the priest should be dead to the world and should have his heart closed to things earthly, to trample them underfoot as dangerous, to utterly scorn them, and have his heart open to seeing and desiring only heavenly goods.

Liturgical comb in ivory

CHAPTER III: THE CELEBRANT COMBS HIS HAIR AND WASHES HIS HANDS

1. The Pontiff as well as the priest, having put on his shoes or sandals, combs his hair and washes his hands and face. Now, in the ancient law the priest, in preparing to offer the sacrifice, first of all washed his hands and feet, and then put on foot-wear called *manastasis* which today are replaced by sandals. We have spoken of the *manastasis* in the third section in the chapter dealing with the vestments prescribed in the ancient law.

2. Thus the priest, in combing his hair and washing his face, does this first of all to follow the example of Mary who, to anticipate the future passion of Christ, anointed His head with oil, and the Mass is in fact a representation of the passion of Christ. Secondly, he does this to obey the commandment of Christ who said: "When you fast, anoint your head and wash your face," thus showing that in our pious works we should remove from us all that is false and all dissimulation. Thirdly, the priest combs his hair for the hair signifies the superfluous thoughts and the unnecessary solicitude we have for earthly matters: the head is the mind (*mens*) and functions to dominate all the acts of the soul as the head is above all the other members. Thus the hair is suitably smoothed down by its combing and put in order, the hair that falls down is put up, to indicate that, above all when approaching the altar, the priest should set his behavior in order and chase away superfluous thoughts, in accordance with the words of the prophet: "Get rid of the burden of your thoughts," so that his mind, through prudent discernment, might be separated and purged of earthly cares, pacified, and clothed with the virtues.

3. Now the comb with its symmetrical teeth functions to arrange the hair in order, and as such indicates the quality of discretion which should serve to adorn the intention of the soul, just as a comb arranges the hair in proper order.

4. The priest also washes his hands out of respect for this great sacrament which he wishes to approach with the greatest possible purity and, as St. Gregory says (in *Pastoral.*, lib. 1, cap. xii): "It is necessary that one who is charged to be pure and who is dirty, should try to have clean hands. He washes his hands according to the bodily sense to purify his actions from a spiritual point of view, according to the psalm *Lavabo inter innocents manus meas*, etc. so that he is not seen approaching the heavenly table with soiled hands, lest he should soil the divine sacraments, because one who eats and drinks unworthily eats and drinks his own judgment.

This is why we read in the *Gospel of Matthew*: "Eating with soiled hands does not affect the man, but that which proceeded from the mouth and comes from the heart, namely, the evil thoughts, the murders, the adulteries and other similar crimes—that is what defiles a man." And so we must make a great effort to purify, not only the exterior soiling of the hands, but the interior contamination of the mind.

5. The washing of the hands, as we have said, draws its origin from the ancient law, for one reads in chapters 30, 38, and 40 of *Exodus* that Moses made a bronze basin with the mirrors of women, in which the priests washed prior to entering the Tabernacle of Witness when they went before the altar. Now the resounding bronze basin indicates the confession of sins, the golden altar bitterness of the soul, and the mirrors of the women meditation on the lives of the saints.

6. The priest then, before going to the altar, should be washed and purified by confession or by tears of penitence. He purifies himself by the bitterness of his soul and tears of penitence, and reforms himself by meditating upon the lives of the saints. With regard to the first of these obligations, it is said: "Be ye pure, ye who carry the vessels of the Lord." With regard to the second: "Purge yourself of the old leaven etc.," and with regard to the third, by the light which proceeds before us, we are relieved of the heavy burden of sin and flee from the evil which is all around us." The priest should so act as to place himself among the numerous innocents who sing with a loud voice: "Judge me, O Lord, because I have walked in my innocence etc." And a little later, "I raise my hands in the company of innocents and I shall approach your altar." After that the priest dries his hands with a towel, because after having shed his tears of contrition, he should abhor sin and counteract it by works of satisfaction. The linen of which the towel is made has been blanched by the labor of men to whom it submits, and penitents come to eternal glory by means of satisfaction. The care of the hair, hands and face is not a sensual refinement, and it was our Lord Himself who gave this command to the priests of the ancient law, and it is a completely symbolic act.[7]

Winchester Bible (1160-1175)

CHAPTER IV: HOLY WATER, ITS CONSECRATION AND SPRINKLING

1. The priest who is about to celebrate Sunday Mass, starts by putting on the alb and stole without the chasuble (*planetam*), so to be free in his movements. In this state he blesses the water, according to the rule established by Pope Alexander I, and he sprinkles the church, the people, and altar with holy water in order to chase away every impurity of the unclean spirits from the place as well as the hearts of the faithful. He does this by the power which resides in the exorcised water, and also because all Christians, born anew in the sacrament of Baptism, are washed in this manner, just as the blood of the lamb was placed on the doors of their houses by the ancient people [of God] to turn aside the destroying angel.

2. From this derives what we read in the rule or canon of Pope Alexander I: "For the faithful we bless the water tinctured with salt, so that all those on whom it falls may be sanctified and purified, and we wish that all priests should perform this sprinkling. For if the ashes of a heifer sprinkled over the people sanctified and purified them, namely removed their venial faults, how much more is this the case with water tinctured with salt and consecrated by the prayers which are addressed to God. This sprinkling sanctifies and purifies the people of their venial faults. And if Eliseus was able to purify the sterile water with a little salt, how much more is this the case when the salt is consecrated by prayers addressed to God. It destroys the sterility of human things, sanctifies and purifies those who are sullied as well as bestows on them a multitude of other benefits; it turns aside the snares of the devil and protects men from his misleading fantasies. The priest then appropriately sprinkles the tabernacle while imploring the mercy of God.

3. Pope Cyprian also says that the sprinkling of the faithful with Holy Water has the power to sanctify them. For as Ezechiel says: "I will spread over you pure water and you will be purified of all your sins, and I will give you a new heart, and I will send a new spirit amongst you." One also reads in the Book of Numbers that "one who touches the body of a dead person or animal remains impure for seven days and will receive the sprinkling of this water on the third and seventh day, and he will in this manner be purified from sin. If he doesn't receive this sprinkling on the third day, he cannot be purified on the seventh." And again, "He who has not received the sprinkling with this water contaminates the tabernacle"; which is to say, as an impure person, he cannot enter with others into the taber-

nacle, which is to say, cannot enter into the tabernacle of the Lord which is the Church. And "he will be cut off from Israel." And again: "He who has not been purified by the water of expiation, remains impure and his impurity remains attached to him." And again, "You will purify the Levites by sprinkling them with the water of purification... The water used for sprinkling is a purification." We can see from these quotations that the sprinkling with water is like a sacred bath. However, some authors understand the above mentioned words as only relating to the water of Baptism.

4. Every Sunday one blesses the water in memory of Baptism, as is explained in the sixth part in the section dealing with the Ascension, except however on the Sundays of Easter and Pentecost because on the Sundays that precede these Sundays, the blessed water is set aside in order to sprinkle our persons and homes, and this before the infusion of chrism in the holy fonts as one sees in the canon *Cautum*, etc.

Thus we sprinkle our bodies and every place with Holy Water in remembrance of our Baptism. This is not done to re-baptized, but to call down the grace of the name of God and at the same time in remembrance of our Baptism; although on the two Sundays of Easter and Pentecost we sprinkle the altar, however, without chanting the ancient *Asperges me, Domine*, etc., because at these times we should weep because we recall that we have been purified by the suffering and Passion of Christ according to the words "I shall always recall these things to my memory and my soul will annihilate itself in them." And so it is that on Sundays, before the Mass and only before the high altar the people are sprinkled, although one incenses all the altars, or at least the main ones at the time of the nocturns and vespers.

5. Beyond this we must consider that this sprinkling of people and altars is done for yet another reason: because God has placed all men under the yoke of sin, at least of venial sin, for the just fall seven times a day. This is why the faithful, entering a church to assist at the Divine Mysteries, are sprinkled with this sanctified water, which is for the washing away of their daily faults, as was done with the ashes of the heiffer in the Old Testament. After that he who is unclean is kept apart from the assembly of the people (*ecclesiam*), until he has been washed by the water. The altar is sprinkled out of respect for the sacrament about to be consecrated on it so to keep away all evil spirits. And just as Christ is symbolized by the altar which should be made of stone according to the words of the Apostle: "Christ is the rock," and our faith is in the one Christ and not in several; this is why the sign corresponds to the thing signified, and a single altar

and all the people are sprinkled because it is the one Christ who bears the sins of the world.

6. Incensing can represent the outpouring of various spiritual graces, and, as grace is found not only in the head (*in capite*), but also in those are submissive to the head, so it is only reasonable that, after incensing the high altar, it is customary to also incense the others which symbolize the various saints. The incense in the censer signifies the heart ablaze with the fire of prayer, because our prayer should principally be directed to God and to Christ our mediator. This explains the custom of incensing the altar and the crucifix. At Eastertide we chant the *Vidi aqauam* during the sprinkling, words drawn from Ezechiel, chapter 40. Our Lord showed him a city built on a mountain which extended south, and in which was a wondrous temple. This city is the Church, of which it is said: "A city built upon a mountain that cannot be hidden." The temple is the Body of Christ about which it is said: "Destroy this temple and I will rebuild it in three days." The water which comes out of the temple is the fountain of Baptism which flows from the side of Christ.

7. But since Christ was pierced with a lance on his left side, why do we say that this water comes from the right side? There are two sides of Christ, the right and the left. The right is His divinity and the left His humanity. Thus the water comes out of the right side because it is from the divine nature of Christ that the invisible water of the Holy Spirit is derived, and He gave us this visible water which flows from the left side, which is to say, from the humanity of Christ pierced by the lance and having the power of salvation. It is thus appropriate that during the procession on Easter we should chant the words of praise for this flowing forth, in the flood of which we have been given a second life by the death of Christ. But after the octave of Pentecost, on Sundays during the sprinkling, one sings the ancient *Asperges me, Domine* etc. After Easter it was omitted because the Prophet had predicted everything that is connected to the faith about the Passion and the humility of Baptism.

8. Finally, when the water is blessed some salt mixed in, a practice which takes its origin from Eliseus; and this to show that the people, symbolized by the water, are imbued with the Word of God by the voice of the priest, who has the power to sanctify. Three signs of the Cross are made over the water and the salt which symbolizes the Word of God, to teach the people to give thanks to the Holy Trinity to which they are indebted for instruction and redemption. Water also represents confession and salt the bitterness of repentance. From the water and salt proceeds a double birth,

the division or separation from faults and the origin of the virtues and of good works.

9. But why does the priest bless the salt before the water? I answer: because the salt brings to mind the bitterness of penitence and the water brings to mind Baptism; therefore, since the contrition of heart should precede absolution, this is why the salt is blessed before the water. And it should be noted that there are four kinds of holy water.

10. The first, in which is accomplished the judgment said to be of purgation, which is no longer used. The second is that which sanctifies at the time when the Church and the altar are dedicated, ceremonies spoken of in the first part in the chapters dealing with the consecration and dedication of a church and its altar. The third is that with which we are sprinkled in church, the kind we have been discussing. The fourth is the water of Baptism which we discuss in the sixth part in the chapter on Holy Thursday. It was customary to moisten people before the chrism is added to the water, which still occurs in some places, but is forbidden today. They thought that this sprinkling washed them of their sins a second time, but it is the constant teaching of the Church that one cannot be baptized twice. And, as that which is more worthy draws to itself that which is less worthy, so a unblessed water is mixed with a blessed water to become a blessed water by the very fact of this mixing.

The Baptism (Limoges, France)

Medieval baptismal font detail

CHAPTER V: THE INTROIT OF THE MASS

1. The Mass is begun with the *Introit.* The Holy Fathers and the Prophets, before the advent of Christ, hungered after these times and predicted them. Long before His coming, they offered Him their desires, their works, their praises and their prayers, all of which things are figured in the Mass. With regard to the Introit, it is the antiphon that provides us with the title of the Mass and which provides us with their poetical and prophetical predictions, the desires of their holy prayers as they patiently await the coming of the Son of God and the incarnation of God Himself. As an indication of this, on the first Sunday of Advent, the Church chants in the Introit "I have elevated my eyes towards you." Then the choir of priests, representing the prophets and the multitude of saints, kings, priests and faithful, full of desire for the coming of Christ, chants in these imploring terms: "Lord, send for the Lamb who should rule on earth, *etc.*… Come Lord, do not delay, *etc.*," And this is why the elderly and saintly Simeon blessed God and said, "Now thou dost dismiss thy servant O Lord, etc." because "my eyes have seen." And the Evangelist: "A great number of kings and Prophets have desired to see what you have seen, and they have not so seen." Their desires are fulfilled in chanting the Introit according to this statement: "When He introduced his first born into the world, he said: "All the angels of God adore Him." The short verse (*versiculus*) follows drawn from the Psalms or even the same Psalm indicating that the desire has been fulfilled. This is also called a verse (*versus*), because by it we return once again to the Introit which symbolizes the works and predictions of the saints of the ancient law.

2. Pope Damasus instituted the saying of the *Gloria Patri* etc., which signifies praise because glory follows after great actions as a gift and recompense. One also says the *Gloria* to show that the Father, Son and Holy Spirit have an equal glory and coeternal majesty, in the beginning, now, and for ever and ever, which is to say, in the past, the present and the future. The interposition of the *Gloria* between the first chant and its repetition indicates a seeking after the supreme good. For, in order to more easily obtain that for which they ask, the saints cry out to the entire Trinity, glorifying it with heart and voice. "Lord, show us your mercy and give us your Savior, You who sit upon the cherubim, come to us." And the Holy Spirit, responding to their clamor, anoints the Savior with the oil of joy far greater than that of all other men, his brothers according to the flesh, and authorized him to announce the good news (*evangelisandum*) to the poor

as indeed the Son of God Himself attests through the Prophet when he said: "the Spirit of the Lord is on me. It is for this that He has anointed me and has authorized me to evangelize the poor." After this the antiphon is repeated to express most clearly the desire of the ancient patriarchs, its repetition indicating the multiplicity of their hopes and their cries. And as the prophet said, "Cry out, repeat, be patient, always waiting, for yet a little while longer, and yet a little time more because He will come and will not delay." The Introit however does not always present the desires of the ancients in the same terms, rather it does so by the vigor of the chant.

3. On the vigil of major feasts the Introit is chanted twice in praise of the divine and human natures united in the person of the Son of God. And in certain churches on major feast days it is repeated three times in praise and honor of the Trinity as if one wished to leap in cadences before it (*quasi ei tripudiemus*).[8] It is in memory of the Trinity that we offer the Mass, and that one says once the *Gloria Patri* in honor of the Incarnation. Sometimes one says the Introit in a low voice to give expression to our humility; then the response is given in a louder voice to indicate His humanity; and then in a still higher voice signifying that one has chased away the sleep of sin which the low voice gave expression to. The Apostle said, "The hour has come for us to rise from sleep." One can also say the Introit in yet another manner as is discussed in the section on the invitatory in the fifth part in the chapter on the Nocturnes; however the Introit is always repeated in its entirety, in order to symbolize a perfect joy. Some churches first say the entire Introit (*perfecte*), because the Church wishes to praise God in a perfect manner; then in sections (*impefercte*), because in this world praise is always imperfect; and lastly in its entirety because any panegyric of the celestial homeland is always perfect.

4. The Introit is so called either because the priest chants it before celebrating the sacred mysteries, or because this antiphon introduces the divine office, as is explained in the preface to the fifth section. Pope Celestine ordered that the hundred and fifty psalms of David be chanted with an antiphon at the start of Mass, and prior to the sacrifice. Before this it was the custom to read only the Epistles of Paul or the Gospel, following which one celebrated Mass.

5. All the usual Introits are drawn from these psalms, as are the graduals, the offertory and the communion verses, and thus they became the practice in the Roman Church. Saint Gregory put the Introit to music and specified the psalm verse that should be sung. The "irregular" Introits are those instituted in accordance with specific feasts, such as *Puer natus est nobis*, and *Spiritis Domini replevit*. And there are others such as *Viri Galilaei*,

and *Nunc scio vere, quia misit*, and still others used in individual churches. It is interesting to note that when the first verse of a psalm is used in the *Introit*, several of the following phrases are taken from the same psalm, as is seen for example in the Introit for the third feria of the first week in Lent which starts out with *Domine refugium*, of which the subsequent verse is *Priusquam montes fierent.* If on the other hand, it is not taken from the first verse of a psalm, but from some other place, then the first verse will be in the Introit later, as occurs on Christmas: *Dominus dixit ad me*, etc, the verse of which is *Quere fremuerunt gentes*. Similarly on the Feast of the Holy Innocents the Introit of which is *Ex ore infantium,* etc., and the verse *Domine, Deus noster*, etc. This practice demonstrates the union and connection between the head and the members. Sometimes the verse is double, sometimes simple, and sometimes split apart. This is discussed in greater detail in the sixth part in the section dealing with Saturday in the third week of Lent. During the chanting the priest and congregation stand, because this part of the Mass relates to the public preaching of Christ, for in this public preaching the predestined are called to the true worship of God. In some churches the tropes are said instead of the psalms, according to the order established by St. Gregory to indicate the tremendous joy resulting from the advent of Christ.

6. Properly speaking a trope is a small verse which is chanted on the principle festivals just before the Introit both as a preamble and a continuation. For example, on Christmas, before the Introit *Puer natum est*, the trope *Ecce adest, de quo Prophetae cecinerunt, dicentes: Puer natum est.* The trope is drawn from the ancient law. We read in chapter 10 of Numbers that when they lifted the tabernacle they sang "Arise O Lord", and when they carried it they sang "Return O Lord to the multitude of the hosts of Israel."

7. The word trope comes from the Greek *tropos*, meaning conversion, because ordinarily one would return to the Introit which is also why it is sometimes also called a verse (*versus*), It is also called *cord* (*zona*), *quae convertitur ab umbilico ad umbilicum cum circumeundo*.

8. We can understand the Introit in another way, as the praise which the Church offers to God for the conversion of the Jews. In this view the trope contains three things: the antiphon, the verse and the Gloria. And this relates to the three orders of the faithful which in the Hebrew language are referred to as patriarchs, prophets and apostles. The repetition of the antiphon is as it were the affirmation of what has been proclaimed by the prophets and evangelized by the apostles, and which had formerly been figuratively exemplified by the actions of the patriarchs. And, with regard

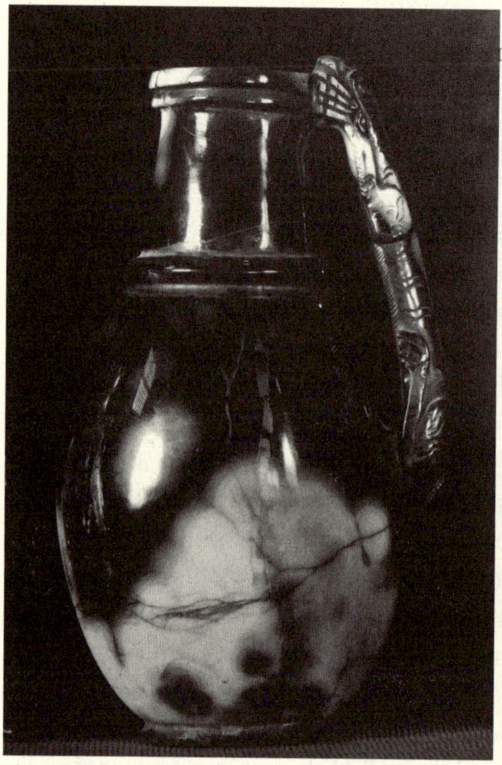

(St. Mark's, Venice, Italy)

(St. Mark's, Venice, Italy)

"Thus we sprinkle our bodies and every place with Holy Water in remembrance of our Baptism."

(Byzantine, 6-7th Century)

(13th-14th Century)

(Musée Cluny, Paris, France)

"The incensing can represent the effusion of various spiritual graces, and as grace is found not only in the chief, but also in those are submissive to the chief. So it is only reasonable that after incensing the High Altar, it is customary to also incense the others which symbolize the various saints. The incense in the censor signifies the heart enflamed with the fire of prayer, because our prayer should principally be directed to God and to Christ our mediator. This explains the custom of incensing the altar and the Crucifix."

Note the weeping sun and moon and rent curtain (Hortus Deliciarum, 12th Century)

(Hortus Deliciarum, 12th Century)

"The water which comes out of the temple is the fountain of Baptism which flows from the side of Christ. But since Christ was pierced with a lance on his left side, why do we say that this water comes from his right side? There are two sides of Christ, the right and the left. The right is His divinity and the left is His humanity. Thus the water comes out of the right side because it is from the divine nature of Christ that the invisible water of the Holy Spirit is derived, and He gave us this visible water which flows from the left side, which is to say, from the humanity of Christ pierced by the lance and having the power of salvation. It is thus appropriate that during the procession on Easter we should chant the words of praise for this flowing forth, in the inundation of which we have been given a second life by the death of Christ."

to this conversion, it should be noted that the solemn tropes are grafted onto the Introits, since the praises which they contain are intimately linked to the Introit, and the Greek word *trope* is translated in Latin as conversion.

(Notre Dame, Paris, France)

"The incensor walks before the acolytes carrying the candles in order to show that the mystical meaning of incense is the same in both the Old and the New Testaments, and in both it represents the saints. The incensor is a clear symbol of the human heart, which should be open to what is above and closed to what is below to guard and retain what is given. It should contain the fire of charity and the incense of devotion..."

CHAPTER VI: THE ENTRANCE PROCESSION AND THE ARRIVAL OF THE PRIEST OR BISHOP AT THE ALTAR

1. While the Introit is being chanted, the bishop or priest, dressed and adorned with sacred vestments leaves the sacristy (*de sacra aede*) and advances towards the altar, manifesting to us how Christ, waited for by the people, having drawn his most holy flesh from the incorruptible flesh of the Virgin, goes forth to the world. He departs from His impenetrable dwelling place in heaven, and from his secret retreat in the womb of the Virgin, like a husband from his nuptial bed. The priest or bishop advances from the sacristy towards the altar between two individuals, namely another priest and a deacon. He in turn is preceded by a subdeacon who carries the closed book of the Gospels. And before him two acolytes bearing candles and another priest carrying the censer or the incense. Last of all the priest or bishop arrives at the altar, removes his mitre, and says the *Confiteor,* opens the book and kisses it. The priest or bishop represents in a most excellent manner the High Priest which is Christ,—as the Apostle said, "Christ, the High Priest of future blessings, etc." The priest and deacon that accompany him represent the law and the prophets, as Our Lord Himself made clear in the parable of the wounded Samaritan: "A priest," he said, " passed by the road and seeing the wounded man avoided him; a Levite passed by and did the same." Again on Mt. Tabor, Moses and Elias appeared along with Christ, signifying the Law and the Prophets. The priest and the deacon lead the bishop because the Law and the Prophets foretold the coming of Christ. With regard to this Moses said "God will send you a prophet who will arise in the midst of you and you will listen to him as you do to myself." And Isaiah said "a great prophet will come and will renovate Jerusalem."

2. The bishop or priest walking between the two people mentioned symbolizes Christ between the Old and New Testaments. Christ is clearly announced to the world by both Testaments, by the Prophets and by the Apostles. And as Christ, who had to enter into the world, sent before him prophets, sages and scribes, so also the priest is preceded by the subdeacon, who carries the Scriptures and is qualified to prepare the sacred vessels for use in Sunday Masses. Sometimes an archdeacon and a priest accompany the bishop and they are preceded by the deacon and subdeacon, symbolizing the Apostles and the disciples that Christ sent before him; and again, each day the preachers and the bishops of the Church are sent to prepare, in a spiritual sense, the paths before the Lord. The subdeacon preceding

the bishop represents also John the Baptist, who with the spirit and virtue of Elias, was the precursor destined to prepare a perfect people for the Lord. And the sub-deacon carries before him the book of the Gospels, because John the Baptist initiated the Gospels by preaching "Be ye penitent, for the Kingdom of God is at hand." As for the deacon, he represents the prophets who announced the future life taught and promised by the Gospel. The bishop follows the Gospel to indicate that he should always have his eyes fixed upon the Gospel and have it present in his heart. It is carried before him because the doctrine of the Gospels prepares us for the way of Christ which leads to life.

3. One can also say that the subdeacon, who carries the book of the Gospels, and deacon who is its herald, also designate the saints of the New Testament. The book of the Gospels symbolizes the New Testament. The candle bearers and those that carry the incense represent the saints who have opened the pathways of the New Testament; the candle bearers represent the prophets and the law which foretold Christ, the light of the world.

4. Now one should not sacrifice without fire, for as it says in Leviticus (Chap. 7): "fire always burns upon my altar." We said in the first part, in the chapter discussing paintings, what light and candlesticks signify. Candles carried in the candlesticks signifies a principle, namely that the light of preachers should burn brightly before men and be founded on the Gospel. And this explains in a wonderful manner why the deacon and subdeacon follow behind the candle bearers which go before the Gospels, for the Law and the Prophets go before the law of grace. In some churches there are three candles, the one in the center being linked to these words: "Where two or three are gathered together in my name, I am in the midst of them." In other churches seven candles are used because the seven gifts of the Holy Spirit illuminate the entire Church. We will speak of this elsewhere when dealing with the subject of the Gospel.

5. The incensor walks before the candle-carrying acolytes and the others in order to show that the mystical meaning of incense is the same in both the Old and New Testaments, and in both it represents the saints. The censer is a clear symbol of the human heart which should be open to what is above and closed to what is below to guard and retain what is given. It should contain the fire of charity and the incense of devotion, or a most sweet prayer and a good example leading to what is above, thus showing the sweet odor which raises up from the censer. Just as the incense exhales a sweet scent which is put forth from the fire in the censer and which ascends on high, so our good works and prayers on earth which proceed from charity are more scented than all other perfumes. The censer filled

with incense also represents the Body of Christ so full of sweetness. The burning coals represent the Holy Spirit, and the incense and scent good works. We also speak of this in the fifth part in the chapter on Matins and Lauds, and later in the chapter on incensing.

6. When they arrive at the altar, the candles which went before are now placed on the side which indicates the teachings given before the birth of Christ as well as the light which followed after this event. The acolytes hold the candlesticks in their hands until the start of the *Kyrie eleison,* showing that those who preach should put into practice the teachings which they give out, and that they should not abandon the people who are ignorant before they learn to say "Lord, have mercy on us." When the *Kyrie* has started, the acolytes place the candlesticks on the floor, because, after performing good actions we should humble ourselves and recognize that we are but dust, and because doctors in the middle of their good actions and preaching ought to recognize that they are but slime. But when the Office starts we should rise up from the earth because each person, and especially the priest, ought to be raised up by good works, for from this point of view they allow others to glorify their Father who is in Heaven. The bishop, on arriving at the altar, removes his mitre and then says the *Confiteor*.

7. During the time that the Pontiff says the *Confiteor*, the subdeacon holds the book of the Gospels closed before his face. He stands on the left side because he to some degree represents the Prophets which are often read in the Church. He holds the book before the eyes of the Pontiff to remind him that he should always keep in mind the preaching of the Gospel, and the book is closed because the law of the Gospel is contained and mystically shut up in the sayings of the Prophets. When finished, he opens the Gospels and kisses the book as is spoken of in the chapter dealing with the kissing of the altar.

8. According to Pope Innocent III, when the Roman Pontiff offers a solemn High or "stational" Mass, he walks in procession from the sacristy or the place where he vests to the altar. He is likened to Christ coming forth from the Father and entering the world. He is accompanied and assisted by six orders of priests spoken of in the preface to the second section of this work. These six orders of priests represent the order of generation of Christ which St. Matthew describes in his Gospel, where one reads of the six orders or persons from which Christ, according to the flesh, drew His origins. These are the patriarchs, prophets, kings, princes, pastors and leaders. The patriarch Abraham, the prophet David, the king Solomon, the prince Solomon, the pastor Judas, and the leader Zorobabel.

9. The two deacons that accompany the Bishop represent Abraham and David who both prophesied the coming of Christ. The first said "in your race, all the nations shall be blessed," and the second, "I will place someone from your seed upon your throne." And this is why the Evangelist in providing the genealogy of Christ, places these two at the head, saying "concerning the book of genealogy of our Lord Jesus Christ, son of David and son of Abraham." These are the two columns that the ancient high priest placed in the vestibule of the temple, before the door connected by a rope with twelve segments, which represents the faith which the twelve Apostles embraced, by means of which Christ opened the door to those who believe.

10. Four ministers carry a canopy raised on four poles which shields the Bishop. They are called *mapularii* and the covering a *mapulam*. This cloth is richly ornamented and covered with various figures or images taken from Holy Scripture and indicative of various mysteries. The *canopy* is carried aloft on four poles or standards because the Holy Scriptures relate to Christ in four ways, for the Scriptures are understood historically, allegorically, anagogically and tropologically, as explained in the preface to the first volume. It is like the river which waters the terrestrial paradise because, like it, it springs from four sources. It is the Table of Proposition which stands on four legs. One thus carries this canopy over the Pontiff to show that He who formerly spoke through the Prophets and gave the Law has come. For Christ, starting with Moses and the prophets, is the object which the interpretation of all the Scriptures points to, for they speak of Him, which is why it is said, "If you believe in Moses you will believe also in me, for it is of me that he wrote."

11. The four ministers who carry the supports of the canopy are the four Evangelists who preach Holy Scripture and exalt the Faith, hence their images are placed at the upper end of these supports. And two lighted candles and incense precede them because the law and the prophets, along with the psalms, have announced in advance the coming of Christ, as Christ himself bears witness when He says "Moses wrote in the law about me, as do the psalms and the words of the prophets." On major feasts seven candles are carried before the Bishop, recalling what St. John describes in the Apocalypse: "When I turned I saw seven candelabras of gold, and in the midst of which was someone who resembled the Son of man, dressed like him in a long robe." By this it becomes clear that He has arrived, the One on whom the spirit of sevenfold grace reposes, as the prophet Isaiah says: "A stalk will come out of the root of Jesse, and a flower shall rise up out of his root, and the spirit of the Lord shall rest upon him, etc."

12. In some basilicas, a handful of oakum is suspended in the middle of the choir which the pontiff lights as he passes on the way to the altar, in order that all may see the moment when it is reduced to ashes. This fire brings to mind the Second Coming in which Christ judges the living, the dead, and the entire age by fire. For fire always burns in his presence (Lev. 6) and he is surrounded by a violent tempest (Psalm 49), so no one should relax with a false sense of security. Christ is good and gentle in his first coming, but will be terrible in His second. He first came to be judged, but the second time He will come to judge. The bishop in lighting the cotton should himself consider that he also will be reduced to ashes, and that his vestments and signs of office will also be so reduced; for just as the cotton is readily burnt, so also the world with its desires readily and instantaneously passes away. For, according to the Apostle James, "our life is like smoke which only lasts for a moment." Whosoever is bedecked in glory should not take pleasure in temporary honors, for "all flesh is like the green grass, and one's glory is like the flower in the field." When he approaches the altar, the master of ceremonies removes his outer cape, and kisses the right shoulder of the bishop, before all the assistants, because, when Christ came into the world, the angel who was part of the multitude of the heavenly host praising God, announced to the shepherds the birth of Him of whom the Prophet said: "A child is born to us, and a son is given to us, and he carries the mark of government on his shoulder." Lastly, the three priests who come with reverence before the bishop as he goes to the altar, and who bow to him and kiss him on the mouth and chest, symbolize the three kings who came to Jerusalem saying "Where is the king of the Jews that has just been born?" and who, falling to the ground, adored him and opened their gifts, offered Him gold, incense and myrrh. The double kiss proclaims the two-fold nature of Christ who is both man and God—the divine is as it were hidden in the chest, while the human is as it were expressed by his lips. These two natures were also symbolized in a mystical manner by the gifts of the Magi. Now the kiss is a sign of respect, as is discussed in the chapter dealing with the Kiss of Peace.

13. The procession recalls by its disposition, an army ordered for battle. For the greatest and strongest, as advance- and rear-guard, begin and end it, while the minor orders, like the weaker soldiers, are ranked in the middle. The bishops march in front and the priests follow directly behind them. Then come the pontiff and the deacons. In the middle are placed the subdeacons and the acolytes. As for the cantors, like trumpeters they march at the head of an army to encourage and inflame the army in its combat with the demons. The Apostle said, in speaking of this battle: "We are not

fighting with men of flesh and blood, but against the spirits of evil that are in the air all around us." "This is why we blow the trumpet on the new moon, on the noted day of your solemnity."

14. We have spoken first of all of the procession of a sovereign Pontiff; we should now say something about other processions. With regard to this it should be noted that, just as the Mass presents to us the mission of Christ on earth for our sake, so also our processions symbolize our return to our fatherland, these celebrations imitating in nearly every detail the departure of the Israelites from Egypt. And just as Moses wrested the people from the hands of Pharaoh, so also God's people are delivered by Christ from the jaws of the lion. And just as the Tables of the Law were received by Moses on Mount Sinai and brought before the people (Exod. 34 and 45), so also the Gospel book is taken from the altar and carried in procession. A pillar of smoke preceded the Israelites, while a burning candle goes before us. Standards were carried before the tribes, while we carry the Cross and banners. Marvels occurred there, while, with us, miracles never cease. There Levites carried the tabernacle of the covenant, while our deacons and subdeacons carry the *pax*[9] and reliquary. The ark of the Lord was carried by the priests, while, with us, they carry relic chest. For them Aaron, the high priest, followed adorned in sacred vestments; for us the bishop, with his miter on his head. Moses carried his staff; with us, the king follows the procession, scepter in hand, and the bishop, supported by his crozier. In those days the din of trumpets resounded; with us, the ringing of bells. In those days the people carried arms; now the priests are arrayed with holy vestments and the people with their virtues. In those days the people were sprinkled with blood; now we are sprinkled with salt-imbued holy water. Bloodthirsty Amalech came to meet them; while, for us, a host of demons ever set traps. Their champion was Joshua, while it is our Jesus who has won the victory for us. When we go in procession towards some church or other, it is as if we are leaving for the Promised Land. When we enter singing into the church, it is as if we are full of joy because we have arrived at our homeland. When we circle the church with the relics, and the bells are rung, it is as if, with the ark, the sound of the trumpets and the cries of the faithful, we were encompassing Jericho. Jericho crumbles and is destroyed when concupiscence is vanquished in us. And when we go in choir to an altar and stop there, this signifies that our souls are going to Christ and desire to be associated with the angelic hosts.

15. Secondly, David and Solomon also formed processions when these two carried the ark of God, the first into the tabernacle and the second into the temple; and this with the chanting of hymns and canticles, and placed

it under the wings of the cherubim. Likewise the humanity of Christ rises from the earth to enter heaven, where the angels eternally adore it and where faithful souls accompany it. Thirdly, also, the procession reminds us that Christ has come into the world from the bosom of His Father, from the crib to the temple, from Bethlehem to Jerusalem, and from Jerusalem to the mountain where we also desire to return from this world to our homeland or to one Church from another, which is to say, from the Church militant to the Church triumphant, which is achieved by following the cross, or rather in the footsteps of the Crucified One, and by crucifying in ourselves our vices and concupiscence. This is also achieved by following the footsteps of the saints and the precepts of the Gospel, by being clothed in sacred vestments: the armor of justice, the belt of continence, the shield of faith and the mantle of eternal salvation. The priest, in celebrating the holy mysteries, should be dressed in the sacred vestments as a soldier in armor ready for battle "against the spirits of evil present in the air" as we pointed out in the preface to the third part.

16. In some churches processions are arranged in the following manner. Leading in front are seven acolytes with torches; they symbolize all those who, thanks to the seven gifts of the Holy Spirit, have given light and knowledge to the faithful. They are followed by seven subdeacons carrying the *pax*, signifying those who, by the same grace, have taught that the fulness of divinity dwells bodily in Christ. After them come seven deacons, representing all those who, by the same gifts, have spiritual understanding, which is to say that which the Gospel instructs us about Christ. Next come twelve priors, representing all those who shine both with their faith in the Holy Trinity, the three Persons, and by the works of the four virtues; these twelve priors are accompanied by three acolytes carrying censers and incense-box who symbolize the three Magi who brought presents to Christ. They are followed by a sub-deacon who carries the book of the Gospels; he symbolizes the Law, and he immediately precedes the Pontiff, because the Law, which contains the mystery of the Passion about which the Gospels speak, preceded the coming of Christ. The book is carried closed to indicate that under the Law much was obscure before the Lamb opened the seal of the seventh book (as described in the Apocalypse). The Pontiff is carried by two people, as if in a chariot, and he is accompanied by a crowd praying, and this indicates that the faithful follow Christ into heaven. The train of the Pontiff is composed of the ten orders, namely, porters, readers, exorcists, acolytes, subdeacons, deacons, priests, cantors, and the laity, both men and women, for it is said that the chariot of God is surrounded by more than ten thousand to indicate their

perfection. The procession is composed mainly of the deacons, the subdeacons and the acolytes dressed in their appropriate vestments, according to the word: "See those which I have sent you, the prophets, the sages and the scribes." The prophets are the deacons, the sages the subdeacons and the scribes are represented by the acolytes. The Vicar of Christ, Christ himself, is as it were conducted by them in public, much like a host of young girls playing on the tambourines. And then the cantors, divided into two choirs, receive with transports of joy those who sing the Introit, and they respond with the *Gloria in excelsis*; these rejoicing singers and clergy dressed in albs are like the angels who received Christ at the time of His ascension, with glory and praise reaching to the highest heavens. The two choirs chanting praises are the two races, the Jews and Gentiles, who came before Christ singing praises. The procession itself is the way that leads to the celestial homeland. The holy water which is carried in front represents purity of life. The lights are the works of mercy, according to the words of Scripture: "Let your loins be girt, and burning lamps carried in your hands." Then the Pontiff or the priest, who is more or less in the middle between the clergy and the cross which is carried before him, and the people who follow, presents in him the type of a mediator between God and man. Beyond all this the leaders of the choir are the last in the procession, because salvation is achieved by means of humility. Thus it was that Zacchaeus, prince of the publicans, because he was short, had climbed up on a sycamore to see Jesus pass; and Jesus said to him, "Zacchaeus, come down, for today I must stay at your house." And Zacchaeus came down and received Jesus with joy in his home. The Jews seated themselves on raised chairs, and their leaders had first place in the synagogues.

17. Now the cross, like a royal standard and a triumphal sign, is always at the head of processions, first of all so that "those who hate it, have it before their face (Psalm 67). It is, in point of fact, the sign of Christ's victory according to the word "the standards of the king go before him, etc." By him the demons are conquered; for, on seeing it, they tremble and flee. And for this reason, in certain places the cross is used to oppose the fury of storms, in order to make those demons that inhabit the airy spaces cease their activities and put them to flight. The mystery of the holy cross is in effect our rallying sign and our banner, as is said by Isaiah "The root of Jesse which standeth as an ensign for the people, him the Gentiles shall beseech, and his sepulcher shall be glorious" (Isaiah 10:10). Secondly, the standard of the cross goes before because, as the Apostle wrote to the Galatians, "But God forbid that I should glory, save in the cross of our

(St. Martin's of Tours, Louisville, Kentucky)

"When they arrive at the altar, the candles which went before are now placed on the side which indicates the teachings given before the birth of Christ as well as the light which followed after this event."

(Church of Our Lady of Tyn, Prague)

"The Cross, like a royal standard and a triumphal sign, is always at the head of the processions."

(Church of Our Lady of Tyn, Prague, 14th Century)

Crystal Procession Cross

(St. Vitus Cathedral, Prague)

Dome in mosque courtyard protecting the Ascension site atop the Mount of Olives

"The fourth procession occurs on the day of the Ascension of Our Lord, in order to represent the last gathering of the disciples with our Lord on the day of His Ascension to Heaven- gathered together on the Mount of Olives from where he was raised before their eyes; and it is to this gathering that the processions that occur on every Sunday represent."

This dome in the courtyard of the Mosque of the Ascension, atop the Mount of Olives, marks the spot where Muslims and Christians believe that Jesus ascended into Heaven.

Candle marks the place of the Ascension. Here preserved are Christ's footprints.

Detail of a capital on a column supporting dome above, which includes the Tree of Life motif.

Lord Jesus Christ; by whom the world is crucified to me and I to the world" (6:14). We will speak more about this in the chapter on the Gospels. And sometimes the banners lead the procession, as is spoken of in the sixth part in the chapter about Rogation Days.

18. It is for a good reason, as was mentioned above, that the bells are rung during a procession. For, just as the kings of the world when marching with their armies carry signs of their military might, such as flags and trumpets, so also Christ, the eternal king in the Church Militant, has the sound of bells which take the place of trumpets, and the cross which is His standard. This is discussed in the first part of the chapter on bells. The reverberating sound of the bells calls to mind the prophets who announced in advance, in a figurative manner, the coming of Christ. Moreover, drappery and other objects indicate the places where the passing procession should stop to chant, in accordance with the words of Tobias, towards the end: "Its places will be paved with pure and shining gold, and in the streets they will sing Alleluia."

19. There are known to be four solemn processions, namely that of the Purification of the most Blessed Virgin Mary, that of Palm Sunday, that of Easter—of these three we will speak in their proper place. The fourth occurs on the day of the Lord's Ascension, so to represent the disciples' last walk with our Lord on the day of His ascension into heaven, coming with Him to the Mount of Olives where he was taken from their sight; and it is this last walk with the Lord that is represented in the processions made every Sunday.

20. You should also know that the early Church solemnized Sunday in the same way that we do today, and that on Sundays the procession was made in memory of the Resurrection. She also had a procession on Thursday in memory of the Ascension of the Lord, but when the daily festivities of the saints became abundant, it was necessary to suppress the Thursday practice, and Pope Agapetus transferred it to Sunday so that it could be solemnly performed with the large number of faithful who gathered together on this day. For this reason, the fifth day of the week retained its common name of Thursday (*dies Jovis*, the day of Jove), which it shared with Sunday from ancient times. Thus it is that the Sunday processions recall to us the resurrection of the Lord, next we are representing the disciples walking after the Lord, not however that they did this on a Sunday, as was said above. In our leave-taking and return, we are somehow returning from Jerusalem to Jerusalem, as they did, and we follow the cross, as they followed the Crucified One. And yet they returned without Jesus, while we return carrying the Cross, because as He Himself has said "I am

with you until the end of time." This procession should occur before tierce is said, as is explained in the sixth part dealing with the Ascension.

21. Neither should we fail to mention that on the Sunday processions we should only chant some passage from the New Testament, or salute the Virgin Mary by singing something directed in some special way to her glory. This is reflected in the practice of having an oratory dedicated to the Virgin in the majority of cloisters, where she is greeted first during the station, according to ancient practice.

22. Although it is said that when Christ rose, the first person he appeared to was Mary Magdalen, and yet it is truer to believe that He showed Himself to His Mother before anyone else. But it was not the Evangelists' place to tell us this, as their function was to bring forth witnesses to His resurrection, and it would hardly be appropriate to have a mother bear witness for her son. If in fact the words of women who had no familial connections were not believed and thought to be the result of delirium, how much more would this be the case with His mother who so tenderly loved her Son! And the Roman Church apparently felt this to be so, for the first day after His Resurrection, namely on Easter Sunday, she established the practice of having the first station at St. Mary Major, which is a way of giving Jerusalem pride of place, which is to say, the Virgin who first before all others saw peace and who possesses the firstfruits of His joy.[10] This is why, from the very first day, we have recourse to her mercy, in going to St. Mary Major; thus we consecrate the first station in Sunday processions in her honor so that, lavishing her with praise and crowding about her oratory, we might seem to say with her Spouse: "I will go to the mountain of myrrh, and to the hill of frankincense." This mountain is the chaste Virgin to whom the risen Son came and appeared, and to whom we go in adoring Him. But we need not say: *Quia nunquam disparuit, et quod simul melius est,etc.*; but one does so because of ignorant souls, and only for those who perceive but do not understand. Finally, it is worth noting that in some churches, after the procession, all the clergy bow before the crucifix and say "Hail to our blessed King." And those who have worn the *pluvial* or other festal vestments place them before the altar: first of all to demonstrate that they, like the Hebrew faithful, are casting their garments on the road to allow for the passage of Christ when He enters Jerusalem, and secondly to show that those called to perform the Divine Office should cast far from their mind all worldly superficialities.

CHAPTER VII: THE CONFITEOR OR CONFESSION

1. The bishop or priest, before mounting the steps before the altar, and before preparing to offer the Holy Sacrifice, bows down before the altar, imitating the humility of Christ who bowed the heavens and came down (Psalm 17:10), reducing himself to a nothing in taking the form of a servant. The priest then, following the words of Solomon to the effect that the just man is the first to accuse himself, and confident in the prophet's consoling word: "I have said: I will declare to the Lord, and will accuse myself of my own injustice; and You will quickly remit the impiety of my sin (*De poen.*, dist. i, *Dixi*). He confesses all his sins in general, along with his assistants. He firstly says, in accordance with the instructions of Pope Celestine (I, q. 1), a psalm in perfect accord with his confession: "*Judica me Deus*—Judge me O Lord," so that, separated from the impious and delivered from the sinful man, he might be found worthy to approach the altar. He asks to be freed from temptation and illuminated by grace, as the words of the same psalm indicate. He also asks God to give him that which he is about to offer, which is to say, His Son, for if he does not give him a victim such as he gave to Abraham, he would have nothing to present to God.

2. He makes his confession so that he can approach the altar with purity and without stain. This points out that he must not wound the consciences of those who hear him (as do some who are none too careful), but confess his sins in a general way, for such requires no secrecy and can be done publicly, as did the priests in the temple of Solomon, saying "Confess to the Lord, because He is good, because His mercy shines forth in all ages." After this a cloud filled the house of the Lord and veiled the faces of the priests so that they could not see one another. And Solomon said: "The Lord said that He has His habitation in the clouds, and He confirmed this, for He appeared in a cloud on Mount Sinai; He also marched before Israel, and He passed in a cloud before Moses who had entered into a cave."

3. We strike our breast when we confess our sins, following after the example of the publican who struck his breast when he said "Lord have mercy on me for I am a sinner." There are three things in the act of striking one's breast: the stroke, the sound, and the touching, which symbolize the three qualities necessary for any true repentance: contrition of heart, oral confession, and works that make satisfaction, and this because when we sin we do so in three ways, with the heart, by our words, and in our actions. Next the priest prays for those that surround him, and implores pardon for

their sins; for Christ, coming into the world from the bosom of the Father, and from the Virgin through the patriarchs, entered into Jerusalem to suffer on our behalf. He bowed down on the mount of Olives, crying out to God for the sake of deceitful and sinful mankind, and, confessing to His Father, said: "Father of Heaven, I confess to you, etc." And He also, in a most generous manner, took and bore on His own body the weight of our sins."

4. And it is reasonable for the deacon, in front of the altar, to place the maniple on the priest or bishop who has to confess his sins. First of all to show that he should accept and administer the temporal charges which are granted to him through the hands of strangers, be they the subdeacon or someone else, and that they are not his own property. Secondly, to indicate that oral confession is insufficient if it is not followed with the fruits of good works that the people represent. Thirdly, so that, seeing himself fitted out by the lowest function of the ministry, he will be humble in spirit. The bishop does not put on the maniple before the chasuble, but after, because Christ, a type of whom he is, did not gather in the sheaves (*manipulos*), the reward of his labors, until after he had lived the heavenly life which the chasuble represents, as is explained in the third part of this work in the article on the dalmatic. The priest, on the other hand, dons the maniple before the chasuble, because he cannot achieve the heavenly life before partaking of the fruits of the works of the saints. The bishop, before approaching the altar, receives the maniple to indicate that we will finally receive the true recompense for our good works only when we appear before the seat of the eternal judge.

5. The priest, during the recitation of the *Confiteor*, and often throughout the celebration of the Mass, joins his hands which action symbolizes devotion. And, just as a person's devotion varies with each individual, so the number of times he joins hands has not been set. Hands so joined also signify, on the part of the priest, the union and harmony of all the goods that flow from God into him. And. because infinite blessings proceed from God in an infinite and indeterminate variety of ways, this is way the number of times the priest joins hands has not been set.

6. The number of bows that the priest makes before the altar during the celebration of Mass are specified, and hence can be determined with certainty according to the practice in most churches; for usually the priest makes eight profound bows before the altar, and thirteen lesser bows at the altar itself. The eight profound bows before the altar are to give thanks to Christ for the eight chief things that He did before His immolation which the priest re-presents during the celebration of the Mass. The first was His

admirable incarnation. The second, the gratuitous vocation of his disciples. The third, the overcoming of the devil in His temptations. The fourth, the performance of His miracles. The fifth, the curing of the sick. The sixth, the raising of the dead. The seventh, the resolving by His wisdom of all questions and other matters put to Him. The eighth, the instruction given to the people in order to make possible their salvation. According to St. Bernard, all these things were accomplished before His immolation.

7. As for the thirteen bows that the priest makes at the altar, these are connected to the thirteen actions which Christ performed at the altar of the Cross, when He entered into His passion. The first was the sweet reprimand which He addressed to the traitor, in saying to him: "Judas, have you betrayed the Son of Man with a kiss?" The second, when he allowed Himself to become a prisoner, saying to the soldiers: "Who are you looking for? — Jesus of Nazareth — I am he." The third was his response, so full of mercy, to the false witnesses and rulers. The fourth, when he accepted the insults and blows without a murmur. The fifth, in what he saw and heard without troubling Himself or others. The sixth, the pardon that he extended to the disciple who denied him three times. The seven others are enumerated by St. Ambrose as being accomplished on the tree of the Cross. This holy doctor says: "The author of mercy, suspended from the cross, distributed responsibilities and offices. He bequeathed persecution to His apostles, peace to His disciples, His body to the Jews, His spirit to His Father, a protector to the Virgin, paradise to the thief and hell to a sinner." The kisses are also fixed at eight in number as is explained in the article on the fourth part of the Canon.

Winchester Bible (1160-1175)

Incensing the altar (1160-1175)

CHAPTER VIII: THE BLESSING OF INCENSE AND THE PREPARATION OF THE CENSER

1. After the *Confiteor* and the absolution the priest goes onto say: *Deus, tu coversus,* etc, and then he blesses the incense and puts it into the censer which is presented to him. This follows the pattern of the high priest of the Ancient Law, who, covered with blood from the sacrificed victims, also filled the censer with incense so that, during his prayer, the perfumed smoke covered him with a cloud, as mentioned in the preface to this section. This is also to remind us that an angel came and stood before the altar, carrying in his hands a golden censer which he filled with fire from the altar, and to him was given a great quantity of incense, the result of the prayers of the saints. This angel is Christ, the golden censer is His immaculate body. The altar is the Church, the fire is charity, the incense is prayer, all according to the words of the prophet: "Let my prayer arise as the smoke of incense before you." The angel, that is Christ, has come; He is standing before the altar which is His presence in the Church, holding a silver censer, that is to say a body without stain, full of the fire of charity, and He has received a great quantity of incense from the faithful, that is to say their prayers, to be offered up, which is to say to make worthy the prayers of the saints before His Father.

2. Observe that the celebrant does not say all the prayers: Christ did not, in fact, grant every prayer; but he hears some of them, knowing which are important for salvation. Hencc it is that when Paul asked the Lord three times to remove from him the thorn in his flesh, the Lord responded, "My grace is sufficient," for virtue is refined by the tribulations of this world. Therefore the priest or bishop places the incense in the censer, because it is Christ who inspires prayer in our mind, so that a sweet-smelling incense is offered. And the assisting priest offers incense to the bishop, or the deacon to the priest, because ancient law had adopted this precious perfume, which it offers as a most agreable odor to the Most High. Touching upon this perfume, the Lord says in the thirtieth chapter of Exodus: "You shall not make it for your own use, because it is consecrated to the Lord, and any person who makes it for his own pleasure and to enjoy the smell, will perish from among his people." And with regard to this statement there are those who say that if, after the offering of the blessed incense at the altar, the censer passes to the hands of the clerics or laity, it should then be filled with unblessed incense to perfume the clerics as well as the laity, the first kind of incense being consecrated to the cult of *latria,* the second to that of

dulia. It is better however to act in this manner from the point of view of the spirit rather than the letter, for the letter kills and the spirit gives life. And this is why those betrothed are not to inhale blessed incense in church.

3. The consuming and consecration of the incense indicates that the priest should pray with both ardor and devotion. For the incense has the virtue of rising upwards because of the smoke's lightness, it has the tendency to harden because of its nature, to constrict because of its resin; and to comfort because of its scent. Thus, while prayers mount upwards in remembrance of God, it reminds the soul about prior faults for which it seeks pardon, constricts our tendency to commit faults in this world, and provides at least a temporary comfort. We have also spoken of this in the chapter dealing with the arrival of the pontiff at the altar and will speak of it again in the article on incensing. The censer is called a boat (*navicula*). This indicates that, through prayer, symbolized by the incense, we should strive to navigate the great and vast sea of this world in such a way that we arrive at our heavenly homeland. Hence we read in Proverbs words regarding a strong woman: "She is like a vessel of a merchant which brings his bread from far off lands." The censer can also represent the heart of man, the fire the fervor of devotion, the incense the prayers that angels carry up to God. The vessels (*vascula*) which receive the fire, these are the children who imitate the heart of their Father by the piety and goodness, and who strive to draw into their souls the flame the heavenly sacrifice which they perceive in the soul of their neighbor. The instruments used to carry the fire to the altar are the preachers who, by the examples given us by the saints, spread the fire of charity and convey sentiments to the hearts of the faithful, sentiments which they will regard as does a father his children. We will speak more of the symbolism of the censer in the chapter on incensing the altar.

(Hortus Deliciarum, 12th Century) Censor (Notre Dame, Paris, France)

(Berlin)

(Berlin)

"We follow the Cross, as they followed the Crucified One. And as they returned without Jesus, we return carrying the Cross, because as he said, "I am with you until the end of time."

SACRAMENTALITY: A PRINCIPLE OF ECCLESIASTICAL DESIGN

INTRODUCTORY ESSAY FROM THE 1893 EDITION OF THE SYMBOLISM OF CHURCHES AND CHURCH ORNAMENTS

INCLUDING AN EXTRACT FROM THE FARDLE OF FACIONS PRINTED IN 1555 A.D.

This essay has been included to give the reader an idea of various views that were held in the early 1800s, several of which we would no longer find acceptable. It is humbling to realize that even *our* own attitudes and conventions are not final. Only the Eternal Truth endures.

St. Mary the Virgin

(Oxford, England, begun in 1280 C.E.)

FROM THE FARDLE OF FACIONS, PRINTED 1555.

The following very curious passage ought to have come in the Introductory Essay, but was not accessible at the time. It is an extract from the Fardle of Facions, printed A.D. 1555.

> Oratories, temples, or places of praier (whiche we calle churches) might not to be built without the good will of the bishoppe of the diocese. And when the timbre was redy to be framed, and the foundacion digged, it behoved them to sende for the bishoppe, to hallowe the firste corner stone of the foundacion, and to make the signe of the Crosse thereupon, and to laie it, and directe it juste easte and west. And then might the masons sette upon the stone, but not afore. This churche did they use to builde after the facion of a crosse, and not unlike the shape of a manne. The channcelle (in the whiche is conteined the highe altare and the quiere) directe fulle in the easte, representeth the heade, and therefore ought to be somewhat rounde, and muche shorter than the body of the churche. And yet upon respect that the heade is the place for the eyes, it ought to be of morelighte, and to bee seperate with a particion, in the steade of a necke, from the bodye of the churche. This particion the Latine calleth cancelli, and out of that cometh our terme channcelle. On eche side of this channcelle peradventure (for so fitteth it beste) should stand a turret; as it were for two ears, and in these the belles to be hanged, to calle the people to service, by daie and by night. Undre one of these turretts is there commonly a vaulte, whose doore openeth into the quiere, and in this are laid up the hallowed vesselles and orna-mentes, and other utensils of the churche. We call it a vestrie. The other parte oughte to be fitted, that having as it were on eche side an arme, the reste mave resemble the bodye with the fete stretched in breadthe, and in lengthe. On eche side of the bodye the pillers to stande, upon whose coronettes or heades the vaulte or rophe of the churche maye reste. And to the foote beneth aulters to be joyned. Those aulters to be orderly alway covered with two aulter clothes, and garnished with the crosse of Christe, or some little cofre of reliques. At eche ende a candelsticke, and a booke towarde the middes. The walls to be painted without and within, and diversely paineted. That they also

should have in every parishe a faire round stone, made hollowe and fitte to holde water, in the whiche the water consecrate for Baptisme maye be kept for the christening of children. Upon the right hand of the highe aulter that ther should be an almorie, either cutte into the walle, or framed upon it, in the whiche they woulde have the sacrament of the Lorde's Bodye, the holy oyle for the sicke, and chrismatorie, alwaie to be locked. Furthermore they would that ther should be a pullpite in the middes of the churche, wherein the prieste maye stonde upon Sondaies and holidays to teache the people those things that it behoveth them to knowe. The channcelle to serve only for the priestes and clerks; the rest of the temporalle multitude to be in the bodye of the churche, seperate notwithstanding, the men on the righte side, and the women on the left.

(Sainte-Chapelle, Paris, France)

SACRAMENTALITY: A PRINCIPLE OF ECCLESIASTICAL DESIGN

INTRODUCTORY ESSAY FROM THE 1893 EDITION OF THE SYMBOLISM OF CHURCHES AND CHURCH ORNAMENTS

ANALYSIS OF THE INTRODUCTORY ESSAY

INTRODUCTION

1. Spread of the study of Church Architecture.
2. Obvious, but indefinable, difference between old and new churches.
   Wherein this consists.
   Not in association,
   Nor in correctness of details,
   Nor in the Picturesque,
   Nor in the Mechanical advantages,
   But in Reality considered, in an enlarged view, as Sacramentality.
3. This probable,
   from examples, and
   promises in Holy Scripture.
   Catholic consent,
   examples to the contrary,
   philosophical reasons.
4. Enunciation of the subject.
5. Writers on the subject,
   Pugin, Poole, Lewis, Coddington, the writers of the Cambridge Camden Society.

A. ARGUMENTS FOR SYMBOLISM.

I. À PRIORI.
   Symbolising spirit of Catholic Antiquity, in
   (a) Interpretation of Holy Scriptures.
   (b) Analogy of the Jewish Ceremonies.
   (c) Private manners.
   (d) Emblems in Catacombs, etc.
   (e) Symbolical interpretations of heathen writers.

II. ANALOGICAL.
  i. Examples of other nations.
    (a) Jews.
      (1) Temple rites.
      (2) Legal observances.
      (3) Sacred books.
    (b) Turks.
    (c) Infidels.
      (1) Hindu and Egyptian Mythology.
      (2) Persian Poetry.
    (d) Heretics.
  ii. From Nature.
    (a) Trinity.
    (b) Resurrection.
    (c) Self-sacrifice.
  iii. From Art.
    (a) Sculpture.
    (b) Painting.
    (c) Music.
    (d) Language of Flowers.
  iv. Parabolic teaching.

III. PHILOSOPHICAL.
  Objective answering to Subjective.
  All effect sacramental of the efficient.
  Sacramentality of all Religion.
  Ritualism peculiarly and necessarily sacramental.
  Church Architecture, a condition of Ritualism.
  Necessities include accidents: and these material expressions.
  Example:
  Necessities of Ritualism, and their expressions in earlier and later ages.
  Hence Symbolism.
      Essential.
      Intended.
      Conventional, which again becomes intended.

IV. ANALYTICAL.
  1. Cruciformity.
  2. Ascent to Altar.
  3. Orientation.
  4. Verticality.

V. INDUCTIVE.
  Express and continuous testimony.
    (a) Apostolical Constitutions.
    (b) Eusebius.
    (c) Symbolical writers.
  Actual Examples.

VI. RECAPITULATION.

B. EXAMPLES OF SYMBOLISM.

I. DOCTRINES.

(a) The Holy Trinity, set forth in
- (i) Nave and Two Aisles.
- (ii) Chancel, Nave, and Apse.
- (iii) Clerestory, Triforium, and Pier Arches.
- (iv) Triple windows.
- (v) Altar steps.
- (vi) Triplicity of mouldings.
- (vii) Minor details.

(b) Regeneration.
- (i) The octagonal form of Fonts.
- (ii) " " " Piers.
- (iii) Fishes.

(c) Atonement.
- (i) Cruciformity.
- (ii) Deviation of Orientation.
- (iii) Double Cross.
- (iv) The great Rood.
- (v) Details.

(d) Communion of Saints.

II. DETAILS.

(a) Windows: a series of examples.

(b) Doors.
- (i) Norman tympana.
- (ii) Double doors in Early English.

(2) These explained in two ways,
- a. Christ's entrance into the world.
- b. Our entrance into the kingdom of heaven.

(3) Difference between mouldings of Chancel arches and doors.

(c) Porches.

(d) Chancel Arch and Rood Screen.

(e) Monuments.

(1) Difference of ancient and modern symbolism in these.
- (i) Sceptical character of the present age.
- (ii) Paganism of modern design.
- (iii) Reality of ancient design.

(2) Historical details of Monuments.

(f) Gurgoyles and Poppyheads.

(g) Flowers used in architecture.

C. OBJECTIONS ANSWERED.

1. Inequality of type and antitype.
2. Difference of Symbolism in the same arrangement.
3. Mechanical origin.

D. HISTORY OF SYMBOLISM.

1. Norman; as symbolising facts.
2. Early English; as symbolising doctrines.
3. Decorated; as symbolising the connection of doctrines.
4. Perpendicular; as symbolising the progess of Erastianism.
5. Flamboyant, etc.
6. Post Reformation Symbolism.

E. CONCLUSION.

Contrast between a modern and ancient Church.

Laus Deo

CHAPTER I: INTRODUCTORY

The study of Church Architecture has within the last few years become so general, and a love for it so widely diffused, that whereas, in a former generation it was a task to excite either, in the present it is rather an object to direct both. An age of church-building, such as this, ought to produce good architects, not only from the great encouragement given to their professional efforts, but from the increasing appreciation of the principles and powers of their art. And yet it cannot be denied, however we may account for the fact, that (at least among those for whom we write, the members of our own communion,) no architect has as yet arisen, who appears destined to be the reviver of Christian art. It is not that the rules of the science have not been studied, that the examples bequeathed to us have not been imitated, that the details are not understood. We have (though they are but few) modern buildings of the most perfect proportions, of the most faultless details, and reared with lavish expence. It is that there is an undefined—perhaps almost undefinable—difference between a true "old church," and the most perfect of modern temples. In the former, at least till late in the Perpendicular era, we feel that, however strange the proportions, or extraordinary the details, the effect is church-like. In the latter, we may not be able to blame; but from a certain feeling of unsatisfactoriness, we cannot praise.

The solution of the problem,—What is it that causes this difference? has been often attempted, sometimes with partial, but never with complete, success. That most commonly given is the following:—The effect of association in old buildings,—the mellowing power of time,—the evident antiquity of surrounding objects,—the natural beauties of foliage, moss, and ivy, that require centuries to reach perfection;—as on the other hand, the bareness, the newness, nay even the sharpness and vigour of new work; these, it is said, are sufficient to stamp a different character on each. There is doubtless something in this; but that it is not the whole cause is evident from the fact, that give a modern church all the above mentioned advantages on paper, and an experienced eye will soon detect it to be modern.

Those writers who, as Grose, Milner, and Carter, lived before the details of Christian art were understood, seem to have placed its perfection in a thorough knowledge of these: experience has proved them wrong. Others, as Mr. Petit,[1] have made a kind of ideal picturesque; and, having exalted the phantasm into an idol, have fallen down and worshipped it. Others, again, have sought for an explanation of the difficulty in mathematical contrivance and mechanical ingenuity; and the result has been little more than the discovery of curious eave-drains, and wonderful cast-iron roof-work. Lastly, Mr. Pugin (*cum talis sis, utinam noster esses!*) has placed the thing required in Reality. That is, to quote his own words,[2] in making these the two great rules of design:—"1. That there should be no features about a building which are not necessary for convenience, construction, or propriety: 2. That all ornament should consist of enrichment of the essential construction of a building." And we may add, as a corollary, still quoting the same writer: "The smallest detail should have a meaning or serve a purpose: the construction itself should vary with the material employed: and the designs should be adapted to the material in which they are to be executed." Still, most true and most important as are these remarks, we must insist on one more axiom, otherwise Christian art will but mock us, and not show us wherein its great strength lieth.

A Catholic architect must be a Catholic in heart. Simple knowledge will no more enable a man to build up God's material, than His spiritual temples. In ancient times, the finest buildings were designed by the holiest bishops. Wykeham and Poore will occur to every churchman. And we have every reason to believe, from God's Word, from Catholic consent, and even from philosophical principles, that such must always be the case.

Holy Scripture, in mentioning the selection of Bezaleel and Aholiab, as architects of the Tabernacle, expressly asserts them to have been filled "with the Spirit of God in wisdom, and in understanding, and in knowledge, and in all manner of workmanship, to devise cunning works, to work in gold and in silver and in brass, and in cutting of stones to set them, and in carving of timber, to work in all manner of workmanship." And this indeed is only a part of the blessing of the pure in heart: they see God, the Fountain of Beauty, even in this life; as they shall see Him, the Fountain of Holiness, in the next. From Catholic consent we may learn the same truth. Why else was Ecclesiastical Architecture made a part of the profession of Clerks, than because it was considered that the purity and holiness of that profession fitted them best for so great a work?[3]

Nay, we have remarkable proofs that feeling without knowledge will do more than knowledge without feeling. There are instances of buildings—Lisbon Cathedral and S. Peter's College Chapel, Cambridge, are cases in point—which, with Debased or Italian details, have nevertheless Christian effect. And we have several similar cases, more paticularly in the way of towers.

Now, allowing the respectability which attaches itself to the profession of a modern architect, and the high character of many in that profession, none would assert that they, as a body, make it a matter of devotion and prayer; that they work for the Church alone, regardless of themselves; that they build in faith, and to the glory of God.

In truth, architecture has become too much a profession: it is made the means of gaining a livelihood, and is viewed as a path to honourable distinction, instead of being the study of the devout ecclesiastic, who matures his noble conceptions with the advantage of that profound meditation only attainable in the contemplative life; who, without thought of recompense or fame, has no end in view but the raising a temple, worthy of its high end, and emblematical of the faith which is to be maintained within its walls. It is clear that modern architects are in a very different position from their predecessors, with respect to these advantages. We are not prepared to say that none but monks ought to design churches, or that it is impossible for a professional architect to build with the devotion and faith of an earlier time. But we do protest against the merely business-like spirit of the modern profession, and demand from them a more elevated and directly religious habit of mind. We surely ought to look at least for churchmembership from one who ventures to design a church. There cannot be a more painful idea than that a separatist should be allowed to build a House of God, when he himself knows nothing of the ritual and worship of the Church from which he has strayed; to prepare both Font and Altar, when perchance he knows nothing of either Sacrament but that he has always despised them. Or, again, to think that any churchman should allow himself to build a conventicle, and even sometimes to prostitute the speaking architecture of the Church to the service of Her bitterest enemies! What idea can such a person have formed of the reality of church architecture? Conceive a churchman designing a triple window, admitted emblem of the Most Holy Trinity, for a congregation of Socinians! We wish to vindicate the dignity of this noble science against the treason of its own professors. If architecture is anything more than a mere trade; if it is indeed a liberal, intellectual art, a true branch of poesy; let us prize its reality and meaning and truthfulness, and at least not expose ourselves by giving to two contraries one and the same material expression.

It is objected that architects have a right to the same professional conscience that is claimed, for instance, by a barrister. To which we can only reply, that it must be a strange morality which will justify a pleader in violating truth; and how much worse for an architect to violate truth in things immediately connected with the House and worship of God! It may be asked, Do we mean to imply then that a church architect ought never to undertake any secular building? Perhaps, as things are, we cannot expect so much as this now: but we can never believe that the man who engages to design union-houses, or prisons, or assembly-rooms, and gives the dregs of his time to church-building; is likely to produce a good church, or, in short, can expect to be filled from above with the Spirit of Wisdom. The church architect must, we are persuaded, make very great sacrifices: he must forego all lucrative undertakings, if they may not be carried through upon those principles which he believes necessary for every good building; and particularly if the end to be answered, or the wants to be provided for, are in themselves unjustifiable or mischievous. Even in church-building itself, he must see many an unworthy rival preferred to him, who will condescend to pander to the whims and comfort of a church-committee, will suit his design to any standard of ritualism which may be suggested by his own ignorance, or others' private judgement, who will consent to defile a building meant for God's worship with pews and galleries and prayer-pulpits and commodious vestries. But hard as the trial may be, a church architect must submit to it, rather than recede from the principles which he knows to be the very foundation of his art. We would go further even, and deny the possibility of any architect's success in all the different styles of Pointed architecture, not to mention the orders of Greece and Rome, Vitruvian, Palladian, Cinque Cento, Wrennian, nay even Chinese, Swiss, Hindoo, and Egyptian at once. We have not even now exhausted the list of styles in which a modern architect is supposed to be able to design. It is even more absurd than if every modern painter were expected, and should profess, to paint equally well in the styles of Perugino, Francia, Raphael, Holbein, Claude, the Poussins, Salvator Rosa, Correggio, Van Eyck, Teniers, Rubens, Murillo, Reynolds, West, Gainsborough, Overbeck, and Copley Fielding all at once! An architect ought indeed to be acquainted, and the more the better, with all styles of building: but if architecture, as we said before, is a branch of poesy, if the poet's mind is to have any individuality, he must design in one style, and one style only. For the Anglican architect, it will be necessary to know enough of the earlier styles to be able to restore the deeply interesting churches, which they have left us as precious heirlooms; enough of the Debased styles, to take warning from their decline: but for his own style, he should choose the glorious architecture of the fourteenth century; and, just as no man has more than one handwriting, so in this one language alone will he express his architectural ideas.

We cannot leave this topic without referring to what the Cambridge Camden Society has said with respect to architectural competition.[4] *It is a fact* that at this time many competing designs are manufactured in an architect's office, by some of his clerks, as if by machinery: if a given plan is chosen, the architect is summoned, and sees *his* (!) design for the first time, when he is introduced to the smiling committee-men. It is another fact that there is at this time in London a small body of persons, with no other qualification than that of having been draughtsmen in an architect's office, who *get up* a set of competing designs for any aspirant who chooses to give them a few instructions, and to pay them for their trouble. How much it is to be wished that there were some examination of an architect's qualifications, before he should be allowed to assume the name! It seems strange that the more able members of the profession do not themselves feel some *esprit de corps*, and do not at least endeavour to claim for their art its full dignity and importance. We fear however that very few, as yet, take that *religious* view of their profession, which we have shown to be seemly, even if not essential. If, however, we succeed in proving that religion enters very largely into the principles of Church architecture, a religious *ethos*, we repeat, is *essential* to a church architect. At all events, in an investigation into the differences between ancient and modern church architecture, the contrast between the ancient and modern builders could not be overlooked: and it is not too much to hope that some, at least, may be struck by the fact, that the deeply religious habits of the builders of old, the hours, the cloister, the discipline, the obedience, resulted in their matchless works; while the worldliness, vanity, dissipation, and patronage of our own architects issue in unvarying and hopeless failure.

We said that there were philosophical reasons for the belief that we must have architects—before we can have buildings—like those of old. If it be true that an esoteric signification, or, as we shall call it, *Sacramentality*,[5] ran through all the arrangements and details of Christian architecture, emblematical of Christian discipline, and suggested by Christian devotion; then must the discipline have been practised, and the devotion felt, before a Christian temple can be reared. That this esoteric meaning, or symbolism, does exist, we are now to endeavour to prove.

We assert, then, that *Sacramentality* is that characteristic which so strikingly distinguishes ancient ecclesiastical architecture from our own. By this word we mean to convey the idea that, by the outward and visible form, is signified something inward and spiritual: that the material fabric symbolizes, embodies, figures, represents, expresses, answers to, some abstract meaning. Consequently, unless this ideal be itself true, or be rightly understood, he who seeks to build a Christian church may embody a false or incomplete or mistaken ideal, but will not develop the true one. Hence, while the Parthenon, or a conventicle, or a modern church, may be conceived to have, on the one hand, so much *truthfulness*, as to symbolize respectively the graceful, but pagan, worship of Athene,—the private judgement of the dissenter—and the warped or ill-understood or puritanized religious ethos of the modern churchman; and, on the other hand, to have so much reality as to carry out most satisfactorily Mr. Pugin's canons; yet, inasmuch as in neither case was the builder's ideal the true one, so in neither case is his architecture in any way adapted to, or an embodiment of, the ideal of the Church. Reality, then, is not of itself sufficient. What can be more real than a pyramid, yet what less Christian? It must be Christian reality, the true expression of a true ideal, which makes Catholic architecture what it is. This Christian reality, we would call *Sacramentality*; investing that symbolical truthfulness, which it has in common with *every* true expressson, with a greater force and holiness, both from the greater purity of the perfect truth which it embodies, and from the association which this name will give it with those adorable and consummate examples of the same principle, infinitely more developed, and infinitely more holy in the spiritual grace which they signify and convey,—the Blessed Sacraments of the Church.

The modern writers who have treated on Symbolism seem to have taken respectively very partial views of the subject. Mr. Pugin does not seem in his books to recognize the particular principle which we have enunciated. We have shown that his Law about Reality is true so far as it goes, but that it does not go far enough. He himself, for example, is now contemplating a work on the reality of domestic, as before of ecclesiastical, architecture. Now, nothing can be more true, nothing more useful, than this. Yet even he does not seem to have discerned that as contact with the Church endues with a new sanctity, and elevates every form and every principle of art: so in a peculiar sense the sacred end to which Church architecture is subservient, elevates and sanctifies that reality which must be a condition of its goodness in common with *all* good architecture; in short, raises this principle of Reality into one of Sacramentality. We should be sorry to assert that Mr. Pugin does not feel this, though we are not aware that he has expressed it in his writings: but in his most lasting writings, his churches namely, it is clear that the principle, if not intentionally even, and if only incompletely, has not been without a great influence on that master mind. Yet even in these we could point to details, and in some of his earlier works to something more than details, which show that there is something wanting; that in the bold expedients and fearless licence which his genius has led him to employ, he has occasionally gone wrong; not from the fact of his departure from strict precedent, and his vindication of a certain architectural freedom, but because in these escapements from authority, he has not invariably kept in view the principle now advocated. However the author of the "True Principles" might point to his churches, to prove that a reverent and religious mind, employed in administering to the material wants of the Church, (even though that reverence be misapplied, and that Church in a schismatical position,) cannot fail to succeed, at least in some degree, in stamping upon his work the impress of his own faith and zeal, and in making it, at least to some extent, a living developement and expression of the true ideal.

Mr. Poole, the author of the "Appropriate character of Church Architecture," would appear to believe the symbolism of details rather than any general principle. He was the first, we think, to reassert that the octagonal form of fonts was figurative of Regeneration. In the latter edition of his Book he has adopted several of the symbolical interpretations advanced by the writers of the Cambridge Camden Society.

Mr. Lewis, in his illustrations of Kilpeck Church, (in an appendix to which he has printed a translation of some part of the "Rationale" of our Author) has given a treatise on symbolism generally, and has applied his principles to the explanation of the plan and details of that particular church. His book excited some attention at the time of publication, and was met by considerable ridicule in many quarters. To this we think it was fairly open, since the author did not seem to have grasped the true view of the subject. He appears to believe that, from the very first, *all* church architecture was *intentionally* symbolical. Now this is an unlikely supposition, inasmuch as till church architecture was fully developed, we do not think that its real significancy was understood to its full extent by those who used it. That it was, in its imperfect state, symbolical, we should be the last to deny; but it seems more in accordance with probability, and more in analogy with the progress of other arts, to believe that at first certain given wants induced and compelled certain adaptations to those wants: which then *did* symbolize the wants themselves; and which afterwards became intentionally symbolical. Now such a view as this will explain satisfactorily how a Christian church might be progressively developed from a Basilican model. Mr. Hope, in his essay on Architecture, carries us back to the very earliest expedient likely to be adopted by a savage to protect him from weather, and from this derives every subsequent expansion of the art. Which may be true, and probably is true, so far at least as this: that, however first acquired, the elementary knowledge of any method of building would be, like all other knowledge, continually receiving additions and improvements, till from the first bower of branches sprang the Parthenon, and from that again Cologne or Westminster. But then it is clearly necessary to show some moral reason for so strange a developement, so complete a change of form and style. Now the theory that the ethos of Catholic architects working upon the materials made to hand, namely, the ancient orders of pagan architecture and (say) the Basilican plan, gradually impressed itself upon these unpromising elements, and progressively developed from them a transcript of that ethos in Christian architecture, is intelligible at least, and presents no such difficulty as Mr. Lewis's supposition that ancient architects, (he does not say when, or how long—but take Kilpeck church and say *Norman* architects,) designed intentionally on symbolical principles. We want in this case to be informed when the change took place, from what period architects began to symbolize intentionally, at what time they forgot the traditions of church-building, which they must have had, and commenced to carry new principles into practice. Nor, on this supposition, do we see why there should have been any progressive developement, why the Basilican and Debased-Pagan trammels were not cast away at once; nor why, if the *ideal* of the Norman architect was true and perfect (that is if he were a true Catholic,) its expression should not have been so too: nor why any Norman symbolism, thus originated, should ever have been discarded (as it has been in later styles) instead of remaining an integral and essential part of the material expression of the Church's mind. Now our view appears to be open to no such objection. On the one hand there are given materials to work upon, and on the other a given spirit which is to mould and inform the mass. The contest goes on: mind gradually subdues matter, until in the complete developement of Christian architecture we see the projection of the mind of the Church. It is quite in analogy with the history and nature of the Church, and with the workings of God's providence with respect to it, that there should be this gradual expansion and developement of truth. We foresee the objection that will be raised against fixing on any period as that of the full ripeness of Christian art, and are prepared for many sneers at our advocacy of the perfection of the Edwardian architecture. But we are assured that, if there is any truth (not to say in what is advanced in this essay, but) in what has ever been proposed by any who have appreciated the genius of Pointed Architecture—to confine ourselves to our own subject—no other period can be chosen at which all conditions of beauty, of detail, of general effect, of truthfulness, of reality are so fully answered as in this. And from this spring two important considerations. Firstly, the decline of Christian art—which may be traced from this very period, if architecture be tried by any of the conditions which have been laid down—was confessedly coincident with, and (if what we have said is true) was really symbolical of, those corruptions, which ended in the great rending of the Latin Church; the effects of, and penalties for, which remain to this day in full operation in the whole of Western Christendom. Secondly, the Decorated style may be indeed the finest developement of Christian architecture which the world has yet seen; but it does not follow that it is the greatest perfection which shall ever be arrived at. No: we too look forward, if it may be, to the time when even a new style of Church architecture shall be given us, so glorious and beautiful and true, that Cologne will sink into a fine example of a Transitional period, when the zeal and faith and love of the reunited Church shall find their just expression in the sacramental forms of Catholic art.

But besides the above objection to Mr. Lewis's theory we may mention the arbitrary way in which he determines on things which are to be symbolized, and then violently endeavours to find their expected types. This is quite at variance with the practice of any sober symbolist; and more especially (as we shall hereafter have occasion to point out) with that of Durandus. This forced sort of symbolism naturally leads to a disregard of precedent and authority: and accordingly we remember to have heard of a design by this gentleman for the arrangement of a chancel which professed to symbolize certain facts and doctrines; but which, whatever might be the ingenuity of the symbolism, was no less opposed to the constant rule of arrangement in ancient churches, than it was practically absurd and inconvenient for the purpose which it was meant to answer. Indeed, while Mr. Lewis insists strongly on the symbolizing of facts, he does not succeed in grasping any general principle, any more than he sees the difficulty there is in the way of our receiving his supposition of an intention to symbolize from the first. No architect ever sat down with an analyzed scheme of doctrines which he resolved to embody in his future building: in this, as in any other department of poesy, the result is harmonious, significant, and complete, and may be resolved into its elements, though these elements might never have been laid by the poet as the foundation upon which to raise his superstructure. That were like De La Harpe's theory that an epic poet should first determine on his moral, and then draw out such a plan for his poem as may enable him to illustrate that moral.[6]

The writers of the Cambridge Camden Society have carried out the system more fully and consistently than any others. It has evidently grown upon them, during the process of their enquiries: yet in their earliest publications, we trace, though more obscurely, the same thing. Their "Few Words to Church Builders" acknowledged the principle to a far greater length; and the *Ecclesiologist* has always acted upon it, even when not expressly referring to it. As a necessary consequence, they were the first who dwelt on the absolute necessity of a distinct and spacious chancel; the first who recommended, and where they could, insisted on, the re-introduction of the rood-screen; and the first to condemn the use of western triplets. The position and shape of the font, the necessity of orientation, and some few details, they have, but only in common with others, urged.

The Oxford Architectural Society have never recognised any given principles: and in consequence Littlemore is proposed by them as a model,—a church either without, or else all, Chancel; and either way a solecism.

As might have been expected from a separatist, Rickman, in his treatise, gives not a single line to the principle for which we contend. Mr. Bloxam, in his excellent little work, though often referring to it—more especially in the later editions which have appeared since the labours of the Cambridge Camden Society—yet hardly gives it that prominence which we might have expected from one, who possesses so just an idea of mediaeval arrangements and art.

Among the chief opposers of the system we may mention Mr. Coddington of Ware, who sees perfection in the clumsiness of Basilican arrangements, and schism in the developed art of the middle ages. This writer, as it has been observed in the Ecclesiologist, contends for two things:—1. That one great object of Romanism was to abolish the distinction between the clergy and laity: 2. That another great object of the same Church, acting by its monks, (or, as he calls them, schismatical communities,) was to exalt the clergy unduly above the laity. The former assertion he does not attempt to prove: the latter he supports by pointing to the arrangement of the rood-screen, which, therefore, like the French Ambonoclasts, he wishes to pull down both in cathedrals and churches.

This brief review of the principal writers who have treated on the Symbolism of Churches and Church Ornaments, concludes our first chapter. In it we have endeavoured to point out an acknowledged desideratum; to show what suppositions have been advanced on the subject; to set forth wherein, and for what reason, they fail of being satisfactory; to enunciate the principle of *Sacramentality* as essential for the full appreciation and successful imitation of ancient church architecture; and finally, in referring to the works of some later symbolists, to show why their hypotheses are incomplete or untenable. We have also brought under review the glaring contrasts between the methods of life of an ancient and modern architect; and, if we may so say, between the machinery of designing and the habit of mind in the two cases. We shall now proceed to examine those arguments which may lead us to suspect that some such principle as Sacramentality really exists.

(Saxon Tower, St. Michael's, Oxford, England, 1100's)

(St. Bartholomew the Great, London, England, begun in 1123)

Floriated Cross

(St. Michael's, Oxford, England)

CHAPTER II: THE ARGUMENT À PRIORI

It will first be proper to consider whether, regarding the subject *à priori*, that is, looking at the habits and manners of those among whom the symbolical system originated, if it originated anywhere, we have reason to think them at all likely to induce that system. Now, as matter of fact, we know that the train of thought, the every-day observances, above all, the religious rites of the early Christians, were in the highest degree figurative. The rite of Baptism gave the most forcible of all sanctions to such a system; and while it sanctioned, it also suggested, some of the earliest specimens of Christian symbolism. Hence, when that rite was found to be, so to speak, connected with the word formed by the initial letters of our Blessed Saviour's name and titles, arose the Mystic Fish: hence, as we shall see, the octagonal baptistery and font. Indeed, almost every great doctrine had been symbolized at a very early period of Christianity. The Resurrection was set forth in the Phoenix, rising immortal from its ashes: the meritorious Passion of our Saviour, by the Pelican, feeding its young with its own blood: the Sacrament of the Holy Eucharist, by grapes and wheatears, or again by the blood flowing from the heart and feet of the Wounded Lamb into a chalice beneath: the Christian's renewal of strength thereby in the Eagle, which descending grey and aged into the ocean, rises thence with renewed strength and vigour: the Church, by the Ark, and the vessel[7] in which our Lord slept: the Christian's purity and innocence by the Dove[8]: again, by the same symbol, the souls[9] of those who suffered for the Truth: again, though perhaps not so early, the Holy Spirit: the Apostles were also set forth as twelve Doves[10]: the Ascension of our Saviour by the Flying Bird; concerning which S. Gregory[11] teaches, "rightly is our Redeemer called a Bird, Whose Body ascended freely into heaven:" Martyrs also by birds let loose; for so Tertullian,[12] "There is one kind of flesh of fishes, that is of those who be regenerate by Holy Baptism; but another of birds, that is of martyrs." The caged bird is symbolical of the contrary; this has been found upon the phial containing the blood of a martyr. Of this, Boldetti says, "It is represented on the mosaic of the ancient Tribune of S. Mary beyond Tiber; one being seen at the side of Isaiah the Prophet, the other at that of the Prophet Jeremiah." In the same way, partridges and peacocks, each with its own meaning, are represented. So, again, lions, tigers, horses, oxen, strange fishes, and marine monsters, represent the fearful martyrdoms to which God's servants were exposed: a point which the reader will do well to bear in mind, because in treating of Norman mouldings we shall have occasion again to refer to this matter. So, again, the extended hand symbolised Providence. We have also the seven stars, the moon, and many other symbols of a similar kind. Nor must we forget the *Agnus Dei*, by which our Blessed Lord Himself was represented; nor the *Pastor Bonus*, in which His own parable was still further parabolized. The Christian gems found in the Catacombs are all charged with some symbolical device. Upon these is the ship for the Church, the palm for the martyr, and the instrument of torture: as well as the sacred monogram expressing our Saviour's name. The same symbol blazed on the *labarum*, of the first Christian Emperor; and the very coins symbolically showed that the Church had subdued the kingdoms of this world. That fearful heresy, Gnosticism, which arose from an over-symbolizing, shows, nevertheless, how deeply the principle, within due limits, belonged to the Church. The Gnostic gems exhibit the most monstrous perversions of symbolical representations: the medals of Dioclesian bear a lying symbol of a crushed and expiring Christianity. Later still, new symbols were adopted: mosaics, illuminations, ornaments, all bore some holy emblems. The monogram IHS is found in every Church in Western Christendom: the corresponding symbol stamps the Eucharistic wafers of the East.[13]

The symbols of the Evangelists were also of very early date, though not, in all cases, appropriated as now: for the angel and the lion fluctuated between S. Matthew and S. Mark. Numbers, too, were fruitful of allegorical meaning; and the most ingenious combinations were used to elicit an esoteric meaning from them. By *one*, the Unity of the Deity was understood: by *two*, the divine and human Natures of the Saviour: by *three*, of course, the doctrine of the Most Holy Trinity: by *four*, the doctrine of the Four Evangelists: by *six*, the Attributes of the Deity: *seven* represented the sevenfold graces of the Holy Spirit: *eight*, (for a reason hereafter to be noticed,) Regeneration: *twelve*, the glorious company the Apostles, and, tropologically, the whole Church. And when a straightforward reference to any of these failed, they were added or combined, till the required meaning was obtained. A single instance may suffice:—S. Augustine, writing on that passage of S. Paul's, "What? know ye not that the saints shall judge the world?" after explaining (*Expos. super Psalm.* lxxxvi.) the twelve thrones, which our Saviour mentions, of the whole Church, as founded by and represented in the Apostles, finds a further meaning. "The parts of the world be four; the east, the west, the north, and the south:" and (adds the Father) "they are constantly named in Holy Writ." From these four winds, saith the Lord in the Gospel, shall the elect be gathered together: whence the Church is called from these four parts. Called, and how? By the Trinity. It is not called, except by Baptism, in the name of the Father, and of the Son, and of the Holy Ghost. So "four, multiplied by three, make twelve." In accidental numbers, too, a meaning was often found. No wonder that some beheld, in the three hundred and eighteen trained servants wherewith Abraham, the Father of the Faithful, routed the combined kings, a type of the three hundred and eighteen Fathers of Nicaea, by whom the Faithful rose triumphant over the Arian heresy.

Again, types and emblems without number were seen in the language of the Psalmist, occuring so continuously in the Services of the Church. "His faithfulness shall be thy buckler," gives rise to a fine allegory of S. Bernard's, drawn from the triangular shape of the buckler used at the time when that Father wrote; even as we still see it, in the effigies of early Knights. It protects the upper part of the body completely: the feet are less completely shielded. And so, remarks the Saint, does God's Providence guard His people from spiritual dangers, imaged by those weapons which attack the upper, or more vital parts of the body: but from temporal adversities He hath neither promised, nor will give so complete protection.

To mention the symbolism which attached itself to the worship of the early Church, would be to go through all its rites. Confirmation and Matrimony, and above all, Baptism, were attended by ceremonies in the highest degree symbolical. But it is needless to dwell on them; enough has been said to prove the attachment which the Catholic Church has ever evinced to symbolism.

But the Sign of the Cross is that which gave the greatest scope to symbolism.—Our readers will probably remember the passage of Tertullian in which he says, "we cross ourselves when we go out, and when we come in; when we lie down, and when we rise up," etc. Indeed, as in every thing they used, so in every thing they saw, the Sign of the Cross. The following lines from Donne are much to the purpose:

Since Christ embraced the Cross itself, dare I
His Image, th' Image of His Cross, deny?
Would I have profit by the Sacrifice,
And dare the chosen Altar to despise?
It bore all other sins, but is it fit
That it should bear the sin of scorning it?
Who from the picture would avert his eye,
How should he fly His pains, Who there did die?
From me no pulpit, nor misgrounded Law,

Nor scandal taken, shall this Cross withdraw:
It shall not—nor it cannot—for the loss
Of this Cross were to me another Cross:
Better were worse: for no affliction,
No cross were so extreme, as to have none.
Who can blot out the Cross, which th' instrument
Of God dewed on him in the Sacrament?
Who can deny me power and liberty
To stretch mine arms, and mine own Cross to be?
Swim—and at every stroke thou art thy Cross:
The mast and yard are theirs whom seas do toss.
Look down, thou seest our crosses in small things,
Look up, thou seest birds fly on crossed wings.

We will mention but one symbolical feature more in the trains of thought which were common among the early Christians. We refer to the esoteric meaning which was supposed to exist in the writings of heathen authors: as for example, when the Pollio of Virgil was imagined to point to the Saviour, and the Fortunate Isles of Pindar to Paradise. It were easy but needless to dwell on this subject. The few instances we have given are already amply sufficient to prove to some, to remind others, how symbolical was the religion of the early Church, and (we think) to establish our case *à priori*.

CHAPTER III: THE ARGUMENT FROM ANALOGY

Having dealt with the argument à priori, we now proceed to show that, from analogy, it is highly probably that the teaching of the Church, as in other things, so in her material buildings, would be symbolical.

Firstly, let us look at other nations, and other religions. It need not be said that the symbolism of the Jews was one of the most striking features of their religion. It would be unnecessary to go through their tabernacle and temple rites, their sacrificial observances, and their legal ceremonies. The Passover, the cleansing of the leper, the scape goat, the feast of tabernacles, the morning and evening sacrifice, the Sabbatical year, the jubilee, were all in the highest degree figurative. The very stones in the breast plate have each, according to the Rabbis, their mystical signification. And, as if still further to teach them sacramentality, not only of things, but of events, it pleased God to make all their most famous ancestors, chiefs, and leaders, *e.g.* Abraham, Isaac, Jacob, Joseph, Moses, Joshua, David, most remarkable types of the Messiah: nay, from the beginning the principal doctrines of Christianity were, in some form or other, set forth. Regeneration and the Church, in the Flood and the Ark: the Bread and Wine in the Manna and the Stricken Rock: the two dispensations in Sarah and Hagar. Indeed the immense extent of symbolism in the Old Testament was the mine of the Fathers. Every day they brought to light some new wealth; and, if we press the symbolism of the Church further than it was actually intended, we are only treading in the steps of her bishops and doctors. For while, of course, in commenting on and explaining the sacrifice of Isaac, the covenant of circumcision, the captivity and exaltation of Joseph, they were only developing the real meaning which God seems to have intended should be set forth by those events, there are,—as we have already hinted,—many instances where their piety found an interpretation which was perhaps never intended. Thus, because Job, while all else that belonged to him was restored double, had only the same number of children which he had lost,—they have argued, that thus the separate existence of souls was represented, as the Patriarch could not be said to have lost those who were in another state of existence.

And if in the Old Testament we find authority for the principle of symbolism, much more do we in the New. We shall presently have occasion to allude to the rise and progress of the sacramentality of Baptism: we may now refer more particularly to the frequency with which S. Paul symbolizes the enactments of the Law; as in the case of the ox forbidden, while treading out the corn, to be muzzled. So again, the Revelation is nothing but one continued symbolical poem. The parabolic teaching of our Lord we shall presently notice.

To this we may add, the exoteric and esoteric signification of certain books, e. g., the Song of Solomon: the double interpretation of many of the prophecies, primarily of the earthly, principally of the heavenly Jerusalem: we may refer to the symbolical meaning attached, under the Christian dispensation, to certain previously established rites, as, for instance, Holy Matrimony. With symbolical writings, enactments, events, personages, observances, buildings, vestments, for her guides and models, how could the Church Catholic fail of following symbolism, as a principle and a passion?

But not only is Christianity symbolical: every developement of religion is, and must necessarily be so. On the Grecian mythology, we shall have occasion to say something more presently. The symbolism of Plato, and still further developement by Proclus and the later philosophers of his school, will occur to every one. If it be asserted that the more it was touched and acted on by Christianity, the more symbolical did it become,—we only reply, So much the more to the purpose of our argument. But not only in Roman and Grecian Paganism is this the case. The Hindoo religion has much of symbolism; and some of its most striking fables, derived from whatever source—whether from unwritten tradition, or from contact with the Jews—possess this character wonderfully. Take, for instance, the example of Krishna suffering, and Krishna triumphant; represented, in the one case, by the figure of a man enveloped in the coils of a serpent, which fastens its teeth in his heel; in the other, by the same man setting his foot on, and crushing the head of the monster. Now here, it is true, the doctrine symbolised has long been forgotten among those with whom the legend is sacred: we, on the contrary, have a very plain reference to the promise concerning the Seed of the Woman and the serpent's head. This is an instance of the fact, that Truth will live in a symbolical, long after it has perished in every other, form: and doubtless, when the time for the conversion of India shall have arrived, thousands will receive the truth the more willingly, in that they have had a representation of it, distorted it is true, but not destroyed, set, for so many centuries, before their eyes. Some truths, accidentally impressed on a symbolical observance, may still live, that otherwise must have perished: just as the only memory of some of the beings that existed before the flood, is to be found in the petrified clay on which they accidentally happened to set their feet.

The Mahometan religion has also, though in an inferior degree, its symbolism; and the reason of its inferiority in this respect is plain—because, namely, it is a religion of sense. Now Catholicity, which teaches men constantly to live above their senses, to mortify their passions, and to deny themselves;—nay even Hindooism, which, so far as it approximates to the truth, preaches the same doctrine, must constantly lead men by the seen to look on to the unseen. If everything material were not made sacramental of that which is immaterial, so, as it were, bearing its own corrective with its own temptation, man could hardly fail of walking by sight, rather than by faith. But now, the Church, not content with warning us that we are in an enemy's country, boldly seizes on the enemy's goods, converting them to her own use. Symbolism is thus the true Sign of the Cross, hallowing the unholy, and making safe the dangerous: the true salt which, being cast in, purified the unhealthy spring: the true meal which removed death from the Prophet's provision. Others may amuse themselves by asserting that the Church in all that she does and enacts, is not symbolical:—we bless God for the knowledge that she is.

We need not dwell on the symbolism of heretics, insomuch as we shall have occasion to refer to it in other parts of this essay. We will rather notice, that those to whom we have been but now referring, heathens and Mahomedans, have a way of discovering a subtle symbolism in things which in themselves were not intended to have any deeper meaning. We may mention the odes of Hafiz—the Anacreon, or rather perhaps, the Stesichorus, of Persia. These poems, speaking to the casual reader of nothing but love, and wine, and garlands, and rosebuds, are seriously affirmed, by Persian critics, to contain a deep esoteric reference to the communion of the soul with God; just as it has been wildly supposed, that under the name of Laura, Petrarch in fact only expressed that Immortal Beauty after which the soul of the Christian is constantly striving, and to which it is constantly advancing. So, in Dante Beatrice is not only the poet's earthly love, but, as it has been well shown by M. Ozanam, the representative of Catholic Theology.

To dwell on the symbolism of Nature would lead us too far from our point. But we must constantly bear in mind that Nature and the Church answer to each other as implicit and explicit revelations of God. Therefore, whatever system is seen to run through the one, in all probability runs through the other. Now, that the teaching of Nature is symbolical, none, we think, can deny. Shall we then wonder that the Catholic Church is in all her art and splendour sacramental of the Blessed Trinity, when Nature herself is so? Shall God have denied this symbolism to the latter, while He has bestowed it on the former? Shall there be a trinity of effect in every picture, a trinity of tone in every note, a trinity of power in every mind, a trinity of essence in every substance,—and shall not there be a trinity in the arrangements and details of church art? It were strange if the servant could teach, what the mistress must be silent upon: that Natural Religion should be endued with capabilities not granted to Revealed Truth.

Is not, again, the doctrine of the Resurrection wonderfully set forth by Nature? This symbolism is the more remarkable, in that to the ancients the rising of the sun and the bursting forth of the leaf must have appeared false symbolism, although they knew too well that of which autumn and evening were typical. So, to quote only one other example, the Law of self-sacrifice is beautifully shadowed out by the grain that "unless it die, abideth alone; but if it die, bringeth forth much fruit."

We may argue next from the analogy of all art. Sculpture, perhaps, has least to offer in our support. But in painting we may refer to the conventional colours appropriated to various personages: and the mechanical symbolism of poetry is known to all. Nor must we forget the conventional use of language. Archaisms, studied inversions, quaint phrases, and the like, have always been affected by those who were treating of high and holy subjects. None has employed these with happier effect than Spenser, whose language, it need not be said, never was and never could have been really used. The solemnizing effect of a judicious employment of this artifice is no where more strongly felt than in works of Divinity. Compare for example the English language, where the conventional Thou is always addressed to the Deity, and where a stern simplicity runs through the whole of our Divine Offices, with the French which can only employ *Vous* in prayer, and with the Portuguese, where, in the authorized translation of the Holy Scriptures, Apostles, and Prophets—nay, our Blessed Lord Himself, speak in the polite phrases of conversational elegance.[14]

Music, however, has the strongest claims to our notice. We know, for example, that each instrument symbolizes some particular colour. So, according to Haydn, the trombone is deep red—the trumpet, scarlet—the clarionet, orange—the oboe, yellow—the bassoon, deep yellow—the flute, sky-blue—the diapason, deep blue—the double diapason, purple—the horn, violet:—while the violin is pink—the viola, rose—the violoncello, red—and the double-bass, crimson. This by many would be called fanciful:—therefore let us turn to a passage of Haydn's works, and see if it will hold. Let us examine the sun-rise in the "Creation." At the commencement, as it has been well observed, our attention is attracted by a soft-streaming sound from the violins, scarcely audible, till the pink rays of the second violin diverge into the chord of the second, to which is gradually imparted a greater fulness of colour, as the rose violas and red violoncellos steal in with expanding beauty, while the azure of the flute tempers the mounting rays of the violin: as the notes continue ascending to the highest point of brightness, the orange of the clarionet, the scarlet of the trumpet, the purple of the double diapason, unite in increasing splendour—till the sun appears at length in all the refulgence of harmony.

This may serve as a specimen of the manner in which the expressions of one art may be translated into that of another, because they each and all symbolize the same abstraction.

Again, the language of flowers is a case much in point. This is a species of symbolism which has prevailed among all nations, and which our devout ancestors were not slow in stamping with the impress of religion. Witness, for example, the *Herb Trinity*, now generally called *Heartsease*, the *Passion Flower*, and the *Lacrima Christi*. And in the present day, who knows not that the rose is for beauty—the violet for modesty—the sunflower for faithfulness—the forget-me-not for remembrance—the pansy for thought—the cypress for woe—the yew for trueheartedness—the everlasting for immortality? The flowers introduced into the ornament of churches we shall consider presently.

Furthermore, whatever was the character of our Lord's teaching—such is likely to be that of His Church. If the former were plain, unadorned, setting forth naked truths in the fewest and simplest words; then we allow that there is a *primâ facie* argument against the system which we are endeavouring to support. But if it were parabolic, figurative, descriptive, allegorical—why should not the Church imitate her Master? His parables are at once the surest defence, and the most probable originators, of her symbolism.

We shall have occasion in another place to draw from a consideration of the nature of our Lord's parables an argument in behalf of symbolism against one of the most formidable objections that has been raised against the system. It would here be sufficient for our purpose to notice the figurative character of our Lord's general teaching. But we have His own authority for much more than a general adoption of such a principle. Tradition hands down that He was within sight of the Temple when He pointed towards it, and uttered those gracious words, *I am the Door*. Be this as it may, we have from it a sufficient precedent to justify us in seeking for an emblematical meaning in the external world, and more particularly in the material sanctuary. S. Paul, on the same principle, allegorizes the Jewish Temple, detail by detail:—the Holy of Holies was heaven; the High Priest,

Christ; the veil even, His flesh. It is inconceivable that the Temple should be so symbolical, and so holy that our Lord Himself cleansed it from its defiling moneychangers: and yet that a Christian church, wherein the Great Sacrifice is commemorated and our Lord is peculiarly present, should be less symbolical,—particularly when its arrangement is in exact conformity to that of the Temple—or should be less holy. At any rate the *Door* must be significant: at any rate the Altar, which S. Paul claims for the Christian Church, in opposition to those who "serve the tabernacle."

Again, the holy Sacraments of the Church are examples, in the highest degree, of this principle of figurative or symbolical teaching. They, indeed, are not only signs of unseen things, but the channels and instruments of grace. The latter quality we do not claim for the speaking symbolism of a material church: but architecture is an emblem of the invisible abstract, no less than Holy Baptism and the Lord's Supper. Besides the two Sacraments κατ' ἐξόχην, our Church recognizes other offices, such as Marriage, Confirmation, and the like, as Sacramentals. In short the whole Church system is figurative from first to last: not indeed therefore the less real, actual, visible, and practical; but rather the more real and practical, because its teaching and discipline are not merely material and temporary, but anticipative of the heavenly and eternal. This quality, then of symbolism cannot be denied to one, and a most important, expression of the teaching of the Church, namely its architecture. The cathedral (to repeat the general in the particular) is not the less material, the less solid, the less real, because we see it in the figurative exhibition of the peculiarities of our religion and the articles of our creed.

Tympanum over the Norman Prior's Door (Cathedral of Ely, England)

CHAPTER IV: PHILOSOPHICAL REASONS FOR BELIEVING IN SYMBOLISM

We now propose to offer a few remarks on the philosophical reasons there seem to be for concluding that Ecclesiastical Architecture has some esoteric meaning, some figurative adaptation, more than can be appreciated, or even discerned, by the casual observer, to the uses which produced it, and which have always regulated it. We venture to approach this consideration, however, rather from a feeling that our Essay would be incomplete without some reference to this kind of argument, than from any idea of our own ability to treat on subjects so abstract and infinite; and fearing that we may not be able clearly to express or dissect those thoughts which, nevertheless, appear to our own minds both true and very important.

It is little better than a truism to assert that there is an intimate correspondence and relation between cause and effect: yet this thought opens the way to a very wide field of speculation. Mind cannot act upon matter without the material result being closely related to the mental intention which originated it: the fact that anything exists adapted to a certain end or use is alone enough to presuppose the end or use: who can see a ποίημα, without distinguishing its relation to the want or necessity which brought about ποίησις? In short, the ἐργόν, whatever it may be, not only answers to that which called it forth, but, in some sort, represents materially, or symbolizes, the abstract volition or operation of the mind which originated it. Show us a pitcher, a skewer, or any of the simplest utensils designed for the most obvious purposes: do not the cavity of the one, and the piercing point of the other, at once set forth and symbolize the τέγος which was answered in their production? Now, from this thought, we might proceed to trace out the truthfulness and reality of every ποίημα considered in relation to the τὸ ποιοῦν; for even a deceptive thing is true and real in its relation to the mental intention of deceiving: but we intend merely to consider the way in which the abstract movements or πρέξεις of mind are *symbolized* by the material operations or results which they have produced. In other words, we would allege that everything material is symbolical of some mental process, of which it is indeed only the developement: that we may see in everything outward and visible some inward and spiritual meaning. It is this which makes "books in everything:" finding in everything objective the material exhibition of the subjective and unseen: not claiming for the abstract mind an independence of matter, but acknowledging its union with it; and thus learning from the speculations of reason, to perceive the fitness for our nature of that system of sacramentality in which God has placed us, and to bless Him more and more for the Church, a sacramental institution, and for *the* Sacraments κατ' ἐξόχην, which it conveys. This method of viewing the subject will be our excuse for attempting on the one hand to learn by analysis from a material church itself, considered objectively, the symbolism which may be supposed to have directed its design; and on the other hand to show from the abstract necessities of the case that a material church might have been expected to be symbolically designed. But if this theory of symbolism gives light and meaning and connection to the acknowledged facts, whether abstract or material, with which we have to do;—while no other view will explain *all* the phenomena;—it certainly recommends itself by its simplicity and harmony to a general reception. Considered in this light, the whole group of separate facts become linked together and adjusted, and so resolve themselves into a great fabric of truth, which (like the Pyramid of Cheops) is consistent and real and intelligible, when seen from any point, under any circumstances, or in any light.

But if it be granted that there is this mutual connexion between the abstract and its material exhibition in every case, it will be readily admitted that a principle of sacramentality must be especially a condition of all religious acts. If we were merely spirits, without bodies or any necessary connexion with matter, it would be possible perhaps for us to worship the Great Spirit in an abstract way by a sort of volition of devotion; but not being so, our souls cannot engage in adoration without the company of their material home. Hence every effort of devotion is attended by some bodily act. Whether we lift our eyes or hands to heaven, or kneel in prayer, we show forth this necessity of our being: our body has sinned, has been redeemed, will be punished or glorified, no less than the soul: it must therefore worship with the soul. Now the symbolism of the bodily acts of devotion is understood by all. We have even personated Prayer by a prostrate figure with uplifted hands.[15] It has been felt not only right but necessary, in all ages and places, to accompany the inward feeling of devotion with some outward manifestation of it. In other words, all religious actions are from their nature symbolical and figurative. But if the most obvious corporeal accompaniments to spiritual worship show this clearly, how much more evidently must all ritual systems appear to be symbolical? A system of worship, whether heathen, Christian, or heretical, is only the development and methodizing of the simplest figurative acts of devotion; the whole affected by the peculiar relation between the object of adoration and the worshippers which in each particular system may have been presupposed. Why does the Mussulman take off his shoes, kneel on his carpet towards Mecca, and perform his stated ablutions? Is not each act in itself figurative and full of meaning? How could such a system, or any other system, have been originated, but with some intended typification of certain given facts or doctrines or feelings? Why does the heartless Quaker go with covered head into his bare conventicle, and sit in enforced silence? He will answer, to *express* his independence of idle forms, the spirituality of his worship, his repudiation of any *media* in his intercourse with the Divine Being. We thank him for his admission of a symbolical purpose, but we read the symbolism differently. We perceive it to express clearly enough the presumptuous pride and vanity of his sect, his rejection of all Sacraments, and his practical disbelief in the Communion of Saints. Again, is the pulpit of the Brownist symbolical; and shall not our font and altar be so at least as much? The Catholic ritual is indeed symbolical from first to last. Without the clue to its figurative meaning, we should never have understood its pregnant truthfulness and force. No one, in short, ever ventured to regard the ancient ritual as anything but highly figurative: this was claimed as its highest excellence by its observers and commentators, this was ridiculed and despised by the enemies of the Church; but was confessed by all. The more any one meditates on the ancient ritual of the Church, the more this will be found not only the most prominent characteristic, but the only satisfactory explanation of many otherwise unintelligible requirements. This is not the place to go at any length into the consideration of the whole symbolism of the ritual system: it will be enough if it is granted that some prescribed ritual, however meagre, must be a necessary part of all religion; and that every such system is in some degree figurative or symbolical. Now to apply this to church architecture. No one will deny that, in a general point of view, the form of our churches is adapted to certain wants, and was chosen for this very adaptation. Indeed this is allowed by modern writers and builders: who defend a church which has no more than an altar-recess, on this very ground, that there is no longer any want of a deep chancel. "I object to aisles," says a modern architect, "because the great end of a church is to be an auditorium." "The cross form," says another, "I always adopt, because then every one can see the preacher if I place the pulpit in the middle." But why not take a circle or octagon at once, or the form which is always adopted for the lecture-rooms at Mechanics' Institutes? For these plans are obviously most convenient for hearing and seeing. But then, every one knows that these are not *church* forms. The modern builder then, trammeled, at least in this respect, by rule and precedent, chooses the cruciform plan, not (perhaps) for its true symbolism; but, by a wrong arrangement of this plan, still further symbolizes (for example) his own undue estimation of the ordinance of preaching. So true it is that those who would most object to symbolism, as a rule of design, are themselves (did they but know it) symbolizing, in every church they build, their own arbitrary and presumptuous ideas on the subject. It is not our intention to prove here, (what has been pointed out however many times,) the duty incumbent upon us of following in our modern churches the ancient principles of design: we are not writing with the immediate practical end of improving modern church architecture; but are endeavouring to illustrate the symbolical principles of ancient design. We shall, however, before finishing this chapter, choose an example, which will apply to us, as well as to any other branch of the Church, to show how essentially church architecture in that respect at least is a part of the Ritual system. And if Catholic worship is expressed and represented by Catholic ritual, and if church architecture is a part of this ritual, then is church architecture itself an expression and exponent of Catholic worship. A conclusion this which will well warrant the very strong language in which the Cambridge Camden Society have always asserted the great importance of this art, and have exacted from its professors such qualifications of personal holiness and liturgical knowledge as are no less above the attainment than the aspirations of the modern school.

It may not be clear to some how in any sense architecture can be called symbolical, or the outward sign of something invisible: or rather what the process is by which a given arrangement, suggested perhaps by some necessity, becomes in turn suggestive and figurative of the very purpose for which it was planned. But let us take the case of a theatre. Here it is clearly necessary that there shall be a stage or orchestra, accommodation for spectators, and means of easy exit. Accordingly every theatre displays all these requisites. And does not the building then in turn emblem the purpose for which it was planned? The ruins of Roman theatres are not uncommon: do we fail to be recalled by them to the idea of the Roman stage? are not the several parts of the material building highly figurative and suggestive of the rules and orders of the abstract drama?

With respect to churches: let us suppose the institution and ritual of the Church to be what we know it was; and that we have to adapt some architectural arrangement to the performance of this ritual. Is there anything which will dictate any general form rather than another? Surely there is. We will not speak now of the propriety of setting aside a place for the celebration of the Holy Eucharist, or of the propriety of retaining the plan of the typical Temple; but we are considering simply what is required by practical necessity. The worshippers who are to assemble in our church are not all on an equality. There are some who are endowed with high privileges as being those consecrated to the immediate service of the sanctuary. In early times so real a thing was the distinction between the clergy and the laity, that the Church being divided into these two classes, the material edifice displayed a like division: and the nave and chancel preach to posterity the sacredness of Holy Orders, and the mutual duties arising from the relation in which the flock stand to their shepherds. But in early ages the laity were not all classed *en masse* as with us now. Among them were the Faithful, the Catechumens, who had not yet been admitted to Holy Baptism, and the Penitents or those who had lapsed. True to itself, church architecture provided then a separate place for each of these divisions. Does not the ground plan of such a church symbolize minutely the then state of church discipline and the conditions of church worship? The reality and meaning of such an arrangement may be shown thus also. After the Reformation the great distinction between clergy and laity became lost or undervalued: accordingly the chancel-screens in many places disappeared, as symbolical in their absence as in their existence. But still there was a necessity for some material arrangement to protect the Altar from insult: and so altar-rails came in, manifest symbols of that spirit which made their introduction allowable, if indeed not necessary[16]: still these very rails, and the penned up reading-pew, teach that the clergy, at least when performing a function, are divided from the laity.

Now it is of no consequence whatever, whether the early builders of churches intended this particular arrangement to be symbolical. The arrangement being adopted becomes necessarily, even if unintentionally, symbolical, by the process we have endeavoured to trace, and so things essentially symbolical give rise to intended symbolism: for it is a simple historical fact that the weathercock, whatever practical utility may have first suggested its use and peculiar form, has been for many centuries placed on the church spire for its *intentional symbolism*. And the process is repeated: for suppose one only of the conventional symbolical meanings of the weathercock had been discovered: the thoughtful mind goes on to find out other figurative senses in which its use is appropriate, and these conventional meanings become in their turn intentionally symbolized by future church builders. This may be illustrated also in the following way. The Jews, in the rite of Baptism, had probably no other idea than a reference to "the mystical washing away of sins." But when S. Paul had once given to that rite the new idea of a burial with Christ in the Baptismal

Abraham and Isaac (Hortus Deliciarum, 1100's)

"Indeed the immense extent of symbolism in the Old Testament was the mine of Fathers."

The altar rail (St. Mary the Virgin, Oxford, England)

"After the Reformation, the great distinction between clergy and laity became lost or undervalued: accordingly the chancel-screens in many places disappeared, as symbolical in their absence as in their existence. But still there was a necessity for some material arrangement to protect the Altar from insult: and so altar-rails came in."

water, and a rising again with Him, this typical meaning became an example of intended symbolism to all those who should hereafter use it.

As we began this part of our subject with hesitation, so we finish it with some degree of apprehension. To some what has been said may seem more than ordinarily visionary, and ridiculous: yet others, we hope, will feel that, however feebly and inadequately expressed, there is some truth in what has been advanced concerning the relation between the material and immaterial: that the latter wielding and moulding the former into an expression of itself, makes it in turn a type of that which it expresses. So that if on the one hand, to take our particular branch of the subject, the theoretical ritual and ordinances of religion imply and require certain peculiar adaptations of the material building in which they are to be celebrated; then in turn the circumstances of the material fabric suggest and symbolize the peculiar conditions of ritual which induced them. In short we have endeavoured to prove that from our very nature every outward thing is symbolical of something inward and spiritual: but, above all things, outward religious actions are sacramental; and particularly *any* prescribed ritual, of which the first characteristic is that it is figurative: that the Catholic ritual is eminently symbolical, and from its nature very strikingly influences all its material appliances: that church architecture is the eldest daughter of Ritual: that the process, according to which architecture was influenced by the requirements of Ritualism was at first as simple as that by which the form of a theatre sprang from the conditions which were to be fulfilled by its builder: that thus a church (built in the fully developed style of Christian architecture) even if not built with any intention of symbolizing, (though it is an historical fact that the symbolism of each part was known and received *before* the erection of any church of this style,) became nevertheless essentially a "petrifaction of our religion": a fact which, once admitted and realized, becomes to succeeding church builders, whether they will or not, a rule and precedent for intentional symbolical design.

Symbolic tree of life and cross motif on the altar cloth (St. Mary the Virgin, Oxford, England)

CHAPTER V: THE ANALYTICAL ARGUMENT

We must arrive at the same conclusion, if we consider the subject in an analytical way. For example; suppose a person, hitherto unacquainted not only with the general peculiarities of Christian churches, but also with Christianity itself, were to enter a cathedral; or (which will be a fairer case) were to visit a Catholic country, and examine its churches as a whole, would he not, if possessed of only ordinary intelligence, observe that the cross form, for example, was of most common occurrence, and, in the case of the larger buildings, was perhaps the only plan adopted? And would he not then naturally enquire why there should be this marked preference for a form, in itself inconvenient for purposes of hearing or seeing, and open to great mechanical objections, such as the almost resistless pressure of the four arms on the piers which stand at the angles of intersection?[17] But if he learnt that the religion for which these temples were designed was that of the Cross, he would at once see the propriety of this ground plan, and would confidently and truly conclude that this form was chosen in order to bring the Cross, by this symbolism, vividly and constantly before the eyes of the worshippers. To deny intended symbolism, in the case of such a person, would clearly be absurd: shall it be less obvious to us? Our traveller would probably, being satisfied on this point, examine these buildings more closely. He would find an altar raised conspicuously above the surrounding level; and for this he might discover a practical reason; but why in so many cases (so many as well nigh to make a rule) are the steps in either *three* or some multiple of three? Surely the fundamental doctrine of the Holy Trinity would, if explained to him, sufficiently account for this all but universal arrangement. Why, again, in every case does a screen separate one part of the church from the other? When our inquirer learns the principle of the separation of laity and clergy, this arrangement will be at once intelligble and figurative. How unreasonable would the position of the font by the door appear to him, till he learnt the symbolical reason for it being placed there! And we may here remark that the practice of the last generation in removing old fonts, or using basins for substitutes, or in placing new fonts, near the altar, shows clearly enough that convenience and utility would have pointed out a very different place for the font from what is assigned by the canon, on symbolical grounds; grounds adduced in this case, it would seem to give weight to a decision so clearly opposed to all merely practical and obvious reasons. Again, the marked deviation of the orientation of the chancel from that of the nave, would be quite inexplicable till the beautiful and affecting symbolism of the arrangement were pointed out.

Again, it has not been left merely to the meditative ecclesiologist to observe that Christian architecture has as decided a characteristic of verticality, as Pagan architecture had of horizontalism. A mere artist could not fail of marking the contrast between Beauvais and the temples of Paestum. The contrast must then be admitted: but how must we explain it? Surely no accident could have developed the grovelling Pagan into the aspiring Gothic. What mechanical reasons could produce Westminster from even the Parthenon? But is not the phenomenon explained when we see in towering pier, spire, and pinnacle, the symbolical exhibition of that religion which alone aspires to things above, nay more, the figurative commemoration of that Resurrection itself, which alone originates, and only justifies, the same heavenward tendency. But if this be true; if these acknowledged peculiarities in Christian architecture be utterly unintelligible on any other supposition than this of a symbolical meaning, surely it is not unreasonable to receive so ready a solution of the difficulty: and, the principle admitted, why may not reasons of the same figurative nature be assigned for other arrangements, in themselves on any other interpretation not only meaningless but obviously useless or absurd?

(St. Mary the Virgin, Oxford, England)

(St. Mary the Virgin, Oxford, England)

"The altar is raised above the surrounding level by 3 steps or some multiple of 3."

CHAPTER VI: THE INDUCTIVE ARGUMENT

We have next to show, by a process of induction, that some principles of symbolism have always been observed in designing churches: that is to say, that without any actual acquaintance with the plan, details or arrangement of existing churches, we might gather from other sources, not only the probability, but the fact, that there was some reason (not merely mechanical or accidental) for the selection and universal observation of particular forms and ornaments, and peculiar rules of distribution.

First, we shall refer to the celebrated passage of S. Clement of Rome, about performing the Divine Offices decently and in order, as to time, and place, and circumstance. "Where and by whom God willeth these to be performed He hath Himself defined by His most supreme will."[18] "But where," says Mede, (discussing the passage with the view of establishing a particular point namely, bowing towards the altar) "hath the Lord defined these things, unless He hath left us to the analogy of the Old Testament?"[19] This indeed is obviously S. Clement's meaning: and not to go at any length into the consideration of all the particular forms or ceremonies of the Old dispensation which were perpetuated in the New—as the threefold Ministry deduced by S. Jerome, from the High Priest, Priests, and Levites; the Canonical Hours; the Gospel anciently laid on the altar, answering to the Two Tables, and the like—it will be sufficient to refer once more to the remarkable parallel between a Christian church and the Jewish Temple.[20] There can be little doubt that Mede proved his point of the propriety of genuflexion towards the altar. We are contending for a much simpler thing: for no more indeed than the concession of a probability that in the earliest Christian churches there was at least this resemblance to the Temple; that there should be in both a Holy of Holies and an outer-court. Supposing this distinction to have been only made by a curtain, our point is nevertheless gained: and we would rest here on this one particular of resemblance only, (though others might be insisted on); because, any one designed parallel being granted, the inference for others is easy. And here it will be enough to observe that the almost constant practice in ancient writers of applying to some one part of a Christian church a name or names derived directly from the *Holy of Holies* is a strong argument in our favour: though the passages are often too incidental to be adduced as evidence of an intended symbolism.[21] But, we repeat, the fact that a particular part of a church—(if we were now arguing for rood screens, we should show that any such distinction of parts made a *screen of some sort* necessary, even if we did not know what sort of screens really existed)—the fact that a particular part of a church was distinguished by names directly carrying us back to the exactly corresponding particular part in the Temple, shows that in the arrangement at least, if not in the building, of the earliest churches there was, at least in this one point, an intention to produce an antitype to the typical Tabernacle. It is observed in a note to Neander's history that if the interpretation of Michaelis be received there is evidence of a Christian church being built at Edessa, A.D. 202, with three parts, expressly after the model of the Temple.[22]

Whatever may be the authority allowed to the Apostolical Constitutions, the fact that they touch at some length upon the form of churches is enough for our purpose. "The church," they say, "must be oblong in form, and pointing to the East."[23] The oblong form was meant to symbolize a ship, the ark which was to save us from the stormy world.[24] It would be perfectly unnecessary to support this obvious piece of symbolism by citations. The orientation is an equally valuable example of intended symbolism. We gain an additional testimony to this from the well known passage of Tertullian,[25] (A.D. 200,) about "The house of our Dove." Whether this corrupt extract be interpreted with Mede or Bingham, there can be no doubt that its *in lucem* means that the church should face the East or dayspring. The praying towards the East was the almost invariable custom in the Early Churches, and as symbolical as their standing in prayer upon the Festivals of the Resurrection.[26] So common was orientation in the most ancient churches, that Socrates mentions particularly the church at Antioch as having its "position reversed; for the altar does not look to the east but to the west." This rule appears to have been more scrupulously followed in the East than in the West; though even in Europe examples to the contrary are exceptions.[27]

The Apostolical Constitution in its other directions about the position of the bishop, priests, and deacons, and the separate stations for the sexes, shows (as Father Thiers[28] has remarked) that there was even then a marked distinction between the clergy and laity, though the method of division is not described. At any rate, what has been here adduced—compiled from notes taken some time since for another object, and without access (from accidental circumstances) to a Library—seems enough to show that in the earliest notices of Christian churches there is distinct intimation of at least three particulars of intended symbolism.

The circular form given to the church of the Holy Sepulchre was of course appropriate enough in that particular case, where the sepulchre would naturally become the centre. The circular churches of Europe were again imitated from this. The Cross form would appear to have made its first appearance in Constantinople: that is, in the city which was the first to take a completely Christian character. For example, the church of the Apostles built by Constantine was cruciform: and the symbolism of this is pointed out by S. Gregory Nazianzen in his poem, "the Dream of Anastasia," quoted by Bingham.[29] So Evagrius describes the church of S. Simon Stylites, as cited by Buscemi,[30] who also mentions a Cross church founded by King Childebert, about the year 550. The Cathedral of Clermont, mentioned by S. Gregory of Tours, and the church of SS. Nazarius and Celsus at Ravenna, both founded about 450, were cruciform. More than this, we have examples of an oblong church being *intentionally* made cruciform by the addition of *apsides*, as at Blachernae by Justin Junior, instanced by Bingham out of Cedrenus and Zonaras. This has been remarked also in the case of some Italian churches: though the early churches of the West seemed to have retained the oblong form, even when the details and general arrangement were Byzantine, as in the *Cappella Regia* at Messina; the more remarkable from the peculiar influence of Constantinople in the island of Sicily. But in either case there was a symbolizing intention on the part of the founders of churches.

There is mention also of octagonal churches, as at Antioch and Nazianzum: but these seem to have been mere exceptions; and perhaps from being coupled with fonts in the inscription quoted by Mr. Poole from Gruter, may have been intended to symbolise Regeneration. The first two lines are as follows:—

Octachorum sanctos templum surrexit in usus:
Octagonus fons est munere dignus eo.

Bingham mentions that the oblong form was sometimes called δρομικὸν, which he explains as intimating that they had void spaces for deambulation.[31] It seems however more likely that the name was derived from the resemblance between this form of church and a stadium; the apsidal end answering to the curve round the goal.

Some objection may be raised to our theory because Bingham, from whom of course almost all the existing passages in ancient writers about the form of churches might be gathered, does not recognize any such principles, and rather seems on the other hand to believe that there was at first no rule or Law on these points. But it is not detracting from his fame for almost consummate learning to question whether his practical knowledge of church architecture, ancient or modern, was very deep. It might be shown indeed to be far otherwise. But at any rate the principle now contended for never entered his mind, or he would have seen that some of the very passages he adduces to show that the form of ancient churches was accidental, because (for example) they were often made out of Basilicae or even heathen temples, really tell against such a supposition. He quotes from Socrates[32] a description of the conversion of a Pagan island to Christianity, about 380, and the turning the heathen temple into a church. But the words of the original, given in our note, are very remarkable: "The guise of the temple they transformed unto the type (or pattern) of a church." We want to prove nothing more than that there was *some* type of a church. It was not a mere ejection of idols that was required to make a temple into a church: but some change of form and arrangement. So also in a passage from Sozomen, (vii, 15), "The temple of Dionysus which they had, was changed in fittings (μετεσκευάσθη) into a church." Again, a very interesting passage about the conversion of Iberia by means of a female captive in the time of Constantine is cited from Theodoret,[33] to show that churches *did exist* at that date. But we find a particular form of building clearly alluded to in the original: and, more than this, "He Who filled Bezaleel with a wise spirit for building, judged this captive also worthy of grace, so as to design the divine temple. And so she designed, and they built." And this passage brings us at once to the famous panegyric on Paulinus, Bishop of Tyre, and builder of the church there preserved by Eusebius. In this speech the prelate is throughout supposed to have been inspired for his work, and is compared to Bezaleel, Solomon, and Zerubbabel, the builders of the Tabernacle, and the First and Second Temples. And not only is the general spirit assumed to be a directly religious one: but the details are described as having a symbolical meaning.

In the comparison between the material temple and the 'living temple' the Spiritual Church, there are several points worthy of observation. The symbolical explanation of the corner stone as our Lord, of the foundation as the Apostles and Prophets, of the stones as the members of the Church, are of course taken directly from Holy Scripture. It is scarcely necessary to remark the great authority for considering the fabric of the church as symbolical which these passages convey. Many of our readers will remember how S. Hernias carries out into considerable detail the same idea. But the Panegyrist in Eusebius distinctly refers to "the most inward recesses [of that spiritual temple] which are unseen of the many, and are essentially holy and holy of holies"[34]; that is, of course, to a Sanctuary; which he goes on to describe as having "sacred inclosures," and as being accessible to the priest alone; with a distinct reference to S. Paul's[35] illustration taken from the Jewish Temple. Again he proceeds to compare the

Bishop Paulinus with the "great High Priest," not only in being permitted to enter the holy of holies, but in doing what Christ has done, just as the Son did what He saw the Father do. "Thus he, looking with the pure eyes of his mind unto the Great Teacher, whatsoever he seeth Him doing, as if making use of archetypal patterns, has, by building (demiourgwn) as much like them as possible, wrought out images of them as closely as can be; having in no respect fallen short of Bezaleel, whom God Himself, having filled him with the Spirit of wisdom and knowledge and other skilful and scientific lore, called to be the builder of the material expression of the heavenly types in the symbols of the temple. In this way then Paulinus also, carrying wholly like a graven image in his soul Christ Himself, the Word, the Wisdom, the Light.... has constructed this magnificial temple of the most High God, resembling in its nature the pattern of the better (temple) as a visible (emblem) of that which is invisible."[36] This remarkable passage appears to assert (i) the inspiration of the architect, (ii) the fact of this heavenly type, which (iii) material churches ought to follow; and (iv) the general symbolism of the Spiritual Church by the visible fabric. We must pass over a great deal of this oration, with a general request that such as are interested in this discussion will read the whole in the original for the sake of seeing its general spirit and hearing. The description of the details is of great interest. The arrangement of the porticoes, etc., is of course quite adapted to the wants of the Church in that age: it is fair to own that the chief entrance appears to have faced the East in this church. Mention is made also of seats in order for the bishops and presbyters, and of the altar in the midst: the whole being encompassed with wooden network, exquisitely worked, in order to be made inaccessible to the multitude.[37] Further on[38] we read that Paulinus rebuilt his church "such as he had been taught from the delineation of the holy oracles." And again, "More wonderful than wonders are the *archetypes*, and the intelligent and godlike *prototypes* and *patterns* (of earthly church building); namely, I say, the renewing of the divine and reasonable building in the soul"[39]; assuming that material churches are but copies from some heavenly type. Again, a passage, in which the ruined fabric and the persecuted Church are mixed up, speaks of the Church as "having been made after the image of God,"[40] and more to the same effect. The symbolical prophecy of the "fair edification" of the Gentile Church[41] is quoted as being almost literally fulfilled in the Tyrian church, and is still further symbolized by the Panegyrist.[42] The four-square atrium is said to set forth the four Gospels of the scripture.[43] The whole arrangement of the church is symbolised at much length, as setting forth the different divisions of the laity and the states of

Painted wood roof beams (St. Mary the Virgin, Oxford, England)

Stained glass windows (St. Mary the Virgin, Oxford, England)

Octagonal font at entrance to side (St. Mary the Virgin, Oxford, England)

Pulpit/ambo (St. Mary the Virgin, Oxford, England)

Side chapel with altar rails (St. Mary the Virgin, Oxford, England)

The altar and the altar rail

Choir

Choir

rood/chancel screen–entrance to altar & choir

Nave approaching chancel screen

the faithful with respect to advance in holiness. The great portico symbolized God the Father: the side porticoes the other Two Persons of the Most Holy Trinity. The seats represented the souls of the faithful, upon which, as on the Day of Pentecost, the cloven tongues would descend and sit upon each of them. "The revered and great and only altar, what could this be but the spotlessness of soul and holiness of holies of the common Priest of us all?"[44] Once more, the parallel between the spiritual and material Churches being continued, the Word, the Great Demiurgus of all things, is said to have Himself made upon earth a copy of the heavenly pattern which is the Church of the Firstborn written in heaven, Jerusalem that is above, Sion the Mount of God, and the city of the living God.

It appears then that throughout this description a symbolical meaning is found attached to the material church: and this not far-fetched or now first fancifully imagined; but appealing, as it seems, to what the auditors would be prepared to grant, and admitted by the historian without a comment, as one specimen of a class.

We have before remarked that every notice of the particular distribution of a church for the reception of the different classes of Christians, may be taken as an argument on our side: for if it can be shown that the form of churches was not arbitrary, but was adapted to certain peculiar wants, it must be granted that there was some particular Law of design, and that Law connected with Ritual; and then, as before pointed out, this arrangement becomes itself symbolical, and that *intentionally*. We shall only refer here to a passage quoted by Bingham, in which S. Gregory Thaumaturgus[45] describes the places in church assigned respectively to the five degrees of Penitents. Mede[46] argues for the *existence* of churches in the first three centuries, from the universal custom of praying towards the East, the necessity of providing distinct places for the Penitents, Hearers, Catechumens, and Faithful, and from the patterns of the Jewish *proseuchae* and synagogues. But all these arguments seem to tell as much for some particular form of churches as for their existence: that is they prove that the earliest churches were designed on rules which, even if not intentionally symbolical (though we have shown that many were so), became by a natural process intentional among later churchbuilders.

So also with respect to the great division into nave and sanctuary by a screen of some sort: concerning which the passages that might be cited from ancient writers would be innumerable. We shall only give one quoted by Father Thiers from a Poem of S. Gregory of Nazianzum, in which the *balustrade* or rood-screen is said to be "between two worlds, the one immovable, the other changeful; the one of gods (or heaven) the other of mortals (or earth); that is to say, between the choir and the nave, between the clergy and the laity."

We have attempted to prove then that the earliest Christian churches were designed, or described, symbolically: by showing that there was a reason for their shape, whether oblong, cruciform, or circular; for their main division into choir and nave, and their sub-division for the penitents: for their orientation; and even to some extent for their minor internal arrangements: and that some type or pattern of a church was universally recognized.[47] It would require more reading than we can boast of to give a catena of writers who have asserted the symbolism of churches. But if the point has been in any way proved for the first four centuries, enough will have been done: since from that period we can trace from existing edifices the gradual relinquishment of the peculiar Basilican plan, and general adoption of the Latin Cross, or oblong, in the West, while the East consistently retained the Greek Cross. We observe it stated[48] that Mr. E. Sharpe, in a paper read before the Cambridge Camden Society, described the gradual "*typical* additions" to the Basilican ground plan. Indeed symbolism, to any extent, once made known, must have become a rule and precedent to later church architects.

S. Isidore, of Seville, incidentally mentions many symbolical arrangements: they will be found in the notes to the text of the Rationale. Many pieces of symbolism are to be found incidentally in the Decretum of Gratian.

In mentioning Durandus himself, it seems proper to anticipate an objection which may occur to some readers. The authority, it may be said, of that writer must be very small who can give such absurd derivations as *cemeterium* from *cime*, *altare* from *alta res*, *allegory* from *allon* and *gore*. But it must be remembered, firstly, that in the thirteenth century, Greek was a language almost unknown in Europe: next that our author nowhere professes an acquaintance with it: further, that the science of derivation was hardly understood till within the last few years: and lastly, that Cicero's authority led Durandus into some errors; for instance, his derivation of *templum* from *tectum amplum*.

One proof of the *reality* of Durandus's principles we must not fail to notice. It is the express allusion which he makes to, and the graphical description which he gives of, that which we know to have been the style of architecture employed in his time. The tie beams, the deeply splayed windows, the interior shafts, all prove that we are engaged with a writer of Early English date.

It is very remarkable, that Durandus, S. Isidore, Beleth, and the rest, seem to quote from some Canons of church symbolism, now unknown to us. Their words are often, even where they are not very connected nor intelligible, the same. One example may suffice. "In that this rod," says Hugh of S. Victor, "is placed above the Cross, it is shown that the words of scripture be consummated and confirmed by the Cross: whence our Lord said in His Passion, 'It is finished.' *And His Title was indelibly written over Him*." "In that the iron rod," says Durandus, "is placed above the Cross, on the summit of the church, it signifieth that Holy Scripture is now consummated and confirmed. Whence saith our Lord in His Passion, 'It is finished,' *and that Title is written indelibly over Him*, The following, by way of another instance, is the symbolical[49] description of a church, written on a fly-leaf, at the beginning of a MS. "Psaltarium Glossatum," in the public library at Boulogne, though formerly in that of S. Bertin's Abbey, at S. Omer.

The text is either of the tenth or eleventh century; but it will be seen that the words of Durandus, writing at so great a distance of time and place, are, nearly the same in some passages.

Fundamentum ipsius Camerae est Fides.
Altitude ejus est Spes.
Latitudo ejus est Caritas.
Longitudo ejus est Perseverantia.
Latera ejus sunt Concordia et Pax.
Frontes ipsius sunt Justicia & Veritas.
Pulchritudo ejus est exemplum bonorum operum.
Fenestrae ejus sunt dicta sanctorum.
Pavirmentum ejus est humilitas cordis.
Camera est conversatio coelestis.
Pilastri ejus sunt spiritales virtues.
Columnae ejus sunt boni pontifices & sacerdotes.
Interlegatio ejus est vinculum pacis.
Tectum ejus est fidelis dispensator.
* isces ejus sunt mediatio celestis.
Mensa Christi est in camera bona conversatio.
Miuisteriura Christi in camera sua est bona memoria.
Facinus Christi est bona voluntas.
Canterellus Christi est nitor conscientiae.
Cathedra Christi est serenitas mentis.
Sponsa Christi est sancta anima.
Camerariae Christi spiritales virtutes sunt:
Prima Sancta Caritas dicta est; illa Christi regit cameram.
Secunda est Sancta Humilitas; illa est thesauraria in camera Christi.

Tertia est Sancta Patientia; illa facit luminaria in camera Christi.
Quarta Sancta Puritas; illa scopat cameram Christi.

But besides, and in our opinion stronger than, this express and continuous testimony to the fact that Catholic architecture is symbolical, we have the testimony of all other branches of Catholic art, which none ever did, or could deny to be figurative and sacramental. Let us take merely the rites which accompany the close of Easter week. We enter a darkened church, illuminated only by the lighted "Sepulchre": we hear the history of the Passion chaunted by three voices in three recitatives: we have the most mournfully pathetic strain for the "Reproaches" which perhaps the human mind ever imagined:—we pray for Pagans—and we kneel; we pray for Turks—and we kneel; we pray for the Jews, and we kneel not; in abhorrence of the mockery that bowed the knee to the King of the Jews. We enter that church again, now perfectly darkened, except for the one lamp that renders the lectern and the books thereon just visible: the solemn litanies seem in that obscurity, and amidst the silent crowd of worshippers, more solemn than usual. There is a short pause: then in one second, priests and people, voices and instruments, burst forth with the Easter Alleluia: light pours in from every window of the cathedral: showers of rose leaves fall from the roof: bells—silent for three long days, peal from every church tower: guns fire and banners wave: *Dominus esurrexit vere, Alleluia, et apparuit Simoni Alleluia.*

Now, without being concerned to defend, or the contrary, any or all of these ceremonies, we ask,—Is it possible to conceive that the Church which invented so deeply a symbolical a system of worship,—should have rested content with an unsymbolical building for its practice? This consideration, perhaps, belongs to the analogical branch of our essay: yet it may also find a place here, as one of the strongest parts of the inductive argument.

Seeing then that there are strong reasons *à priori* for believing that the ritual and architecture of the Church would partake of a decidedly symbolical character: that by the analogy of the practice amongst all religionists, of the operations of God in nature, of the conditions of Art, and especially of the whole sacramental system of the Church, it is likely that church architecture itself would be sacramental: that from the nature of things every thing material is in some sort sacramental, and a material fabric essentially figurative of the purpose for which it was designed: that an actual Christian church, (taken as we find it) has such accidents as can be explained on no other than a symbolical supposition, and might be analyzed into just those elements from which, by induction we first constructed an hypothetical Christian church: and lastly, that from express and continuous historical testimony without any actual acquaintance with existing fabrics we might have deduced that the material church would be itself, to some extent, a figurative expression of the religion for the celebration of which it was constructed: it does not seem too much to assert that Christian architecture owes its distinctive peculiarities to its sacramental character, and that consequently we can neither appreciate ancient examples nor hope to rival them, at least in their perfection, without taking into account this principle of their design. In other words, the cause of that indefinable difference between an ancient and modern church which we were led to discover at the beginning of this treatise, is neither association of ideas, nor correctness of detail, nor picturesqueness, nor of a mechanical nature, but, (in the most general point of view) is the sacramentality, the religious symbolism, which distinguished and sanctified this as every other branch of mediaeval art.

Stained Glass Window (St. Bart's Kolin, Bohemia, 1365 C.E.)

"The primary idea shadowed forth in every one of the styles, is the saying of our Lord to His disciples, YE ARE THE LIGHT OF THE WORLD."

CHAPTER VII: EXAMPLES OF SYMBOLISM

In endeavouring shortly to develop the practice of symbolism, according to our view of the subject, we are fully aware that to those, who have never yet bestowed a thought upon it, we shall appear mere visionaries or enthusiasts. It has been the fashion of late to smile at the whole theory, as amusing and perhaps beautiful: but quite unpractical and indeed impracticable. We cannot hope to convince by aesthetics those who are deaf to more direct arguments, and who refuse to view every thing, as churchmen ought to do, through the medium of the Church. But those who agree with us in the latter duty, will perhaps suffer themselves to think twice on what will be advanced before they condemn it.

We shall consider the practice of symbolism as connected with, 1. The Holy Trinity; 2. Regeneration; 3. The Atonement; 4. The Communion of Saints; and then we shall notice several parts of a church, such as windows, doors, etc., with their specific symbolical meaning.

I. THE HOLY TRINITY.

The Doctrine of the Holy Trinity has left, as might be expected, deeper traces in the structure of our churches than any other principle of our faith. We have already noticed that possibly the Basilican arrangement might be providentially adduced with reference to this. In Saxon times we find the idea carried out, not only by the Nave and two Aisles, but also by the triple division in length, into Nave, Chancel, and Sanctum Sanctorum. This triple division is most frequently given in Norman buildings, by a central tower; with chancel and nave: we also find in this style a triple chancel arch, an arrangement never occuring at a later epoch. Thus length and breadth were made significant of this Mystery; nor was height less so. The clerestory, the triforium, and the piers cannot fail to suggest it. Indeed, where a triforium was not needed, there is often, as at Exeter and Wells, an arrangement of arcading in niches to resemble it, made that the triplicity might be retained. It is only in late Perpendicular, such as the nave of Canterbury Cathedral, that the arrangement is doubled: there the eye is at once dissatisfied. Again, the triple orders of moulding, which are so much more frequent than any other number, may be supposed to refer to the same thing. The altar steps, three, or some multiple of three, certainly do. So do the three fingers with which Episcopal Benediction is given. And this is a very early symbolism. It occurs in illuminated MS. We may mention one (Harl. 5540) of the thirteenth century, where it forms a part of the

(Winchester Bible, England, 966 C.E.)

(Winchester Bible, England, 966 C.E.)

"The mystic vesica piscis of this form () wherein the Divinity, and (more rarely) the Blessed Virgin are represented has no reference, except in its name to a fish; but represents the almond, the symbol of virginity and self-production."

(Berlin, Medieval)

So do the three fingers with which Episcopal Benediction is given. And this is a very early symbolism. It occurs in an illuminated MS, in the thirteenth century, where it forms a part of the first letter of Saint John's gospel.

(St. Mary the Virgin, Oxford, England)

Grave with cross and tree of life motif

first letter of S. John's gospel. So, as we shall presently see, are Eastern triplets. And reference is constantly made to the same doctrine in bosses: we may mention as a remarkable instance one that occurs in Stamford, S. Mary's, a figure with an equilateral triangle in its mouth: thereby setting forth the duty of the preacher to proclaim the doctrine of the Trinity. In large churches, the three towers undoubtedly proclaim the same doctrine. We shall hereafter show that neither in nave and aisles, in triplets, or any thing else, is the *inequality* any thing else than what might have been expected.

II. THE DOCTRINE OF REGENERATION.

We know, as a fact, that from the earliest times, baptisteries and fonts were octagonal. We know also that the reason assigned, if not by S. Ambrose himself, at least by one of his contemporaries for this form was, that the number eight was symbolical of Regeneration. For as the old Creation was complete in seven days, so the number next ensuing may well be significative of the new.

Now none can deny that very much the greater number of fonts are in this shape. To prove this we will refer to those selected by the Cambridge Camden Society in the appendix to the second edition of their "Few Words to Church-builders." There we find,

	Octagonal	Of all other shapes
In Norman	15	43
Early English	19	30
Decorated	24	1
Perpendicular	57	2
Total	115	76

Now, it is to be remembered, that the superior convenience of a cylindrical or circular form, together with the wont of Norman architects rather to symbolize facts than doctrine, accounts for the comparatively small number of octagonal fonts in that style: in later ages their preponderance is overwhelming.

The symbolism sculptured on the sides of the font hardly falls under our consideration in this place. And besides, it has been fully detailed in the publications of the Cambridge Camden Society, and of Mr. Poole. Whether the general octagonal uses of piers may not arise from a similar design, we do not pretend to decide.

One of the most apposite illustrations in *corbels*, consists in three fishes intertwined in an equilateral triangle; and thus typifying our regeneration in the Three Persons of the Ever-Blessed Trinity. For it need not be said, that the fish is the emblem of the Christian, as being born again of water. The mystical vesica piscis of this form () wherein the Divinity, and (more rarely) the Blessed Virgin are represented has no reference, except in its name to a fish; but represents the almond, the symbol of virginity, and self-production.

III. THE ATONEMENT

We will notice in the third place, the symbolical representation of the great doctrine of the Atonement, in the ground lines and general arrangement of our churches.

As soon as ever Christianity possessed temples of her own, the cruciform shape was, we have seen, sometimes adopted. And so, as we all know, has it continued down to the present day. England, perhaps, has fewer examples of cross churches than any other country: the proportion of those which bear this shape being not so much as one in ten. In France, on the contrary, the ratio would probably be inverted. Into the reason of this remarkable difference we shall not now enquire: but will merely remark, that many churches which do not, in an exterior view, appear cruciform, are nevertheless, from their internal arrangements, really so. The transepts do not project beyond the aisles: but have distinct transept arches, and a window of much larger dimensions than those in the aisles. This principally occurs in city churches, or where the founders were confined for want of room. And this is the case as well in churches which have aisles to the chancel, as in Godalming, Surrey, as where the nave alone has them, as in Holy Rood, Southampton. They will be distinguished readily on the outside by the northern and southern gable. In some cathedral churches, there is a double cross: in York, this perhaps signifies the metropolitical dignity of that church: in other cases, it was probably merely a method of imparting greater dignity to the building. Some churches—though they are not frequent—are in the form of a Greek Cross: that is, the four arms are all of equal length. Darlington, Durham, is an example: in this case there is a central tower. In some, as at Westminster, Gloucester, and S. Albans, the choir runs westward of the transept; in Seville, almost the whole of the choir is locally in the nave: in others, as Ely, it does not extend westward so far. These peculiarities, curious in themselves, do not affect the symbolism: and probably no modification of meaning is to be attached to them.

Mr. Lewis has asserted, that in early churches, a cross was marked on the pavement, the upper part running into the chancel, the arms extending into the transepts, and the body occupying the nave. And some such arrangement, or rather the traces of it, we have ourselves perhaps noticed. The reason it was given up, was probably the anathema pronounced by the second Ecumenical Council, on those who should tread on that holy symbol.

Thus, in the ground plan, the Cross of Christ was preached. It is often said, that the adjacent chapels, more especially the Lady Chapel, obscured the symbolism. But it must be remembered that a ground plan can only be judged of in two methods: either from a height above, for example, the tower of the church; or when marked out on paper. It is surprising, in either of these cases, how easily the most complex cathedral resolves itself to the spectator's eyes into a cross.

In looking at the details of churches, the Cross is marked on the Dos-d'ânes and plain coffin lids of the earliest times: it commences the later inscriptions on brass: it surmounts pinnacle, and gable, and porch; it is often imprinted on the jambs of the principal entrance, showing the exact spot touched in the consecration with chrism,[50] and possibly having reference to the blood sprinkled at the Passover on the Door Post: and finally, in a more august form, is erected in the churchyard. And here we may notice another curious and beautiful expression of Catholic feeling.[51] It is very uncommon to find a plain cross surmounting a church: the whole force of Christian art has sometimes been expended in wreathing and embellishing the instrument of redemption: flowers, and figures, and foliage are lavished upon it. And why? Because that which was once the by-word of Pagans, the instrument of scorn and of suffering, has become the symbol of Hope and of Glory, of Joy, and of Eternal Felicity; and its material expression has altared proportionately. In that the arms frequently end in leaves and flowers, they signify the flourishing and continual increase of that Church which was planted on Mount Calvary. The Crown of Thorns is sometimes wreathed around them: but so, that it should rather resemble a Crown of Glory. The instruments of the Passion are, as every one knows, of the most ordinary occurrence. The commonest of these are—the Cross, the Crown of Thorns, the Spear, the Scourge, the Nails, and the Spunge on the pole. But in the Suffolk and Somersetshire churches many others are added. Their position is various: sometimes, as in Stogumber, Somersetshire, they appear amidst the foliage of a perpendicular capital: sometimes, as in the Suffolk churches, they are found in the open seats: often in bosses, often in brasses, often in stained glass; and sometimes the angel that supports a bracket holds them portrayed on a shield. The Five Wounds are also often found. These are represented by a heart, between two hands and two feet, each pierced; or by a heart pierced with five wounds as in a brass at King's College Chapel, Cambridge. The instruments of the Passion may sometimes be seen amongst the volutes of the stem of the churchyard cross: examples occur at Belleville, near Havre, in Normandy, and Santa Cruz, in Madeira.

Again, the very position of our blessed Saviour on the Cross as represented in the great rood and in stained glass, is not without a meaning. In modern paintings, the arms are high above the head, the whole weight of the body seeming to rest upon them. And this, besides its literal truth, gives occasion to that miserable display of anatomical knowledge in which such pictures so much abound. The Catholic representation pictures the Arms as extended horizontally: thereby signifying how the Saviour, when extended on the Cross, embraced the whole world.[52] Thus, as it ever ought to be, is physical sacrificed to moral truth. Perhaps for a similar reason S. Longinus is represented as piercing the Right Side, instead of the Left: and in a representation of the Five Wounds, it is the right side of the breast that is pierced (as in a brass at Southfleet, Kent); that being the side of the greatest strength, and thereby typifying the strength of that love wherewith our Redeemer loved us. [But this may be doubted. For it appears pretty clear that the ancient Church considered the Right Side to have been that which was really pierced. According to modern ideas, the effusion of the water was not a miracle. S. John undoubtedly considered it not only a miracle, but one of the most extraordinary which he had to relate, seeming to stop the mouth of the objector by insisting on the fact, that he himself was an eye-witness.] In some old roods, a still further departure was made from literal truth: the Saviour was represented on the Cross, as a crowned king, arrayed in royal apparel.[53] And His figure was constantly represented as larger than that of His attendants, His Blessed Mother, and S. John, thereby signifying His immeasurable superiority over the highest of human beings.

Another reference to the Atonement will be found in the deviation which the line of the chancel often presents from that of the nave. It is sometimes to the north, but more frequently to the south. There are many more churches in which it occurs than those who have not examined the subject would believe: perhaps it is not too much to say that it may be noticed in a quarter of those in England. Of our cathedrals, it is most strongly marked in York and Lichfield: among the parish churches in which we have observed it, none have it so strongly as Eastbourne and Bosham, in Sussex, and S. Michael's at Coventry: in all of which the most casual glance could not but detect the peculiarity of appearance it occasions. This arrangement represents the inclination of our Saviour's Head on the Cross. In roods the Head generally inclines to the left.

Mr. Poole, after noticing the fact in York minster, seems inclined to attribute it to a desire of evading the old foundation lines of that church, which induced the builders to deviate a little from the straight line, rather than encounter the difficulty of removing this obstacle. But in the first place, however much modern church builders might bethink themselves of such an expedient, it is not at all in the character of the church architects of other days: and in the second, the explanation is applicable to York alone, one only out of many hundred churches so distinguished.

IV. THE COMMUNION OF SAINTS

Next, we will notice the effect which the Doctrine of the Communion of Saints has exercised in the designs of churches.

In the ground plan of small churches there is little which seems to bear on this subject. The principal references to departed Saints occur in the stained glass, in the rood screen, in niches, in the canopies of monuments, and in brasses. Monuments, in particular, often afford some beautiful ideas, among which we may notice the angels which often are seated at the head of the effigy, supporting the helmet or pillow, and seeming to point out the care of angels for the saints. In cathedrals, however, the chapels have a very considerable effect upon the ground plan: though we cannot agree with Mr. Poole that such a modification of the principal lines of the building for the reception of these shrines and oratories, is necessarily uncatholic. He principally objects to the position of the Lady Chapel at the east end, above, as he expresses it, the High Altar. Now we believe the Lady Chapel to have occupied that place merely on grounds of convenience: not from any design—which it is shocking to imagine—of exalting the Blessed Virgin to any participation in the honours of the Deity. Sometimes, as at Durham, this chapel is at the west end: in country churches, it generally occupied the east end of thc north or south Aisle: and sometimes is placed over the chancel, as in Compton, Surrey, Compton Martin, Somerset, and Darenth, Kent; or over the porch, as at Fordham, Cambridgeshire. At Bristol cathedral it is on the north side of the choir. That the position of the Lady Chapel at the east end adds greatly to the beauty of the building will hardly be denied, on a comparison of York, or Lincoln, or Peterborough with Lichfield, *as it now is*.

CHAPTER VIII: EXAMPLES OF SYMBOLISM CONTINUED

We come now, according to the plan we laid down, to speak of the symbolism of some particular features of a church, which do not fall so well under any of the four heads which we have been considering. And firstly, of windows.

The primary idea shadowed forth in every one of the styles, is the saying of our Lord to His disciples, *ye are the light of the world.* More simply set forth at first, this notion acquired, in the course of time, various methods of expression, and was subjected to different modifications; but we must retain it as the ground work, or we shall be in danger of mistaking the true meaning of ancient church architects.

In Norman, then, and early English, the single lights, north and south, set forth the Apostles and Doctors who have shined forth in their time as the lights of the Church: and the rich pattern of flowerwork wherewith the stained glass in them was decked, represented the variety of graces in each. But to have symbolized the servants without the Master, the members without the Head, had been at variance with all the Catholic Church has ever practised. Looking therefore to the east end, we behold that well known feature, the Triplet: setting forth the Most Holy and Undivided Trinity.[54] Nor is this all: to denote that all that the Church has, and all She is, is from above, the string course, springing from the eastern triplet, runs round the whole church (often both within and without,) binding it, as it were, in and connecting every other light, with those at the east. Again, the Western Door, as we shall see, symbolized Christ: and two lights, typical of His two natures, are therefore generally placed over it. There are, undoubtedly, instances of western triplets: though we think that the Camden Society has well explained these.

In some cases, there is a series of couplets on each side of the church: and, taking the hint from Durandus, we may interpret this arrangement of the mission of the Apostles two and two.

A series of Triplets, as in Salisbury Cathedral, and the Lady Chapel of Bristol, is very rare: and, of course, not objectionable on any other grounds than that of the too cheap use of a most beautiful feature.

So far all is simple: but as we approach the decorated style, the symbolism becomes excessively complicated. The principal doctrines of the Catholic Church are set forth in each window: and to unravel the whole of these is often a task of no small difficulty. We shall proceed to give a few examples, with the explanation which appears to us probable: entreating the reader to remember, that if in any instance our conjectures should appear unfounded, the failure of probability in one case throws no discredit on the others, and still less does it invalidate the system. Durandus's silence on the language of tracery is easily explained by the consideration, that assign as late a date as we will to the publication of his work, it came forth while the Early English style was yet in existence: and his silence on triplets only proves, what is well known to ecclesiologists, that they are far less common in foreign than in our own architecture.

In Norman windows the wheel window is conspicuous. This, whether formed with the *radii* like those of Barfreston, or of the Temple church, represent (as we shall presently observe that Norman symbolism usually *does* represent) an historical fact: namely, the martyrdom of S. Catherine. The celebrity of this Virgin Martyr may tend to explain why she should be so far honoured: a celebrity which has descended to our own day in the common sign of the Cat and Wheel: as well as the firework so denominated.

Of Norman triplets there are not many to which we can refer. The tower of Winchester, however, presenting one on each face, is noble example. The southeastern transept of Rochester, though later, is equally in point: it contains two triplets, far apart, and one disposed above the other. The west front of S. Etienne at Caen is a well-known instance.

The earliest symbolism of Early English triplets represented the Trinity alone: the Trinity in Unity was reserved for a somewhat later period. And this was typified by the hood moulding thrown across the three lights. At other times a quatre-foiled, or cinque-foiled, circle was placed at some little distance above the triplet: thus typifying the Crown which befits the Majesty of the King of Kings. And the same Crown is often exhibited above the western couplet. But, for as much as we are "compelled by the Christian verity to acknowledge every person by Himself to be God and Lord," a crown is sometimes represented over each light of the triplet, as in Wimborne minster.

Another method of representing the same doctrine was by a simple equilateral triangle for a window: whether plain, of which there are many examples, or with the toothed ornament, as in the famous example at York minster.

S. Giles's at Oxford has windows, the tracery of which will serve as an example of many: it has *three tre*-foiled lights, with *three* quatre-foiled circles, arranged triangle-wise in the head.

This type is a little varied in S. Mary Magdalene's church, in the same city, by the introduction of the ogee form.

Berkeley church has a wheel window containing *three* quatre-foils: the *three* spaces left between them and the line being *tre*-foiled.

The east windows of Dunchurch and Fen Stanton have been explained in the publications of the Cambridge Camden Society: the former in their "Few Words to Church-Builders," the latter in their illustrations of monumental brasses, Part iv.

The south transept of Chichester cathedral is a glorious specimen of decorated symbolism. In the gable is a Marygold, containing two intersecting equilateral triangles: the *six* apices of these are *sex*-foiled: the interior *hex*-agon is beautifully worked in *six* leaves. The lower window seven lights: in the head is an equilateral spherical *tri*-angle, containing a large *tre*-foil, intersected by a smaller *tre*-foil. Here we have the Holy Trinity, the Divine Attributes, the perfection of the Deity.

A window in Merton College Chapel has *three* lights: with a circle in the head containing *six sex*-foils.

Broughton, Oxon, has in the head of one of its windows a circle, containing two intersecting equilateral triangles, the *six* apices, and *six* spaces around, being *tre*-foiled.

The east end of Lincoln, though far inferior to the south transept of Chichester, is nevertheless highly symbolical. The east window of each of the aisles has *three* lights, with *three* foliated circles, disposed *triangle*-wise in the head. The great east window has eight lights in two divisions, each whereof has *three* foliated circles in the head: and in the apex of the window is a circle containing seven foliations. The upper window has a circle of eight foliations in the head: and in the apex of the gable is an equilateral trefoil.

The next element introduced was the consideration of the Six Attributes of the Deity. One of the simplest examples was to be found in the west window of the north aisle of S. Nicholas, at Guildford: a plain circle, containing six *tre*-foils: these are arranged in two *tri*-angles, each containing *three tre*-foils, and the two sets are varied.

The clerestory of Lichfield cathedral (circ. 1300), is a series of spherical *tri*-angles, each containing *three tre*-foils.

A similar clerestory occurs in the north-west transept of Hereford cathedral, and the same idea is repeated in its triforium: a series of *three tre*-foiled lights, with *three* circles in the head.

The east end of Lichfield symbolizes most strikingly the same glorious doctrine. The apse is tri-gonal: the windows of each side are the same: each is of *three* lights, with six *tre*-foils (emblematical of the six attributes) disposed above in the form of an equilateral *tri*-angle.

The east end of Chichester is rather earlier, but introduces yet another element. Here we have a triplet: and at some height above it, a wheel-window of seven circles: symbolising therefore eternity and perfection.

The triforium and clerestory of Carlisle are singular symbols of the doctrine of the Trinity. The former has in each bay three adjacent equal lancets. The latter is a series of triplets: the central window in each being composed of three lights. We may observe, by the way, that three *adjacent* equal lancets are hardly ever found, whatever the reason may be. We know but of three examples: in the churches of Bosham, Sussex, Godalming, Surrey, and S. Mary-le-Crypt, Gloucester: and in all these cases they occupy the same position, the south east end of the chancel, or chancel aisle.

Dorchester church, Oxfordshire, has for one of its windows an equilateral spherical triangle with three heads, or knops, one at each angle.

We are now in a purely decorated age. And as one of its earliest windows we may mention that in the Bishop of Winchester's Palace at Southwark. It was a wheel, and contained two intersecting equilateral triangles: around them were *six sex*-foiled triangles, the hexagon in the centre containing a star of *six* greater and *six* smaller rays. Here, of course, the Blessed Trinity and the divine and human natures were set forth.[55]

The symbolism of the more complicated decorated windows it is next to impossible to explain. Carlisle and York have doubtless their appropriate meaning; but who will now pretend to expound it?

One exception we may make:—the east window of Bristol cathedral. It is of seven lights, but so much prominence is given to the three central ones, as strongly to set forth the Most Holy Trinity: over them is a crown of six leaves and by the numerous winged foliations around them, the Heavenly Hierarchy may, very probably, be understood.

II. DOORS

Durandus has given us a clue to the symbolical meaning which these generally present, by directing our attention to that saying of our Lord's, *I am the Door*. And this, uttered as tradition reports it to have been, in reference to the Gate of the Temple, on which the Saviour's eyes were then fixed, gives additional force to the allusion.

In small churches, doors are seldom the subject of much symbolical ornament, except in the Norman style: but in cathedrals, some of the most strikingly figurative arrangements are often thrown into them. The Person, the Miracles, or the Doctrines of our Lord are here frequently set forth. He is sometimes, especially in the tympanum of Norman doors, as at Egleton in Rutland, represented as described in the Apocalyptic vision;

with a sword in His mouth. More frequently, however, with His Blessed Mother; in order, perhaps, to connect His entrance into the world with ours into the Church, which He thereby gathered together. This in the south entrance of Lincoln minster, is enclosed in a quatre-foil: because the birth of Christ is announced by the four evangelists; and angels are represented around it in attitudes of adoration. A singular, and indeed irreverent symbol, is to be seen in a door of Lisieux church: the Holy Ghost descending on the Blessed Virgin, and the Infant Saviour following Him. In the entrance to the cloisters of Norwich cathedral, the door arch is filled by nine niches, the central one being occupied by the Saviour, the others by saints. But this arrangement is much more common in French churches: where two, or even three rows of Saints in the architrave are not uncommon: witness the south and west doors of S. Germain, at Amiens, and a west door of S. Etienne, at Beauvais. This is sometimes, in late Flamboyant work, carried to an absurd extent: in a south door of Gisors, two niches actually hang down out of the soffit. Early English doors are generally double, thereby representing the Two Natures of our Saviour: but embraced by one arch, to set forth His One Person. So the celebrated door in Southwell minster: the west door in the Galilee of Ely Cathedral: the entrance to the chapter House, at Salisbury; the West door of the same; so the decorated west door of York; so the door to the Chapter House there, of which the inscription truly says: *Ut Rosa Phlos phlorum, sic est domus ista Domorum*: so the west door and entrance to the Chapter House of Wells. The west door of Higham Ferrars has the Saviour's triumphal entrance into Jerusalem, over the double Western doors. And this is the case in one of the doors of Seville cathedral. Both these connect the ideas of His entrance into the temporal, with that of ours into the spiritual, Jerusalem. In these symbolical doorways, we have one proof of the immeasurable superiority of English over French architecture: compare any of the above named with the celebrated west door of Amiens, with its twenty-two sovereigns in its soffit. Again, by way of contrast to the second Adam, by whom we enter into Heaven; we sometimes, especially in Norman churches, have the Forbidden Tree, with Adam and Eve in the tympanum; setting forth the one man by whom sin entered into the world.

The Crucifixion seldom occurs over doors: while over porches a crucifix is very common. The cause of the difference is explained by a consideration that the former are shut, the latter open: and "when Thou hadst overcome the sharpness of Death, Thou didst *open* the Kingdom of Heaven to all believers." Indeed it may almost be asserted that a crucifix is never seen over a closed door, except where it forms a part of the usual representation of the Trinity. For the Trinity is also, in Norman churches, there represented: and that not inappropriately: inasmuch as the Trinity is the beginning of all things. A Holy Lamb is sometimes found in Norman tympana: as saith the Saviour, *I am the Door of the sheep*. A hasty glance at Durandus[56] might lead us to imagine that we should find the Apostles set forth under the similitude of doors: but he there probably refers to the well known passage in the Apocalypse. (Apoc. xxi, 14.)

This however leads us to another, and that a totally different, meaning attached to doors. We have already noticed the fact, that many Norman and Early English mouldings refer to various kinds of martyrdom: those which do so, occur more frequently on doors than any where else; for it is written, "We must through much tribulation enter into the kingdom of God." And here we may observe a very curious and beautiful progression in symbolism. In the early ages of Christianity, it was a matter requiring no small courage to make an open profession of Christianity, to join one's self to the Church Militant:—and this fact has left its impress in the various representations of martyrdom surrounding the nave-doors of Norman and the first stage of Early English churches: as well as in the frightful forms which seem to deter those who would enter. But in process of time, as the world became evangelized, to be a member of the visible Church was an easy matter: the difficulty was transferred from an entrance into *that*, to the so living, as to have part in the Communion of Saints:—in other words, to an entrance into the Church Triumphant. And therefore in late Early English, and Decorated, the symbols which had occupied the nave-doors in the former period, are now transferred to the chancel arch.

The different agricultural operations, the signs of the zodiac, and occupations of various kinds, sometimes found on the *outside* of Norman doors, signify that we must turn our backs on, and leave behind us, all worldly cares and employments, if we would enter into the Kingdom of God. In later porches, true love knots are sometimes found on the bosses: because part of the service of Holy Matrimony was performed there. The serpent, in which the handle is so universally fashioned, has probably reference to that text, "They shall lay their hands upon serpents," to signify that God's arm will protect us, when engaging, or about to engage in, His service. For the serpent with his tail in his mouth is not a Christian, and indeed by no means a desirable, emblem of eternity, and therefore the door handle cannot be so interpreted.

The doors are of course placed near the west end: for it is only by way of the Church Militant, that we can hope to enter the Church Triumphant. One door, indeed, the priest's door, conducts at once into the chancel.

Durandus is probably right in interpreting this of Christ's coming into the world; though it involves a little confusion of symbolism, inasmuch as the chancel, properly speaking, denotes the blessed place which He left: not the abode to which He came. It is to be noted as an instance of the decline of symbolism in the Perpendicular age, that in churches which have aisles to the chancel of that date, we sometimes, as at Bitton, Gloucestershire, Godalming, Surrey, and Wivelsfield and Isfield, Sussex, find an entrance at the east end of the south aisle. Though used as a priest's door, this is entirely to be blamed: what shall we say then of modern churches, which have two doors at the east end, one on each side of the altar, as Christchurch, Brighton? In Seville cathedral, a late, although fine flamboyant building, there are large doors at the east end of each choir aisle.

Porches are usually on the south side. For as the east was considered in an especial manner connected with the Kingdom of Heaven, so was the north imagined to be under the Prince of the Power of the Air. It is curious how diametrically opposed in both these ideas were Christianity and Paganism. For as by the latter the west was known as "the better country, where lay the Isles of the Blest in their abundant peace," so in the north dwelt the deathless and ageless Hyperboreans: whose state was the model of good government and secure happiness. That the belief of our ancestors is not yet extinct, a very slight knowledge of our country churchyards will prove: the north side of the churchyard has generally not more than one or two graves. To be buried there is, in the language of our Eastern Counties, to be buried *out of Sanctuary*: and the spot is appropriated to suicides, unbaptised persons, and excommunicates. A particular portion is, in some churchyards of Devonshire, separated for the second class, and called the *chrisomer*. Where the contrary is the case, it may be worth enquiring how far it does not arise from the accidental position of the Churchyard Cross on the north side. There the spell seems broken: and the villagers' graves cluster around it, as if the presence of that sacred symbol were a sufficient protection to the sleeping dust. A remarkable instance of this occurs at Belleville, between Dieppe and Abbeville, in Normandy.

The doors in the transepts are, in small churches, almost invariably east or west: much more frequently the latter. This, however, is probably not symbolical: but an arrangement adopted to prevent any resemblance in the porches and transepts:—and it is a rule which needs to be much impressed on modern church builders.

The rule as to the western position of the doors seems to apply generally to the churchyard.

It is worthy of remark that in the matter of doors, Protestantism presents us, as is so frequently the case, with a very unintended piece of symbolism. When we see, as in the beautiful church of Bisley, Gloucestershire, *thirteen* different openings, with external staircases, made into the church, through windows and elsewhere, can we forbear thinking of him who cometh not by the doors into the sheepfold, but climbeth up some otherway?

III. CHANCEL ARCH AND ROOD SCREEN

We come now to speak of the chancel arch and the rood screen, two of the most important features in a church. These, as separating the choir from the nave, denote literally the separation of the clergy from the laity: but symbolically the division between the Militant and Triumphant Churches: that is to say, the Death of the Faithful. The first great symbol which sets this forth, is the Triumphal Cross: the lineage of Him who by His Death hath overcome Death, and has gone before His people through the valley of its shadow.[57] The images of Saints and Martyrs appear in the lower panelling, as examples of faith and patience to us. The colours of the rood screen itself represent their passion and victory: the crimson sets forth the one, the gold the other. The curious tracery of net work typifies the obscure manner in which heavenly things are set forth, while we look at them from the Church Militant. And for as much as the Blessed Martyrs passed from this world to the next through sore torments, the mouldings of the chancel arch represent the various kinds of sufferings through which they went. Faith was their support, and must be ours: and Faith is set forth either in the abstract, by the limpet moulding on the chancel arch; or on the screen, as in Bishop's Hull, Somersetshire, by the Creed in raised gilt letters: or is represented by some notable action of which it was the source: so in Cleeve, Somersetshire, the destruction of a dragon runs along, not only the rood screen, but the north parclose also. But in that the power of evil spirits may be exercised against us till we have left this world, but not after, horrible forms are sometimes sculptured in the west side of the chancel arch. The foregoing remarks may perhaps explain what has been felt by some ecclesiologists as a difficulty: how it happens, since the Chancel is more highly ornamented than the nave, that it is te western, or nave side, not the eastern or chancel side, of the chancel arch which invariably receives the greatest share of ornament. The straitness of the entrance to the Kingdom of Heaven is set forth by the excessive narrowness of Norman chancel arches. And the final separation of the Church Triumphant from every thing that defileth was almost invariably represented by the Great Doom painted in fresco over the rood screen: of which there are still several examples, as the celebrated one in Trinity church, Coventry: and many more might be found, if the whitewash in that place were scraped off. And not only is the judgement of the world, but that of individuals here set forth: on the south side of the chancel wall of Preston church, Sussex, is a fresco of S. Michael weighing the souls: the Devil stands by, eager to secure his prize, but by the intervention of the Blessed Virgin, the scale preponderates in favour of the sinner. There might probably be an altar to the Blessed Virgin under this picture. Also deeds of faith are represented in similar positions:—so in the same church, on the north chancel wall, is the fresco of the Martyrdom of S. Thomas of Canterbury. We have already noticed the triplicity, in some instances, of Norman chancel arches. A very curious triple chancel arch is to be seen at Capel-le-Ferne, Kent. We may also refer to those singular double ones, Wells and Finedon, and in another manner, Darlington, in Durham, and Barton, in Cumberland. It may be well, finally, to note the entire absence in the ground plans of our churches of any reference to purgatory. The only instance in which chancel and nave are separated by any intervening object, is the chantry of Bishop Arundell in Chichester cathedral. Of the triple division of the church by two (so to speak) chancel arches, we have already spoken.

IV. MONUMENTS

We now proceed to *Monumental Symbolism*. But it will be proper first to consider a very curious subject: namely the reason of the difference between the personages with which the effigies of the departed were of old time, and are now, surrounded. In the former case they were always real: Our Lady, S. John, S. Pancras, S. Agatha, and so on. In the latter, they are always allegorical: Faith, Virtue, Courage, Eloquence and the like. Nay, in the very ground which is common to the two—the representations of angels—we may observe a great difference: in modern monuments any angel is represented: in those of ancient date the particular one is often named: S. Gabriel, S. Raphael, etc. Now there are, we think, three good reasons to be assigned for this.

1. The *enlightened*, or in plainer terms, the *sceptical* character of the present age. naccustomed to view any great examples of heroic devotion and self-sacrifice now, we naturally, though scarcely allowing it to ourselves, begin to doubt whether there ever were any such. In thinking of patience, our forefathers would naturally have had S. Vincent presented to their mind: but we, who, some of us have scarcely heard of his name, and some, are totally ignorant of his character, have of course no such ideas suggested. So again, where our ancestos would have represented S.

Lawrence, we content ourselves with a representation of Fidelity. And it is in accordance with this easy and self-indulgent age, rather to personify a thing, which as having never had real existence, cannot be brought into comparison with ourselves, than by representing a really existing person, to run the risk of a contrast between his virtues and our own.

2. This allegorizing spirit is more in accordance with the general paganism of our architectural designs: though, be it observed, a feature of the very worst and most corrupt state of Paganism. It is worth noting that in heathen countries, evil qualities have always been personified before good. Paganism like every other false system, became worst at its close. In the early times of Grecian mythology the attributes of purity, and truth, and mercy, were so strongly felt to reside in the gods, that a separate personification of them was needless: whereas strife, and violence, and fury, qualities which had no place in heaven, demanded, and obtained, a seperate existence. But in process of time, when the divinities themselves became invested with the attributes of sinful humanity, the qualities of goodness which were no longer supposed theirs, found separate embodiments and expressions.

3. We may assign as a reason for the difference we have noticed the far greater reality with which our ancestors looked on the connections subsisting between ourselves and the other world. Thus, tempests and hurricanes, which we coldly explain on philosophical principles, they considered as directly proceeding from the violence of evil spirits[58]:—earthquakes and volcanoes they regarded as outbreaks, so to speak, of that place of punishment, which they believed locally situated within the earth:—diseases and pestilences they held to be the immediate work of the Devil: madness and lunacy were, in their view, synonymous with possession. Whether theirs, as it certainly was the most pious, were not also the most philosophical view, has been so ably discussed in the "Church of the Fathers" under the chapter *S. Anthony in Conflict*, that we need here only allude to it. But the same spirit led them to adopt the effigies of those saints who had been members of the same Church Militant with themselves and who now were members of that Triumphant Church which they hoped hereafter to join: and its contrary leads us to adopt the cold, vague, dreamy, unsubstantialities of allegorism.

The earliest kind of Monumental Symbolism is that which represents the trade or profession of the person commemorated. And these principally occur on Lombardic slabs and Dos d'Anes. The distaff represents the mother of a family[59]: a pair of gloves a glover[60]: so we have a pair of shears: and the like. But the Cross constantly appears; and in a highly floriated form: sometimes at its foot are three steps representing the Mount: sometimes a Holy Lamb.[61] And so ecclesiastical personages have their appropriate symbols: so the chalice or the ring[62] represents a priest:—another type is the hand raised in benediction[63] over a chalice: brasses abound in symbolical imagery. The animal at the feet varies with the varying circumstances of the deceased: a married lady has the dog, the emblem of fidelity: with which we may compare the speech of Clytemnestra, of her absent Lord,[64]

> γθναῖκα πιστὴν δ' ἐν δόμοις εὕροι μολ◊ν
> οἵαν περ' οὖν ἔλειπε ΔΩΜΑΤΩΝ ΚΥΝΑ.

There are, doubtless, instances (there is one in Bristol, S. Peter's) where the unmarried are so represented: but they are very rare, and quite in the decline of the art. The knight again has, generally, a terrier at his feet: as the emblem of courage: sometimes the greyhound,[65] the symbol of speed. Lord Beaumont[66] has an elephant: it is a bearing in his coat-armour.

Early priests have a lion also at their feet[67]; but this typified their trampling on the devil: as servants of Him concerning whom it is written "and the devil shall go forth before His feet."[68] They have also a dragon for the same reason. And this position doubtless also has reference to the verse, "Thou shalt tread upon the lion[69] and adder: the young lion and the dragon shalt thou trample under feet." In the decline of the art, effigies have the crest of the departed at their feet.

Whether those knights who are represented with crossed legs are to be considered as Crusaders, or at least as having taken the vow, is a question which has been much discussed. The general belief seems now to be in the negative:—and Mr. Bloxam in his work on Monumental Architecture gives it as his opinion that this posture was chosen by the artist, for the more graceful arrangement of the surcoat. And it is to be remarked that some illuminations, as in the Life of S. Edward the Confessor, in the Cambridge University Library, represent the knights as sitting cross legged. For our own parts we must confess that we incline to the old belief:—as better supported by tradition, and more in accordance with the general principles of Catholic artists. The knight's hand is sometimes represented as resting on the hilt of his sword:—or as it is called *drawing it*. We are astonished that a writer in the *Quarterly Review* should fall into this popular error: especially when the idea was completely opposed to the whole course of his argument. There can be no doubt that this typifies the accomplishment of the vow, the taking which was set forth by the crossed legs. The contrary—an act of war in the House of Peace—is not for a moment to be

"Early priests had a lion at their feet, but this typified their trampling of the devil: as servants of Him concerning whom it is written 'and the devil shall go forth before His feet. They also have a dragon for the same reason. And this position doubtless also has reference to the verse, 'Thou shalt tread upon the lion and adder."

Effigy with dragon (Salisbury, England, 1140)

Archbishop of York (1215-1255)

"The symbolism of ecclesiastics, lying principally in their vestments...the mitred abbot and the bishop in the former holding his pastoral staff with the crook inwards, as signifying his dominion to be internal, i.e.- within his own house- the latter outwards, to set forth his external dominion over his diocese."

The Annunciation (Elfenbein, Germany, c. 1000 C.E.)

"The Holy Dove descending or on a ray of light"

thought of. As emblematical of deep humility, some effigies are represented naked: some in shrouds: some, as emaciated corpse: and sometimes, still more strikingly, the tomb will be divided into two partitions: and while the departed appears in rich vests, and with a gorgeous canopy above—below there is a skeleton, or a worm eaten figure. There is a remarkable instance at Tewkesbury, in the cenotaph of the last Lord Abbot.: and we may refer to the monument of William Ashton, in S. John's College Chapel, Cambridge.

The symbolism of ecclesiastics, lying principally in their vestments, does not so much fall within the scope of this essay. The same be said of the allusion to the Holy Trinity in the benedictory attitude of the bishop: and the distinction between the mitred abbot and the bishop in the former holding his pastoral staff with the crook inwards, as signifying his dominion to be *internal, i.e.* within his own house;—the latter outwards, to set forth his external dominion over his diocese.

The reception of the soul of the departed into Abraham's bosom is often represented. Sometimes angels are bearing it, in the likeness of a newborn child, (a figure symbolical of its having now returned into its baptismal state of purity) and presenting it before the throne. The founders or rebuilders of churches are known by the building which they hold in their hands.

The carving of the *open seats* is one of those parts of ecclesiastical symbolism, which it is very hard to explain. The monsters which constantly occur on them may be perhaps regarded as typical of the evil thoughts and bad passions which a life of ease and rest encourages, and it will be observed, that in the choir, a gentler class of ideas often is suggested: we have here flowers and fruit, and birds making their nests, and flocks feeding. There, are however, certain other types to be found here, and also in stringcourses, and corbel heads, of which we shall presently speak in terms of disapprobation.

Nothing, with this exception, shows the exuberance and beauty of ideas which distinguished the architects of the ages of Faith—and the depth and variety of the scriptural knowledge we are pleased to deny them—than their wood carvings.[70] There is perhaps hardly a scriptural subject which they have not handled: and it requires no small degree of ecclesiastical knowledge to be able at all to comprehend many of their allusions: while probably many more are lost to us. The Annunciation is one of the most favourite topics. The almond tree blossoming in the flower pot—the bud terminating in a cross or crucifix—the prayer desk at which the Blessed Virgin kneels—the temple seen in the distance—the Holy Dove descending on a ray of light—these are its general accompaniments. The descent of our Saviour into hell—the delivery of souls—

"Magnaque; de magna praeda petita domo:"

the visions of the Apocalypse: the final doom: the passions and triumphs of martyrs—all here find their expression.

V. CORBELS, GURGOYLES, POPPY HEADS, ETC.

The corbels which occur in the interior of churches generally represent the Heavenly Host—often with various instruments of music, as if taking a share in-the devotions of the worshippers. This idea is most fully and beautifully carried out in late perpendicular roofs: where the various orders of the heavenly hierarchy hover, with outstretched wings, over the sacred building,—an idea evidently derived from the cherubim that spread their wings over the ark, and the apostle's explanation, "which things the angels desire to look into". Often, however, benefactors to the Church are here portrayed. The gurgoyles, on the contrary, represent evil spirits as flying from the holy walls: the hideousness of the figures, so often, by modern connoisseurs, ridiculed or blamed, is therefore not without its appropriate meaning.

We must now say few a words on the least pleasing part of the study of symbolism: we mean the satirical representations which record the feuds between the secular and the regular clergy. Thus, in the churches of the latter, we have, principally as stallwork, figures of a fox preaching to geese: in those of the latter an ass's head under a cowl: or, which is very frequent, both in woodwork, and as a gurgoyle, the cowled double face. As a specimen of these designs, we may mention the stalls[71] in East Brent, Somersetshire. A fox hung by a goose, with two cubs yelping at the foot of the gallows, a monkey at prayers, with an owl perched over his head: another monkey holding a halbert: a fox with mitre and staff, a young fox in chains, a bag of money in his right paw, and geese and cranes on each side. To these objectionable devices we may add those which to us appear simply profane or indecent[72]: such as the baptism of a dog, in one of the Stamford churches, and others in Northampton, S. Peter's, of Norman date. One of the grossest which we have ever seen is to be found on the north side of the chancel arch of Nailsea, Somersetshire.

On the towers of some Norman churches, the evangelistic symbols are represented. So in Stow church, Lincolnshire. Tiles ought not to have the cross on them: for though Christ is indeed the foundation of the Church, yet these holy symbols should not be exposed to be trodden under foot.

Heraldic devices are here more proper, to signify the worthlessness of worldly honours in the sight of God.

(Notre Dame, Paris, France)

(St. Mary the Virgin, Oxford, England)

(St. Mary the Virgin, Oxford, England)

"The gurgoyles, on the contrary, represent evil spirits as flying from the holy walls: the hideousness of the figures, so often, by modern connoisseurs, ridiculed or blamed, is therefore not without its appropriate meaning."

CHAPTER IX: SOME OBJECTIONS CONSIDERED

Several objections to the symbolical system have been noticed and answered in the course of this treatise. We shall, however, devote a greater space to the consideration of one difficulty which has often been raised by opponents, and has often been felt even by such as have adopted the theory. It is said, for example, that to assert the nave and two aisles, or a triplet of lancets, to be symbolical of the Most Holy Trinity, is both false and profane, when, as is almost always the case, the aisles are much less broad than the nave, and the three lancets are unequal both in height and breadth: whereas in the Trinity none is afore or after other, none is greater or less than another. But the difficulty seems only to arise from carrying the similitude too far: the point of resemblance is in these cases a single one: the mere trinity of the arrangement is the only particular which gives rise to the symbol. "Three mystic lines approach the shrine," sings the poet of the Christian year for Trinity Sunday. The number alone is answerable for the emblem. We do not deny that an equilateral triangle is a more perfect symbol of the Blessed Trinity: but even here a captious man might object to the emblem, because the angles gain greater or less prominence according to the position in which the triangle is placed. The Catholic monogram of the Trinity, for example, assigns to the Father and the Son the upper angles of a triangle standing on the third point. On the other hand the modern triangle, generally charged with the Hebrew word Jehovah, has the third angle uppermost. We can quite conceive these differences being thought objectionable. The case is not so strong indeed as when the three members are unequal, but still it is the same in kind and in reality.

It is a condition of emblems that the points of similitude must not be pressed too far. The material Sun indeed typifies the Sun of Righteousness: but in what particulars? in its being created, in its rising on the dark world every day, in its being matter? Surely not: but in this one point, that it brings light and heat to the earth. "I am the Door," said our Lord. In what particulars, we may again ask? It would be profane to show by examples that it is only in this point; that a door is for entrance into a material house just as we enter into the Church through Christ. The ark, our Church teaches us, was an emblem of the Church: not in its human building, nor in its final perishing.; but in that it saved souls by water. Did the Paschal Lamb typify the Immaculate Victim in any thing more than its comparative purity and its bloody death? We need not multiply such examples.

But there is another consideration to be adduced. Our Lord's own parables must not be pressed too far. The history of the five wise and five foolish virgins, must not be adduced to prove that the number of the lost will equal that of the saved. This may be dangerous ground, but the assertion is true. Every parable is figurative to a certain point, and no further. Not that there is much danger of persons not knowing where the line is to be drawn: any more than there would be in the case of one of a reverent mind, who was told that the *triplicity* of aisles and windows typified a great doctrine. The *British Critic* made a very just observation on this point, that it argued a great blindness of spiritual vision to deny such an emblem, because the similitude was not complete in all points. Indeed if all points answered so closely and exactly to each other, it is not clear how a similitude would differ from a fac-simile. The very notion of a thing being like another involves the fact that the two are not identical. Nothing more is found or expected, than a similarity, an analogy, in certain qualities. For in all symbolism it is quality and not essence in which resemblance is sought.

Which leads us to consider another objection sometimes urged to the effect that if a thing mean one thing it cannot mean another. For example, if the nave and aisles represent the Holy Trinity, they cannot also represent the Church Militant here on earth, or in another point of view the true fold. Again, if the piers and arches set forth the foundation of the apostles and Prophets, they must not bear a part in the representation of the Trinity together with the clerestory and triforium. But this difficulty vanishes if we remember that the resemblance, for the most part, is derived from grouping independent things together and viewing them in a particular light. We do not deny the *real* essential symbolism of a material result: but this its particular significancy need not obtrude itself at all times: the thing itself in other combinations, and viewed under other aspects, may acquire an additional and occasional meaning. For example, it is the union of the rose, thistle, and shamrock, which is the emblem of our United Empire: they have each their own figurative sense; in combination they acquire a new meaning. The harp is not less the emblem of Ireland, because it must primarily represent music. Leaven was of old the symbol of wickedness: our Lord spake of the leaven of the Scribes and Pharisees: yet we hear from His own lips, the Kingdom of Heaven is like unto leaven.[73]

Another objection is as follows: If this theory be true, how will you account for churches with nothing but a nave, or with only one aisle; how for churches with neither clerestory nor triforia; or, on the other hand, for those with double triforia, or with four or five aisles? Now we never asserted that it was necessary that all, or indeed any, given things should be intentionally symbolized. We have pointed out that some things are essentially symbolical; others accidentally and occasionally. We might attempt to classify what *must* be symbolized in church building, and what *may* be. But we decline to do so because we do not think that the principles of symbolism are yet sufficiently investigated or apprehended. However, in a general way, *every* building must, from the nature of things, have some accidents, as of material, of parts, of plan; every particular building must have particular accidents, as of use and purpose. These accidents *must* be symbolical, from their nature, in a general way: they may derive, from purpose added to their nature, a further or modified symbolism in a particular way. With the first sort it is that Durandus chiefly concerns himself. A building must have walls, must have roof, piers, windows, corners, and floor. For each then he finds a meaning. He does not quite neglect the second sort. Early English windows must have a splay: the spire may have a weathercock: for these then there is an appropriate signification. So we do not mean to insist that certain things *shall* be symbolized; we say they *may* be symbolized. Perhaps when more is known, we shall be able to criticize ancient buildings, to show their faults or their shortcomings in this particular. As it is, we have framed a sort of *beau ideal* of a church, fully formed and developed, which we should propose as a perfect model. We are not qualified as yet to blame the ancient churches which do not come up to this ideal, but we cannot be wrong in praising such as do.

In discussing Mr. Lewis's illustrations of Kilpeck church, we touched upon the Basilican origin of churches considered as an argument against the reception of the symbolical theory. Our last remarks will apply to the same question. It has been thought quite sufficient ground for turning into ridicule the whole principle, that the Roman justice halls had three or more aisles, or that a barn or banquetting room may have three longitudinal divisions. But what if mechanical convenience suggested the arrangement? (though we do not grant this). It is clear that many churches, many barns, and many refectories have never had a triple arrangement. It has never been asserted that every church shall have nave and aisles: but if a church has nave and aisles it will be symbolical of a great doctrine; and for this reason it is better for a church to have nave and aisles. Why do not such writers argue that the cross form is not symbolical, because many barns are cruciform? Now it is instructive to observe that there is a great and obvious utilitarian advantage in this shape for a barn: but not in the case of churches *as anciently arranged*; in which the transepts were utterly useless for the accommodation of worshippers; and in which there is a mechanical evil (as before mentioned) from the lateral pressure on the lantern piers. Yet it is undeniable that the cross form was chosen for its symbolical meaning: and this in spite of mechanical disadvantages. A mechanical reason fails here, as in the former case, in accounting for the fact. How will they account for the cross form? Their own argument tells against them. We may still further remark that in modern times we have had some curious practical lessons upon this cross form. Messrs. Britton and Hosking, in their atrocious plan for rearranging S. Mary Redcliffe church, unwittingly testified to the inconvenience, and want of any utilitarian end, of this plan by placing the pulpit under the lantern, and arranging the congregation in the four arms so as to face it. On the other hand, some modern architects confessedly employ the cross form because it allows of people arranged as in the last case, all seeing the preacher. But why do they not look deeper into things? Why have the cross at all? Why not have an amphitheatre, an octagon, an acoustically designed Mechanic's Institute Lecture Room? Then all could hear, all could see much better, and the building would not cost half so much. They may think that they are designing on utilitarian principles. In truth they are unknowingly, unwillingly, symbolizing the Cross.

The Mourning Virgin (Naumberg, Germany, 1220)

(Naumberg, Germany, 1220)
The Crucified Christ from a Triumphal Cross

CHAPTER X: DEVELOPMENT OF SYMBOLISM

It is now our intention to attempt a brief sketch of the history of symbolism, confining ourselves to its rise, progress, and decline in England. For of its earlier development we have already had occasion to speak, both in the first and in the eighth chapter, when we referred to its use among the primitive Christians, and to such particulars of information as could be gained concerning it from the later fathers, and from mediaeval authors.

Among all nations, the facts of Christianity have been received before its doctrines. The inhabitants of a heathen country are first called on to believe, as matter of history, that our Blessed Lord was conceived by the Holy Ghost, born of the Virgin Mary, suffered under Pontius Pilate, was crucified, dead, and buried, before any attempt is made to set before them the doctrine of the Atonement, the Mystery of the Trinity, or the compatibility of God's foreknowledge with man's free action. And it is in the infancy of individuals, as in that of nations. We may therefore, from all analogy, conclude, that the things set forth in the earlier development of church art, would be facts rather than doctrines.

Now, if we look to Norman buildings, we shall find this to be the case. Excepting the doctrine of the Holy Trinity (which after all, perhaps rather ranks, through all the stages of Christian Art, under the head of essential, than under that of intended symbolism), we shall find an almost exclusive reference to history, in arrangements and details. That God was the Creator of heaven and earth, is set forth in door mouldings, and capitals, sometimes by the heavenly constellations or signs of the zodiac, sometimes by the animals brought to Adam to be named, sometimes by the references to agriculture, which, as we have before seen, often occur. The Incarnation of our Saviour is set forth, as it has been already hinted, by representations so physical and earthly, as to be to our eyes almost profane. The Fall of Man, which appears on the sides of Fonts, well reminds us of that stain which must be washed away in Holy Baptism. A great many of the events of our Lord's life are sculptured in various positions: above all, of course, His Passion. Again, duties are symbolically represented, so in the chancel arch of Egleton, Rutland, we have the figure of a deacon ringing a bell; doubtless to remind the worshippers of the duty of attending God's house. And a still more practical method of representing the evil consequences attending the breach of duty, and one which speaks much of the rudeness of the age, is where some local event well known at the time of the erection of the church, finds a commemoration in it. Thus (though at a later epoch) among the capitals of the south transept of Wells cathedral, the architect has represented a theft, which doubtless, at the time, had made considerable noise in that place. In the first group, a man is seen stealing apples: then follows the struggle and apprehension: finally, his trial and condemnation. And such practical admonitions might not have been without their use. Sometimes they are refined and exalted into such an one as may be seen in the northern apse of S. Mary's, at Guildford, where heavenly and earthly judgement are portrayed. Victory over the devil is singularly enough symbolized in Oxford, S. Peter's, by the piers which rest on, and crush, a monster. We have before noticed that Norman architecture, true to its love of facts, delighted in the representation of instruments of martyrdom, or the deeds of faith, as the victory of S. George. The final doom was also a favourite subject; so was the descent of Christ into hell. In fact, its whole character, whether in stringcourses, tympana, capitals, or chancel arches, was graphicalness, and that obtained sometimes at the expense of grace, sometimes almost at that of decorum, but probably well adapted to the particular development which the minds of the people had then reached. One point we must remark, to the eternal honour of the Anglo-Norman, and indeed also of the Saxon church, deadly as was the hatred existing between the two peoples, for at least a hundred and fifty years after the conquest, it has left no symbolical trace, either in the churches of the vanquishers, or of the vanquished. Much as the one had suffered, and much as the other despised the conquered nation, this feeling vanished in the house of God.

In advancing to Early English, we still find strong traces of the historicalism of ornaments, both in some of the mouldings, as in the toothed, and in the capitals, though the latter begin now to assume a more allegorical form. Indeed, the observation seems worth making, that this style is the only one which appears to have dealt much in allegory, we mean in that sense which we have already attached to the word. That is, it employs fictitious representations to set forth real truths; as in Wells cathedral, the fall of the barren tree forms a beautiful corbel. We do, however, find some traces of this in Norman work, as the fable of the crow and the fox may occasionally be discovered in it. The works of the Creation were often set forth, rather with reference to their beauty than from any other reasons. Such as the birds making their nests in the thick foliage, flowers, and fruit. Yet, on the whole, facts such as those which principally occupied the attention of Norman architects, began rather to find expression among the details, than to usurp any important part in church arrangement. We are in possession of too little wood work of this date—and in that many references of this kind were probably to be found—to be able to speak with so much certainty as we can in the later styles: but that this was the tendency of the progress of architecture, it requires but little knowledge to discover. Impressed, but evidently, now, not only essentially but intentionally, on every building, was the doctrine of the Ever Blessed Trinity: for triplets were so common at the east end as to form the rule of Early English design. Fonts, instead of bearing a representation of the Fall of Man, and thereby implying our need of regeneration, began to be octagonal, thereby setting forth the doctrine itself, a strong confirmation of our previous observation respecting facts and doctrines. The shape of piers is also to be noticed. For there appears to have been almost a rule, either that the octagonal and circular shape should altarnate; or that one aisle should present the one kind, the other the other. This we can hardly, in our present state of knowledge, profess to explain. Durandus's observations about windows, their splay and shafts are very curious: and again, he evidently recognises in the tiebeams, the knitting together of the elect in one communion and fellowship: a strong argument, this, that we are justified in regarding arrangements, which arise from mechanical necessity, as nevertheless truly and really symbolical. In the bases of piers we now often find flowers, which indeed, sometimes, as in Rochester cathedral, occur in transition work; principally the fleur de lys, which we may interpret to signify that humility is the foundation of all Christian graces.

On the whole, however, we conclude that in this style, while churches taken as a whole became more symbolical, their details, *as* details, became less so.

In proceeding to the next development of Catholic art, we are almost afraid of expressing a belief, that Decorated, in its early dawn, gave promise of a brighter day than it ever reached. It had not shown its wonderful resources and capabilities in windows and flying buttresses, before the boldness of its capitals and bases began to decline. We can imagine that, had it so been ordered, Christian architecture might, about the year 1300, have taken a different direction, and attained to a glory, inconceivable to us—perhaps attainable only when the whole Catholic Church shall be at unity. As it is, we cannot but consider, that about that period, or a few years later, it took a wrong turn, and being hurried in a short space through the hectic of a rare flush of beauty, declined thenceforward slowly but surely. Now, if we ask, why was this? It will lead us to look at Church history as connected with the development of church architecture. Contemporary with the change from Saxon to Norman (for we are none of those who hold that the former extended till Oct. 14, 1065, and the latter began the next day), was finally the victory of the Anglican Church over Paganism in the conversion and civilization of the Danes. Contemporary with the appearance of Early English, was the great victory of the Church over Erastianism, by the martyrdom of S. Thomas of Canterbury, and the abrogation of the constitutions of Clarendon. But, hardly had Early English finished its course of splendour, when while traces, of rare glory were developing daily, the statute of Mortmain began to tell upon the Church: and though the impulse already given yet continued for some time to act, the end was near. No magnificent cathedral was built after the full effects—not so much of that act, as of the Erastianism which contrived and allowed it—were felt. The nave of Winchester can hardly be called a solitary exception; because, in truth, it may be doubted whether the pious exertions of William of Wykeham were not, so far as concerns the actual beauty of his cathedral, misplaced. Thenceforward, the State interfered more and more with the Church; and not allowed to carry out her own designs, it is no wonder if the latter quickly began to forget her own symbolical language. After, for the first few years of the fourteenth century, using it with precision and elegance before unattainable, she thenceforward began to disuse it. We need not give examples of decorated symbolism, because all that was new in it lay in its windows: and these we have already discussed at considerable length. And having sufficiently explained why there should be a decline, we have only now to examine why that decline should have been so different in England, France, and Italy. In England, from the time that Edward IV directed the execution of Archbishop Scrope, when the State interfered, it was with a strong arm, cramping and confining, obliging the Church to confine herself to ritual observances, and forbidding her to expatiate in the grand objects for which she was ordained. Now could there be a more fitting expression of this than the Perpendicular style? Does not its stiffness, its failure in harmony, its want of power and adaptation, its continual introduction of heraldry, its monotony, its breaking up by hard continued lines, its shallowness, its meretriciousness, its display,—set forth what we know to have been the character of the contemporary Church? Above all, do not the reintroduction of horizontality, the Tudor arch, the depressed pier, speak of her want of Spirituality? Everything teaches us that there was no want of power in her architects; considered merely as specimens of art, King's College, and Henry the Seventh's chapels, are matchless. And here and there we may trace some tokens of vastness and holiness of conception worthy of a better age; such as the Suffolk roofs, which, as it has been well said, never attained their full development. It must be borne in mind, that Perpendicular[74] was the first style, which in its full developement was used first for a secular building. Far be it from us, however, to depreciate the excessive magnificence it assumes in shrines and chapels: indeed, this is one of the features which Decorated has not, and the absence of which in that style renders it possible to believe that a still more magnificent may be in store for us. Perpendicular introduced no new element of symbolism.

But if this were the state of the Anglican Church, the Gallican, though not better off, was acted on in a very different manner. The State gradually interfered with it, embraced it with its dangerous friendship, made its observances meaningless, while sustaining their splendour; secularized its abbeys, by appropriating them to political ends; made statesmen of its bishops, gave it outside show, while eating out its heart. Does not Flamboyant express this? A vast collection of elegant forms, meaninglessly strung together: richness of ornament, actually weakening construction: vagaries of tracery, as if the hand possessed of church art, were suddenly deprived of church feelings: nothing plain, simple, intelligible, holy: parts neglected, parts ostentatious: the west front of Abbeville to a choir that would disgrace a hamlet.

In Spain again, where Christianity unfolded itself later, so also was church art later in its development. San Miguel, at Seville, which was actually built in 1305, would, in England, be set down to the date of about 1180.

In Italy, where there was no State to interfere with the Church, Paganism, which had always been more or less at work, sprang up at once, at the time of the Great Schism, and has ever since prevailed.

But to return to England. Perpendicular, unable to express any idea by its ornaments, soon began to imitate those of earlier styles: first Early English, in the wretched banded capitals of the western counties, and then Decorated in its windows. While, however, the Church was yet united with the rest of Christendom, Paganism interfered but in a very slight degree: the Italian example of Henry the Seventh's tomb was not followed. Even after the Dissolution, there were some good churches built: the symbolism which lingered longest was that of the chancel and nave. Nor was this destroyed summarily: the importance of the chancel had been gradually, all through the Perpendicular era, weakened by chancel aisles, and the omission of the chancel arch: it was but to omit the rood screen and parclose, and (as at Hawkshead, Lancashire, circ. 1564) the mystical division vanished.

The symbolisms which Protestantism introduced were few and easily understood.

The removal, and material, of the altar, the change of vestments, the gradual introduction of close pews, the innovation of a reading pew, were all figurative enough. Something like a return to church art was made just before the great Rebellion: chancels became elongated, altars resumed their old position, copes reappeared, and the like. Details began to improve: and (which we could hardly have expected) intentional symbolism is sometimes to be discovered in them. So, in Baltonsburgh, Somersetshire, a stone pulpit of the date of 1621, has among other devices, an equilateral triangle, containing, and surrounded by, a *tre*-foil: and evidently setting forth the Holy Trinity. After the Rebellion, but still more after the Revolution, those faint traces of symbolism died away into that *ne plus ultra* of wretchedness, the Georgian style.

CHAPTER XI: GENERAL CONCLUSION

It is very remarkable, as has been already observed, that the buildings of those who most strongly object to the principle of symbolism, do in effect contain as striking an exemplification of it as it would be possible to find.

Let us look at a Protestant place of worship. It is choked up and concealed by surrounding shops and houses, for religion, nowadays, must give way to business and pleasure: it stands north and south, for all idea of fellow-feeling with the Church Catholic is looked on as mere trifling, or worse: the front which faces the High Street is of stone, because the uniformity of the street so required it: or (which is more likely) of stucco, which answers as well, and is cheaper: the sides, however, are of brick, because no one can see them: there is at the entrance a large vestibule, to allow people to stand while their carriages are being called up, and to enter into conversation on the news of the day, or the merits of the preacher: it also serves the purpose of making the church warmer, and contains the doors and staircases to the galleries. On entering, the pulpit occupies the central position, and towards it every seat is directed: for preaching is the great object of the Christian ministry: galleries run all round the building, because hearing is the great object of a Christian congregation: the altar stands under the organ gallery, as being of no use, except once a month: there are a few free seats in out-of-the-way places, where no one could hear, and no pews would be hired, and therefore no money is lost by making the places free: and whether the few poor people who occupy them can hear or not, what matters it? The font, a cast-iron vase on a marble pillar, stands within the altar rails; because it there takes up no room: the reading pew is under the pulpit, and faces the congregation; because the prayers are to be read to them and not addressed to God. Look at this place on Sunday or Thursday Evening. Carriages crash up through the cast-iron gates, and, amidst the wrangling and oaths of rival coachmen, deposit their loads at the portico: people come, dressed out in the full fashion of the day, to occupy their luxurious pew, to lay their smelling-bottles and prayer-books on its desk, and reclining on its soft cushions, to confess themselves—if they are in time—miserable sinners: to see the poor and infirm standing in the narrow passages, and close their pew doors against them, lest themselves should be contaminated, or their cushions spoilt, at the same time beseeching God to give their fellow-creatures the comfort which they refuse to bestow: the Royal Arms occupy a conspicuous position; for it is a chapel of the Establishment: there are neat cast-iron pillars to hold up the galleries, and still neater pillars in the galleries to hold up the roof; thereby typifying that the whole existence of the building depends on the good-will of the congregation: the roof is flat, with an elegant cornice, and serves principally to support a gas-lighted chandelier: and the administration of this chapel is carried on by clerk, organist, beadle, and certain bonnetless pew-openers.

We need not point out how strongly all this symbolizes the spiritual pride, the luxury, the self-sufficiency, the bigotry of the congregations of too many a pew-rented Episcopal chapel.

In contrast to this, let us close with a general view of the symbolism of a Catholic church.

Far away, and long ere we catch our first view of the city itself, the three spires of its cathedral, rising high above its din and turmoil, preach to us of the Most Holy and Undivided Trinity. As we approach, the transepts, striking out cross-wise, tell of the Atonement: the Communion of Saints is set forth by the chapels clustering round choir and nave: the mystical weathercock bids us to watch and pray and endure hardness: the hideous forms that seem hurrying from the eaves speak the misery of those who are cast out of the Church: spire, pinnacle, and finial, the upward curl of the sculptured foliage, the upward spring of the flying buttress, the sharp rise of the window arch, the high-thrown pitch of the roof, all these, overpowering the horizontal tendency of string course and parapet, teach us, that vanquishing earthly desires, we also should ascend in heart and mind. Lessons of holy wisdom are written in the delicate tracery of the windows: the unity of many members is shadowed forth by the multiplex arcade: the duty of letting our light shine before men, by the pierced and flowered parapet that crowns the whole.

We enter. The triple breadth of nave and aisles, the triple height of pier arch, triforium, and clerestory, the triple length of choir, transepts, and nave, again set forth the Holy Trinity. And what besides is there that does not tell of our Blessed Saviour? that does not point out "Him first," in the two-fold western door: "Him last," in the distant altar: "Him midst," in the great rood: "Him without end," in the monogram carved on boss and corbel, in the Holy Lamb, in the Lion of the tribe of Judah, in the Mystic Fish? Close by us is the font; for by regeneration we enter the Church: it is deep and capacious; for we are buried in baptism with Christ: it is of stone; for He is the Rock: and its spiry cover teaches us, if we be indeed risen from its waters with Him, to seek those things that are above. Before us, in long drawn vista are the massy piers, which are the Apostles and Prophets: they are each of many members, for many are the graces in every saint: there is delicate foliage round the head of all; for all were plentiful in good works. Beneath our feet are the badges of worldly pomp and glory, the charges of kings and nobles and knights: all in the Presence of God as dross and worthlessness. Over us swells the vast "valley" of the high-pitched roof: from the crossing and interlacing of its curious rafters hang fadeless flowers and fruits which are not of earth: from its hammer-beams project wreaths and stars, such as adorn heavenly beings: in its centre stands the Lamb as It had been slain: from around Him the Celestial Host, cherubim and seraphim, thrones, principalities, and powers, look down peacefully on the worshippers below. Harpers there are among them harping with their harps: for one is the song of the Church in earth and in heaven. Through the walls wind the narrow cloister galleries: emblems of the path by which holy hermits and anchorites, whose conflicts were known only to their God, have reached their home. And we are compassed about with a mighty cloud of witnesses: the rich deep glass of the windows teems with saintly forms, each in its own fair niche, all invested with the same holy repose: there is the glorious company of the apostles: the goodly fellowship of the Prophets: the noble army of martyrs: the shining band of the confessors: the jubilant chorus of the virgins: there are kings who have long since changed an earthly for an heavenly crown: and bishops who have given in a glad account to the Shepherd and Bishop of souls. But on none of these things do we rest; piers, arch behind arch, windows, light behind light, arcades, shaft behind shaft, the roof, bay behind bay, the saints around us, the heavenly hierarchy above with dignity of pre-eminence still increasing eastward, each and all, lead on eye and soul and thought to the image of the crucified Saviour as displayed in the great east window. Gazing steadfastly on that, we pass up the nave, that is through the Church Militant, till we reach the rood screen, the barrier between it and the Church Triumphant, and therein shadowing forth the death of the faithful. High above it hangs, on His Triumphal Cross, the image of Him Who by His death hath overcome death; on it are portrayed saints and martyrs, His warriors, who fighting under their Lord have entered into rest and inherit a tearless eternity. They are to be our examples, and the seven lamps above them typify those graces of the Spirit, by Whom alone we can tread in their steps. The screen itself glows with gold and crimson: with gold, for they have on their heads golden crowns; with crimson, for they passed the Red Sea of martyrdom to obtain them. And through the delicate net-work, and the unfolding holy doors, we catch faint glimpses of the chancel beyond. There are the massy stalls; for in heaven is everlasting rest: there are the sedilia, emblems of the seats of the elders round the throne: there is the piscina; for they have washed their robes and made them white: and there, heart and soul and life of all, the altar with its unquenched lights, and golden carvings, and mystic steps, and sparkling jewels: even Christ Himself, by Whose only merits we find admission to our heavenly inheritance. Verily, as we think on the oneness of its design, we may say: *Jerusalem edificatur ut civitas cujus participatio ejus in idipsum*.

POSTSCRIPTUM

On concluding their work, which from circumstances that need not be specified has been a year in the press, the writers must apologize for the numerous typographical errors which have been allowed to remain. Their separation from each other, and distance from the printer, must plead in excuse.

They take this opportunity of expressing their thanks to the Reverend Dr Mill, Christian Advocate of the University of Cambridge, and to F. A. Paley, Esq., M.A., of S. John's College, Cambridge, Honorary Secretary of the Cambridge Camden Society, for their advice and assistance.

It remains to say that some doubt has been felt by persons who have read the Introductory Essay in proofs, whether the writers have given Mr Pugin sufficient credit for several passages in his works which seem to *involve* the principle now contended for. We had thought that no misapprehension could be feared on this head. It was enough to know that the principle in question, even though *felt* (as we indeed allowed) by this architect, had not been *expressed in terms*. In short, we took this fact for our ground: that whereas Mr Pugin's book professed to assert the *true principles* of Christian architecture, yet reality, according to his definition, was not at least so accurately a "true principle" as sacramentality. The principles themselves, as enunciated by Mr Pugin, apply as well to any secular building as to a church: they are true for *construction*, but not adequate in themselves to form a rule for ecclesiastical design.

KEMERTON, August 16, 1843.

NOTES

MYSTICAL MIRROR OF THE CHURCH

1. Apocalypse iii, 7.
2. Psalm lxxx (*Fundamenta ejus*), 1.
3. Cant. iv, 4.
4. 1 Corinthians ix, 27.
5. 1 S. Peter iv, 2.
6. S. John xix, 30.
7. Galatians vi, 14.
8. 2 Corinthians v, 13. Vulgate.
9. Isaiah lx, 8.
10. S. John x, 7, 9.
11. Cant. iii, 10.
12. Cant. iii, 10.
13. Cant. i, 17.
14. Cant. iii, 9.
15. Eccles. iii, 18.
16. Isaiah xlix, 18.
17. Cant. iii, 10. Vulgate.
18. The fifteen Psalms, cxx-cxxxiv of our version, are called Songs of Degrees.
19. S. Matthew v, 14.
20. S. Matthew v, 16.
21. Here is an allusion to Psalm xlv (*Eructavit cor meum*), 14.
22. Cant. i, 5.
23. Psalm xvi (*Conserva me Domine*), 7.
24. Psalm xvi (*Judica me Domine*), 8.
25. Cant. iii, 10.
26. Cant. vi, 10.
27. Genesis xxviii, 17.
28. The hymn, *Vexilla Regis*, occurs in the office for Passion Sunday.
29. Apoc. xxi, 2.
30. See note 4 on the Rationale, I. i, p. 13.
31. Psalm lxxxvii (*Fundamenta ejus*), 2.
32. Cant. iv, 6.
33. Psalm xix (*Cœli enarrant*), 5.
34. Psalm xxiv (Domini est terra), 7-10.
35. S. John xvii, 17.
36. Genesis xxviii (? xlviii ?)
37. Psalm cxxxiii (*Ecce quam bonum*), 2.
38. Psalm xxx (*Exaltabo te Domine*), 12.

THE SYMBOLISM OF CHURCHES AND CHURCH ORNAMENTS

THE SYMBOLISM OF CHURCHES: CHAPTER I: OF A CHURCH AND ITS PARTS

1. It has been found advisable to print the word church in the following pages with a great or small initial letter, according as 'The Blessed Company of all Faithful People,' or the material building, were intended.

2. Psalm lxviii (*Exsurgat Dues*), 6.

3. See below, chapter vi.

4. So the hymn in the Parisian Breviary for the dedication of a church:

Urbs beata, vera pacis
Visio, Jerusalem.

5. Compare Cicero de Senect. xxiii. Et ex vita ita discedo tanquam ex hospitio, non tanquam ex domo: commorandi enim Natura diversorium nobis, non habitandi dedit.

6. Chapter vi, sect. 5, ad fin.

7. Durandus, II. 10. 8. 'In many places, priests be called chaplains. For of old the Kings of France, when they went forth to war, carried with them the Cope of Blessed Martin, which was kept in a certain tent (where Mass was said), and from the cope (cappa) the tent was called chapel (capella).'

We may observe that chapel was used in former times with much greater latitude than now. An additional aisle or chantry was so called. So in Haddenham, Cambridgeshire, on a brass in the north aisle, *Orate pro Animabus fundatorum hujus Capellæ:* that is, the aisle itself.

8. 2 Cor. xi, 2.

9. S. John iii, 29.

10. Psalm xlv (*Eructavit cor meum*), 16.

11. S. John ii, 17.

12. Psalm xi (*In Domino confido*), 4.

13. Hebrews xiii, 14.

14. S. Matthew vii, 25. In general illustration of the foregoing sections the reader is referred to the first chapter of the eighth book of Bingham's 'Antiquities.'

15. In the account of the dedication of S. Michael the Archangel, in the Isle of Guernsey, preserved in the 'Black Book of the Bishop of Coutances,' it appears that the ceremony was performed by a priest: though it is believed that such has seldom been the case in the Anglican Church. But see chapter vi, section 2.

16. A cross was not only inscribed on the foundation stone, but a cross was placed where the church was to be: and this in the Eastern Church; where the *Stauropegia* was a ceremony of much importance.

17. This passage is valuable as proving that in the country of our Bishop nothing was known of a practice undoubtedly prevalent in England; the direction of a church to that part of the sky in which the sun arose on the Feast of the Patron Saint.

18. Psalm cxxii (*Lœtatus sum*), 3.

19. Ephesians ii, 20.

20. Psalm lxxxvii (*Exudamenta ejus*), 1.

21. Ephesians vi, 16,17.

22. Exodus xxv, 2.

23. The sanctuary of course means that the eastermost division in churches consisting of three parts, which still remains in many Norman buildings, and of which Kilpeck,

in Herefordshire, may be taken as a type. These churches are generally apsidal: but there are instances to the contrary, as Bishopstone, in Sussex. A view of sanctum sanctorum and chancel arches in this church is given in the Cambridge Camden Society's 'Illustrations of Monumental Brasses,' part iv.

24. This passage is somewhat obscure; but the difference between the virgins and the continent appears to be this: by the former are meant those who have taken vows of celibacy; by the latter, those who practise it, without, however, having bound themselves to it by vow.

25. Psalm xxvii (*Dominus illuminatio*), 13.

26. 1 S. Peter iv, 8.

27. S. Matthew xix, 17.

28. Psalm cxix (*Adhœsit pavimento*), 25.

29. Rev. xxi, 16.

30. S. John xiv, 23.

31. S. Matthew xvi, 18.

32. This of course refers to the Church of the Holy Sepulchre, the prototype of these buildings. There are four, as it is well known, in England yet standing, and two in ruins—namely, Temple Aslackby, in Lincolnshire, and the church in Ludlow Castle.

33. Psalm xix (*Cœli enarrant*), 4.

34. We may observe that Prynne perverts the fact, that the westernmost seats in the choir are the most honourable, to a depreciation of the Catholic custom of the position of the altar. See his 'Pacific Examination,' s.v.

35. Canticles iv, 4.

36. Ephesians v, 14.

37. 1 Cor. ix, 27.

38. S. John x, 12.

39. 1 S. Peter iv, 11.

40. This passage is particularly to be observed, for the reason given in the Introduction.

41. See Appendix I.

42. S. John x, 9.

43. Canticles viii, 9.

44. Prov. viii, 1.

45. Compare the *Veni Creator:*

Thou the anointing Spirit art,
Who dost Thy sevenfold gifts impart.

46. Gal. ii, 9.

47. That is, it may be supposed, bishops of those sees which were founded by the apostles themselves, *e.g.* Rome, Crete, Ephesus.

48. *Beams*. That is, probably, tie-beams: here is another reference to the architectural arrangements of Early English date.

49. See Appendix I.

50. It is very difficult to find the right meaning of the word *ferculum* here. The English version gives the passage from the Canticles, 'King Solomon made himself a *chariot* (marg. reading, *bed*) of the wood of Lebanon. In the extremely beautiful treatise of Hugo de S. Victore, *De Nubtiis Spiritualibus* (cap. iii), the *fercula nuptialia* appear to mean the *marriage feast*, which is to perform its part of the general *Sensuum refectio*, by its sweet savours; as the bed or chariot of Solomon is noted for the odour of its cedar

wood. However, the same writer devotes five Tituli of his *Erudit. Theolog. Ex Miscellan.* namely, lix-lxii of the first book, and exxi of the second, to the consideration of the Ferculum Solomonis: which he decides to be a *lectica seu vehiculum*, a litter or sedan (such as is now used in Sicily under the name of *lettiga*), differing from the *lectulus* or *bed* (Cant. i, 16.), inasmuch as this denotes the repose of the contemplative life, while the ferculum typifies the laborious exercise of the active life; and differing again from the *currus* or chariot (the only other vehicle mentioned in Holy Scripture), since the latter is drawn on the earth with a grating noise, and represents a depraved heart clinging to earthly things. But the former is borne smoothly and quietly above the ground, an image of the righteous soul despising earthly and seeking heavenly things. Lastly, the *ferculum*, or litter, typifies the Church, from carrying, *a ferendo*, as doth the Church her children unto Heavenly Rest.

51. The fact that in many unaltered and unmutilated churches the chancel is lower than the nave, appears to have been unnoticed by ecclesiologists. Wherever it occurs, William Dowsing, or some of his puritanical coadjutors, have been supposed agents in the matter. But there exist chancels, which, whether from the height of the piscina and sedilia, or on other accounts, cannot have been lowered, to which nevertheless there is a descent from the nave. Such an one is that of S. Giles's at Cambridge; and the arrangement is very common in the little churches of the south-west part of Sussex.

52. This is another very remarkable passage: and one which proves that the injunction of Abp. Laud for the erection of altar rails was not a novelty. And though their abolition is much to be wished, as well from the ugliness of all existing specimens, as from the irreverence which they seem to pre-suppose, the Church in England can scarcely be charged with the adoption of an innovation in giving her sanction to them.

53. 3 Kings vi, 13.

54. This is, of course, a false derivation. The important subject of Rood-lofts has been treated with admirable learning by Father Thiers, in his treatise 'Sur les jubés,' to which the reader is referred. See also Appendix C.

55. Psalm (cxix), *Beati immaculati*, 164.

56. This passage deserves to be noticed, as proving that lead was not the only roofing employed in the Norman churches.

57. Exodus xxxviii, 8.

58. S. John viii, 12.

59. S. John i, 6.

60. S. Matthew v, 14.

61. S. Matthew v, 16.

62. Lev. xxiv, 2.

63. Isaiah lxi, 1.

64. Cantic. iii, 10.

65. Numbers i, 47; xviii, 6.

66. 1 Corinth. xv, 28.

67. S. John xv, 2.

68. Such is probably the meaning of this passage. The original is *ut ili bona sive mala judicia audiamus.*

69. This is the practice in some parts of England even to this day: more especially in Somersetshire. Bp. Montague in his 'Visitation Articles' (reprinted Camb. 1841) asks (p.17), 'Do men and women sit together in those seats indifferently and promiscuously? or (as the fashion was of old), do men sit together upon one side of the church, and

women upon the other?' And, indeed, of old there was a still further separation on each side, into the married and unmarried. The restoration of the practice recommended by Bp. Montague is much to be wished.

70. 1 Corinth. x, 13.

71. Apocalypse x, 7.

72. Ephesians v, 23.

73. Coloss. iii, 16.

74. The passage referred to is as follows:—'Regiam quidem ingrediens, et habitu et aspectu et incessu et omnibus aliis te ornas et componis: Hic autem vere est Regia et plane hic talia qualia cælestia:—et rides? Atque scio quidem quod tu non vides. Audi autem quod ubique adsunt angeli, et maxime in Domo Dei adsistunt Regis, et omnia sunt impleta incorpoeis illus Potestatibus.'

75. Exod. iii, 5. Josh. v, 15.

76. 2 Kings i, 28.

77. See Appendix.

THE SYMBOLISM OF CHURCHES: CHAPTER II: OF THE ALTAR

1. Genesis viii, 20.

2. Genesis xxvi, 25. xxxiii, 20.

3. Genesis xiii, 18.

4. Exodus xxviii, 1.

5. The true ecclesiastical distinction between *altare* and *ara* is that the former means the altar of the true God, and is therefore alone used in the Vulgate, answering to the Greek θυσιαστήριον, as opposed to *ara* (βῶμος), an altar with an image above it. See *Mede*. Folio 386.

6. Exodus xx, 26.

7. Psalm li (*Miserere mei*), 19.

8. Exodus xx, 25.

9. Psalm cxviii (*Confitemini*), 27.

10. III Kings vi, 22.

11. Exodus xx, 26.

12. This prayer, which immediately precedes the Commemoration of the Dead, runs thus: Supplices Te rogamus, omnipotens Deus, jube hoc perferri per manus Sancti Angeli Tui, in conscpectu Divinæ Majestatis Tuæ: ut quotquot ex hac Altaris participatione sacrosanctum Filii Tui Corpus et Sanguinem sumpserimus, omni benedictione cælesti et gratia repleamur. Per.

13. Psalm lxxxiv (*Quam dilecta*), 4.

14. Exodus xxv, 16.

15. Exodus xix, 8.

16. It is very remarkable that no notice whatever is taken of these relics by Ciampini in his very minute description of the Lateran Basilica: although in his account both of this, and of all the other Basilican churches built by Constantine, he copies *verbatim* the list of the donations of the Emperor which is given in the life of Pope S. Sylvester, compiled by an unknown librarian of the Vatican. It is clear that either Durandus was misinformed, or that the present passage is corrupt. Again, it is not likely that the vests of S. John the Baptist, or the scissors of S. John Evangelist would have been kept in the ark besides its proper contents. Yet Durandus had obviously some facts to go upon, since the Lateran Church, having been originally dedicated to the Saviour, was now under the

Invocation of the two SS. John; and the sufferings of both of these saints were depicted in a very ancient mosaic, those of the Evangelists having over them the following inscription, which we give as describing a Confession of this *Martyr in will*, now little known.

Martyrii calicem bibit hic Athleta Johannes
Principium Verbi cernere qui merit.
Verberat hunc fuste Proconsul, *forfice tondet*,
Quem fervens oleum lædere non valuit.
Conditus hic oleum, dolium, cruor, atque capilli,
Quæ consecrantur libera Roma tibi.

To return, we may be satisfied that these Jewish memorials did not exist, since Ciampini, while composing his account, consulted the former writers upon the Lateran Basilica; viz. the poet Prudentius, an unedited MS, of Panvinius, Severanus De Septem Urbis Ecclesiis, and the work of Cæsar Cardinal Rasponus.

17. Exodus ix, 2.
18. Psalm xxiii (*Dominus regit me*), 5.
19. Jeremiah xvi, 7.
20. S. Matthew v, 15.
21. S. Matthew vi, 22.
22. Psalm xxxiv (*Benedicam Dominum*), 8.
23. Prov. xxxi, 18. Marg. Reading.
24. Exodus xxiii, 15.
25. S. Mark viii, 3.
26. Ecclesiasticus xxii, 2.
27. Psalm ii (*Quare fremuerunt*), 12.
28. See Appendix I.
29. Lev. vi, 9.
30. Canticles viii, 7.
31. 1 Corinth. xii, 31.
32. S. Matthew xxii, 40.
33. Psalm lxxi (*Juste, Domine*), 21.
34. This passage does not appear in the edition of Durandus published at Venice, in 1609.
35. Apocalypse iii, 18.
36. Ecclesiastes ix, 8.
37. This passage also is not found in the Venetian edition.
38. This passage also is not found in the Venetian edition.
39. This passage also is not found in the Venetian edition.
40. Psalm lxxxiv (*Quam dilecta*), 7.
41. Exodus xx, 26.
42. This passage also is not found in the Venetian edition.

THE SYMBOLISM OF CHURCHES: CHAPTER III: OF PICTURES, ETC.

1. Exodus xx, 4.
2. *Veneramur.*—We here use the word *adore* in the sense given to it by the great and good Bishop Montague, in his 'Just Treatise of Invocation': where he says, speaking of the Saints, 'I do admire, reverence, *adore* them in their kind.'
3. Effigiem Christi, quum transis, pronus honora:
Non Tamen effigiem, sed quem designat, adora.

4. Esse Deum, ratione caret, cui consulit esse:
   Materiale lapis, effigale manus.
5. Nec Deus est, nec homo, quam præsens cernis imago;
   Sed Deus est et Homo, quem sacra figurat imago.

The later editions add—

Nam Deus est, quod imago docet, sed non Deus ipse ;
Hunc videas, sed mente colas, quod noscis in ipsa.

6. Deut. v, 8.
7. Lev. xxvi, 1.
8. Deut. iv, 16.
9. Exodus xx, 20.
10. Psalm cxv, 4.
11. Psalm xcvii, 7.
12. Deut. iv, 19.
13. I Corinth. viii, 4.
14. Wisdom xiv, 11.
15. A more solemn protest against the sin of idolatry can hardly be found than the above passage: and they who brand every return to, and every wish for the restoration of, Catholic practices, by so hateful a name, would do well to bear it in mind.
16. Ezekiel viii, 10.
17. Ezekiel iv, 1.
18. S. Luke xvi, 29.
19. A. D. 605
20. Durandus had doubtless in his mind the ancient mosaic over the apsides of the earliest churches in Rome. The extremely beautiful one in San Clemente represents our Lord as crucified. The frescoes with which the walls of our own churches were anciently adorned, seem usually to have represented the Saviour as seated on the Throne of His Majesty. In the chancel of Widford, Herts, is, or was till lately, a fresco of the Saviour seated on a rainbow, a sword proceeding from His mouth. His feet and His hands pierced. In Alfriston, Sussex, there was, we believe, before it was whitewashed over by Bishop Buckner's order, a painting of a similar kind. This is a singular, and, we believe, undescribed painting over the altar in Llandanwg church, Merion. The Saviour is seated in judgment, as before: at His side is His Blessed Mother in a kneeling posture: around Him are angels blowing trumpets, and S. Peter in eucharistical vestments. There is a representation of the souls under the altar. Below are devils torturing souls in cauldrons of brimstone. The evangelistic symbols are also represented.

In a fresco at Beverstone, Gloucestershire, our Saviour is represented on the Cross, with blood flowing from His side into a chalice. (See App. I.) There are remains also of a crucifixion in fresco, in the exquisite, but descrated chapel of Prior Crauden, in the Deanery, Ely. On the Iconostasis of the Greco-Russian Church, all the three positions are to be found.

In stained glass, the Crucifixion generally supplies the place of any other representation of the Saviour. Brasses occasionally, as a very curious one in Cobham, Surrey, represent His nativity or epiphany: but most commonly the Crucifixion, or a Trinity.

There can be no doubt, that many of the most graphic pictures in our old poets owed their origin to the then undestroyed fresco paintings of churches. Some painting, like that above described, of hell, very probably suggested the noble lines of Spenser (I. ix. 50. 6):

He showed him painted in a table plaine,

The damned ghosts that doe in torments waile,
And thousand feends that doe them endless paine
With fire and brimstone, which for ever shall remaine.

Who can estimate the effect of such pictorial representations on the minds of our ancestors? or the good which might be the result, if our churches were again frescoed with similar subjects, wrought with the genius and Catholic feeling of an Overbeck or Cornelius?

21. S. John i, 29.

22. S. Matt. xxviii, 18.

23. Isaiah vi, 1.

24. Psalm lxxx, 1.

25. Exodus xxiv, 10.

26. S. Matthew xxiv, 30.

27. Isaiah vi, 2.

28. Many of our readers will call to mind the peculiar expression always given to the countenances of angels in Catholic illuminations or paintings, a conventional propriety uniformly neglected by modern artists. The same character was beautifully given in the relieved figures of angels upon the shrine of S. Henry lately exhibiting in London.

29. Apocalypse xii, 7.

30. Apocalypse iv, 4.

31. This very obscure passage is an instance of the symbolism in the combination of numbers. It seems to mean that faith in the Holy Trinity preached through the four quarters of the world, may be represented by three multiplied into four or twelve: and again, this symbolical fact multiplied by general good works and keeping of the Gospels, may be set forth in twenty-four. It is to be remarked that the princeps edition alone gives *Evangeliorum*: the later have *Evangelistarum*, which with *observantia* is scarcely intelligible. Compare S. August, Expos. in Psalm lxxxvi. Non solum ergo illi duodecim (sc. Apostoli) et Apostolus Paulus, sed quotquot judicaturi sunt, propter significationem universitatis ad sedes duodenas pertinent...partes enim mundi quatuor sunt, Oriens, Occicens, Aquilo, et Meridies. Istæ quatuor partes assidue inveniuntur in Scripturis. Ab istis quatuor ventus, sicut dixit Dominus in Evangelio vocatur Ecclesia. Quomodo vocatur? Undique in Trinitate vocatur. Quatuor ergo ter ducta duodecim inveniuntur. See also S. Isitore, Alleg. in S. S.: folio 353, C. D.

32. Psalm xxx (*Exaltabo Te*), 5. These symbols, however, were not at first definitely settled, and as we are informed by S. Austin, the lion was sometimes given to S. Matthew and the angel and or man, to S. Mark. The reasons of the appropriation of the various symbols are beautifully expressed in a hymn quoted in the Camden's Society's 'Illustrations of Monumental Brasses,' Part I, p. 30.

33. This passage is very obscure. Durandus's words are, *quasi quatuor evangelistorum sententias*. We cannot but think that the two sentences have been misplaced. The sense is then plain. Christ is also signified by the ox—as containing in Himself the Law and the Gospel—and accomplishing that which is written of Him by the four Evangelists, *e. g.* His promises of the descent of the Holy Ghost, of being always with His Church, etc. S. Peter Chrysologus, Sermo v. de Christo, Hic est *Vitulus*, qui in Epulam nostram quotidie, et jugiter immolatur.

34. S. Mark is painted with a contracted brow, a large nose, fair eyes, bald, a long beard, fair complexion, of middle age, with a few grey hairs. Durand. vii, 44, 4.

35. S. John i, 1.

36. Psalm ciii (*Benedic, anima mea*), 5.

37. Durandus, book vii, 44. 'S. Matthew is signified by a man, because his Gospel is principally occupied concerning the humanity of Christ: whence his history beginneth from his human pedigree. S. Mark by a lion, which roareth in the desert: for he chiefly describeth the Resurrection: whence his Gospel is read on Easter day. But the lion is said to rouse his whelps on the third day after their birth. His Gospel beginneth, 'The voice of one crying in the wilderness.' S. Luke by the ox, an animal fit for sacrifice: because he dwelleth on the Passion of Christ. S. John by the eagle, because he soareth to the Divinity of Christ, while the others walk with their Lord on earth. The Evangelists be likewise set forth by the four rivers of Paradise: John by Pison; Matthew by Gihon; Luke by Euphrates; Mark by Tigris:—as is clearly proved by Innocent III, in a certain sermon on the Evangelists.'—We may add, that the finest representation of the evangelistic symbols with which we are acquainted in this country, occurs in the chancel of Oxted church, Surrey.

38. S. Matthew xxv, 31.

39. S. Bartholomew is represented with black and grizzled hair, fair complexion, large eyes, straight nose, long beard, few grey hairs, moderate height, with a high white neck, clothed in purple, with a white pall, having purple gems at each angle. Durand. vii, 25, 2.

S. Andrew had a dark complexion, long beard, moderate height. This is therefore said, that ye may know how he ought to be painted: which should be known of the other apostles and saints. Durand. vii, 38, 1.

40. Ephes. iv, 11.

41. Apocalypse v, 2.

42. S. John viii, 12.

43. S. John xiv, 6.

44. Psalm xcii, 12.

45. This explanation differs from that usually received: namely, that the righteous flourishes best in adversity: as the palm-tree grows fastest when loaded with weights.

46. So in the beautiful hymn at Lauds in the commemoration of a virgin martyr, of the Parisian Breviary:

> Liliis Sponsus recubat, rosisque;
> Tu, tuo semper bene fida Sponso
> Et rosas Martyr, simul et dedisti
> *Lilia Virgo.*

47. S. Matthew xxv, 1.

48. This is undoubtedly a mistake: the sword represents in this case, as in others, the instrument of martyrdom.

49. Exodus xxviii, 22.

50. Canticles iii, 11.

51. Psalm viii (*Domine Dominus*), 5.

52. Wisdom v, 16.

53. Psalm v (*Verba mea*), 12.

54. See Appendix I.

55. This does not appear to have prevailed in England. The nearest contemporary effigy of a saint which we have observed in stained glass, is that of S. Thomas, of Hereford, in the church of Cothelstone, Somersetshire. Here the glory is, as usual, of the circular form. As also in the fresco of the martyrdom of S. Thomas of Canterbury, in Preston church, Sussex, which is nearly contemporary. (See Appendix I.)

56. This refers to the account given by Paulus Diaconus of the visible effulgence which surrounded the head of this great doctor when he was dictating his works.

57. 'A monk named Constantine set before the prince those judgments of God which are in all the world, and the retribution of the life to come: his discourse powerfully affected the heathen monarch (Vladimir, afterwards, S. Vladimir); and this was particularly the case when the monk pointed out to him on an icon, which represented the Last Judgment, the different lot of the good and the wicked. "Good to those on the right hand—woe to those on the left," exclaimed Vladimir, deeply affected.'—Mouravieff's 'Hist. of the Russian Church,' p. 11. On which his translator, the Rev. R. W. Blackmore, sensibly remarks, 'Whatever may be the right view of the abstract question respecting icons, and the showing outward respect to them, the Russians at least cannot reasonably be blamed for revering a usage which was made the means, in part at least, of so blessed a result as the conversion of the great Prince Vladimir, the Constantine of their church and nation.'

58. This flower work is excessively common in Norman churches: that of S. Sepulchre's, at Cambridge, was a notable example of it.

59. I Corinth. xii, 8.

60. These are often to be found round Norman doors: as in that of S. Laurence, at York, and Egleton, Rutland.

61. A false reading, of course; yet not without its appropriate sense—the power of *adding* any ornamental circumstance to the main subject.

62. *Ecclesiæ*: here undoubtedly the nave: as often *church* is so used in our prayer-book.

63. Psalm cxxxii (*Domine, memento*), 8.

64. S. Matthew xxiii, 5.

65. Ais, Vigilantium, qui κατ' Ἀντίφρασιν hoc vocatur nomine (nam Dormitantius rectius diceretur), os fœtidum rursum aperire, et putorem spurcissimum contra sanctorum martyrum proferre relliquias, et nos, qui eas suscepimus, appellare *cinerarios*.—S. Hieron, in Epp. See also the 'Church of the Fathers,' 2nd ed. chapter xv.

66. This use of *two* candlesticks is very remarkable: as giving fresh authority to the custom of the English Church.

67. S. Luke ii, 10.

68. Genesis xvii, 17, 19.

69. Isaiah lx, 1.

70. Ephesians v, 8.

71. Numbers xxiv, 7.

72. Leviticus xxvi, 10.

73. S. Matthew xiii, 52.

74. S. Matthew v, 15.

75. Ephesians ii, 14.

76. Exodus xxvii, 4.

77. I Corinth. xiii, 13.

78. S. John viii, 59.

79. St. Matthew xiii, 11.

80. Exodus xxxiv, 33.

81. 2 Corinth. iii, 15.

82. There is much difficulty in this passage. We conceive that Durandus while writing it had in his mind's eye the arrangement of many of the Basilican churches, in which

the choir was raised over the crypt (called Confessio, or Martyrium), in which the ashes of the saints were laid, and was detached from the nave by two flights of steps, one on each side of the descent to this undercroft. In this case the *appodiatio* would mean the elevation of the choir, itself considered as a sufficient distinction from the nave. The usual representations of Basilican churches, however, always show some rails, or cancelli, besides this *appodiation.* The learned Father Thiers devotes the third section of his 'Dissertation sur la Clôture du Chœur des Eglises' to the consideration of this passage. 'Guillaume Durand, Evêque de Mande, assure que dans la Primitive Eglise, le chœur etait séparé de la Nef par une *muraille d'appui*, afin que le peuple voïant la Clergé chanter les louanges de Dieu en fût édifié. Mais comme il parle d'un fait beaucoup éloigné de son temps, et qui n'est attache par aucun ancien auteur, je ne pense pas que l'on doïve faire grande fonds sur son temoignage.' We suspect that Thiers is wrong in construing *appodiatio* by *muraille d'appui* : the latter would well express the real Basilican arrangement, with which the translator was probably acquainted. Durandus, therefore, is wrong in his fact; and Thiers wrong in his understanding of Durandus, as well as in the theory stated in the next section, that 'Depuis Constantin le chœur de quelques Eglises etoit distingué de la Nef par de tapisseries ou des voiles.' For he grounds this chiefly on the next assertion of Durandus about the use of curtains, 'hoc tempore. vers la fin du 13 siècle.' If we did not know from facts that before this time roodscreens were in ordinary use, the words of Durandus *velum aut murus* would show us that he means the *wall* to be taken metaphorically for a *veil.* And so Thiers may have seen, since he concludes his section thus—'Mais peut être que Theodoret parle des tapisseries et Durand des voiles qui convroient la Clôture du Chœur par le dedans, et que sous ces tapisseries et ces voiles il y avait une veritable clôture de balustres, ou de murailles pleines.'

83. Psalm cxix (*Beati immaculati*), 37.

84. 3 Kings iv, 20.

85. For an explanation of the whole Catholic system of feasts, double, semi-double, and simple, the reader is referred to the *Tracts for the Times*, vol. iii.

86. S. Burchardus of Worms flourished in 1025: and is not to be confounded with John Burchardus, who wrote an explanation of the Mass for the use of the Venetian Church, which was published in 1559.

87. In accordance with this feeling, the first Psalm at the second vespers of the nativity in the Benedictine Breviary is the *De profundis*.

88. Philip. ii, 7.

89. Philip. ii, 7.

90. Psalm xlv (*Eructavit*), 6.

91. Cantic. i, 5.

92. The bishop probably refers to Psalm xvi (*Conserva me*), 6. The words in reality spoken by David are understood by him as if spoken by the Almighty.

93. Psalm xxvi (*Judica me*), 8.

94. Job xxxix, 14.

95. Perhaps this custom was introduced by the Crusaders. 'As the ostrich is good for food, so, it seems, are its eggs: to say nothing of their being objects of attention, as being used much in the East by way of ornament; for they are hung up in their places of public worship, along with many lamps.' Harmer's 'Observations,' vol. iv, p. 336, who refers to Pococke's 'Travels,' vol. I, p. 31, and imagines that Dr Chandler, in his travels in Asia Minor, was mistaken when he supposed that the Turkish Mosque of Magnesia was ornamented with lamps pendent from the ceiling intermixed with balls of polished ivory, p.

267. Ostrich eggs might easily be mistaken for ivory balls. The following passage from De Moleon is curious: 'At the conclusion of matins,' he says, speaking of the rites of S. Maurice at Angers on Easter Day, 'two chaplains take their place behind the altar curtains. Two corbeliers (*Cubiculares*) in dalmatics, amices, and *mitallæ*, with gloves on their hands, present themselves before the altar. The chaplains chant, *Quem quæritis?* The corbeliers representing the Maries, reply, Jesum *Nazarenum Crucifixum*. The others answer, *Resurrexit, non est hic*. The corbeliers take from the altar *two* ostrich eggs wrapped in silk, and go forth, chanting, *Alleluia resurrexit* Dominus, *resurrexit Leo Fortis,* Chrisus, *Filius* Dei.'—Voyag. Lit. p. 98.

96. S. Luke xxii, 61.

97. See Martene, Tom. IV, ii, 9; the *Ducretum*, fol. 395.

98. 'A. D. 874, Vid. Concil. Coll. Reg. Tom. I. p. 288.' See also P. Tunoc, iv, Ep. Ad Otton. Carel. Xiii *Hardouin* vii, 365.

99. Jeremiah li, 7.

100. Psalm lxxv (*Confitebimur*), 8.

101. Psalm cxvi (*Dilexi*), 13.

102. S. Matthew x, 22.

103. S. Matthew xxvi, 27.

104. Coloss. ii, 3.

105. S. Matthew viii, 17.

106. S. Matthew xxvi, 9.

107. A. D. 535. Decret. viii. See also the Council of Tribur. A. D. 1036.

108. Daniel v, 1.

109. 'A. D. 524, Concil. Coll. Reg. Tom XI, p. 24.'

THE SYMBOLISM OF CHURCHES: CHAPTER IV: OF BELLS

1. See the account of the consecration of several churches in the island of Guernsey, taken from the Black Book of the Diocese of Contances, in a paper by the Rev. W. C. Lukis, B. A., Trinity College, published in the First Part of the Transactions of the Cambridge Camden Society.

2. Psalm xcii (*Bonum est confiteri*), 2.

3. Exodus xxviii, 35.

4. I Cor. xiii, 1.

5. Ezekiel iii, 8.

6. I Corinthians ix, 27.

7. Psalm l (*Deus deorum*), 16.

8. The passage is very unintelligible in the original, and is probably corrupted or transposed.

9. Gal. vi, 14. *Cavilla* is thus explained by Belethus. Expl. Divin. Off. xxiv. Cavilla, sic enim ferrum illud pensile vocat, quod Græci rectius ῥόπαλον nominant, cujus pulsu campana sonum reddit.

10. This appears to be a reference to 2 Cor. v, 13.

11. The reader will scarcely need reminding that the day is canonically divided into two parts of twelve hours each, beginning at six o'clock respectively. Prime therefore is at our six a.m., tierce at nine, sexts at twelve, nones at three p.m., vespers at six p.m., and compline at bedtime.

Hæc sunt septenis propter quæ psallimus horis
Matutina ligat Christum, qui crimina purgat:

Prima replet sputis; causam dat *Tertia* Mortis:
Sexta Cruci nectit: latus Ejus *Nona* bipertit:
Vespera deponit: tumulo *Completa* reponit.

Which may thus be translated;

At *matins* bound: at *prime* revil'd: condemn'd to death at *tierce*:
Nail'd to the cross at *sexts*: at *nones* His blessed side they pierce:
They take him down at *vesper*-tide; in grave at *compline* lay
Who thenceforth bids His Church to keep her sevenfold hours alway.

The twelve hours of the night are divided into three nocturns, which may be supposed to be said at twelve, two, and four, and are immediately followed by lauds at five. Nocturns and lauds (together called matins), with the six hours above-mentioned, make the seven canonical hours. On this subject we can but refer our readers to the extremely beautiful fifth book of Durandus, and particularly his first chapter, in which all the pregnant symbolism of the canonical hours is set forth. Hugo de Sancto Victore has briefly touched upon the same in the third chapter of the *In Speculum Ecclesiæ*, but nearly the whole of his account is contained in Durandus. See also S. Isidore 'De Eccles. Offic.' lib. I, cap. xix—xxiii; and Belethus whose account is valuable for its conciseness. 'Explic. Divin. Offic.' Caps. xxi—xxix.

The twelve ringings mentioned in the text as being in 'the twelve hours of the *day*' are thus to be made out. At prime, one; at tierce, three; at sexts, three; at nones, three; at vespers, one (the ringing 'many times' being only thus accounted); and at the last hour, one; in whole twelve. Hugo de S. Victor has a passage almost identical with this. 'The bells be also rung twelve times. At prime, once, and again at the last hour once; because all things be from One God, and the Same will be All in All. But at tierce, three times for the second, third, and fourth hours; and so at sexts, for three hours, namely, the seventh, eighth, and ninth; but at vespers many times, because in the time of grace the preaching of the Apostles was multiplied. Also at matins oftentimes, because we should often exclaim, 'Arise, thou that sleepest.' It will be observed that this passage is corrupt, nones being omitted, and its three hours given to sexts. Matins also, as in the text, are belonging to the twelve hours of the *night*.

12. Ephesians v, 14.

13. *Squilla* is properly a *sea onion*. We conceive that the sort of bell here meant is a kind of hand-bell, formed out of a hollow ball of metal, furnished with a slit for the sound, and with a loose pellet inside. This answers to the squilla in shape and utters a very shrill sound. We find below that it was used chiefly in the refectory. So in a note to Martener vol iv, p. 32, we read 'ad gratiarum actionem Sacrista sciliam (the other form of squillam) pulsabat. Cons. S. Benigni, cap. 9. Fratribus exeuntibus de prandio sive de cœna scillam pulsare non negligat Hebdomadarius Sacrista.'

14. It is to be remarked that throughout this chapter there is no allusion to ringing the bells by raising them and causing them to revolve on axes as practised in England. This and the beautiful science of bell-ringing consequent on it are peculiar to ourselves. The method of sounding the bells here understood is by a hammer acting on the rim, or by pulling the clapper, as is used with us for chimes, and where the bell frame is weak. This accounts for the much larger bells which are found abroad, and which were never meant to be poised and swung. Owing to the above difference between the Continental and English methods of bell-ringing, it is not easy to express the difference between *simpulsare*, *compulsare*, and *depulsare*.

Depulsare is to ring by tying a rope to the clapper of a bell, and pulling the rope to and fro: we have accordingly translated it, to *chant a bell.*

Simpulsare is to ring by tying a rope to the hammer, and pulling it back; this we have translated *to toll.* Tolling is of course performed by swinging the bell round: but as there is no English word which expresses *simpulsare*, we thought it better to use an old term in a new sense, than to coin a new one.

Compulsare is to do several bells what *depulsare* is to do to one: and we have translated it to *chime.*

Pulsare we have translated *to ring.*

It may be worthy of remark, how completely the ringing of the bells is here considered a part of the priest's office.

15. In Book V, chapter iii, 'of Nocturns,' Durandus says, 'When the nocturns be finished, the bells be rung and the *Te Deum laudamus* is chanted with uplifted voice, to denote that the Church doth openly and wonderfully laud God in the time of grace, and to show that if by good works we answer rightly to holy doctrine, we shall attain to singing heavenly praises in concert with the angels. The chant also is then made with a loud voice, to signify the joy of the woman at finding the lost 'piece of silver.' And the versicle *Day by day we magnify Thee*, and the following, be chanted still more loudly to set forth the gratulations of the neighbours over the finding of the piece of silver: and the ringing of the bells representeth the calling together of the neighbours. In some churches also the candles be lighted, because the woman also 'lighted a candle and sought diligently till she found it.' This also signifieth that the Church Catholic is drawn by Christ out of hell. And the hymn itself representeth the future joy and gladness, which the Church resting from her labours shall attain in the day of judgment.' Hugo de S. Victore, and Belethus agree as to this ringing of the bells at matins: a practice of which perhaps we may find the shadow in our own use in many places of ringing the bells at eight o'clock on Sunday mornings, to which day our services are now chiefly confined.

16. For an account of the 'passing-bell,' and the authority for its right use among ourselves, the reader is referred to Bp. Montague's 'Articles of Inquiry.' Camb. 1841, pp. 76, 116. It is to be observed that the bells are here said to be rung, not *tolled*, as is generally the case now. Many will remember a beautiful passage upon this custom in one of the Rev. F. E. Paget's 'Tales of the Village.' The practice of their distinguishing the sex of the dying person is still in most places retained.

17. '*Wherefore the second day had no benediction.*' It will be observed that of this day only it is not said expressly that 'God saw that it was good.' We give a chapter of Hugo S. Victore upon this question:

'But it is admirable wherefore God did not see the works of the second day that they were good: since in each other day He is said to have seen them, and that they were good. For either it was not His work, and so not good; or if it were His work, it was good. But if it was good, it was also His work: and then He saw it was good, Who could not be ignorant what it was, whether good or bad. Wherefore then is it not said here as elsewhere "God saw that it was good"? For if this be said elsewhere only because the work was made, why ought it not also to be said here since it was made? Perhaps because *dual* is the sign of division; since it first recedeth from *unity*: and so here we perceive some sacrament. Thus the works of the second day be not praised, not because they were not good, but because they were signs of evil. For God made His first works "and behold they were all very good:" in the which neither was corruption present, nor perfection absent. But afterwards cometh the devil and man, and they also made their works: and these second works came after the first; the evil after the good: and God was unwilling to behold these works because they were evil; but beholding them by His wisdom, He disapproved them by His judgment.' 'De Sacramentis,' Lib. i, Pars I, cap. xx. S. Isodore (Sentent. I, xx de Mundo) does not allude to this, nor S. Augustin upon Genesis.

18. 'The bells be rung in processions. For as an earthly monarch hath in his army royal insignia, namely trumpets and banners; so Christ the Eternal King hath in His Church Militant bells for trumpets, and crosses for banners. Thus the ringing of the bells doth signify the Prophets, who foretold the advent of Christ.' Durandus, book iv, chapter 6, 'Of the priest's approach to the altars,' sec. 19. The same idea is applied by Belethus to the matin bells in his 24th chapter.

19. See note 1 to this chapter.

20. See Appendix.

21. Ezekiel iii, 26.

22. Durandus, in his fourth book, chapter xxxiv, *'Of the Sanctus*,' says, 'Moreover in this concert of angels and men, the organs do from time to time add their harmony: the which was introduced by David and Solomon, who did cause hymns to be sung at the sacrifice of the Lord, with the concert of organs and other instruments of music, and the people also to join in chorus.'

SYMBOLISM: CHAPTER V: OF CEMETERIES, ETC

1. It has been thought right to give a few of the bishop's derivations, lest his translators should be accused of concealing a circumstance which may weaken, with some, his testimony on other points (though, as we have before shown, most unjustly): it has not, however, been thought necessary to follow him through all his names of a cemetery: since to do so would be a mere waste of the reader's time.

2. Genesis xxiii, 9: 'We take this word Machpelah for a proper name, as many others do: but the Talmudists generally think it to have been a double cave, as the lxx also, with the vulgar Latin, understand it. Yet they cannot agree in what sense it was so: whether they went through one cave into another, or there was one above the other.'—Bishop Patrick, s. l.

3. One might almost have thought that this is a false reading for Leah and Rebecca. For the common tradition was that Adam and Eve were buried in Mount Calvary: so that where the first Adam fell before death, the second Adam triumphed over death. And the bishop speaks below of three patriarchs, and their three wives buried in Machpelah: which is at variance with the text as it stands: but would agree with the proposed emendation.

Yet S. Isidore says, 'De morte Abrahæ,' fol. 295: 'Sepultusque est in spelunca duplici: in cujus interiore parte Adam esse positum traditio Hebræorum testatur.' S. Victor upon Spelunca duplex: 'Domus quædam fuit subterranea, in qua erat solarium, et multi fuerant sepulti, in ea et diversis foveis et subter et supra:' and in another place, 'Spelunca in qua est sepulta spiritualem designat vitam, quæ recte duplex vocatur; propter bonam actionem et contemplationem.'

4. A similar story has been parodied in the 'Ingoldsby Legends': a work which for irreverence and profanity has hardly an equal. Disgraceful as it would be to any author, it is trebly so, if (as it is said) that author is a clergyman.

5. *Sub propriis podiis*. For some account of the curious word *podium*, whence *pew* or *pue* is derived, see the Cambridge Camden Society's 'History of Pews' (or the 'Supplement,' pp. 6, 7).

6. Tobit xiv, 10.

THE SYMBOLISM OF CHURCHES: CHAPTER VI: OF THE DEDICATION OF A CHURCH

1. Appendix H.
2. Exodus xxx, 23-34.
3. I Kings iii, 6.
4. Daniel iii, 2.
5. Book iii, ch. I.
6. S. John i, 17.
7. 'The solemnities of the consecration of churches and of priests ought to be celebrated year by year, after the example of our Lord Himself, Who at the feast of the Dedication of the Temple did set us a pattern of this in that He celebrated this festival with the rest of the people; as it is written in S. John, "And it was at Jerusalem the feast of the Dedication, and it was winter and Jesus walked in the Temple in Solomon's porch." Felix Papa in 'Epist. Ad Episc. Per divers. Provincias', cap. i.
8. The editors have not been able to find any other account of this legend.
9. S. John, xvii, 5.
10. Psalm cxvii (*Nisi Dominus*), 1.
11. I Kings viii, 30.
12. See chapter i, 4.
13. See the Appendix on the 'Dedication of a Church.'
14. 'Pope Boniface the Fourth did consecrate to the most Blessed Virgin and All Saints the famous monument of Agrippa, the Pantheon, having purified it from the base herd of vain gods.' Ciampini IV, vi, 55. This is now called Santa Maria Rotonda. Doard.
15. S. John iii, 5.
16. S. Mark ix, 50.
17. S. Mark v, 13.
18. Isaiah xi, 4.
19. Ps. ix (*Confitebor tibi*), 13, 14.
20. Ps. cxviii (*Confitemini Domino*), 19, 20.
21. Ps. xxiv (*Domini est terra*), 'Attollite portas principes vestras.'
22. This hymn, by S. Gregory, is used in the office of matins in the Roman Breviary.
23. S. John, xvii.
24. We understand this to mean that the cross described in the church is a saltire, or S. Andrew's Cross, and not a plain one. Upon this again consult the Appendix.
25. S. Matt. xxviii, 19.
26. Psalm lxviii (*Exsurgat Deus*), v, 5.
27. Compare the hymn, *Vexilla Regis prodeunt*.
28. Genesis xxviii.
29. Cant. viii, 6.
30. I Cor. ii, 2.
31. This passage is obscure. A confession or martyrium was built over the place of S. Peter's martyrdom in the earliest times, and is now covered by the Vatican. See Ciampini de Vaticana Basilica. The expression probably means, in honour of the martyrdom.
32. Psalm li (*Miserere mei*), 7.
33. Levit. xv, 31
34. Psalm lxxix (*Deus, venerunt*), 1.
35. Some of our readers may not know that *reconciliation* is the technical term for the restoring a desecrated church to a state fit for the performance of the divine offices.

36. The editors have ventured to make a few omissions in this and some of the following sections.

37. Malachi ii, 2.

THE SYMBOLISM OF CHURCHES: CHAPTER VII: OF THE CONSECRATION OF AN ALTAR

1. Genesis viii.

2. S. Luke xxii, 19.

3. Genesis xii.

4. Eccles. xlvii, 9.

5. The word *horn* appears to be used simply for *corner*, evidently with reference to the altar of the temple, which had raised projections, or horns at its angles.

6. We shall use the word *table* to denote the *mensa* or upper surface of the altar, on which the chief part of the ceremonies of consecration were performed.

7. This passage is obscure, and receives no light from other ritualists who have not spoken much on the consecration of altars. From the 25 of the chapter we apprehend that this slab, or cover of the sepulchre, was marked with a cross of chrism before it was fitted on to the cavity.

8. S. John xv, 5.

9. Tobit xiii, 18.

10. Jonah iii, 6.

11. Psalm cii (*Domine exaudi*), 9.

12. Genesis xviii, 27.

13. S. John vii, 38, 39.

14. S. John iii, 5.

15. Genesis i, 2.

16. S. Mark i, 4.

17. 'There be four kinds of holy water, one, by which is made the judgment of expurgation, which is no longer used; a second, which doth sanctify in the consecration of a church or an altar; a third, with which aspersions be made in the church; and a fourth, the water of baptism.'—Durandus, Lib. IV, iv, 10.

18. The *tables*, or upper slabs of the altar, were inscribed with five crosses, one at each corner and one in the middle: as are also the altar stones which are found in the middle of the frightful wooden altars abroad at this day. See an interesting list of altar slabs in the 'Few Hints' of the Cambridge Camden Society.

19. Cant. 5, 7.

20. 2 Cor. vi, 16.

21. Heb. xiii, 10.

22. Psalm li (*Miserere mei Deus*), 17.

23. Isaiah lv, 1.

24. Psalm cxi (*Confiteor tibi*), 10.

25. I Corinthians x, 4.

26. S. Matthew xxi, 13.

27. Psalm xxii (*Deus Deus meus*), 22.

28. Exodus xxix, 12.

29. See chapter ii.

30. Romans ii, 13.

31. I Corinthians xi, 1.

32. I Kings viii, 2, 6, 7.

33. The Venice edition of 1609 reads *Apostoli* here.
34. I Kings, viii.
35. Romans i, 17.
36. Hebrews xi, 6.
37. See above, section 4, note 7.
38. I S. Peter iv, 8.
39. Romans v, 5.
40. S. Matthew xvi, 18.
41. Wisdom xv, 3.
42. Jeremiah ix, 24.
43. Ephesians ii, 20.
44. Psalm cxviii (*Confitemini Domino*), 22.
45. S. Luke, xix, 14.
46. Philippians ii, 10.
47. S. Matthew v, 44.
48. Psalm xlv (*Eructavit cor meum*), 8.
49. Exodus xxvii, 1, etc.
50. The same examples are briefly adduced in the notes to the Decretal. Ciampini describes the wooden altar of the Lateran , and mentions its numerous escapes from fire. It was made of firewood, because 'abies non cedit vermibus unquam, nec putret facile.' See also Stephen Durantus, *De Rit. Ecc. Cathol.* Lib. I, xv, 3, quoting from De Turrecremata, about the Lateran altar, and generally about the subject of this chapter.
51. According to the Golden Legend, S. Mary Magdalene, with other saints, amongst whom was S. Lazarus, were placed by the Jews in a ship which was borne by the sea to Marseilles. The country was converted, and S. Lazarus became the first bishop. The people of Vezelay, in Burgundy, also claimed the honour of possessing the relics of S. Mary Magdalene. Durandus, a native of Provence, gives it to the latter country. This curious passage of our author seems to have been overlooked by some who have attempted to adjust the dispute.
52. Genesis xxviii, 18.
53. Isaiah ii, 3.
54. Isaiah x, 27.
55. I Corinthians xii, 8.
56. Psalm xlv (*Eructavit cor meum*), 8.
57. S. Matthew vi, 17.
58. Psalm cxlv (*Exaltabo te Deus*), 9.
59. S. James ii, 13.
60. Job xix, 21.
61. Eccles. xviii, 12—*Vulgate.*
62. Jeremiah viii, 6.
63. Isaiah vi, 5—*Vulgate.*
64. S. Luke xvii, 10.
65. Eccles. xxx, 24—*Vulgate.*
66. Psalm cxii (*Beatus vir*), 5.
67. S. Matthew v, 16.
68. 2 Corinthians i, 12.
69. S. Matthew xxv, 20.
70. Hebrews i, 9.

71. Genesis xxvii, 27.
72. 2 Corinthians ii, 15.
73. Romans viii, 35.
74. S. Matthew xx, 34.
75. Wisdom iii, 7.
76. Psalm li (*Miserere mei Deus*), 17.
77. The blessed Bernard saith, My brethren, let us in sacrificing add the sacrifice of praise unto our words, let us add sense to sense, affection unto affection, exaltation unto exaltation, maturity unto maturity, and humility unto humility. Wherefore, he that is about to celebrate must offer unto the Highest that sacrifice of which the Psalmist speaketh 'The sacrifices of God are a troubled spirit.' And again, 'Offer unto God the sacrifice of thanksgiving.' And the Apostle, 'Present your bodies a living sacrifice holy acceptable unto God which is your reasonable service, mortifying upon the altar of your heart your members which are upon the earth; fornication, uncleanness, inordinate affection, evil concupiscence, and covetousness, which is idolatry'; in order to sacrifice yourselves with a pure heart and chaste body unto God.—Proeme lib. iv,. 17.
78. Quoted also in the Decretal *De Consecrat. Distinct. I.*

THE SYMBOLISM OF CHURCHES: CHAPTER VIII: OF CONSECRATION AND UNCTIONS

1. Exodus xxx, 22.
2. S. James v, 14.
3. I S. John ii, 27.
4. See Acts xxviii, 8.
5. It has not been thought necessary to translate the passages referred to.
6. I S. Peter ii, 9.
7. Habakkuk ii, 4.
8. Romans x, 10.
9. S. James ii, 26.
10. Gal. v, 6.
11. This clause does not occur in the *Princeps* Edition.
12. I S. Peter iii, 15.
13. Ecclesiasticus ii, 14.
14. The passage referred to speaks of the diverse graces conferred by the several unctions, and does not illustrate our more particular object.
15. 'For Christ is named of *chrism*, and meaneth the Anointed One. For it was commanded the Jews to make a holy unguent for such as were called unto the priesthood or the kingdom: and as now the vestment of purple is unto kings the mark of kingly power, so upon these did the unction with sacred unguent bestow the name and kingly power: and hence they were called Christi, from chrism, which is unction. For *chrisma* in Greek is *unctio* in Latin. And this unction did aptly give this name unto our Lord, because He was anointed of the Father by the Spirit, as is said in the Acts of the Apostles, "Against Thy Holy Child Jesus, Whom Thou hast anointed, were they gathered together": not, that is, with visible oil, but with the gift of grace, which is denoted by the visible oil.' S. Isidore of Seville, *Orig.* vii, 2. See also *Orig.* vii, 4, and *De Off. Ecc.* i, 1.
16. 'Christians be named from Christ, and Christ from *chrism*, being *anointed*. For He was anointed by God from the beginning "with the oil of gladness above His fellows." In the Old Testament priests and kings be called *Christs* (or Anointed), because they were anointed with a temporal unction. As it is written, "Touch not my Christs" (*i.e.* mine

anointed). Wherefore, Christ is not a peculiar name of our Saviour, but is a common appellation of dignity. But the name Jesus is peculiar to the person of our Saviour alone, and was given Him, as the Evangelist doth testify by the angel, Gabriel, at the Conception, and by men at His Circumcision.'—Durand. *loco cit.* This will explain the reason, to many persons so puzzling, why it is only to the name of Jesus that our Church, after the Apostle, commands due obeisance to be made: and will reprove the erroneous, though pious, zeal which makes so many of the poor even now bow at the other names of our Blessed Lord.

17. S. Matthew xxiii, 4.

18. S. Sylvester was the contemporary of Constantine. *Circa* A. D. 325.

19. Our author mentions another heresy of the Arnaldistæ in the 19th section of the proeme of book iv. These heretics were the followers of Arnaldus de Brixio (of Bresse), a disciple of Abelard. His opinions were condemned in the second General Lateran Council, 1139.—*Baron. Sub. Anno.* tom. xviii. See also S. Bernard, *Epist.* 195.

20. It has not been judged necessary to translate the passages referred to, for the same reason as stated above in note 13.

21. See note 19.

22. Leviticus xi, 10.

23. 2 Corinthians i, 12.

24. Psalm xlv (*Eructavit cor meum*), 14.

25. 2 Corinthians ii, 15

26. 1 Timothy iii, 7.

27. There appears to be here some mystical reference to the coupling of the curtains of the tabernacle. See Exod. xxvi.

28. Apocalypse xxii, 17.

29. S. Matthew vi, 17.

30. Canticles v, 5.

31. Psalm cxxxiii (*Ecce quam bonum*), 2.

32. Isaiah lxi, 1.

33. Galatians vi, 10.

34. Proverbs xxxi, 20.

35. Eccesiasticus xiv, 15.

36. 2 Corinthians ii, 15.

37. 1 Kings xix, 15.

38. See Acts iv, 27, and Hebrews i, 9.

39. Ephesians v, 23.

40. Isaiah ix, 6.

41. 1 Samuel x, 24.

42. S. Matthew xxv.

43. Apocalypse xix, 14.

44. Philippians iii, 20.

45. S. James v, 20.

46. 1 S. Peter ii, 21.

47. The consecration of a bishop, in the which the Holy Ghost is present unto such as receive it worthily, is administered always on the Lord's day, and at the third hour. For bishops do obtain the office of apostles, unto whom the Holy Ghost was given on the Day of Pentecost and at the third hour. When a bishop is to be ordained, the suffragans of the province should assemble with their metropolitan, and two bishops place and hold a vol-

ume of the gospels above his head and neck, or upon his shoulders, one shedding the benediction over him, and the rest, such as are present, touching his head with their hands. This book is held above his head; first, that the Lord may confirm the gospel in his heart; secondly, that he may understand by this, unto what burthen and labour he is subjected: because everyone that is pre-eminent, that is, a prelate, is more troubled with griefs than rejoiced with honours; thirdly to denote that he ought not to be backward to carry with him everywhere the burthen of the preaching of the gospel; fourthly, to admonish him to submit himself more than ever to the yoke, and to obey the gospel.—*Rationale*, Book II, c. xi, 6.

48. Hebrews ix, 2.

49. S. James v, 24.

50. 'On this day also ashes are blessed, and scattered over the head in token of humiliation. "Dust thou art, and unto dust thou shalt return," was said unto Adam (Genesis iv). And Job "repented in dust and ashes" (Job xlii, 6). And the Lord saith, "In the house of Aphrah (marg. read dust) roll thyself in the dust" (Mic. I, 10). Also in Judith we read, "The children of Israel humbled themselves in fasting, and dust on their heads" (Chronicles iv). And Abraham saith, "Shall I speak unto the Lord, who am but dust and ashes?" (Genesis 18). And "Mordecai put on sackcloth with ashes" (Esther iv, 1). And "the daughters of Zion have cast ashes on their heads" (Samuel iii). Hence, we read in the Pontifical, penitents and the dying, in token of repentance and humility and that they are dust and ashes, do prostrate themselves in ashes and put on sackcloth—an use drawn from the Old Testament. For we read in Isaiah the fifty-eighth, that penitents do lie in sackcloth and ashes. And Hieremiah saith the same in the twenty-fifth chapter, "Wallow yourselves in the ashes, for the days are accomplished." Also in the third of Jonah, "The king of Nineveh put on sackcloth and sat in ashes." Also in the Lamentations, "The virgins of Jerusalem are clothed in sackcloth."'—*Rationale* vi, 28, 18.

51. Hebrews x, 1.

52. Exodus xxxix.

53. The history, use, and symbolism of the sacred vestments would themselves require a volume to be fully illustrated.

54. 'Observe that when a person in confirmaton is blessed on the forehead, and when salt, and water, and palls, and vestments, and the like be consecrated, the hands are held over them, because there is a certain virtue in consecrated hands, which is as it were stirred up when benediction is poured out over anything with the hands suspended in this way. Whence the Apostle admonishing his disciple Timothy, saith, "I put thee in remembrance that thou stir up the gift of God, which is in thee, by the laying on of my hands." So that devotion may be stirred up in the body by the suspension of hands, just as in the heart by the effect. For virtue existeth not only in animate things, but also in inanimate. Whence some do affirm that by the virtue of a church, if anyone entereth therein from devotion, his venial sins be forgiven. Again, the hands are thus held in cases of exorcism especially, as if the priest by the bodily act would put to flight and threaten the devil by the virtue of the consecration of his hands.'—Durandus ii, 9, 16.

55. This point is not sufficiently connected with our subject to need illustration.

THE SYMBOLISM OF CHURCHES: CHAPTER IX: OF THE SACRAMENTS OF THE CHURCH

1. The seventh part of the Canon of the Mass is, 'Likewise after supper He took the cup into His holy and venerated hands; and when He had given thanks, He blessed it and gave it to His disciples, saying, Take and drink ye all of this; for this is the chalice of My

blood, of the New and Everlasting Testament, *the mystery of faith*, which is shed for you and for many for the remission of sins: Do this as oft as ye shall drink it in remembrance of me.'—See Rationale iv. 42, 20.

2. The chapter referred to treats of holy baptism doctrinally, and does not therefore fall within the province of this volume.

3. What we call *Maunday Thursday*, from *Mandatum novum* ('A new commandment I give unto you,' etc.), which the Church of England retains as a Lesson for the day, is more properly called *The Cœna Domini*, or Lord's Supper, in remembrance (as Bishop Andrewes says) *of the mighty mystery of Thy holy body and precious blood, instituted on the evening of this day.*—See S. Isidore, *De Offic. Eccles.* I, 28. The chapter referred to (73 in the sixth book), shows that penitents were restored to communion on this day, and with what ceremonies.

4. These, besides their great length, are not required for the explication of our more immediate subject.

5. See note 4.

6. Bp. Cosins says that marriages are not to be solemnised from Advent Sunday, until eight days after (or the octave of) the Epiphany; from Septuagesima Sunday until eight days after Easter; and from Rogation Sunday until Trinity Sunday. Some of these being times of solemn fasting and abstinence, some of holy festivity and joy, both fit to be spent in such holy exercises, without other avocations. See his 'Devotions', republished by Messrs Rivington.

7. We are accustomed to celebrate only the manifestation of Christ to the Gentiles, on the Epiphany. But S. Isidore (*De Off. Ecc.* I, 26) gives two other objects of commemoration upon this day: viz. the baptism of our Lord, and his first miracle at the marriage in Cana. And so the hymn in the Breviary:

Ibant Magi, quam viderant, Stellam sequentes præviam;
Lumen requirunt lumine, Deum fatentur munere.
Lavacra puri gurgitis Cælestis Agnus attigit ;
Peccata quæ non detulit, Nos abluendo sustulit.
Novum genus potentiæ! Aquæ rubescunt hydriæ,
Vinumque jussa fundere Nutavit unda originem.

Our own Church, however, retains the old Gospel for the second Sunday after the Epiphany.

8. Martinmas is the 11th November. The forty days are not exactly made out between this and the Nativity.

9. See S. Paul 1 Corinthians vii, 5. The whole of this passaage is quoted from S. Isidore, who is, however, more circumstantial than Durandus, and much more elegant and intelligible in his language. The extreme corruption of the printed copies of our author may be exemplified by referring the reader to the original in S. Isidore.—*De Off. Eccles.* ii, 19. See also Hugo de S. Victore, *Exercit. Theol. Summ. Sent.*, Tract vii.

10. 1 Corinthians vi, 17.

11. S. John i, 14.

12. It is laid down that a widow on taking the vows is not veiled by the bishop, as is the case with a virgin. 'A priest,' Durandus continues, 'is prohibited from taking a part in second marriages and from giving the benediction to such as are twice married. But a widow taking the vows is married as it were twice, first to her late husband, and secondly unto Christ in her profession, wherefore the veil of consecration, or even of profession, is not given unto her, but she herself takes it from the altar. ... Yet in the Pontifical, accord-

ing to the Roman Order, we find the benediction of a widow professing continence, and also of her veil. For the Lord also comforted the widow of Serepta by the hand of Elias the prophet. And I have myself seen in the city (Rome, of course) the [Cardinal] Bishop of Ostia bless two widows among the virgins who took the vows' (Proeme II, c. 47).

THE SYMBOLISM OF CHURCHES: EPILOGUE TO THE WHOLE WORK

1. Book viii, chap. 14
2. Job xxxviii, 31. See the Proeme towards the beginning.
3. See the Preface.
4. S. James i, 17.
5. Wisdom ix, 17.
6. The passage seems corrupt: but the sense appears to be, 'reciting them, as testimonies in my favour, and not presuming to add my testimony to their worth.'

THE SYMBOLISM OF CHURCHES: APPENDIX A: CHANCELS

1. After the *Sanctus*, which, as we shall find, was performed with the full choir and the accompaniment of organs, came the secret, which embraced the whole *Canon of the Mass*, performed by the celebrant alone, and the celebration of the Holy Eucharist. 'It is called the secret because these things be hidden from us, since the nature of man can in no wise fully comprehend so great a mystery: for the denoting of which it is rightly performed secretly. To signify the same also, the priest when entering upon the secret is veiled as it were with the side curtains.' See other mystical reasons adduced in the remainder of this passage, Book IV, Chapter 35, and in Chapter 39 an account of the side curtains. Upon the use of these see also the *Dublin Review*, vol. x, p. 339.
2. See Leviticus xvi; Exodus xxviii, xxxix, and xl.

THE SYMBOLISM OF CHURCHES: APPENDIX B: ORIENTATION

1. S. John Lateran is an instance. We may observe that the reasons for the orientation of churches must have been very strong to have caused an universal disregard of an example thus set at the centre of Western Christianity.
2. S. Luke i, 79.
3. Malachi iv, 2.
4. Zechariah vi, 12.
5. Wisdom xvi, 28.
6. Jeremiah xxiii, 24.
7. Psalm cxxxix (*Domine probasti*), 7.
8. Malachi iv, 2.
9. S. John i, 9.
10. *Quatuor orationes*. We should probably read, *rationes*.
11. Genesis ii, 8.
12. Acts i, 11.
13. This section is in several places corrupt: for example—from Damascenus the quotation in the sixth head belongs properly to the seventh.

Our readers may perhaps be reminded of the anecdote of the good Earl of Derby (who, if the Reformed Church in England should ever have a calendar of her own, will assuredly be one of its martyrs), when on the scaffold. The church of Bolton was in sight: and the Earl requested that he might be allowed to kneel on the western side of the block, so that the last object on which his eyes were fixed might be God's house. His executioners showed their poor malice to the last, by denying him this wish.

THE SYMBOLISM OF CHURCHES: APPENDIX C: ON THE DESIGN, ETC.

1. As is well known, double staircases to rood lofts appear to have been almost as common in England as single ones: and there are sometimes, especially in Norfolk churches, two corresponding rood turrets.

2. S. Luke xvi, 16.

3. Canticles ii, 6.

4. S. Mark xvi, 5.

5. S. Luke vii, 37.

6. Micah iv, 2.

7. Jeremiah xxxi, 31.

8. Exodus xx, 24.

9. Canticles ii, 6.

10. Romans xi, 26.

11. Micah iv, 2.

12. Romans x, 15.

13. S. Matthew ix, 38.

14. Isaiah vi, 8, 9.

15. S. Matthew x, 7.

16. Psalm l (*Deus Deorum*), 16.

17. S. Matthew x, 10.

18. *Per dextram partem*. We are to imagine, in the whole of this description, the spectators supposed to face the altar. So in the fifteenth chapter of this book, the epistle is said to be read *in dextera parte*.

19. Psalm xxxvi (*dixit injustus*), 6.

20. S. Matthew x, 22.

21. Acts i, 1.

22. S. Matthew ii, 12.

23. Acts xiii, 46.

24. I Corinth. ix, 11.

25. I Corinth. ix,13.

26. S. Luke x, 7.

27. Deuteron. xxv, 4.

28. S. Matthew xi, 30.

29. Psalm lxviii (*Exurgat Deus*), 10.

30. Psalm cxix (*Beati immaculati*), 103

31. S. Matthew x, 41.

32. S. John xv,16.

33. Colos. iii, 17.

34. 2 Corinth. ii, 15.

35. Isaiah xi, 9.

36. S. Matthew v, 1.

37. Psalm xix (*Cœli enarrant*), 4.

38. Psalm lxxv (*Notus in Judea*), 1.

39. Psalm xviii (*Diligam Te*), 10.

40. Ezekiel xi, 19.

41. Isaiah xliii, 6

THE SYMBOLISM OF CHURCHES: APPENDIX E: ON THE FOUR COLOURS, ETC.

1. Lamentations iv, 7.

2. The bishop here confuses two passages, Apocal. iii, 4, and xiv, 4. Of the same subject Lævinus Torrentius says beautifully in his hymn on the Holy Innocents:

Ergo supremi parte cœli, lactea qua lucidum fulget via,
Qua picta dulci stillat uva nectare, et nectar exhalant rosæ,
Lœti coronis luditis, et insignium mixti puellarum choris
Sacrum canentes itis agnum candido quacunque præcedat pede.

3. A misquotation of the bishop's. The words are addressed to Job. Job xxxviii, 7.

4. That is, on the 27th of December, the day of his 'deposition': the other feast, kept in memory of his deliverance from the boiling oil, before the Latin gate, and therefore called *S. Joannes ante Portam Latinam*, is the 6th of May.

5. The 22nd of February.

6. Which are S. Stephen, the Holy Innocents, S. Thomas of Canterbury.

7. Isaiah xix, 3.

8. S. Luke i, 35.

9. Jeremiah i, 3

10. S. Luke i, 15.

11. Isaiah lx, 3.

12. A very harsh construction: but surely preferable to that by which the Blessed Virgin herself is spoken of as the promised light.

13. S. John xiii, 10.

14. S. Matthew xxviii, 3.

15. Acts i, 11.

16. 2 Corinthians ii, 11.

17. Canticles i, 15.

18. Apocalypse vii, 14.

19. Isaiah lxiii, 2.

20. Both retained by our Church. The former (May 3) instituted in commemoration of the discovery

21. Acts i, 1.

22. S. John xv, 13.

23. Apocalypse vii, 9.

24. This alludes to the history of the feast of all Saints. Pope Boneface obtained a grant of the Pantheon from the Emperor Phocas: and dedicated it in honour of S. Mary and All Martyrs. This was on the 11th of May: and the feast of All Martyrs was kept on that day under the title of *S. Maria ad Martyres*. S. John, having confessed before the Latin gate on the 6th, the feast was subsequently kept on that day. But Gregory IV transferred it to Nov. 1st, because the harvest was then gathered in: and because the feast of All Apostles being kept on May 1st, the other would answer to it half-yearly. *All Martyrs* occurs, in a solitary instance, as an English dedication: *All Apostles*, not to be found in this country, has been adopted in Germany.

25. Canticles I, 5.

26. Jeremiah xxi, 15; S. Matthew ii, 18.

27. Apocalypse vi, 9.

28. Palm Sunday.

29. This refers to the celebrated golden rose blessed by the Roman Pontiff on that day: and sent in token of approval to some Catholic prince. Some of our readers may remember that which was lately exhibited along with the golden altars of Basle.

30. Canticles iii, 6. But the quotation is not exact.

31. This passage seems very corrupt.

32. 'Whether there be any superstitious fasting on S. Mark's Day?' is a question which sometimes occurs in the Visitation Articles of Archbp. Parker and his contemporaries.

33. Isaiah liii, 5.

THE SYMBOLISM OF CHURCHES: APPENDIX H: ON THE DEDICATION OF A CHURCH

1. In the treatise of the Mart. Remigius, *De Dedicatione Ecclesiæ*, we have the following explanation of this singular custom: 'A thing which might appear puerile, unless it had been instituted by men, great in dignity, spiritual in life, apostolical in discipline. In all things of this kind, the Lord by His example hath gone before us: and what He hath done, remaineth unchangeable in His successors. What is understood by the alphabet save the beginnings and rudiments of sacred doctrine? Whence S. Paul, "Ye have need that one teach you again, which be the first principles of the oracles of God." Therefore the bishop writeth the alphabet, to signify that he teacheth the pure doctrine of the gospel. He writeth the alphabet twice, and that in the figure of a cross, to signify that the Passion of Christ is set forth by the gospel in its purity. He writeth it in the angles of the church, because by them be set forth the four corners of the world. He beginneth from the east, because the gospel began from the Jews.'

There is probably some reference to the Saviour's stooping down, and writing in the sand. We may also compare those singular and rare bells, in which the only inscription round the crown consists of the letters of the alphabet.

THE SACRED VESTMENTS

THE SACRED VESTMENTS: CHAPTER I: PROEME

1. Vide 'Epist. Stephani R. P.' ap. Baron. ad An. 260, n. 6; Hieron. *in c.* 44 *Ezechiel*: 'Religio diuina altarum habitum,' etc. Pelliccia thinks that anciently the Altar-dress was identical in shape with the ordinary civilian dress, which the clergy merely changed for a similar garb of better quality, when about to celebrate (Lib. II. i. 8). The Church's Vestments certainly seem to have become the peculiar dress of the clergy through growing obsolete among the laity. This is worthy of the consideration of those who condemn them as innovations.—Bingham dates the distinction from the beginning of the fourth century, on the ground that Constantine is said (Theod. lib. ii. c. 27) to have given a rich gold-embroidered Vestment to Macarius, Bishop of Jerusalem, to be worn by him when celebrating Baptism.

2. Gratian, Decretum, 'De Consecratione,' Distinctio I. c. xliii. ('Vestimenta'). Stephani Episc. Hilario (Epist. i. c. 5).

3. *v.* 19.

4. Louis I., called *le Débonnaire*, who reigned from 814 to 840 A.D. From the beginning of the sixth century right through the middle ages there were constant canons forbidding the gradually-increasing secularity and magnificence of the dress of the clergy; notably at the Second Council of Nice (A.D. 787), the Council of Aix (A.D. 816), etc.

5. Exodus xxviii, 2.

6. Durandus says this either (i.) on the authority of some tradition, or (ii.) by analogy from the heathen practice recorded in 2 Kings xxiii. 7, 'the houses where the women wove hangings for the grove.'

7. *v*. 10

8. V.1. *mysterium Incarnationis*.

9. S. Matthew viii. 17.

10. *Tapeta*: called in Old English 'tapets', 'coverlets', or 'pede cloaths' (Pugin).

11. *Succinctorium*, a sash, called also *succingulum*, *succincta*, and *praecinctorium*, formerly worn by all Bishops, but now by the Pope only. (Pugin.) See Ch. iv. of this work, note 4.

12. 2 Cor. x. 4.

13. *vv*. 13-17.

14. S. Matthew xxiii. 27.

15. From this point to the end of the Section Durandus is quoting, in a somewhat inverted manner, the words of the Pontificale. They occur in a prayer offered by the Consecrator ('De Consecratione Episcopi', xx.). See also Greg. Sacram., Muratori, Lit. Rom. Vet. ii. 357. The passage had existed, however, in the Gelasian form 100 years before S. Gregory (Murat. i. 625). In connection with the Pontificale, it may be interesting to state that Durandus himself wrote the MS. version of it at the Vatican Library, No. 4744.

16. Durandus says elsewhere: 'The Deacon, being about to read the Gospel, taketh off his Chasuble, and folding it in seemly manner, placeth it upon his left shoulder, and fasteneth it beneath his right arm, so that it shall fall from his left shoulder unto his right side after the manner of a Stole; and keepeth it in this wise bound upon him until the last Collect after the Communion, when he putteth it on again as before.' (*Rat. ii.* 'De Diacono.')

17. A small plate, generally of metal, was kissed by the Priest after the *Agnus Dei*, and then handed to the people, in token of the Kiss of Peace. But it is doubtful whether this was in common use so early as Durandus' time, as the first definite mention of it was in a Council held at Oxford in 1287, about the time of Durandus' appointment to the see of Mende. Doubtless he means the Kiss of Peace as given personally. See *Rat. iv.* 51 'De Pacis Osculo.'

18. The concluding words of Holy Mass—'Go, it is done.'

19. Durandus gives these as follows: to baptise, to preach, to celebrate Mass, to bind, and to loose; the nine peculiar to the Bishop, to ordain, to bless virgins, to consecrate Bishops, to lay on hands (confirm), to dedicate Churches, to degrade clerics, to call Synods, to consecrate the Chrism, and to consecrate vestments and vessels. (*Rat.* ii. 'De Episcopo.')

20. Ezek. xxviii. 13.

21. Pss. cxx.—cxxxiv.

22. Ps. cxxxii. 9.

23. S. Matthew v. 20.

24. S. Matthew xxxviii. 19.

25. Eccles. ix. 8.

26. Fur robes were worn of old in choir, as a protection against cold, especially in northern countries such as England; and hence the word *superpellicium* is found often in old English monuments.

27. 'Priests about to celebrate Mass shall not be without a Surplice (*vestis camisialis*) under their Albes' (Council of Cologne, A.D. 1260). So also the Canons of the Church of Liège, A.D. 1287. Durandus is one of the earliest writers who mention the Surplice, though it had been in use long before his time.

28. Ps. xxv. 21 (Vulgate).

29. *Pace* those who loudly boast the special antiquity of the Surplice, it seems certain that it was a modification of the Albe, made fuller and ampler, to enable it to be worn over the fur garments of which Durandus speaks; and that the very *rationale* of its existence was to be *full*, unlike its modern Anglican development. As late as 1339 a Constitution of Benedict XII orders that Surplices be 'large and ample.' We hear much of the 'beauty' and 'grace' of the close-fitting cathedral surplice. It is as ugly and ungainly as the girded Albe, its prototype, is dignified and beautiful.

30. 1 S. Peter iv. 8.

31. Gal. v. 24.

THE SACRED VESTMENTS: CHAPTER II: OF THE AMICE

1. The Amice (amictus), which is now put round the neck, is thought by some to have been originally a head-vestment. There was an old French custom of wearing it on the head at certain times of the year and in certain parts of Mass, and letting it fall down over the shoulders at others to signify reverence. To this day the Priest, in vesting for Mass, rests it on his head before letting it down over his shoulders. The strings which are fastened to its corners are crossed over the breast, passed behind the back, and tied before the breast. It is nowhere mentioned as a Vestment until the ninth century.

2. Exodus xxxviii. 30. See the last Chapter of this work, § 12.

3. Ephesians Vi. 17.

4. Martene tells us that the Amice was formerly put on over the Albe.

5. So Hugh of S. Victor, L. i. *Erudit. Theolog.* C.45, and Innocent III., Lib I, *De Myst. Missae*, c. 50.

6. Genesis xlix. 15.

7. 1 Cor. v. 8.

8. 2 Tim. ii. 3.

9. See Proeme, p. 15, *n*. 3.

10. So Fortunato, Archbishop of Trèves, L. ii. *De Divin. Offic.* c. 17

11. Rev. x. 1.

12. Isaiah xix. 1. Vulg. says *levem*, not *candidam*, as Durandus.

13. 1 Cor. xi. 3.

14. The Fanon or Orale, which (as Georgius tells us, Lib. I. c. xviii.) is a striped veil of four colours, put on by the Pope after the Girdle, and turned back over the head. After the Chasuble is put on, it is brought down over the shoulders and breast. Durandus gives a similar description of it in the chapter referred to.

15. Ps. lxxvi. 1.

16. *Ibid.* lx. 8.

17. *Ibid.* xcvii. 2.

18. S. Matthew xxvi. 68.

THE SACRED VESTMENTS: CHAPTER III: OF THE ALBE

1. Eccles. ix. 8.

2. Rev. xix. 8.

3. 'Comme elle [l'Aube] se blanchit dans l'eau, et avec des grands soins, cela nous marque que notre pureté nous vient de l'eau spirituelle, des larmes qu'une sainte pénitence nous fait couler de nos yeux' (*Explication du Breviaire et du Missel*, par M. Raymond Bonal, prêtre de Lyons, 1679). See Pugin under 'Albe'.

4. 1 Corinthians ix. 27.

5. So also had the Chasuble, which S. Isidore describes as 'casula, uestis cucullata'; and the Colobium, which was probably the prototype of the Tunicle; also the Cope, with most Vestments originally designed for outdoor use.

6. *Cf.* Rom. viii. 15.

7. Gal. v. 1.

8. These 'Apparels', as they are called, which the Albe has in common with its correlative the Amice, are very ancient. They formed part of the Vestment even in the old time when it was a civilian's dress, and were then usually purple (Vopisc. *in Aureliano*, c. 48). They were, and still are, sewn in round the sleeve-edges and the bottom of the skirts; were very various in their decoration, and usually angular in shape; and were beginning to be specially ornate and extensive at the time when Durandus wrote.

9. Ps. xlv. 10. All this is closely borrowed from Innocent III.

10. S. Luke xii. 35.

11. Durandus thus tells the story elsewhere:—'When he [S. Martin] was Archbishop of Tours, there came a poor and needy man unto him, begging for a coat. The Saint granted the hest, and sent his steward to buy one. The latter went into the market, and returned after a long while with a cheap cloak, which one might well have called a *paenula* (mantle) for it was *paene nulla*, next to nothing! The holy man bade show it to him; now it was very short, reaching but unto the knee, and the sleeves to the elbow; wherefore he took off his own cloak and gave it to the poor man, and himself put on this pauper garment. Not long after this, the Saint made him ready to say Mass; when, as he stood at the Altar and at the Preface, as is the wont of priests, uplifted his hands unto the Lord, the loose sleeves of the mantle aforesaid slipped back—for his arms were not much covered with flesh—and so let his arms bare. Whereupon there came miraculous bracelets of gold, and covered his bare arms in seemly manner; whereby it was made plain that the Holy Spirit had come down upon him to his comfort, as upon the Apostles at Pentecost. And hence he is not undeservedly called Peer of the Apostles, with whom we place him on a par in the Offices of the Church.' (*Rat.* L. vii. '*De beato Martino.*') His day (Nov. 11) is a double in the Roman Calendar.

12. Rom. viii. 24.

13. Col. iii. 9, 10, and Ephesians iv. 24.

14. S. Matthew xvii. 2, and S. Mark ix. 3.

15. 1 S. Peter ii. 22.

16. S. Luke xxiii. 11.

THE SACRED VESTMENTS: CHAPTER IV: OF THE ZONE, OR GIRDLE

1. See Exodus xxviii. 4, Vulg. 'Balteus' is allied with our word 'belt'. The Girdle, like most other Vestments, has dwindled in size. In early times it was larger, and more ornate; as Bishop Riculfus in his will bequeaths 'five girdles, one adorned with gold and precious stones, and four more with gold.' Girdles were used by the ancients as purses; hence their old Greek name καταθεσίςι—repositories. See Pelliccia, Lib. I. c. viii. 2. S. Chrysostom (Hom in Psal. 48; vol. v, 521) inveighs against luxury in dress, and espe-

cially against golden girdles. Which secular sumptuousness the Girdle preserved, long after it had become a Vestment of the Church.

2. S. Luke xii. 35.

3. Job xl. 16. It is also good to think of the Girdle as a type of continence because it is the means of keeping the skirts out of the mire.

4. 'In the Caeremoniale S.R.E., it is ordered that the Pope be vested with a Girdle having a Succinctorium, or sash, hanging down on the left side. . . . Pope Boniface was found in his tomb with a rochet girt about with a sash of leather, covered with red silk, like to a belt, with four cords of red silk hanging in front, which fastened the Girdle.' (Pugin, *Gloss. Ecc. Orn.*, under 'Girdle.') See Proeme, note 11, p. 156.

5. S. Matthew xvii. 21.

6. Ephesians vi. 14.

7. Sec. 4.

8. Those mentioned in 1 Kings xviii. 13 as slain by Jezebel.

9. 1 Cor. ix. 27.

10. Rev. i. 12, 13.

11. Ephesians iii. 19.

12. Isaiah xi. 5.

13. Ps. xi. 8.

14. *Ibid.* cxlv. 17.

15. Expanded from S. Luke vi. 31.

16. S. John xix. 1.

THE SACRED VESTMENTS: CHAPTER V: OF THE STOLE

1. Thought to be derived from *ora*, a border. It has been thought that the Orarium was in some way distinct from the Stole. In the Life of S. Livinus we are told that the Saint was given by S. Augustine of Canterbury, on the day of his ordination, a *Stole with an Orarium*, enriched with jewels. It may be that the word was formerly applied to the ornamental *border* of a large Vestment now obsolete, which was called *Stola*; and that this Vestment gradually dwindled in size, until nothing was left of it but the said border, which survived under the interchangeable names of Orarium and Stole. For the old classical word στολή, *stola*, as is well known, meant a feminine garment with sleeves, covering the whole person: Hor. *Sat.* Lib. I. ii. 99,'Ad talos Stola demissa.' And Pugin tells us that in the plates of Bosio's *Roma Sotterranea* the Stole is represented in its ancient form, with the present Stole as a stripe or orfrey. Durandus himself, in § 6, implies that the Stole was once larger than it was in his time. Others, however, condemn this view, and connect Orarium with *os*, the face, regarding the Stole as having originated from a kerchief or napkin. The etymology of the word is further touched on in note 16, p. 169.

2. 2 Cor. vi. 7.

3. This the Pontifical directs the Bishop to say, while he arranges the Stole before the Priest's breast in the form of a cross. *Pontificale Rom.* Pars I. Titul. XII. § viii.

4. Heb. x. 36.

5. S. Luke xxi. 19. The A.V., 'possess ye,' represents the other reading, κτήσασθε. But κτήσεσθε (Vulg. *Possidebitis*, and R.V. 'ye shall win') is preferable both as regards authority and meaning.

6. See Col. iii. 14.

7. More correctly, the Bishop says these words while unfolding the Chasuble which the Priest wears folded over his shoulder. Pontificale, P. I. Tit. XII. § xxviii.

8. See p. 70, *n*. 18.

9. *I.e.* as being still a Deacon.

10. Tit. ii. 12.

11. The Fourth Council of Braga, c. 3 (A.D. 675). Grat. *Decr.* I. Dist. Xxiii. C. 9 ('Ecclesiastica'). This refers to the Priest who is about to celebrate Mass. The Stole was of course never crossed in this way until it had become contracted in size. Bishops and Priests alike formerly wore it pendent on both sides, as do Bishops now.

12. Durandus has 'preparare.' In the canon it is 'preparet'; but there is another reading 'praeferat,' 'bear before him the Sign of the Cross,' which seems much more natural.

13. From this it appears likely that the present custom which is in accordance with the Decree, was not very prevalent in Durandus' time. This seems strange, for it has been usual since about the ninth century, as is testified by ancient representations, and discoveries of the Stole in tombs crossed over the breast. However, Durandus says below (§ 5) that 'upon Bishop and Priest it falleth down upon either side evenly.'

14. 'When he is ordained, the Deacon receiveth the Stole, which signifieth the yoke of Christ, because it will pertain unto him to read the Gospel, wherewith he is encompassed as with a yoke.' (*Rat.* Lib. II. 'De Diacono.')

15. So Josephus, *Ant.* Lib. III. c. 11: 'When they prepare for the ministry of sacrifice, they carry their girdles on the left shoulder, so as not to be hindered.'

16. This etymology of the word (oro, to pray) is assigned by the Fourth Council of Toledo (c. 28; A.D. 633). But it bears the look of being what Bingham calls an 'ecclesiastical derivation,' and is hardly probable. There was a post-classical *orarium*, a handkerchief, which was derived from *os*. 'Oculum ligauit orario' (S. Aug. Civ. Dei, xxii. 8, no. 7). This was used for wiping the face (ἐκμαγεῖου τοῦ προσ√που). *Vide* Du Cange, *sub voce*. From a scholar's point of view this etymology is far more satisfactory than either *oro* or *ora*.

17. A.D. 895. Burchardus, Lib. Vi. C. 'Presbyteri.' The Stole seems to have been the invariable everyday garment of Bishops and Priests until quite a late date. The Council of Mayence (A.D. 813) ordered that priests should wear it 'constantly.' S. Thomas of Canterbury always wore his Stole. Martene quotes these verses of S. Maur, Abbot:

'Deponendo Stolam, quam toto tempore caram
Anni portabat.'

18. The thought is involved. Durandus seems to transfer in fancy the primal innocence of Adam to the patriarchs, who were wont, he says, upon receiving their father's blessing, to put on a large garment called a Stole or robe, and to sacrifice to the Lord in token that their innocence claimed such blessing as a right. Whereas for fallen man the birthright can only be regained through the Sacrifice of Christ, symbolised by the Fatted Calf, and the Stole with which he is invested is now a yoke, suggestive of his willingness to submit to that allegiance which alone shall win him back the garment of righteousness. Though he does not mention it, Durandus seems to be thinking of the 'best robe,' which so many Fathers, from Irenaeus downwards, interpret as the robe of righteousness, as put upon the Prodigal by his Father.

19. Philippians ii. 6, 7, 8.

20. In Conc. Laodic. Can. 22 and 23 (A.D. 361): οὐ δεῖ ὑπηρέτην (the Subdeacon) ∫ ρΩφιον φορεῖν ... οὐ δεῖ Ωναγν√στας ή ψάλτας ∫ ρ. φορεῖν. The Vestment which the Subdeacons were to wear was the Tunicle; the Stole was the mark of Bishops and Priests. (Grat. *Decr.* I. Dist. xxiv. C. 'Non oportet.') The office of the Readers (lectores) was to

take care of the Sacred Books, and to read the Scriptures in Church; that of the Psalmist or Cantor, to precent and sing.

THE SACRED VESTMENTS: CHAPTER VI: THE MANIPLE

1. This Vestment was called indifferently *manipulus, mappula, sudarium*, and *phanon*; though the two latter were strictly speaking names of quite distinct Vestments, as will be seen in Chs. ix. and xvi. The Maniple was originally merely a napkin for wiping the hands, carried on the arm, especially at Mass. After the sixth century it passed, like many other Vestments, from an utilitarian to a ceremonial purpose. Its ornamental use seems to have been at first confined to the Roman clergy. S. Gregory the Great allowed the chief Deacons of the Church of Ravenna to wear the Maniple while attending on the Bishop at Mass, as a great concession (L. ii. *Ep*. 54 and 55). The Maniple was anciently worn on the hand, rather than on the arm; Archbishop Stigand is so represented in the Bayeux Tapestry. It is now worn by Bishop, Priest, Deacon, and Subdeacon, on the left arm; it varies in colour and texture with the Chasuble, and, like the Chasuble, is discarded for processions.

2. Ps. cxix. 28.

3. S. Matthew xxv. 13.

4. Cant. v. 2.

5. Ps. cxix. 28.

6. Lat. *manipulus*, a handful: hence a small bundle of corn, or sheaf; also a 'hand-thing,' in our sense of the Maniple. The word also means a band of soldiers, as we should say a handful of men, or because of the handful of straw on the pole which in primitive times served for a military standard.

7. Lat. *manipulos*—Ps. cxxvi. 6. A kind of *paronomasia*, or play upon words.

8. *I.e.* as ideally supposing virtue to increase in the measure of ecclesiastical rank.

9. Arsenius, called the 'Great,' was one of the most famous of the monks of Egypt. With great asceticism and rigorous sternness of character he combined deep penitence for sin. A mediaeval Collect in commemoration of him speaks of his 'ceaseless floods of tears' (A.D. *c*. 354-450).

10. The passage following strikes me as one of singular beauty.

11. Cant. ii. 6.

12. S. John iii. 13.

13. *Ibid*. xviii. 12.

14. All Bishops now put on the Maniple after the *Confiteor*, after the Chasuble. Pugin says that formerly the great Chasuble hung down all round the Bishop, and he struck his breast at the 'Meâ Culpâ' beneath its folds. Then the ministers raised it, folded it back over his arm, and affixed the Maniple. However, Durandus confines this to the Roman Pontiff, and says elsewhere that in his time Bishops put it on *before* the *Confiteor*. These are his words, in effect:—'The Bishop, ere he say *Confiteor*, hath the Maniple put upon him by the Subdeacon, before the Altar. This for three reasons. First, because he must receive and administer temporal goods, not through his own hands, but through the hands of another. Secondly, because confession with the lips sufficeth not, save it be followed by the fruit of good works. Thirdly, that he may be made humble of heart, when he findeth him arrayed with the badge of an inferior ministry. The Bishop, again, putteth on the Maniple after the Chasuble, because Christ, Whose vicegerent he is, did live an heavenly life, or ever He might win to the reward of His labour. But the Priest putteth on the Maniple first, for that he cannot attain unto heavenly conversation, unless he first bear the

sheaves of holy works. Wherefore also the Bishop receiveth the Maniple after that he is come to the Altar, in token that we shall then at length receive the reword of our labour, when we are come to the tribunal of the Eternal Judge.' (Rat. iv. 7). But the Maniple was *anciently* assumed by Priests as well as Bishops *after* the *Confiteor*. Martene says that in a MS. of the Monastery of S. Denis, written in Charlemagne's time, there occurs after the prayer for putting on the Chasuble, the following prayer for the Maniple:—'Praecinge me, Domine, virtute, et pone immaculatam uiam meam.'

THE SACRED VESTMENTS: CHAPATER VII: THE CHASUBLE

1. The word is derived from *casula*, a little house. So S. Isidore (c. A.D. 600), who explains that 'like a hut, it covers the entire person' (*De Origin*. xix. cap. 21). It is called also *amphibalum*, *planeta*, and *paenula*. It seems to have been a somewhat humble garment at first, being confined to peasants and artisans; and it had a hood, as a protection against the weather. It was long the ordinary outdoor dress of the clergy and monks, before it passed into the present ecclesiastical Vestment, so indispensable to, and characteristic of, the Holy Sacrifice of the Altar. The Council of Ratisbon (A.D. 742) directs that Priests and Deacons shall wear the 'Casula' out of doors.

2. So Isidore, *De Etymol*. xix. 24. But some ascribe this name to its starlike appearance when folded back. The name is used more strictly of the *folded*-chasuble. (Dr. Littledale thought that the Planeta is represented now by the Chasuble, and the Casula or Casacula by the Cassock.)

3. 1 Cor. xiii. 1.

4. 1 S. Peter iv. 8.

5. Rom. xiii. 10.

6. The primitive Chasuble, being quite round, enveloped the whole body. Certain schools sigh for this 'ancient perfection' of the Chasuble, with its 'graceful folds.' How it can be possible to desire the renewal of so cumbersome a garment, with its sides continually slipping over the hands, to the great peril of the Holy Sacrifice in both paten and chalice; or what especial dignity or beauty can reside in a mere circle of cloth with a hole in the middle for the head, it is hard to conceive. Were the human figure spherical, it would be all that could be desired. It was appropriate in its own time and place. But here is such a thing as 'old-fashion' in the Church as in the world. We do not revive ordinary garments after they have become unsuitable; and there are few sights so ludicrous or so unbecoming the dignity of Divine worship as that of a short Priest in an enormous Chasuble. It is not well that their prevailing horror of 'modern Romanism' should drive Englishmen to absurdities. Moreover, antiquarian punctilio is apt to forget that external matters, in the Church, are subject to development. Surely the almost universal adoption of a smaller form of this and of other Vestments by the great Latin Church is more authoritative and more convincing than the private 'fads' of scholars, who forget that logical consistence demands of them the rejection of the whole principle of ritual evolution, and a return, along the entire range of worship, to the models of whatever century they happen to have honoured with their preference. Surely in these, as in greater matters, the Holy Spirit was to 'guide into all truth'; and to appeal from the Holy Ghost in the nineteenth century to the Holy Ghost in the first, or second, or thirteenth, whether in things great or small, is dangerously near to stultifying that promise of perpetual guidance. Antiquarianism is a good thing. But Antiquarianism in conflict with Catholicism helped to produce the Anabaptist heresy.

7. 1 Cor. xiii. 1.

8. 1 Cor. xiii. 2.

9. S. Matthew xxii. 12.

10. 'Bonum opus debet ad charitatem referri.'

11. 1 Tim. i. 5.

12. S. Matthew xxii. 37-40.

13. Ps. cix. 96.

14. Durandus doubtless means the natural gathering of the Vestment over the arms on each side, to leave the hands free. This, of course, necessitated a limp material, for it would have been impossible with our thickly-embroidered Vestments. The raising of the Chasuble on either side by the Ministers, which was then necessary to free the Priest's hands for censing, etc., survives now only ceremonially. In Durandus' time it had developed from its primitive circular shape into that of a vesica, which hung down in long points when the arms were raised, behind and before. The effect of this must have been very graceful.

15. So also Honorius, Bishop of Autun. It is not obvious what kind of 'doubling' is referred to. Durandus may (i.) be referring to the folded-chasuble, or to the ancient practice of throwing back the borders of the Planeta for convenience before celebrating; or (ii.) perhaps the Chasuble was made of a double thickness in the regions named (though he says below that it was 'of one piece'); but more probably (iii.) the natural folds of the Vestment are meant, which would be caused by the raising of the arms.

16. Gal. vi. 10.

17. Doubtless this refers to the natural folds upon the raised arms.

18. Ps. cxxxii. 9.

19. Lev. xxi. 12.

20. Gal. iii. 27. So Rupert, Bishop of Tuy, in his comments *De Divinis Officiis*. It will be observed that Durandus says nothing about the orfreys or ornamentation of the Chasuble, and does not allude to the **Y** cross upon it. Yet this undoubtedly existed in his time. Agnellus, in his Life of S. Maximian, who was Bishop of Ravenna in the sixth century, says that Maximian had an altar-cloth embroidered with pictures of his predecessors, and that these Bishops were depicted as wearing Chasubles with the 'auriclave' in front, in shape like the Pallium, which is thus (**Y**). It is well known that this cross represents the raising of Our Blessed Lord's arms in the Crucifixion, and that the straight orfrey often found on the front of the Chasuble is symbolical of the stake to which He was bound when scourged. These significations are of course instances of the evolution of symbolism from utility.

21. Ps. cxxxiii. 2.

22. S. John i. 16.

23. S. Matthew xxi. 9.

24. S. John xix. 2.

THE SACRED VESTMENTS: CHAPTER VIII: OF THE BUSKINS AND SANDALS

1. S. Matthew xxviii. 19.

2. As ordered in the Roman Missal. According to the Prayer Book computation, they are Pss. lxxxiv., lxxxv., lxxxvi., cxvi. (*v*. 10 to end) and cxxx.

3. Ephesians vi. 15.

4. Isaiah lii. 7

5. Ephesians vi. 15.

6. S. Mark vi. 9.

7. S. Luke x. 19.

8. *Caligae*, called also *Compagi*. These are a kind of stocking of some precious material, quite distinct from the Sandals, and reaching to the knee, where they are fastened. Sicardus of Cremona (twelfth century) says that they were of silk. They were originally peculiar to the Pope, but towards the ninth century seem to have become an universal Episcopal Vestment. The earliest writer who mentions 'caligae' as regularly included in the Sacred Vestments to be worn by Bishops and Cardinals is Ivo Carnotensis (*c*. A.D. 1115).

9. Heb. xii. 12, 13.

10. S. Matthew v. 19.

11. Sometimes crimson, sometimes cloth of gold. The Buskins found in the tomb of Boniface VIII were of black silk.

12. Isaiah xxxv. 4.

13. It appears that no mention of the Sandals as a distinctively Episcopal Vestment occurs before the ninth century, unless S. Gregory, in forbidding Deacons to wear 'sandalia' (L. vii. *Ep*. 28), be speaking of them. They were originally worn by all Holy Orders, as might be expected from their purely secular origin. Amalarius says they were worn by Priests as late as the ninth century (*De Eccles. Offic*. L. li. C. 25). They were often embroidered in the most costly manner. In old representations they are generally red, but sometimes purple, or white.

14. Sandaraca, σανδαράκη, a red mineral colouring matter; (Vitr. Vii. 12, 2; Du Cange, *sub voce*). But the derivation is improbable, as there is also a Persian word *sandal*. The Greek word σάνδαλον is more probably connected with σανίς, a wooden board, as being a sole of wood for the foot. Durandus' alternative derivation, 'the plant of that name,' is not obvious. There was a *white* kind of corn mentioned by Pliny, called *sandala*, and a kind of palm called *sandalis*; but it is difficult to connect either with the sandal.

15. S. Matthew x. 14.

16. Ps. cxix. 18.

17. S. Luke viii. 10.

18. S. Matthew vii. 6.

19. S. Luke x. 35.

20. S. John xiii. 10. See Chap. xix. of this work, p. 165, n. 2.

21. *Centones rubei*. 'Cento' usually means patchwork. It probably refers here to the red cross sometimes found on a white sandal.

22. Ps. lx. 8.

23. S. John i. 27.

24. The sequence of thought is obscure. Durandus seems to mean one of two things: (i.) that the feet are a type of the Godhead, and the Sandals of Our Lord's Human Soul. But the thought of Our Lord's Godhead being united with His Human Soul through the medium of His Flesh seems strange. One might have thought rather that His Godhead was united with His Flesh through the medium of His Soul; but this, too, is strained. But the passage more probably means (ii.) that the feet are the Godhead, and the Sandals man's soul, which is brought to God by the medium of the Incarnation, typified by the Buskins.

25. Ps. xcix. 5.

26. Grat *Decret.* I. Dist. xciii. c. 20 ('compagis uero calciari absque apostolica licentia diaconibus non permittitur, sicut nec mappulis') And Greg. 'Ioanni Episcopo Siracusano,' L. vii. *Epist.* 28, Indict.I.

27. 'Et sicut noster senatus calceamentis utitur cum udonibus, idest candido linteamine illustratis, sic utantur et clerici, ut sicut coelestia, ita et terrena ad laudem Dei decorentur.' ('And whereas our senate wear sandals enriched with socks of white linen, let the clergy wear the same, that both heavenly and earthly things may be adorned to the praise of God.') 'Donation of Constantine,' Grat. *Decr.* I. Dist. xcvi. c. 14.

THE SACRED VESTMENTS: CHAPTER IX: THE UNDERGIRDLE AND VEIL

1. See Proeme, § 4, and Chap. iv. throughout, with Notes. In Durandus' time the Undergirdle was the common property of all Bishops, but it is now a Papal Vestment. This chapter is borrowed almost bodily from Innocent III. *De Myst. Miss.* Lib. I. c. 53.

2. A striped veil like a coloured amice, which the Pope puts on after the Girdle, turned back over the head, until the Chasuble is put on, when it is brought down over the shoulders and breast.

3. Durandus, with Innocent III. and also S. Thomas, seems to confine the Pectoral Cross to the Pope. It is of course now the common property of all Bishops. Yet in Durandus' time, though not a part of the exclusively Episcopal dress, it was worn by Bishops. Georgius says that Pectoral Crosses were called ἐγκόλπια by the Greeks; for the practice of wearing a Cross seems to have come from the East, where all the faithful, but especially the Bishops, wore them. The use probably originated in the wearing of a reliquary, containing the wood of the Holy Cross, in the bosom, the reliquary itself becoming cruciform in shape. Nicephorus the Emperor (A.D. 811) sent Pope Leo III. a golden Pectoral Cross, containing relics of the true Cross.

4. Exodus xxviii. 38.

5. For this mystery, see Chap. xix., § 16.

6. Ephesians Iii. 18.

7. Rom. x. 10.

8. 1 Cor. vi. 2, adapted, with a reminiscence of Gal. vi. 17.

THE SACRED VESTMENTS: CHAPTER X: OF THE TUNIC

1. The word occurs in Isaiah xix. 9, Vulg. ('confundentur texentes subtilia') and Ezek. xvi. 10 ('indui te subtilibus,' LXX τὴν βύσσον).

2. Genesis xxxvii. 3 ('fecitque ei tunicam polymitam').

3. S. Matthew x. 22.

4. Rev. ii. 10.

5. Exodus xxxix. 22 and 27; or xxviii. 31 ('tunica superhumeralis,' the Robe of the Ephod) and 39 ('tunica byssina,' the coat of fine linen.)

6. *I.e.* Dalmatic and Tunicle. The words were almost interchangeable in Durandus' time. In the *Pontificale Ecclesiae Cameracensis* occurs this prayer, to be said in putting on the Dalmatic: 'Indue me, Domine, vestimento salutis, *et Tunica iustitiae.*' And in most old English inventories the two Vestments are called indifferently 'Tunicles'. The early Dalmatic was a little larger than the Tunicle, and had ampler sleeves. See following chapter, § 3.

7. S. Matthew xiii. 52.

8. Evidently the Dalmatic, which Pope Silvester ordered to be of white.

9. § 1.

10. Rom. xii. 15.

11. Exodus xxviii. 33-35.

12. § 10.

13. Isaiah xl. 9 (Vulg. 'super montem excelsum ascende, tu qui euangelizas Sion'—where 'Sion' may be either vocative or accusative).

14. S. John xv. 15.

15. *Ibid.* xix. 23.

THE SACRED VESTMENTS: CHAPTER XI: OF THE DALMATIC

1. But in the account of the martyrdom of S. Cyprian, long before Pope Silvester's time (which was 315-325 A.D.), we read that S. Cyprian, being led to martyrdom, 'cum se Dalmatica exspoliasset et diaconibus tradidisset, in linea stetit' ('Ex Passione S. Cypr. Pontii Diacon.' In *Act. Mart. sincer.* p. 205, *in fine*). Pope Silvester probably made the Episcopal use of this Vestment general. Walafrid Strabo says that before that Pope's time Bishops and Priests both wore Dalmatics, but that when they began to use Chasubles they allowed Deacons to wear Dalmatics (*De Reb. Eccl.* c. 24). And S. Isidore calls the Dalmatic 'a sacerdotal Vestment.'

2. This was a short under-tunic, anciently an under-garment of the Romans, and worn originally by all freemen, and latterly by senators. It appears to have been the Vestment of a Deacon at the time when the Dalmatic distinguished Bishops and Priests. It is derived from κολοβός, short, or stunted.

3. The monastic 'cowls' known to Durandus probably reached to the feet. 'Cuculla quae nostro singulariter convenit ordini, quod uestimentum antiquitus uocabatur Colobium, idest tunica sine manicis, tantum debet habere longitudinis antea, quod ad callum pedis usque pertingat.' ['The Cowl of our Order, formerly called Colobium, a tunic without sleeves, ought to be long enough in front to reach the sole of the foot.'] *Guidonis Disciplina Farfenis*, cap. 4, 'De uestimentorum mensura.'

4. Bingham (Orig. Eccles. Vol. I. Bk. vi. ch. 4, § 20) says the Dalmatic was otherwise called χειρόδοτος or Tunica manicata, because it had these sleeves down to the hands.

5. *Reperta*. 'Dalmaticas testatur Isidorus Episcopus in Dalmatia primum contextas' (Onuphrius Panvinus, *Interpr. Voc. Eccles.*, sub 'Dalm. ; S. Isidore, Etym. xix. 22).

6. Tit. i. 7 and 8.

7. Isaiah lviii. 7.

8. So S. Isidore, in the place last referred to. He calls the Dalmatic a 'sacerdotal Vestment with purple stripes' ('tunica sacerdotalis candida cum clauis ex purpura'). At present the Dalmatic is usually crossed also behind by two transverse stripes at top and bottom, to distinguish it from the Subdeacon's Tunicle, which has only one, at the top. It has also tassels hanging from the meeting-points of these stripes at the back, supposed to be a survival of strings or laces by which the mouth of the Dalmatic was anciently opened to admit the head, and then drawn tight again.

9. S. Luke x. 27.

10. 1 S. John ii. 7, 8.

11. 2 Cor. xi. 28.

12. Pss. cxx.—cxxxiv.

13. 1 Cor. xiii. 4-8.

14. Ps. cxlviii. 11, 12.

15. Ps. xlv. 10.

16. S. Luke vi. 36.

17. S. Matthew v. 7.

18. S. Luke x. 34.

19. S. Luke i. 78.

20. Tit. iii. 5.

21. S. Matthew ix. 13.

22. Grat. *Decret.* I. Dist. xxiii. c. x. 'Communis.'

23. In the Roman rite the Deacon and Subdeacon leave off their Dalmatic and Tunicle respectively on Fast-days (except the Vigils of Saints' Days); on all days of Advent and Lent; on the Vigil of Pentecost before Mass (but not on Gaudete and Laetare Sundays, nor on Christmas Eve, Holy Saturday at the Blessing of the Candle and at Mass, nor on the Pentecostal Ember Days); also at the Blessing of Candles and Procession upon the Purification of Our Lady, at the Blessing of Ashes and of Palms, and at the Procession of Palms. At these times, in Cathedrals and principal Churches, they substitute the Folded-Chasuble, a Vestment which they take off before the Gospel and Epistle respectively, the Deacon folding it over his left shoulder, and the Subdeacon ministering in his Albe. But in inferior Churches, at these times, they minister in Albes alone.

24. Grat. *Decr.* I. Dist. xcviii. c. 24, 'Legimus' *ad finem*. A maxim whose truth must have been felt by all who have much to do with the Service of the Altar.

25. 'Upon Fasts the Deacon hath a Chasuble folded over his left shoulder, because whatever labour we undergo in this life is borne in a figure upon that part; until from the Left we pass over unto the Right, wherein we have our rest.' Rat. ii. 'De Diacono.'

26. *I.e.* the Ember Days.

THE SACRED VESTMENTS: CHAPTER XII: OF THE GLOVES

1. But formerly they were the common property of both Bishops and Priest. The first extant mention of them as an ecclesiastical Vestment is in the twelfth century, by Honorius Augustodunensis (died *c.* A.D. 1152). They were often very ornate. Bp. Riculfus in his well-known Will (*c.* A.D. 914) mentions 'annulum aureum unum cum gemmis pertiosis, et vuantos (gants, gloves) paria unum' (*Patrol.* cxxxii. 468)

2. S. Matthew vi. 3.

3. S. Matthew v. 16.

4. *Ibid.* vi. 1.

5. Gal. v. 9.

6. Like most other Vestments, it appears that the Gloves were originally white. But they were ornamented with jewels from an early date.

7. Genesis xxvii. 16.

8. Not a theological dogma, but a poetical and mystic conceit; and to be taken as such.

9. S. Matthew iv. 2.

THE SACRED VESTMENTS: CHAPTER XIII: OF THE MITRE

1. This was always a peculiar ornament of Bishops. For the first six centuries the Mitre was, in Pelliccia's opinion, a simple linen fillet or cap, which began to grow ornate in the time of John of Cappadocia. The word *Mitra* originally denoted the headgear of an Asiatic woman; and in early times the *mitella* was worn by Christian women as a badge of virginity. The early Episcopal Mitre was called *uitta*, or *infula*, a fillet. When its use

became distinctively ceremonial, it came to be called a Crown, and was regarded as strongly symbolical of the Episcopate, Bishops taking oath 'per coronam meam.'

2. Ps. viii. 5.

3. 'Beato Siluestro...et omnibus eius successoribus Pontificibus...de praesenti contradimus...diadema, uidelicet coronam capitis nostri, simulque frigium, necnon et superhumerale, uidelicet lorum, quod imperiale circumdare assolet collum; uerum etiam clamidem purpuream, atque tunicam coccineam, et omnia imperialia indumenta.' ['To Blessed Silvester and all his successors in the Holy See we donate from this present the Diadem, to wit the Crown of our head, the Tiara, the Imperial Pall which is wont to surround the imperial neck, the purple cloak, the scarlet tunic, and all the Imperial robes.'] Donation of Constantine, Grat. *Decret.* I. Dist. xcvi. c. xiv. 'Constantinus.' The Frigium, or Phrygium, was so called because the Emperor's tiara was 'opere contexta Phrygio' (Du Cange, *sub voce*). (The reader will understand that I am not concerned to discuss the *genuineness* of the Donation of Constantine.)

4. The Mitre was originally single in form, the division into two horns having come into general vogue about the tenth century.

5. This is the 'Dark Ages,' when the Bible is popularly supposed to have been a sealed or unknown book! We are very proud of our days of an 'Open Bible'; but if we read, marked, learned, and inwardly digested it as much as we talk about it, our national humility, learning, and piety might be materially increased.

6. Exodus xxxiv. 29, 30. In E. V. we read, 'the skin of his face shone.' But the Hebrew verb *kăran*, to shine, is connected with *keren*, a horn; and hence we have the verb rendered 'horned' in Aquila's version and in the Vulg. The latter reads 'et ignorabat quod cornuta esset facies sua ex consortio sermonis Domini.' Thus it comes to pass that so many representations of Moses are horned.

7. Rev. xiii. 11. The wresting of the Apocalypse to purposes of this sort was plainly not unknown before the Reformation; cf. Proeme, § 14.

8. *Fimbriae*. Called also *infulae*.

9. S. Matthew xiii. 52. This, and much else of the Mitre hitheto, is to be found almost word for word in Innocent III.

10. *Ibid.* xv. 14.

11. Hos. iv. 6.

12. The Mitre seems to have gradually grown in height, from its low stature at the beginning, to its present towering form.

13. *Vigent*. Durandus's physiology is unimpeachable here, as regards the reflex action of physical sensations.

14. To do so was strictly forbidden before the thirteenth century. But Pope Innocent IV (A.D. 1243) allowed the resident monks of Canterbury to wear the Almuce, a fur hood which covered the head and hung down to the shoulders, because they found themselves 'grauissimis morbis implicitos' through worshipping bareheaded. The present biretta, or more properly berretta, took its origin in an ordinary layman's cap in the sixteenth century. It is regarded as the official headgear of the clergy, and so is worn in Church. Many object to the biretta on the ground of its being 'Italian.' To which it may be answered—all honour to Italy for having evolved a vestment which for simplicity, convenience, and seemliness leaves little to be desired! The objection raised by some that the use of the biretta involves 'unfaithfulness to the Church of England,' speaks volumes for the conscience of the objectors, but little for their sense of humour.

15. There are now three kinds of Mitre. (i.) *Mitra Simplex*, of plain white silk or linen. (ii.) *M. Aurifrigiata*, adorned with orfreys of gold. (iii.) *M. Pretiosa*, richly embroidered and adorned with gold and precious stones. *Caeremoniale Episcoporum*, Lib. I. c. xvii. Durandus gives only the two former.

16. Ch. xviii. § 6, *q. v.*

17. Gaudete Sunday (the Third Sunday in Advent) is so called because the Introit for that day begins 'Gaudete in Domine semper'; and Laetare Sunday (the Fourth Sunday in Lent) because its Introit begins 'Laetare Jerusalem.' See Ch. xviii. § 6.

18. I.e. the Ember Days, which fall in the four seasons of the year respectively.

19. The *Caeremoniale Episcoporum* says: 'The Bishop uses the Precious Mitre on the greater Feasts, and generally when *Te Deum* and *Gloria in Excelcis* are said. Nevertheless the Orfreyed Mitre may be used on these same Festivals, but rather for convenience than of necessity. The Orfreyed Mitre is used from Advent Sunday until Christmas Day, except upon Gaudete Sunday, when the Precious is used; from Septuagesima until Wednesday in Holy Week inclusively, except Laetare Sunday; upon all Fasted Vigils, Ember Days, and Rogation Days, and in Litanies and Processions of a penitential nature; on Holy Innocents' Day, unless it fall on a Sunday; in Offices having three Lessons, and at private Benedictions and Consecrations. The Simple Mitre is used on Good Friday, and at Offices and Masses for the Dead.' Thus it will be seen that Durandus, roughly speaking, assigns to his 'Orfreyed Mitre' the present use of the Precious, and to his 'Simple' those of the present Orfreyed and Simple combined; the Precious Mitre being evidently a subsequent evolution from the old Orfreyed, and having thrown the two others, as it were, each a step downward.

20. *I.e.* the Papal Tiara, now a triple crown, called cometimes Frigium, the token of Temporal Power. It is usually represented as worn first by S. Silvester (A.D. 315) as granted to him by the Donation of Constantine (see p. 94, n.2), and Platina, *Vit. Pont., sub Silvestro*). The second crown was added, it is said, by Boniface VIII., in token of the union of the Spiritual and Temporal Powers; and the third, by Urban V.

21. So Innocent III.

22. Genesis x. 10.

23. *Ibid.* ix. 20.

24. Ps. viii. 5, 6.

25. Philippians ii. 9, 10.

26. The Fathers say that S. James, Bishop of Jerusalem, and S. John were in the habit of wearing this Golden Plate.

27. Exodus xxviii. 36-38.

28. Ch. xix. § 16, and notes.

29. Ps. xcix. 5.

THE SACRED VESTMENTS: CHAPTER XIV: OF THE RING

1. An integral part of the Episcopal ornaments from very early times. It is mentioned by S. Isidore of Seville in the sixth century. It is placed upon the right hand of the Bishop by the priest assistant, who first kisses the Ring and the Bishop's hand. The Ring has usually been large and massive, with with a jewel and adorned with devices.

2. Cant. iii. 3.

3. S. Luke xv. 22.

4. 2 Cor. xi. 2.

5. S. John iii. 29.

6. Exodus viii. 19.
7. S. Luke xi. 19, 20. The clauses are transposed.
8. S. John iii. 34.
9. Col. ii. 9.
10. S. John iii. 31.
11. S. John i. 33.
12. Isaiah xi. 2.
13. 1 Cor. xii. 9, 10.

THE SACRED VESTMENTS: CHAPTER XV: OF THE PASTORAL STAFF

1. This, the sceptre of spiritual authority, has many names; it is called *virga, cambutta, sambuca, pedum, crocia*, and *ferula*. Its use may be traced at least as far at the sixth century (S. Greg. Tur. De Mirac. S. Mart. L. i. c. 4). And tradition carries it back to the time of S. Peter himself. The essential notion of it is threefold—it may be called a Crook, a Sceptre, and a Rod; in other words, it expresses the threefold function of the Prelate, as a Shepherd, to gather in the wanderers to the true Fold; a King, to rule his spiritual subjects, under Christ; and a Master, to correct the froward and spur on the indolent. Baronius (*c.* A.D. 504) says that the Pastoral Staff was used by Bishops as early as the fourth century.

2. The Pontifical has these words:—'Accipe baculum pastoralis officii, ut sis in corrigendis uitiis pie saeviens, iudicium sine ira tenens, in fouendis uirtutibus auditorum animos demulcens, in tranquillitate seueritatis censuram non deserens.'

3. 1 Cor. iv. 21.

4. Josh. v. 6.

5 So always in primitive times; generally either of elder (hence probably the name *sambuca*, 'sambucus' meaning elder) or of cypress. Martigny says most commonly the latter (*Dict. des Antiq. Chrét.* s.v. 'Evêques').

6. These developed into most elaborate pieces of tabernacle-work, like the knops of chalices, octagonal, and adorned with images set with precious stones. In Dugdale's *Monasticon* the following is quoted from an inventory of Lichfield Cathedral: 'Imprimis, a head of a Bishop's Staff of silver and gilt, with one knop and pearls, and other stones, having an image of our Saviour on the one side, and an image of S. John Baptist on the other, weighing eighteen ounces.' Visitors to Oxford are familiar with the exquisite Pastoral Staves preserved at New, Corpus Christi, and S. John's.

7. 'Modice tamen reconditur.'

8. Hab. iii. 2.

9. The full quatrain is thus:

> In Baculi forma, Praesul, datur haec tibi norma:
> Attrahe per curuum, medio rege, punge per imum;
> Attrahe peccantes, rege iustos, punge uagantes;
> Attrahe, sustenta, stimula—uaga, morbida, lenta.

10. S. Matthew xviii. 3, 4.

11. *Cir.* A.D. 362. In the legend of Maternus, Bishop of Cologne, the see of Trèves is said to have been founded in the first century, and Maternus, Eucherius, and Valerius were its first Bishops.—Greg. Tur. *Vit. Pat.* c. 17, § 4, p. 1237.

12. This variant of the story is also given by S. Thomas Aquinas, *In IV. Sententiarum*, Distinct. xxiv. Qu. 3; and by Honorius of Autun, and Peter of Clugni.

13. Georgius says that Egbert, Archbishop of Trèves, A.D. 980, obtained this Staff from Werinus, Archbishop of Cologne, whither a former Bishop, Bruno, had transferred it. The Case in which the Staff is contained preserves the above history, in a very ancient inscription. This case is covered with plates of silver, curiously gilt, and adorned with jewels; and round the knop of the Staff are small images of the Twelve Apostles. See Pugin's *Glossary*, under 'Pope'.

14. The last-quoted authority questions whether the Popes did not at one time carry a Pastoral Staff, and cites from the ceremonies of the election of Pope Pascal II. (A.D. 1099) a statement to the effect that 'a Staff was given into his hand.'

15. As wielder of a jurisdiction extending to all the baptised. S. Thomas Aquinas makes the curvature of the Pastoral Staff denote a limited jurisdiction. The Triple Cross may be said to have taken its place as a Papal emblem. It is, however, an open question whether the Popes ever used the Pastoral Staff. There are three distinct ancient representations of S. Gregory with one; and the tendency to deny its use by the early Popes seems to date from the twelfth century.

16. Ps. xlv. 7, 8.

17. *Ibid.* ii. 9. Vulg. *reges* ; E.V. 'thou shalt bruise.'

18. *Ibid.*

19. *Ibid.* xxiii. 4.

THE SACRED VESTMENTS: CHAPTER XVI: OF THE SUDARIUM

1. 2 Sam. xii. 20.

2. Job xlii.

THE SACRED VESTMENTS: CHAPTER XVII: OF THE PALL

1. The Pall, the emblem of full jurisdiction in the Bishop, was, according to Gregory Nazianzen, originally an ornament of the heathen emperors in the character of Pontifex Maximus, and was first presented by Constantine the Great to the Bishop of Jerusalem. But from very early times there was a large woollen Vestment worn by Bishops generally, properly called ʃ μοφόριον, and worn, according to Liberatus, by S. Mark, at Alexandria. This Vestment, which Isidore of Pelusium says was a figure of the lost sheep borne on the shoulders of the Good Shepherd, was, according to Pelliccia and others, the prototype of the Pallium; having been gradually cut down, until only its outer edges remained. After a time it acquired a jurisdictional meaning, and Emperors and Patriarchs began to bestow it upon chief Bishops; then the right of conferring it passed by degrees into the hands of the Roman Pontiff, and it became customary in the Roman Church for Metropolitans to go to Rome to receive it; until, at the Fourth Lateran Council (A.D. 1215), it was formally decreed that Oriental Patriarchs must receive the Pall from the Pope. And from that day to this its bestowal has been, in the Roman Catholic Church, an indispensable condition of the full exercise of Metropolitan authority.

2. § 14.

3. Prov. i. 8, 9.

4. 1 Cor. ix. 24.

5. 'When the Pall is put upon the Archbishop, it is always placed over the Chasuble, so that its double part shall lie on the left shoulder' (*Caer. Ep.* I. xvi. 'De Pallio').

6. The following account of the putting-on of the Pall, when the Bishop celebrates High Mass, may be of interest:—'If the Bishop may wear the Pall, and it be convenient for him to do so upon that day, it is brought by a Subdeacon from the Altar, in both hands,

covered with a veil. The Deacon then takes it and offers it to the Bishop, that he may kiss it upon the cross behind; and he has a care, in holding it, to take the double part in his right hand, and the single in his left. And while he puts it on, the Subdeacon raises with his right hand the part which must hang down from the back, and they arrange it evenly over the Bishop's shoulders, so that the double part goes over his left shoulder. This done, the Deacon takes one of the three pins, which are brought by an Acolyte; and the fairest of these he fixes into the front cross of the Pall, which is before the breast, and another into that on the left shoulder; while the Subdeacon fixes the third into the cross behind; and all are fixed in such a manner that they may go through the Cross, but not pierce the Pall nor touch the Chasuble, and that the jewels fixed to the pins may lie on the right-hand side of him that puts them in' (*Caer. Ep.* L. II. c. viii. 'De Missa Solemni Episcopo celebrante').

7. 'The office of making and keeping the Pallia belongs to the Subdeacons Apostolic, who prepare them of pure white wool in the following manner. The holy women of the Monastery of S. Agnes . . . offer yearly two white lambs on the Altar of that Church on S. Agnes' Day, while *Agnus Dei* is sung in the High Mass. These lambs are received by two Canons of the Church of S. John Lateran, and are afterwards consigned by them to the Subdeacons Apostolic, who send the lambs out to pasture till shearing-time. Their wool, and other wool mixed with it, is spun into yarn from which Pallia are woven of the breadth of three fingers, of a round form, to encircle the shoulders of Prelates. The Pallium has a band hanging down about a Roman foot long, and at the ends small leaden weights with bosses, covered with black silk sewn on the bands, which hang down before and behind, and on each shoulder. The Pallia, thus prepared, are carried to the Church of S. Peter, and there placed by the Canons of that Church over the bodies of the Apostles Peter and Paul beneath the High Altar; where, having kept vigil according to custom, they leave them all night, and then return them to the Subdeacons, who reserve them in a convenient place' (*Caer. Rom.* L. I. § 10; Pugin, *sub* 'Pall'). The form of granting the Pall in the *Pontifical* is:—'Tradimus tibi Pallium de corpore B. Petri sumptum, uel Archiest plenitudo Pontificalis officii, cum Patriarchalis, uel Archiepiscopalis nominis appellatione,' &c. The form of the Pallium is yet to be found upon the Arms of the See of Canterbury.

8. Ecclus. i. 25.

9. Isaiah liii. 7, as quoted Acts viii. 32

10. S. Luke x. 34.

11. Not Solomon, but Eccles. i. 21, 22.

12. 'Ut his posthabitis in seipsum redire intelligatur.' The play in the word 'posthabitis' is necessarily impaired in translation. *Posthabeo* means 'to throw off, disregard, a thing.'

13. Wisdom ix. 15.

14. S. Luke x. 41, 42.

15. Ps. xxvii. 4.

16. S. Matthew v. 20.

17. Cant. vii. 5. A difficult passage. Vulg. 'Comae capitis tui sicut purpura regis vincta canalibus.' A.V. 'the hair of thine head is like purple; the king is held (marg. *bound*) in the galleries.' R.V. 'the king is held captive in the tresses thereof.' Durandus gives 'purpura regis *tincta* canalibus,' which would doubtless bear the signification I have assigned in the text.

18. 2 Cor. xi 29.

19. *Ibid.* 28.

20. 1 S. Peter iv. 18. Any connection of these words with Job, except in an imaginary point of view, is of course a mistake. But there is something like it in Prov. xi. 31, 'Si

iustus in terra recipit, quanto magis impius et peccator?'

21. Rev. xxi. 4.

22. S. Matthew xiii. 45, 46.

23. *Confertur*, v.l. *confortatur* (so latest ed.) which is perhaps better, as it is of course needless to say that the virtue of the Pall is purely *jurisdictive* and not *sacramental*, making the Bishop no more a Bishop, strictly speaking, than he was before.

24. Nor that of Patriarch or Primate, nor have his Cross borne before him, not even though he be consecrated, nor even though he may have had another Pall in another Province. See, for this and remainder of Section, *Pontificale*, Pars I. Tit. xiv. 'De Pallio,' §§ v. viii. &c.

25. The passage seems corrupt.

26. And if he be buried outside his own province, he may be buried with his own Pall; but not *wearing* it; it must be place, folded, under his head. *Caer. Ep.* I. c. xvi. *in fine*.

27. Easter Sunday, Monday, and Tuesday.

28. Formerly May 1, the present Feast of SS. Philip and James. Micrologus (eleventh century) says that on that day 'inuenitur in Martyrologiis siue in Sacramentariis festiuitas SS. Phil. et Jac., *et omnium Apostolorum*.' This Commemoration was also associated, and more naturally, with the Feast of SS. Peter and Paul (June 29) ; and it is to this day observed upon the morrow of that Feast in the Greek Church, and called 'σύναξις τῶν δ√δεκα 'Αποστόλων .'

29. *I.e.* Purification (February 2), Annunciation (March 25), Assumption (August 15), and Nativity (September 8).

30. Durandus says elsewhere (L. vii. 'De B. Martino') that this name was given to S. Martin, not so much on account of the multitude of his miracles, as on account of one miracle, which the reader will find in Ch. iii. of this work, p. 63, n. 11.

31. And now upon Corpus Christi Day, the Thursday after Trinity Sunday. Durandus does not include this, because it was not yet a regular Feast of the Church when he wrote the *Rationale* (About A.D. 1290). It was decreed as a Festival by Pope Urban IV. in 1264, but, Urban dying, it lapsed until his Bull was promulgated and confirmed at the Council of Vienne in 1311; and did not come into general observance until even later.

32. *I.e.* the Metropolitan Church, or Cathedral.

33. And of Virgins.

34. Anastasius Bibliothecarius says of Marcus, Bishop of Rome (c. A.D. 336), 'Hic constituit, ut Episcopus Ostiensis, qui consecrat Episcopum Urbis (sc. Romae) Pallio uteretur, et ab eodem episcopo [lege episcopus] Urbis Romae consecraretur' (Vit. Pontif. 49). ['He appointed that the Bishop of Ostia should wear the Pall, and should consecrate the Pope.'] Ménard quotes from an ancient MS. at Corbey (of unknown date) an Order of Papal Consecration in which the Bishops of Alba, Portus, and Ostia took part.

THE SACRED VESTMENTS: CHAPTER XVIII: OF THE FOUR COLOURS, ETC.

1. Lam. iv. 7.

2. Rev. iii. 14.

3. *Ibid.* xiv. 4. Neale and Webb, who have given an epitome of this Chapter in their Symbolism of Churches, quote here the beautiful words of Laevinus Torrentius in his hymn on the Holy Innocents:—

'Ergo supremi parte cœli, lactea qua lucidum fulget via,
Qua picta dulci stillat uva nectare, et nectar exhalant rosae,

Lœti coronis luditis, et insignium mixti puellarum choris
Sacrum canentes itis agnum candido quacunque praecedat pede.'

4. Rather, to Job (Job xxxviii. 7).

5. *I.e.* December 27, his 'Deposition'; not May 6, 'S. John before the Latin Gate,' the day of his deliverance from the boiling oil.

6. Called *Cathedra S. Petri Antiochiae*, or 'S. Peter's Chair at Antioch,' a Double, which occurs on February 22. It is explained as commemorating S. Peter's seven years' episcopate at Antioch (Leo, Ep. 119) where he had raised the son of Theophilus of Antioch from the dead, and converted the people; in consequence whereof they built a Church there, with a lofty throne in it, wherein they placed the Apostle, that he might be seen and heard by all. The Enthronement of S. Peter at Rome (Cath. S. Petri Romae) is in the Roman Calendar celebrated on January 18.

7. S. Stephen, Holy Innocents, and S. Thomas of Canterbury.

8. Isaiah xix. 1.

9. *Ibid.*

10. S. Luke i. 35.

11. Jerem. i. 15.

12. S. Luke i. 15.

13. Isaiah lx. 3.

14. I.e. the Purification of Our Lady; so called by its Greek name (ὑπαντΩω, to meet), signifying the meeting of the B.V.M. by Simeon and Anna in the Temple. Lat. *Occursus Domini*.

15. S. Luke ii. 32.

16. On that day the Bishop blesses three kinds of oil: one for Holy Unction; another, for anointing candidates for Holy Baptism; and another, with balsam, called the Chrism, for the anointing of Altars, of Sovereigns, and of candidates for Baptism and Confirmation.

17. S. John xiii. 10.

18. *Ibid.* v. 8.

19. S. Mark xvi. 5.

20. S. Matthew xxviii. 3.

21. Alluding to the ancient custom of baptising on Easter Eve, because we are 'buried with Him in Baptism,' and rise again to newness of life. Upon the newly-baptised linen vestments called 'chrisoms' were placed.

22. Acts i. 10, 11.

23. 2 Cor. xi. 2.

24. Cant. iv. 7.

25. Eccles. ix. 8.

26. Rev. vii. 14.

27. Isaiah lxiii. 2.

28. May 3, whereon S. Helena discovered the True Cross.

29. September 14, whereon Heraclius the Emperor recovered it from Chosroës.

30. Acts ii. 3.

31. Lam. i. 13.

32. S. John xv. 13.

33. Rev. vii. 9, part of the Epistle for the Day. Durandus died on this day.

34. Cant. v. 10. Cp. Hymn at Lauds for a Virgin Martyr, in Paris Breviary:—

Liliis Sponsus recubat, rosisque;

Tu, tuo semper bene fida Sponso
Et rosas Martyr, simul et dedisti
Lilia Virgo.

35. Pope Boniface IV, in the seventh century, dedicated on May 11, in honour of the 'B.V.M. and All Martyrs,' the Pantheon, a heathen temple formerly sacred to 'All Gods and Goddesses.' On that day the Feast of S. Maria ad Martyres was kept until the time of Gregory IV. (A.D. 835), when it was transferred to November 1, our present All Saints' Day, because the harvest was then gathered in.

36. The question of ancient colours is so difficult as to be almost hopeless to any but a specialist upon the subject. Durandus' period seems to have been transitional between the uses of black and violet, for in § 9 he proceeds to give violet as an alternative colour for black. The early Church doubtless regarded black with less strictness than we, and used it interchangeably with other sombre colours, such as 'color uiolaceus' or 'purpureus niger.' It appears also that in Durandus' time the tendency to differentiate the great day of Our Lord's Death from mere penitential seasons was becoming more marked.

37. Cant. i. 5, 6.

38. Jer. xxxi. 15; S. Matthew ii. 18; in substance the 'Communio' of the day in the Roman Missal.

39. The Gloria in Excelsis, alleluia, and 'Ite Missa est' are not said upon this day. But 'Credo' is said.

40. See Rev. vi. 9, 10. An expansion of the Tract for the day.

41. At the end of the Mass on the Fourth Sunday in Lent the Pope used to bless a rose full of musk and balsam, and present it to some Christian sovereign. Fulk of Anjou (In 'Fragment. Hist. Andegav.' in d'Acherii *Spicil.* Tom. X.) mentions this ceremony in the eleventh century, and Durandus gives an account of it in his day (*Rat.* Lib. vi. c. 53).

42. And red, when it does fall on Sunday; but red *always* on its Octave, on whatever day it fall.

43. Cant. iv. 13, 14.

44. This passage seems corrupt and obscure.

45. Because white is used then.

46. Because white is used then.

47. Which is always black.

48. These are the beautiful ceremonies of the Blessing of the New Fire and of the Paschal Candle, the reading of the Twelve Prophecies, the Blessing of the Font, the Baptisms, and the singing of the Litanies. During all these the Priest is vested in violet; but the Deacon wears white for the first two. Then all put on white Vestments for Mass.

49. The Missal says 'in Benedictione Cerei in Sabbato Sancto.... Diaconus *solus* utitur Albo.' But this inclusion of the Subdeacon is probably a slip on Durandus' part; for, a few lines lower, he says 'Subdiaconus uero non mutat uestes.'

50. The 'Greater Litany,' ordered by S. Gregory the Great on the Feast of S. Mark (April 25) to avert God's wrath on the occasion of a pestilence. The 'Lesser Litany' is used on the Rogation Days.

51. Isaiah liii. 5.

52. 'In some Churches at Easter the Altar is arrayed in precious palls, and in veils of three colours, red, pale (*subalbum*) and black; and these denote three seasons. After the first Lection and Responsory finisht, the black one is taken away, which denoteth the time before the Law; after the second, the pale veil, the time under the Law; and after the

third, the red, the day of grace, wherein we have access unto the Holy of Holies through the Passion of Christ' (*Rat.* Lib. I. c. 'De Picturis').

THE SACRED VESTMENTS: CHAPTER XIX: OF THE VESTMENTS OF THE LAW, ETC.

1. The whole of this Chapter should be read *pari passu* with Exodus xxviii. (Vulg.) and with Josephus, *Ant.* Lib. iii. c. 7, from which it is closely borrowed in great part.

2. 'Secundum historiam, allegoriam, tropologiam.' The distinction between the two latter is hard to reproduce succinctly. Perhaps the above comes nearest; for Durandus, in interpreting the ancient Vestments '*allegorice*,' finds in them a representation of the material Universe; and '*tropologice*,' a picture of faith and morals. Elsewhere (*Rat.* Proeme, 9, 10 11), he quotes S. Jerome as saying that 'Scripture must be studied in three ways; (i.) according to the letter; (ii.) after 'allegory,' i.e. the spiritual meaning; and (iii.) according to the blessedness of the future.' And he defines allegory as 'when one thing is said and another meant,' and tropology as 'an injunction unto morality.' We are reminded of Origen's 'literal, moral, and mystical.'

3. All are given in *vv.* 40 and 42.

4 I shall quote the Hebrew words as spelt by Durandus. It must be remembered, as Dr. Neale reminds us, that in his time Greek and Hebrew were little known in Europe. The word he intends here is *michnasim*, from *canas*, to hide.

5. Exodus x. 26; Ezek. xliv. 18.

6. *Cethoneth* (χιτ√ν). This Vestment did not differ in the High Priest and the lesser Priests. It was a long tunic like a cassock, worn, according to Josephus, next the skin, and reaching to the feet, with close sleeves (*Ant.* iii. 7, § 2); uniform in colour, and diapered (Exodus xxviii. 39, 'embroidered').

7. *Subucula*, Lat. for a man's under-garment.

8. Doubtless Durandus means *Abnet*. But that was the name of the Girdle, not of the Linen Coat. Durandus seems to have inadverently transferred Josephus's *Abnet* and *Emissanea* (both of which Josephus applies to the Girdle) to the wrong Vestment.

9. I have adopted the word which in the E. V. distinguishes the headgear of the Priests from that of the High Priest. The former wore caps of a simple make, probably cup-shaped, called *migbaoth*, or turbans.

10. Properly, *meil*. It is called in the Bible the *Robe of the Ephod* ('Tunica Superhumeralis,' Exodus xxviii. 31 *et seq*.). A very simple Vestment, reaching perhaps a little below the knees, and all of blue. Its subdued colour must have been seen above and below the Ephod, as a background to its brilliant hues. A round hole at the top, hemmed to prevent tearing, admitted the head. The bells which hung between pomegranates from its lower hem, like all ritual accessories, had a twofold meaning—Godward and manward. For in the first place they were a witness to God that the Priest was wearing his Divinely-appointed Vestments, 'that he die not.' And secondly, being heard by the people outside the Tabernacle, they conveyed to them the knowledge of their unseen Priest's intercession on their behalf, and so acted, like our own Sanctus Bells, as a spur to their devotion.

11. Exodus xxviii. 35.

12. *I.e.* the 'Vestment worn over the shoulders' (LXX ἐπωμίς). It was the distinctive Vestment of the High Priest (Exodus xxviii. 6-12). *Ephod* (from *aphad*, 'to put on') is Hebrew for Vestment, just as our Chasuble is called 'the Vestment.' It was woven of blue, purple, scarlet, and fine twined linen; and seems to have consisted of two pieces back and front, joined by shoulder-straps, somewhat after the manner of the modern French Cha-

suble. It had also what is called in Exodus xxviii. 8 a 'curious girdle,' *i.e.* a band, attached to it, which the High Priest fastened round his body when he put the Vestment on.

13. Josephus says it had sleeves (Ant. iii. 7, § 5). But it may have altared by his time.

14. I.e. settings of gold wire woven in a sort of filagree-work.

15. 1 Sam. ii. 18; 2 Sam. vi. 14.

16. So Vulg., and Latin Fathers, in reference to its oracular use. Heb. *choshen*, from *chashan*, 'to be adorned.' LXX, Jesus the son of Sirach, Philo, Josephus, and Epiphanius all call it λογεῖν. It was 'a piece of cunning work' like the Ephod (Exodus xxviii. 15 *et seq.*), two spans long and one broad. This, folded lengthways (perhaps for use as a bag), made a square of a span. It must have been something like a burse.

17. The Urim and Thummim. Many are the theories as to the nature of this oracle in the Breastplate. A passage in Philo (*Vit. Mos.* iii 11) has given rise to the notion that they were two small images of precious stone, kept in the bag of the Breastplate (Exodus xxviii. 30). All that seems certain about them, however, is that they were visible objects bound up with the history of the Jews, and that they were the means of revealing God's will to the High Priest, perhaps upon some principle of casting lots. Josephus, with a touch of pathos, remarks: 'Now this Breastplate left off shining two hundred years before I compiled this book, God having been displeased at the transgression of His laws.'

18. Josephus seems to attribute the shining properties to the 'sardonyx' upon the right shoulder-piece of the Ephod, and even to the twelve stones set in the Breastplate. It is more probable that the oracular virtue was resident in two objects *within* the Breastplate itself.

19. Most of them of course defy accurate identification. Durandus gives a list identical with that of the Vulgate, and nearly so with that of Josephus, except that the order of the latter differs slightly.

20. So LXX, and Syriac Version. But were these words *inscribed on* the Breastplate? The Vulgate rendering of Exodus xxviii. 30, 'Pones in rationali Doctrinam et Veritatem,' would seem to have conveyed this impression to Durandus. But 'pones' here surely = *insert* rather than *inscribe*; and it seems more likely that the Urim and Thummim were things put into the Breastplate than words written on it.—As to the meaning of the words, different interpretations exist. LXX gives ἡ δήλωσις καὶ ἡ Ωλήθεια; Symmachus, φωτισμοὶ καὶ τελειότητεσ. Durandus, as usual, adheres to the Vulgate.

21. In other words, the Breastplate had a ring at each corner of its square; the two upper rings hung by twisted gold wire from settings in the upper part of the shoulder-pieces of the Ephod, under the onyx-stones; and the two lower rings, which were out of sight, were fastened by blue laces or strings to two rings sewn into the lower ends of the shoulder-pieces of the Ephod, just above that band for fastening it which was called the 'curious girdle.' Thus the Breastplate was held quite firmly in its place (Exodus xxviii. 13, 14, and 22-28).

22. This seems to have been a sort of augmentation of the 'Bonnet' of the lesser Priests. Josephus makes it double, with a golden crown polished, of three rows, one above the other, out of which rose a cup of gold, which resembled the herb 'saccharus' (Ant. iii. c. 7, § 6).

23. Exodus xxviii. 36, 37.

24. Most of this 'allegorical' interpretation is taken from Philo and Josephus. Both were versed in Gentile lore, as the Western character of this mode of interpretation testifies. The latter makes the *Breastplate* symbolic of the earth, for 'that hath the middle place of the universe' (§ 7).

25. The *little world*, i.e. Man.

26. The *great world*, i.e. the Universe.

27. An obscure and seemingly corrupt passage; but the general sense is that all Nature moves by law, and that the laws which operate on earth are regulated in their turn by the laws of the heavenly bodies.

28. Verse 24.

29. From the prayer *'Unde et memores'* immediately after the Consecration in the Missal. 'Hostiam puram, Hostiam sanctam, Hostiam immaculatam.'

30. S. John xiii. 10. The E. V. rendering, 'he that is washed,' loses all the force of the sentence. ''Ο λελουμένος,' i.e. 'he that is bathed all over' (λούω), 'οὐ χερίαν ἔχει εἰ μὴ τοὺς πόδας νίφασθαι,' i.e. 'needeth only to wash his feet' (νίπτω) as when one comes in from a journey.

31. Ps. cxliv. 1.

32. S. Matthew x. 14.

33. 1 Cor. vii. 25.

34. S. Matthew xix. 12.

35. *Altarnatim*. The reader must interpret this as he may.

36. Eccles. ix. 8.

37. S. Luke xii. 35.

38. Prov. xxxi. 24.

39. Isaiah xi. 5.

40. S. Matthew x. 22.

41. Genesis iii. 15.

42. Acts i. 1.

43. 1 S. Peter ii. 21, 22.

44. From this point, down to the words 'his life's way,' Durandus is quoting from S. Gregory's *Pastoral*, Part II. c. iv. (or xv.).

45. S. Luke xxi. 19.

46. Genesis xlix. 15.

47. 2 Cor. vi. 7.

48. Genesis ii. 1.

49. 1 Cor. v. 8.

50. From here to the end of the Section is a selective quotation from S. Greg. *Pastor.* Pt. II. c. iii (or xiv.).

51. A passage, and indeed a whole Section, of remarkable beauty in the original.

52. 2 Cor. vi. 14, 15.

53. 1 Cor. iii. 12.

54. S. Luke x. 27.

55. 1 Cor. xiii. 13.

56. 1 Tim. i. 5.

57. From here to end of Section is quoted from S. Greg. *Pastor*. Pt. II. c. ii. (or xiii.).

58. Exodus xxviii. 30.

59. The Book of the Gospels has long been held in the Latin Church to be an integral part of the Consecration of a Bishop. The Pontifical directs that it shall be placed by the Consecrator, in silence, upon the head and shoulders of the Bishop-elect.

60. 'Leo III. caused to be made for the Apostle Peter, his patron, a golden Book of the Gospels adorned round about with jewels of marvellous size' (V. Anast. in Vitaliano, Leone III.).

61. Cant. i. 11.

62. S. Luke xiv. 11.

63. S. Matthew xi. 29.

64. *Ibid.* vi. 17.

65. The Bishop, while he anoints the Candidate, says in the Roman rite, 'I sign thee with the Sign of the Cross, and I confirm thee with the Chrism of salvation, in the Name of the Father, and of the Son, and of the Holy Ghost.' That is why 'to confirm' is called in Latin *consignare.*

66. From the Easter Preface in the Missal.

67. Ps. xlv. 10.

68. S. Matthew xix. 29.

69. *Ibid.* iii. 10.

70. See Chap. xiii., §§ 1 and 8, and Chap. xvii., § 14, with notes.

71. 1 Tim. iii. 7.

72. 2 Cor. i. 12.

ON THE MASS

NOTES, UNLESS OTHERWISE INDICATED, ARE BY THE EDITORS OF THE FRENCH EDITION

1. This is why St. Epiphanus calls him the *Leader of the Sacrifice*, and he is commonly known as the *Liturgist* and the *Sacrificer* par excellence. It is also said that he composed the first liturgy which we still have.

2. Honorius of Autun, among others, says that *Actio* and the *Canon* of the Mass are identical (lib. 1., cap. 8).

3. This is why the *Veni Creator Spiritus* is always sung at Masses said at this time.

4. The so called "dry" Mass, or Mass for use on sailing ships, is used in some places as a singular mark of devotion towards the Mass. It is called "dry" because celebrated without any consecration or communion, and by means of the simple recitation of the other prayers. In the mediaeval sailing ships it was called a Mass of navigation because of the danger of spilling the contents of the chalice. The priest dressed with a surplice and stole, takes the missal in his hands and reads the *Epistle*, *Gospel* and *Pater Noster*, after which he gives a blessing. It is also said in conjunction with the viaticum for the sick.

5. For example, the sacrifice of Abraham, a figure of the passion of the new Isaac, which is Christ, the Son of God.

6. This word, as used by ecclesiastical authors, signifies that terminal part of the *Our Father*, namely *Sed libera nos a malo, Amen*, because as St. Cyprien says (Serm. 6, and after him Amalaire, *de Eccl. Offic.*, cap. 29): "In consummatione orationis venit clausula, universas petitiones et preces nostras collecta brevitate concludens." And the Roman Order: "Sequitur in altum praefatio dominicae Orationis, et Oratio dominica cum *emboli* sua, in qua tres articuli orationis inveniuntur."

7. This is well shown, among other examples, by the prayer found in the ancient Pontifical of Paris which the celebrant should recite when combing his hair: *Intus exteriusque caput nostrum totumque corpus et mentem mean, tuus, Domine purget et*

mundet Spiritus almus—May thy Holy Spirit, O God, purify inwardly and outwardly our head, our body and our entire soul.

8. *Tripudialis*, in Du Conge, has the sense of happiness or joy. Dance is, in effect, the liveliest expression of joy and gaiety.

9. Also called a 'peace-board' or 'osculatorium'; a plaque with handle used during the middle ages to transmit the kiss of peace to the faithful. –ED

10. The allusion here is to the name of Jerusalem which signifies vision of peace.

SACRAMENTALITY: A PRINCIPLE OF ECCLESIASTICAL DESIGN

1. See the review of his work in the *Ecclesiologist*, vol. I, pp. 91-105.

2. Pugin's "True Principles", p. 1.

3. Compare the general drift of the Address to Paulinus. *Eusebius*. H.E.X. 4.

4. See *Ecclesiologist*, vol. i., pp. 69, 85.

5. It may be proper to distinguish between five terms, too generally vaguely employed in common, and which we shall often have occasion to use: we mean, *allegorical*, *symbolical*, *typical*, *figurative*, and *sacramental*.

"Allegory employs fictitious things and personages to shadow out the truth: Symbolism uses real personages and real actions (and real things) as symbols of the truth:" [*British Critic*, No. lxv. p. 121.] Sacramentality is symbolism applied to the truth κατ' ἐξόχην, the teaching of the Church, by the hands of the teacher: a Type is a symbol intended from the first: a Figure is a symbol not discovered till after the thing figurative has had a being.

6. It is with pain that we have spoken of Mr Lewis at all, because every Ecclesiologist owes him a debt for his great boldness in turning the public attention to the subject of symbolism. Yet we believe that a prejudice has been excited by him against that subject which it will be hard to get over: for we are constrained to say, that greater absurdities were never printed than some which have appeared in his book. His explanations of the west end of Kilpeck church,—his cool assumption when any bracket appears more puzzling than usual that it is of later work, and therefore not explainable,—his random perversions of Scripture—his puerile conceits about the door—deserve this criticism. This same south door he extols as a perfect mine of Ecclesiastical information, while he confesses himself unable to explain the symbols wrought on the two orders of the arch—that is, about two thirds of the whole! It is strange too, that in his restoration of the church, he should have forgotten all about the bells—and have violated a fundamental canon of symbolism, by terminating his western gable in a plain Cross.

7. Naviculum quippe ecclesiam cogitate,—turbulentum mare hoc seculum.—*S. Aug. de Verb Dom.*

8. Quaeque super signum resident coeleste Columbae,
Simplicibus produnt regna patere Dei.
S. Paulin. ep. 12, ad Sever.

9. Cum nollet idolis sacrificare (sc. S. Reparata) ecce, gladio percutitur: cujus anima in Columbae specie de corpore egredi, coelumque conscendere visa est.—*Martyrol. Rom.* viii. *Id. Oct.*

Emicat inde Columba repens,
Martyris os nive candidior
Visa relinquere, et astra sequi:
Spiritus hic erat Eulaliae
Lacteolus, celer, innocuus.

Pruden. Perist. Hymn. 9.

Compare also the Passion of S. Potitus,—Act. S. Bollandi, 13 Jan. So, in the cemetery of S. Calistus, a piece of glass was found by Boldetti, on which S. Agnes was represented between two doves, the symbols of her Virginity and Martyrdom.

10. Crucem corona lucido cingit globo
Cui coronae sunt corona Apostoli,
Quorum figura est in columbarum choro.
(St. Paulin Epp.)

11. In Evang. 29.

12. De Resurrect. 52.

13. See on this subject the Cambridge Camden Society's "Argument for the Greek Origin of the Monogram IHS."

14. It is on grounds similar to these, that, in our translation of Durandus, we have adopted that conventional style which has been objected to by some recent critics:—not that any one ever naturally conversed or wrote in it, but for the sake of producing the effect which the subject seems to require. The brilliancy of a summer's day is beautiful in its place: admitted into a cathedral, it would be totally out of character.

15. The necessity which the body seems to feel for this symbolism may be seen in the constantly occurring fact, that in making signs, whether of enquiry or adieu, to a person at a distance, we naturally *speak* the words, though inaudible to him, which the gestures we use express.

16. In the correspondence of the Rev. W. Humphrey, whose atrocious treatment by the Church Missionary Society has so lately excited the indignation of all true Churchmen, it appears that one of the noble designs of this zealous priest was to restore for the peculiar congregation over which he was appointed, consisting of Faithful, Catechumens, and Unbelievers, the distinct arrangement of the ancient Church: the modern plan of having but one area for the lay worshippers being found inconvenient and injurious. That is to say, our modern church arrangement may suit and does symbolize the present state of the Church with us, but does not suit and does not symbolize the state of the missionary Church of India.

17. That is, a Catholic *arrangement* of the church being presumed.

18. S. Clem. Rom., ad Corinth, I., 40.

19. Mede, in Epist. lviii. Folio, Lib. iv.

20. See this carried out by Durandus. Appendix A.

21. Compare, amongst others, S. Cyprian, Ep. 55; Euseb. x, 4. τὸ ἅγιον ἁγίων θυσιαστήριον; Id. vii, 18. τό ἁγίασμα. (the word used in the lxx. for the *Sanctuary*): S. Dionys. Areop., Ep. 8, ad Demoph.; S. Athanas., *Edit. Commel*. Tom. ii, p. 255; Theod. H. E. iv, 17, v, 18; Concil. Tours. (A.D. 557), can. 4; S. Germ. Constant. *In Theor. rer. Eccles*.; Card. Bona. *Rer Liturg*. i, xxv, 11; Dionys. *Hierarch*. cap. 2; S. Chrysost. Lib vi, *De Sacerdotio*.

22. Rose's Neander, i, 246.

23. Apost. Const. 2, 57, (61.)

24. See also what is said on this point by Buscemi, in his Notizie della Basilica di San Pietro. ch. iii, p. 7. The church of S.S. Vincenzo and Anastatic at Home, near S. Paolo alle Tré Fontane, built by Honorius I., (A.D. 630) has its wall *curved* like the ribs of a ship. The constitution itself refers to the resemblance of this oblong form to a ship. See also S. Clem. Alex., *Paedag*, iii, 246.

25. Tertull. advers. Valent., cap. 2.

26. See Origen, *Hom. 5, in Numer*. cap. 4. Tertull. *Apol*. cap. 16, and *Ad Nation*., i, 13. S. Clem. Alex. *Strom*., vii., *ante med*. quoted by Mede.

27. Hist. Eccles. Lib. v, cap. κβ.

28. Thiers, *Dissert. de la Clôture du Choeur des Eglises*. cap. 2.

29. Carm. ix. tom. ii, p. 79. πλευραῖς σταυροτύποις τέτραχα τεμνόμενον.

30. Notizie etc. Note al Lib. I, capo terzo. Nota 10, p. 15.

31. Book viii, 3, following Leo Allatius and Suicer.

32. Socrates iv, 24, τὸ δὲ σχδμα τοῦ ναοῦ είσ ἐκκλησίας τύπον μεταποιήσαντες.

33. Theodoret I. xxiv. Τὴν Ωξιόγαστον ἐκείνην καταλαβ◊ν δοριάλωτον, παρεκάλει δεῖξαι τδς οίκοδομίας τὸ σχδμα ʽΟ δὲ τὸν Βεσελεὴλ τδς Ωρχιτεκτονικδς σοφίασ ἐμπλήσας καὶ ταύτην Δξίωσε χάριτοσ, ὡς τόν θεῖον διαγράψαι νε√ν καὶ ἡ μὲν διέγραψεν, ο δὲ ὤρυττόν τε καὶ ᾠκοδομοῦν.

34. Euseb. H. E., x, 4, 21.

35. Hebrews, ix, 6, 7.

36. Euseb. X, iv, 24, 25.

37. Euseb. H. E., x, 43.

38. Ibid 53.

39. Ibid 54.

40. Ibid 57.

41. Isaiah liv, 11.

42. Euseb. X. iv, 60.

43. Ibid 61.

44. Euseb. H. E., x, 65.

45. Greg. Nyssen, iii, 567.

46. Discourse of Churches, Folio Edn., p. 333.

47. Much stress is laid by some on the acknowledged Basilican origin of churches as an argument against the principle here contended for. But we find a great authority on the Antiquities of Christian Rome deciding differently: "There seems to be in the building of churches, as in the mosaics, and other works of art of the old Christian times in Rome, one constant type in which the art of building could show little freedom or variety."—*Beschreibung der Studt Rom. Basiliken*. vol. I, p. 430.

48. Ecclesiologist, vol, i. p. 120.

49. *British Magazine*, 1843, p. 393.

50. It is proper to distinguish between Dedication Crosses, which are generally of considerable size, examples of which may he seen in Moorlinch, Somersetshire, and those small crosses in door jambs, as in Preston, Sussex, the use of which is not very clear, but which were perhaps intended to remind the entering worshipper to cross himself. At Yatton, Somersetshire, inside the northern door, and towards the east, is a large quatre-foil-fashioned cross: this perhaps pointed out a now destroyed benatura.

51. That there are some plain crosses, cannot be denied—more especially that on which the weathercock is placed. A little consideration will, perhaps, clear up this difficulty. The cross may be viewed in two distinct lights. It may either set forth that on which our Redeemer suffered—in which case it is the symbol of glory: or it may image that Cross which every true Christian is to take up—in which case it may still be called the Symbol of Shame. In the latter signification, it may well be quite plain. But, inasmuch as our ancestors looked more to the Passion of Christ than to their own unworthiness, the former symbol is that which generally occurs. Yet not always on the church spire, perhaps for this reason:—the spire urges us, by its upward tendency, to press on

towards our heavenly home,—a home which can only be reached by the cheerful bearing of that cross by means of which (as it were) it points. The cross therefore is here, with propriety, plain.

52. However, in late stained glass, the modern position is sometimes found; as in a Crucifixion represented in the east window of the north aisle, in Wiscombe church, Somersetshire.

53. To this we may add the conventional representation of Royal Saints, such as S. Edmund, wearing their kingly crowns during their passion. That such conventional symbolism is natural to us may be shown by alluding (without irreverence in this connection) to the way in which kings are always figured with crown and orb in popular prints: and even, as in a sign-post at Leighterton, Gloucestershire, King Charles II., hiding himself in the Royal Oak, is arrayed in all the insignia of majesty.

54. We read, in the legend of S. Barbara, that, being confined by her father in a room where were two windows only, she added a third, by way of setting forth this Mystery.

55. We may perhaps be allowed to say a few words here on the subject of those singular windows which the Cambridge Camden Society has called *Lychnoscopes*.

It appears, that in Early English churches, the westernmost window on the south side of the chancel is both lower than, and in other ways (particularly by a transom) distinguished from, the rest. It is sometimes merely a square aperture, as in some churches in the Weald of Sussex: sometimes a small ogee-headed light, as in Old Shoreham: sometimes, where the south side of the chancel is lighted by a series of lancets, the westernmost, as in Chiddingfold, Sussex, is transomed, where the others end, and carried down lower; sometimes the lower part appears to have been originally blocked, as in Kemerton, Gloucestershire, and Kingstone next Lewes, Sussex: sometimes there are remains of clamps, as at Buckland, Kent, sometimes of shutters. Again, sometimes there are two, one north, the other south of the chancel: sometimes the same arrangement is found S. E. of the nave. On the other hand, it is never found in any but a parish church: never in late work: seldom is it ornamented. We will give a few remarkable instances. 1. *Dinder*, Somersetshire. Here there is a double lychnoscope, north and south: the date is late Early English, and the specimen is unique from there being a rude moulding in the window arch. 2. *Othery*, Somersetshire. The lychnoscope itself is here blocked: it is square-headed, and of two lights: date probably Early Decorated. The church is cruciform, and a central Perpendicular Tower was subsequently erected. One of the diagonal buttresses is thrown out at a distance of some three feet from the window, so as to hide it: and an oblique square hole has been cut through the masonry of the buttress. This is the more remarkable, because there are stalls in the chancel, of perpendicular work, which would seem to render any window in that position useless. 3. *Christon*, Somersetshire. Here, *almost close to the ground*, is a horizontal slit which appears never to have been glazed. This is an early Norman church. So at Albury, Surrey, at the S.E. end of the south aisle. 4. *S. Appolline*, Guernsey. This church is of the same date as, or may be earlier than, the last. The windows are rude and square headed slits: the lychnoscope is transomed. 5. *Preston*, Sussex. There are three windows in the south of the chancel, which rise one above the other, like sedilia, to the east. 6. *Loxton*, Somersetshire. This is an Early English church with a south western tower serving as porch. From the eastern side of this a long slit is carried through the nave wall, a distance of some twenty feet, and exactly commanding a view of the altar. It is *grated* at the west end, not glazed: the eastern end has long been blocked up. Way is made for it by a bulge of the wall in the angle formed towards the east by the tower and nave. This seems to form a kind of connecting link between the hagioscope and the lychnoscope.

With these windows we will venture to connect those extremely rare ones, three adjacent, unconnected, equal, lancets, as occurring of the same date at the same position. There is again another kind of lychnoscope only found where the chancel has aisles. A panel of the parclose, or wooden screen, behind the longitudinal stalls, is sometimes found pierced with a small quatrefoil, at the S.W. part of the chancel. This is vulgarly called a confessional. It seems however clearly connected with the lychnoscope. Examples are found at Erith, Kent, and Sundridge in the same county. Perhaps also the curious slit in the south wall of the chancel of S. Michael's church, Cambridge, communicating with a south chantry chapel is another variety.

From the above facts we deduce the following remarks: 1. That the necessity for a lychnoscope must in some cases have been very urgent: as may be proved by the example, at Othery, where a buttress is much injured to form one. 2. But yet this need was not universal, because there are many churches in which the arrangement does not occur. 3. That it appears, strictly speaking, a parochial arrangement, not being found in cathedral or collegiate churches. 4. That smaller buildings rather than larger are marked with it: it seldom occurs where there are aisles to the chancel. 5. That, where employed, lychnoscopes were only used occasionally; else the shutters which have evidently sometimes existed, would have been useless. 6. That they are very seldom ornamented, and never have stained glass. 7. That in the Perpendicular era they generally, though not universally, ceased to be used. 8. That, a large sill seems to have been a requisite to them. 9. That, where the upper part is glazed, the lower part often was not, as in the Decorated lychnoscope at Beckford, Gloucestershire. The principal hypotheses to explain the use of this arrangement are. 1. Dr. Rock's. That it was a contrivance by which lepers might see the Elevation of the Host. But the structure of the greater part of these windows forbids this idea: many instances occur in which it is splayed away from the Altar, none (except that at Loxton, and a doubtful case at Winscombe, Somersetshire, where a perpendicular addition has been made) in which it is splayed towards it. 2. That of the Cambridge Carnden Society, that it was for watching the Paschal light. But this, besides being *à priori*, improbable is refuted by that at Othery. Here the eye has to look through two apertures, at some distance from each other, and therefore can command only a very small field on exactly the opposite side of the chancel. 3. It has been imagined by some that it was for confession. The idea of confession near an altar sufficiently refutes itself: but furthermore, some of these openings are so very low down that the thing would be impossible. Two solitary facts, more, though they throw no light on the subject, may yet be mentioned. 1. In the church of S. Amaro, near Funchal, in Madeira, is a grating at the west-end like that at Loxton. Its use is *now* said to be to cool the church, though in that case one should have expected to meet it elsewhere. 2. In Sennen church, by the Land's End, there is said to have been a lychnoscope (now no longer existing) used to take in the tithe-milk. We may gather on the whole, l. That lychnocopes could not have been used to look into a church 2. Nor to hand anything in or out. Both those are sufficiently disproved by Othery. 3. Nor to speak through. But one can hardly imagine any other use, except it were to look *out* of the church. We are inclined to think that it was in some way connected with the ringing of the bells, or of the sancte bell. Where the tower is central, we very often find it: as at Old Shoreham and Alfriston, Sussex: at Loxton it is evidently for some purpose connected with the tower. So in Beckford, which has a central Tower; and Urfington, Berks, a cross church. And the place where the sancte bell was rung is exactly between a double lychnoscope. But what the particular use might have been, we will not pretend to guess. We will conclude this long note, by a question as to the authority for calling the small chancel door, the *Priest's Door*. It is never (originally) furnished with a lock, but always with an interior bar, thus showing that it could only have been used from the inside. So the priest could never have *entered* the church by this way, unless the door were previously opened for him.

56. Durand. i, 26.

57. "Let us consider Him," says Bishop Hall "now, after a weary conflict with the Devil, looking down from the Triumphal Chariot of the Cross on His Church."

58. A Master of Philosophy travelling with others on the way, when a fearful thunder storm arose, checked the fear of his fellows, and discoursed to them of the Natural Reasons of that uproar in the clouds, and those sudden flashes wherewith they seemed (out of the ignorance of causes) to be too much affrighted in the midst of his philosophical discourse, he was struck dead with that dreadful eruption which he slighted. What could this be but the finger of that God Who will have His works rather entertained with wonder and trembling than with curious scanning? Neither is it to be otherwise in those violent hurricanes, devouring earthquakes, and more than ordinary tempests, and fiery apparitions which we have seen and heard of; for however there be natural causes given of the usual events of this kind, yet nothing hinders but the Almighty, for the manifestation of His power and justice, may set spirits, whether good or evil, on work, to do the same things sometimes in more state and magnificence of horror.—Bishop Hall. "The Invisible World," sect. vi.

59. See on this subject an interesting article in the *Church of England Quarterly*, for September, 1841.

60. As in Fletching, Sussex.

61. As in Lolworth, Cambridgeshire.

62. As in S. Mary, Castlegate, York.

63. As in Hedon, Yorkshire.

64. Agamemnon, 606. (Ed. Dindorf.)

65. As in Sir Grey do Groby, S. Alban's.

66. Engraved in the 5th number of the Cambridge Camden Society's *Illustrations of Monumental Brasses*.

67. As in Watton, Herts, and Cottingham, Yorkshire.

68. Habaccuc iii. V, *Et egredietus diabolus ante pedes ejus.*

69. Psalm xc. *Qui habitat.*

70. The astonishing scriptural knowledge of Durandus may be judged of from the Index at the end of the volume of texts quoted by him.

71. Rutter's *Delineations*, p. 89.

72. It is fair to observe that our designating them so *may* be the effect our own ignorance.

73. We have the highest authority for believing that one type can symbolize two things quite independent of each other, in that the Jewish Sabbath, commanded from Sinai to be observed in commemoration of the Rest after the Creation, is enforced in Deuteronomy as the representation of the rest of the children of Israel from Egyptian bondage. "Remember," says Moses, "that thou wast a servant in the land of Egypt, and that the Lord thy God brought thee out thence through a mighty hand and by a stretched out arm: *therefore* the Lord thy God commanded thee to keep the Sabbath day."—Deut. v, 15.

74. We deeply regret that the Oxford Architectural Society should ever have allowed itself to put on paper the opinions expressed by one of its members, that Perpendicular windows are those best suited to the spirit of Christian architecture.

REFERENCE WORKS

Church Vestments: Their Origin and Development by Herbert Norris, (Dover Publications, Mineola, New York, 2002).

Die liturgische Gewandung im Occident und Orient; nach Ursprung und Entwicklung, Verwendung und Symobolik (Frieburg im Breisgau, Herder, 1907).

INDEX OF SYMBOLS

A selection of symbols beyond those indicated in the chapter headings.

G

H

I

J

K

L

M

N

O

P

R

S

T